Day-by-Day
and
Heart-to-Heart

WENDY PHILLIPS LAZAR

Day-by-Day and Heart-to-Heart
Copyright ©2021 Wendy Phillips Lazar

ISBN 978-0-578-89765-3   Hardback
ISBN 978-0-578-89766-0   Paperback

All rights reserved. No part of this publication may be reproduced, distributed, or transmitted in any form or by any means, including photocopying, recording, or other electronic or mechanical methods, without the prior written permission of the publisher, except in the case of brief quotations embodied in critical reviews and certain other noncommercial uses permitted by copyright law.

Book design by StoriesToTellBooks.com

Day-by-Day and Heart-to-Heart

WENDY PHILLIPS LAZAR

This book is dedicated to all those I've met around the world over many years—young and old and in-between, of all races and religions, who opened my eyes, taught me well, sent me down unexpected paths, changed my life and my worldview, and left their imprints on my heart and mind and soul.

Let's get on with the adventures! Of all the books in the world, the best stories are found between the pages of a passport.

INTRODUCTION

As beauty is in the eyes of the beholder, so, too, are the impressions reaped from travels. The events and situations noted here are of a highly personal nature, colored by my own experiences. And what experiences they were!

What follows is a mix of rambling but informative letters to my parents in Rochester, New York, filled with facts, observations, and experiences. Also included are some of my radio scripts or portions of same: "Orientation" broadcast on educational radio stations in the United States, "Japan and I" broadcast on NHK's Radio Japan short-wave network to English-speaking nations of the world, and NHK's "Radio Japan Journal." NHK, Nippon Hoso Kyokai (Japan Broadcasting Corporation), is Japan's only public broadcaster.

When people ask how I ended up living abroad for almost 2-1/2 years, I tell them I joined the Foreign Legion because my then-boyfriend wasn't ready to get married. That's not entirely true, of course, but it makes a good story!

A lot of things were happening to me personally all at the same time back in 1964. 1) I was dating Marty Lazar, who had no interest in a more serious relationship at the time. 2) My passion for Japan continued for reasons I've never been able to understand, so I applied to the U.S. Army for a position as a recreation specialist in what was, at the time, the hardship post of Korea because it was nearest Japan. 3) I also applied to the U.S. Peace Corps requesting an assignment in Southeast Asia—near Japan was my intent. I was accepted to both the U.S. Army and the U.S. Peace Corps, but they weren't sure where to send me or what to do with me, so both applications were put on temporary hold. I didn't realize how lucky that was until a few months later. 4) I had a job I loved as a broadcaster/producer at the educational radio station of The Riverside Church in New York City. The church had an English as a Second Language (ESL) program and had been asking me to work with one of their students. I turned down every request until Hideaki Hyuga came on the scene. He was a radio broadcaster on assignment in New York from a radio station in Nagoya, Japan. Finally, there was something of mutual interest that I could build English lessons around.

This traditional Japanese man and gentle soul nurtured my passion for his country and its arts. As part of that, Hyuga-san—he was always Mister Hyuga to me through all our years of friendship—introduced me to other Japanese living in New York City, including Michiaki Suma, Deputy Consul of the New York Consulate. He was never Mister Suma to me, but "Michi." He spoke English well, adopted western ways, and allowed me to enjoy a New York City life I would never have been privy to otherwise—like entertaining evenings at the Playboy Club and a former speakeasy where, yes, as the sign indicated, you did have to knock three times and whisper low, identify yourself, and leave your guns at the door! How could I not enjoy this inside look at how some others lived? The three of us—Hyuga-san, Michi, and I—often went together to these places.

Above all, I am eternally grateful for Michi's introduction to his father's friend, Yoshiyuki Wazaki. He set me on a course that would change my life forever. Over the next two years, there was much that happened that I didn't fully understand at the time, exciting events I attended and wondered how I got there—but, wait, I don't want to get ahead of myself. What happened next was one of them. Mr. Wazaki, chairman of the United Nations Association in Osaka and with directorships in several business organizations in both Osaka and Tokyo, let Michi know he would be interested in sponsoring my visit to Japan. I could live with his family till I found a job and a place to live. His sponsorship would entitle me to a six-month renewable visa, rather than the usual two months. It was a dream come true!

In the next couple months, I assured my parents that I had researched this monumental transition carefully; I informed the Army and Peace Corps that I was going directly to Japan but thank you anyway; I quit my job in preparation for my move; I bought a one-way plane ticket to Osaka; and I sold what furniture I had to Marty, the guy I was dating.

Part 1

JAPAN

I arrived October 6, 1964, knowing only one word of Japanese:
Sayonara.
(Goodbye.)

10/7/64

Dear *o-kā-san to o-tō-san*,
(Mom and Dad)

I am in Japan and finding it hard to believe! If it's all right with you, I'd like the letters to be my diary. Please share them with family and friends, as they'll be the most complete ones I write.

Flying over the Pacific the clouds hung over the ocean like many puffs of smoke. My flying mate was Aram Saygin, a Turkish pressman, sports editor for a daily newspaper in Istanbul. He spoke no English; I spoke no Turkish; yet it's amazing how much we were able to communicate—drawing with pen on paper helped. He was fascinating to talk with and proved a point: you need no common language to make friends and understand one another.

I arrived in Tokyo on schedule, though somewhat incredulous, and was immediately met by Toshifumi Iwamoto. He speaks excellent English and has been writing the letters for Wazaki-san. He has become my personal interpreter and is with me constantly. Together we flew to Osaka Airport, where we were met by Wazaki-san and his driver, then taken to Wazaki-san's home where dinner was waiting and I was the special guest. Since then, suffice it to say that Eliza Doolittle has nothing over Wendy Phillips! There was great excitement at my arrival. The family insisted I take a bath first—with careful instructions given to me by Iwamoto-san. We dined on *sukiyaki*. My special treat was to have Miss Kazuko Sarada there. She is one of Japan's most famous opera singers, I was told. Her after-dinner performance was topped off with everyone singing "Row, Row, Row Your Boat," the only English song everyone knew while I accompanied them on the ukulele. I slept Japanese style last night as a test. If I didn't like sleeping on the floor on a *futon*, (a quilted mattress rolled out for use as a bed), Wazaki-san is prepared to buy me an American bed. He is taking care of everything. My time is carefully planned.

As head of the household, Mr. Wazaki is the first to be served at mealtimes and the first to use the hot water bath. His wife,

Mitsuko, is generally the last to eat and often stayed in the kitchen. When he wants her, he claps and grunts, and she dutifully comes running. She is a warm and caring woman, and I liked her immediately. She is my Japanese "mother" and my guide to protocol. We enjoy doing things together—food shopping, cooking, and arranging flowers. The term for housewife is *oku-san*, and that's what I was told to call her, but she meant so much more to me than what that banal term conveys. (I write Oku-san with a capital O to show her importance and my respect). There are three children. Yoshihiko, 24, lives at home, having graduated from Keio University in Tokyo. Ryunosuke, 21, is a student at Keio University. Mariko, 17, is still in high school. Also part of the household: a house maid, the driver, a woman whose function has not yet been explained, and a mutt named Gong. He lies in the garden when he's not out for a walk. Their home is small but pleasant, and I have my own room complete with air conditioning next to the *tokonoma*, the alcove set apart for flower arrangements and art objects. It's the old and the new, and this is the way I've found Japan—full of contradictions. The home has both a foreign toilet (that is, a sit-down western one) and a Japanese one that flushes—but is just a hole in the floor that one straddles. English newspapers have been ordered for me; I was asked if I need to see a doctor and to go to church every Sunday.

This morning I had my first lesson in *yen* when Wazaki-san gave me 20,000¥ in bills and coins—about $55—with instructions to save my own money. Today we had lunch with Mr. Miyoshi, who owns a film company; I was taken to the Hankyu Department Store to meet the directors who will help me when I buy there; then to a special sale of cashmere material, where I was introduced to the directors should I ever want anything in cashmere. Now I'm writing to you between the times when people come in to meet me and assure me that they will do everything they can to make my stay pleasant.

The family is most kind. We have a great many laughs together, though our understanding is limited. Thank heavens for

Iwamoto-san. I've met so many people already that my head is spinning, and I'm being quickly groomed to the Japanese way of life.

It will be very difficult to get this experience on paper, but I'm sure going to try, and it will be through these letters to you. My love to everyone. You can rest assured that I'm in the best of care.
Love, ウエンディー
(Wendy, in Katakana)

10/10/64

My assimilation into the Japanese way of life is coming about quickly. My vocabulary increases daily, and I am able to read some signs now. My learning Katakana, the printed language for foreign words and phrases, makes me feel like a first grader. I get excited when I recognize characters and gradually form words.

There are three Japanese alphabets: Katakana, the printed language for foreign words; Hiragana, the cursive writing for foreign words and phrases; and Kanji, the Chinese-inspired ideograms, of which there are more than two thousand. Each character has its own meaning and corresponds to a word. By combining those characters, more words can be created. In Romaji, a system of writing using the letters of the Roman alphabet, my name is written as Wendy and pronounced "oo-en-dee." Sounds close to correct! Phillips in Katakana, the printed alphabet, is written フィリップス and pronounced "foo-ee-ree-pu-soo" (emphasis on the second syllable and all run together). In Hiragana, the cursive writing, it's the same pronunciation but written as ふいりっぷす

I am becoming very fond of the Wazakis. Wazaki-san now calls me his daughter and treats me as one of the family. Oku-san is teaching me Katakana, and yesterday she took me for a walk in the neighborhood, which included a visit to the Buddhist shrine and the local market. They won't let me go anywhere by myself—it would be *muzukashi* (difficult). It's become a frequently used word!

I dined the other night with the vice-mayor, vice-governor,

American consul general, the directors of the American Cultural Center, and the Chinese consul general. What a fascinating party! It included the above people and their wives, myself, and three entertainers. Before dinner we had cocktails and were entertained by a pianist, a soprano, and an excellent lyric tenor. Dinner itself was elegant. The Japanese savor food with their eyes, as well as taste and smell. One dish appeared to be a chestnut in its shell garnished with a pine needle. It really was a shelled chestnut in a fish paste casing covered with little brown noodles. The pine needle was made of two green noodles attached at one end with green seaweed. One fish dish almost turned my stomach the way it was served, but it turned out to be delicious. I'm having fun with this food. I don't like everything, but I'm giving everything a chance — and that pleases the Japanese. At dinner there were hostesses, trained in the geisha way and paid by the hour, who play various games with customers and create origami treats. They also danced for us. I was surprised to find they pay as much attention to the women as to the men — even to the point of scratching my back where it itched!

Last night, I joined 17 of Osaka's leading businessmen who were giving a dinner to console one of the men who had just lost his wife. The same hostesses were there and, by this time, had taken me on as a friend. During dinner, one of the men painted a picture for me of the *ikebana* arrangement in the room, then another guest, one of the directors of Hitachi, presented me with a Hitachi AM-FM Transistor Radio amid much applause!

I was so overwhelmed with the gift and so pleased, it was decided that the next time we were together, he would give me a Hitachi tape recorder! It is embarrassing for me to receive these gifts, and I find it difficult to accept them. Yet, even now, I know this practice will continue. After we left the restaurant, a smaller group of us went to the Club Ota for cocktails and dancing. The band was playing American music and Wazaki-san requested a song that I think is called "A Light in the Window." He was able to sing all the English words to the music, and I was too surprised to tell him I had never heard of the song! Two of the geisha-type hostesses stayed with us at the club, and it was fascinating to see them servicing us while being serviced by the Ota hostesses in western dress. I suspect rank is involved. One hostess insisted I teach her the American jitterbug. Our demonstration was so successful, many of the people there now want instruction! Somehow I have managed to be a friend to both the men and these hostesses because I'm new and different and they are full of questions about America, New York, my parents, and particularly Harvey. They are fascinated with my photo of him, whom they call *oto-oto*, (younger brother).

One lesson I learned last night is that I'm older than I thought. While only 25 in the states, I'm 26 in Japan. The first year after birth is counted as year 1. As is said, I feel old before my time!

Today I attended a diplomatic reception given by the Republic of China (ROC) Consul General Ping-Chien Sun and his wife to celebrate Double Tenth Day, the National Day of the ROC. It was attended by government officials and business and cultural leaders. I met the Argentine consul general, the Peruvian consul general, members of the American consulate team, and others. It was nice after being in Japan such a short time to be greeted by new friends and by name. Toasts were made to the Chinese Republic and to Chiang Kai-shek. Not speaking either Chinese or Japanese, I understood nothing of the speeches until everyone turned to face me and shouted, "*Banzai! Banzai! Banzai!*" That I knew as the *kamikaze* pilots' final whoop in World War II as they dive-bombed their planes into Allied naval vessels on suicidal missions of destruction.

Movies and books had taught me that battle cry and now it was directed at me. I had a few seconds of sheer panic. It must have been clearly evident because my interpreter quickly explained that, in the world of 1964, *banzai* was the equivalent of "Hip, hip hooray!" for the emperor. People had not turned to face me but to face east. Japan, after all, is called Land of the Rising Sun. Did they look at me? How could they not? I was the only redhead in the room!

After the reception, I was taken to Osaka Castle. From the top of the large castle's dungeon, there is quite a view of the surrounding area. I was stopped twice while visiting the castle by high school students who are members of English-speaking societies. They were anxious to chat with me. Like everyone else here, they are full of questions.

The rest of the weekend was spent by the TV watching the Olympics. We have great fun picking a winner when Japanese and American athletes compete against each other. The Japanese are very proud to have the games here. Their usual six-day work week was cut short on Saturday when everyone had the afternoon off to watch the Olympic opening ceremonies on TV.

Gradually I become attuned to the "Japanese way." Men in Japan, particularly those who are "broad-faced" or prominent, have the best of all possible worlds, and it is this that I am learning to accept or at least understand. Iwamoto-san feared that I didn't comprehend until I gave him a complete report on the way it is. Every time a business, industry, or cultural pursuit is mentioned, Wazaki-san informs me that the president/chairman/director of the organization is his good friend.

It's a wonder the way things happen around here! In restaurants, my coat and purse disappear when I enter and return when I leave. When a group leaves their shoes at the door, each pair is returned to its rightful owner on departure. If I order sherry, it is remembered everywhere I go. If I order scotch and water one time, next time I might get both, because it is known that I also like sherry. I never know where I'm headed till I get there; I'm only told that the Wazaki's driver will pick me up at a certain time. Each day is a surprise to me but, when I return, everyone else asks me how such-and-such was. I'm the only clueless one!

Oku-san, in an official act of acceptance the other day, wrote my name on my slippers so that no-one else can use them. One time she caught me coming out of the bath too early and was afraid I was only taking showers. Now I think she times me. It has become a joke in the family. The bath is so damn hot it takes me 10 minutes to even get in!

For lunch today, I had turtle soup for the first time. It's delicious! Naturally, when I left the restaurant, I was given a gift. Then I toured the Mitsui Trading Company and received a butane lighter and a book about Japanese gardens. They have asked me to teach English to some of their employees.

Mr. Wazaki found a job for me at a film company in Tokyo, but I chose not to accept. Tokyo has a large American population, whereas I prefer staying in Osaka where there are few Americans and where I will have a much better opportunity to immerse myself in Japanese culture and the spoken language. My first break comes with that introduction to the Mitsui Trading Company. I'm also told I will teach at Shinai Women's Junior College four hours a week at 32,000¥ per month, roughly $93, and at Tezukayama College. Mr. Iwamoto and Mr. Wazaki are carefully juggling the schedule.

> **[With the passage of time, events happen, people's views shift, and formerly accepted words change their impact in current political settings. Once simple and descriptive words are now sometimes interpreted with overtones of discrimination, disrespect, and stereotypes. Such it is with words frequently used in this diary and in my radio scripts: Oriental, Orient, Negro--words generally accepted in the 1960s. This book represents common usage at the time of writing.]**

This morning Wazaki-san and I were sitting in the living room chatting. His doctor came to give him a massage and I, quite naturally, left the room. But Oku-san came in and said that Wazaki-san wanted me to watch how they give oriental massages. I thought for sure he'd be partly nude, and I was extremely reluctant to go in. But, with much coaxing, I entered—only to find him fully covered in his *yukata*, or Japanese robe. You can't imagine how relieved I was! I'm sure you think this is all very strange, but you should have seen my reaction last week when I came to a restaurant alone to meet him and his friends there. When I walked into the room, there was his suit lying on the *tatami*! He was—as I was not told but understood—with his *koibito*, (lover), and joined us several minutes later. There is much in Japan to become accustomed to!

10/14/64

In the morning I went to one of Wazaki-san's companies that produces concrete-asbestos boards for construction. One of the directors reported that working conditions are very poor and need to be improved. It was a science lesson, too, for it was explained how asbestos is taken from the rocks. Later I toured an extremely well-automated plant that manufactures steel pipes. I accept it as part of my all-things-Japanese education.

10/21/64

On Friday I attended another reception. It seems that the Japanese Foreign Ministry keeps one ambassador in Osaka to further cement relations with the local people. The ambassador here now is going to Thailand; the one from the Congo is now in Osaka. The reception was for them and, as it turned out, there were about 150 businessmen, about 40 geisha hostesses, and me! I met many new people and received a great deal of attention.

Afterwards, Mr. Wazaki and Mr. Takada, the vice governor, and I went to a dinner given by what could be called the ladies auxiliary of the United Nations Association-Kansai Chapter, where Mr. Wazaki is director. Following the meal, we went back to Club Ota where I've been many times already. It's not unusual for me to go out to a club afterwards with Wazaki-san and some of the other men I've spent the evening with at a dinner or reception. Club Ota has cocktails and dancing and hostesses. The hostesses dance with the male guests (I was always the only female guest) and ply them with drinks, which is good for the club since there is high profit in a high bar bill. I am more of a distraction. Because I'm new and different, hostesses have many questions, both personal and more random. I am often asked to teach the "Americanu Jeeterbugu" (American Jitterbug) and the "Tweest" (Twist).

My first planned weekend away from Osaka was to visit Hyuga-san, who has now been reassigned from New York City back to

Nagoya. Tickets were purchased in advance, and Wazaki-san's driver not only drove me to the train station but escorted me onto the train to make certain I had no chance of getting on the wrong car. Hyuga-san's wife and two children had been taught to say in English, "Welcome, Wendy. It is nice to meet you." Both his wife and son, Sashi-chan, said it but his daughter, Mari-chan, was too shy. I replied in proper Japanese: *Dozo yoroshiku*. (I am glad to meet you.) The three books I brought as gifts went over well, but it's strange to hear the story of Peter Pan in Japanese, especially when Peter and the boys capture the pirates to the shouts of *"Banzai"*! It sent a chill of memories up my spine.

The afternoon I arrived in Nagoya, there was a parade downtown featuring costumed marchers representing various periods of Japanese history. I don't think I've mentioned before that autumn and spring is the time for festivals honoring the Buddhist deities. I've seen many of them but nothing on this scale.

After the parade, we went to a pleasant *ryokan* (Japanese-style inn) in one of the hot spring areas. Upon arrival, guests are given a *yukata* and a jacket for comfort. The *yukata* is a casual robe also used for sleeping and, in resort areas and at festivals, for street wear. Our room had a pretty little balcony overlooking a pretty waterfall and, with the trees on the mountain beginning to change colors, it was overall a pretty sight!

On Sunday we returned to Nagoya and were taken out to dinner by Mr. Nakagawa, one of the vice-presidents of Hyuga-san's firm, Chubu-Nippon Broadcasting Company, a regional radio-TV service. His 22-year-old daughter Sumiko joined us. After dinner, Sumiko drove us to the top of the Higashiyama Driveway from where you can see all of Nagoya. Good timing, too—there was a fireworks display.

Monday I went shopping and bought a camera—a Minolta Minoltina P, which seems to make good picture taking a snap! It is a gift from Hyuga-san for Chanukah, my welcome-to-Japan gift, and my birthday next April! He was with me when I intended on making the purchase and insisted he wanted to give it to me as a gift!

That evening I went to the Nakagawa's home for dinner. I was dressed up in one of Sumiko's kimonos—with hand-painted butterflies that took a year to complete. It was great fun and we took many pictures. I felt like a young girl in my first formal dress. But how difficult it is to wear kimono; you are tied in from every angle! Sumiko also taught me the rudiments of the tea ceremony. Before many girls marry, they go through training courses in the tea ceremony, cooking, and *ikebana*. Only child care is learned from their mothers.

Crowded and noisy Pachinko parlors are everywhere. People are addicted to this pinball game. I played it in Nagoya and can't understand why it's such a big thing. It's a silly diversion and time waster and, since I kept winning with no effort, I'm convinced it takes no skill at all. Beginner's luck, I guess. I brought home as prizes a bottle of port wine for the Wazakis and a pint of whiskey for Iwamoto-san.

Word gets around quickly that I'm back in town, and Mr. Wazaki has received a number of calls from those interested in having me teach English. This afternoon I'm visiting Tezukayama College to discuss conditions of employment. Also interested is Osaka Jo-Gakuen Girl's School; Osaka Junior Women's College; the American Cultural Center; and a Mrs. Ito, whom I met at the Chinese Republic's Reception and is head of a club of distinguished Osaka-area women. Mr. Iwamoto and Mr. Wazaki are carefully juggling the schedule so that I'll be able to take on the least number of assignments for the most money. They seem to be managing my business affairs nicely and are trying, as much as possible, to keep me up to date on developments.

10/26/64

Every year in Japan there are three outstanding festivals. One of them is on Oct. 22nd in Kyoto. Called "Jidai Matsuri" (Festival of the Ages), it is a parade of costumed marchers representing the history of Kyoto while it was the capital of Japan, circa 557-1889. This parade is similar to the one I saw in Nagoya but is much more professionally done and draws a more international crowd. I decided to go to Kyoto for it and stood near the Sakaimachi Gate of the Imperial Palace; the effect was quite nice. After the parade, I went to Nijo Castle, only open for one month every year. The castle is very large and well preserved. Its most unique feature is the "whispering nightingale" floor, which seems to sing as you walk on it. The historical purpose was to warn the shogun of approaching assassins! It was a pleasant day despite the awful rainy weather.

The Japanese are quick to say that their best season is the fall, and this is why the Olympic Games were held in October. But since the weather has been so bad, they are also quick to say that this year is a rare exception.

There are many foreigners in Japan now, most of them Olympic athletes, so the children walk around with autograph books. The way I was being circled at Jidai Matsuri I could tell they were trying to determine if I was one of the athletes and if they should get my autograph. Fortunately, they decided correctly. As it is, I create enough of a stir everywhere I go. I feel somewhat akin to a celebrity and, though people stare in friendship, I find that, unless I'm at home, I have absolutely no privacy. And to think one of the things I loved about New York was the anonymity!

But to go back a minute. On Wednesday I visited Tezukayama and met Kay Nakano, one of the English teachers. I'm sure I'll mention her often. I went back yesterday to sit in on one of her classes. After school the kids called a special meeting of the English Speaking Society. I had been told there were 20 members of the ESS, but somehow 40 appeared to ask me questions about the World's Fair, dating in the United States, our parks versus Japanese parks, and many other curiosities.

Here's a conundrum. We buy subway tickets from illegal ticket sellers at an increased price, so they can earn a little money. Think of it as respectable begging. It is illegal for them to do this, and it is illegal for citizens to buy from them. Yet they do sell tickets and people buy them, and no-one is arrested, for if they were arrested, they would have no way to earn money!

My initial teaching schedule:

At Tezukayama I have 12 teaching hours on Monday, Thursday, and Friday, including five eighth grade classes, one English Speaking Society Club, and three university classes. ESS will have about 20 members, but my other classes will each contain about 50 students. Tuesday and Wednesday mornings I will have four teaching hours at Ashiya College. Wednesday afternoon I teach one hour at Osaka Women's College. On Tuesdays, I'll be teaching English to a group of older distinguished Osaka women, followed by a 30-minute "tea time." Since schools in Japan are on a three-term system, I'll have extended vacations in December, March, and during the summer. It should work out satisfactorily in all ways. Naturally I'm nervous about the whole thing. I've never taught classes above the fourth grade, and I'm worried about making the students understand me. But, since I've never been one to balk at new challenges, I shall tackle the classes head-on. I'm full of ideas and have already ordered *King Arthur and His Knights* and *Gulliver's Travels* for use with my university classes.

Mariko Wazaki and I were having a discussion the other day about Oriental people. She said it was easy to tell Koreans from the Japanese because of their slanted eyes. She doesn't think Japanese people also have slanted eyes. Just shows that it's all in how you look at things!

Let me try to explain the address system based on where I live: 37-5 Chōme, Sakurazuka Hondori, Toyonaka City. Let's start with Toyonaka City, one ward or district of Osaka City. That much is easy. Sakurazuka is one small district of Toyonaka City. Hondori is one small district of Sakurazuka. Things are sub-divided and sub-divided till nothing is left! 5 Chōme is the name of the street, like 1 Street, 2 Street, 3 Street, and 37 is the house number. That all seems relatively easy to figure out until you know that there may be 12 houses with the address of 37-5 Chōme, Sakurazuka Hondori, Toyonaka City. Or, there could be 12 houses with the address of 37-5 Chōme, Sakurazuka Kurigaoka-cho, Toyonaka City. Here's another explanation: Japanese cities are divided into *ku* (wards); each *ku* is divided into *chō*. One *chō* may be 2-1/2 or more acres; a *chō* may have two or more *chōme*, (subdivision of a *chō*); one home is subdivided into several *banchi* (lot number); several houses may have the same lot number. Complicated? You bet it is!

Iwamoto-san was trying to convince me that Toyonaka City itself was only a small town. When I asked how small, he said only 250,000 people live in it!

Beware of room numbers—almost as confusing as street numbers. Room 25 is apt to be on the first floor, and the room opposite number 403 on the fifth foor may be room 629. It's impossible to figure out!

The Olympics finish today, and the Japanese will be sad to see it end. They've loved every minute of it and welcome signs and flags fly from everywhere. I've seen more of this year's games on TV than any other, and I enjoy them even in Japanese!

Japanese teenagers have a new hero: Don Schollander, five-time Olympic champion swimmer. They think he's wonderful and clamor for his autographs and save his newspaper pictures.

Yes, Oku-san is Mrs. Wazaki. All "Mrs." are called *oku-san*. It means "housewife." She does go to some of the functions I attend but usually stays at home. In Japan, a woman's place is clearly in the home!

Most of the functions have many men in attendance, and I'm the only woman. All the men are older and married or younger and married. As for Yoshihiko taking me to parties, no. I hardly ever see him. That reminds me: he is passionate about rugby and teaches me words in gutter Japanese. When I use them at home, his mother reprimands him and tells me that I

Ryunosuke, Mariko, and Yoshihiko Wazaki—my Japanese family

am to immediately unlearn what he has taught me.

You also asked about the hostesses. Yes, they do have a reputation, but it doesn't appear to be shady. Their jobs are considered respectable by the Japanese. They are asked often to go to bed with the men but the choice is theirs, I'm told. They must be nice and courteous to club patrons, but not necessarily go to bed with them, too! One of their chief complaints is that foreigners so often assume they are like high-class prostitutes. Their main duty is to provide pleasing femininity and graciousness—while increasing the patrons' bar tabs for the benefit of the club.

When the Wazakis asked if I have to go to church every Sunday, I told them I am Jewish. They are not familiar with the religion but, when I mention Israel, that seems to clear things up a little. Iwamoto-san, on the other hand, asks many questions about Judaism. Since he speaks such good English, it's easy to explain to him. He is married, by the way—as everyone seems to be!

The Japanese bath is becoming increasingly pleasant. It can't be beat for relaxing tired muscles. Yes, I do soap up under the shower, rinse, and only then hop into the tub. Fortunately, the Wazakis have a device that gives them hot water most of the time, but most places have only ice cold showers. That's when you really need the hot bath!

As far as I can tell, the housekeeper does most of the cooking, while Oku-san merely supervises. She has made it quite clear that I can cook anything for myself that I want, but she doesn't seem too interested in my cooking an American meal for the whole family. She may not want to impose on my time. As for courage in my eating habits, I never knew just how much I had till I came here. I try everything!

But I digress. While Mr. Wazaki played golf with the foreign minister on Sunday, Iwamoto-san and Oku-san took me to Kyoto for another round of temples. First was Seiho-ji, more commonly called the Temple of Moss by foreigners. The chief priest there is a friend of the Wazakis, so he invited us to the temple for tea and cookies. (When cookies or cakes are given in such situations, they are considered gifts and, if you don't eat them there, you must take them home.) After tea, the priest took us on a personal tour of the lovely 1,200-year-old garden. This was followed by a visit to Ryoan-ji with its 500-year-old Zen garden of rock and white sand. Not being a Zen Buddhist, I'm afraid it didn't make much sense; I prefer a garden with trees and plants. Last, we saw Kinkaku-ji, popularly referred to as the Golden Temple. It was the most magnificent of all. In 1950, however, a deranged novice monk burned it down so, while not the original from 1397, it is very picturesque and a place of note for tourists. I want to return when snow is on the ground. I think the gold of the temple will be most spectacular against the white of the snow.

Mr. Iwamoto, my guide, interpreter, teacher, and friend with Mrs. Wazaki (Oku-san), my Japanese "mother" and protocol guide.

Yesterday was the United Nations Day celebration. First was a luncheon, then everyone moved to Festival Hall for speeches. The foreign minister was scheduled to be the featured speaker but had to return to Tokyo after Prime Minister Ikeda announced his retirement. During the speeches, I was filmed by five different television stations. I was sitting with Jim Elliott from the American Cultural Center. He told me he, too, has a problem with privacy. My own dinner plans were interrupted when I was summoned by Mr. Wazaki to join him for dinner with a member of the Japanese delegation to the United Nations and the ambassador to Osaka. We were joined by six other government officials and businessmen. It turned out to be very pleasant, for my dinner companions were all people I knew.

11/1/64

Random thoughts ...

Here they sell a powdered cream for coffee called Creap. It makes me laugh every time I see a commercial advertising delicious Coffee and Creap! My friend Jim Elliott thinks a law should be passed here forcing Japanese men to wear solid black socks, instead of assorted colors and designs, with formal attire. And why do women always wear their sandals too small? They do sell them in larger sizes; I bought a pair.

I have become a full-fledged commuter in Japan, something I would have abhorred in New York! I'm even equipped with season tickets for subways and trains. In Japan the company you work for pays your transportation. The theory is quite logical: if A and B both get the same salary but B lives far from his place of business, the fact that he has to pay larger transportation fees means he actually earns less than A. So by paying all travel expenses, the company then assures that both men earn the same amount. And every year on your birthday you receive a 2,000¥ raise regardless of your output. That's why people sometimes sport beards or mustaches to make them look older!

Remember my mentioning Kazuko Sasada, the opera singer I met the first night I was in Osaka? Friday night she gave a fine recital with the Osaka Philharmonic Orchestra. To give you some idea of prices here, the box seat was only $5.50! Bus rides are only 5¢.

Yesterday I met Ryuzo ("Rick") Kobayashi, son of the president of the cashmere firm. Rick just returned last week after two years of graduate study at London University and one year at the University of Michigan. He spent the summer in New York City working at the Japan Pavilion at the World's Fair. In what turned out to be my first "date" since arriving, Rick took me to the Chrysanthemum Festival in Hirakata. There were chrysanthemums from several countries, and how they were displayed defies description. Also, an exquisite perfumed fragrance pervaded. The feature attraction was life-sized dolls clothed in colorful chrysanthemums that told the famous "Chushingura" story from Japanese history of 47 masterless samurai who beheaded a high-ranking shogunate official they held responsible for the death of their lord two years earlier. The dolls were breathtaking, and I was furious with myself for not having taken a camera! I had always thought there were only two or three varieties of mums. Not so! I have never seen such exquisite blossoms nor such variety. In Japanese culture, the chrysanthemum represents longevity and rebirth. The monarchy is referred to as the Chrysanthemum Throne, and the imperial crest is a stylized mum blossom.

Here's a bit of interesting information. Now that 25-year-old Rick is back in Japan, Wazaki-san thinks he should get married. So in typical Japanese fashion as the go-between, he gave Rick a picture of a "proper mate" and with it was a list of particulars: name, address, age, hobbies, schooling, skills, etc. Since Rick doesn't want to settle down immediately, he won't call the girl and, thus, her picture will be passed on to another eligible bachelor. Were he interested, arrangements would be made for the two of them to meet with both sets of parents at a dinner or Kabuki play. If they are interested in each other after the first meeting, they would start to date. If all worked out, they would eventually become engaged. If it didn't, they would stop seeing each other, and the poor girl would have to try again. Long live the American way!

Contrary to what you might think, the Japan-America Society is made up mostly of Japanese men and women who are interested in the U.S. There are few American members because there aren't that many Americans living in the Osaka area. They seem to congregate in Tokyo, which is why I didn't want to work in Tokyo.

After school I attended a dinner meeting given by Tezukayama Gakuen for junior high school teachers in that area. The purpose was to encourage them to talk up the high school and university to their students. It was brief and included an introduction of both myself and a Mr. Smith, who's from Washington and has been at Tezukayama for 2-1/2 years. He really attracts attention. Not only is he blonde but he stands 6'6"—towering over the Japanese!

Today I'm at home reading, writing, and relaxing. I was finally able to locate the Armed Forces Far East Network and the Voice of America on the short-wave band. I'll be glued to those two stations for election results.

11/6/64

Having just come from my first *ikebana* lesson, I'm so excited I just have to write! I'm learning the Saga School of *ikebana*, one of the top five, I'm told. My teacher, Mrs. Kitaguni, is the Wazaki's next-door neighbor. She teaches the tea ceremony, too, but I don't think it's necessary to learn that. The one-hour lessons are 500¥ a month, about $1.40. Mrs. Kitaguni shows me one arrangement with explanations, then I do it with her help, then I take the flowers home and do it again with Oku-san's help. Finally, the flowers are put in the *tokonoma* in my room for my personal admiration! Mrs. Kitaguni speaks no English, but her daughter stands-by since she speaks a little. Between her English and my Japanese, I'm learning *ikebana*. It looks easy, but there are principles of height, dimension, color, and light that must be followed. I enjoy it very much.

The other night I was helping Oku-san with an *ikebana* arrangement. She had purchased a whole pail of flowers, leaves, and more for 100¥.

Just one of the chrysanthemums would cost twice as much in N.Y.C. Is it any wonder that *ikebana* is popular here? It's quite affordable!

My teaching schedule is in full swing. My favorite class is my women's group. The women are delightful and diverse in their interests. Next are my university students, an easy group to work with. My high school classes are somewhat difficult. The co-educational ones are noisy at times, and those with only girls are too quiet! Having seen the texts they use in other English classes, I know they speak more English than I hear, but they're so embarrassed to speak to me that it's all I can do to get a girl to say "yes"! They are used to repeating everything, though, and if I say "river," they say "reever." If I say "not reever," they say, "not reever." Needless to say, it's most disconcerting. My English Speaking Society sessions are the easiest, for we merely sit around a table and chat, and I don't have to give marks. So that about sums up my teaching. The hardest thing is to keep the classes straight and what I have covered in each.

Even in Osaka I meet someone I know. While going to the train today in the middle of the rush hour, I bumped into Iwamoto-san, who was on his way to see friends at a local beer hall. They get together every week for one hour and speak only English. I went along with him to meet his friends, both named Nakamura, and darned if the young, good-looking one wasn't a bachelor lawyer! Lucky me! He'll be calling me soon—wants to take me to see the famous Girls Revue in Takurazuka. And, I, of course, will be happy to join him!

11/9/64

In my first letter home I mentioned a woman who was at the Wazaki's my first night here and whose function I couldn't figure out. I now know she is the hostess-manager of one of the local restaurants. She was with us last night again, so I was reminded to explain her position. She is hired to serve meals in a gracious manner. It's difficult to say exactly what she does, but she relieves the housewife of the burdensome serving and cooking duties. I say "cooking," because you may remember that most food is cooked on the table in front of the guests.

I received a letter today informing me that whenever I'm ready WUWM in Milwaukee is ready to receive taped reports from Japan. No salary—it's a favor to Ru Hill, the director, but they'll pay tape costs. It will give me some good experience and will look good on future resumés. Ru Hill was staff facility manager at WAER when I was at S.U., and we've been keeping an erratic correspondence with each other since I graduated.

I gave in and bought some long underwear, which is so popular here. I'm finding it difficult to live in a house where the temperature inside is almost the same as it is outside. And my classrooms are even worse! My fingers are numb half the time and winter isn't even here yet. Unlike New York, Osaka's weather is a very wet cold and goes right through me. Winter in the states was always my favorite season, but here I'm already anxiously awaiting spring! The weather is the worst thing about Japan.

11/14/64

I received a note from Sally Small, a high school friend, who was in the Philippines and is now in Japan. She'll be leaving at the end of this month but will be in Osaka next week, staying with a Japanese family around the corner from the Wazakis.

Mom, can you send me a recipe for corned beef and cabbage and a simple white or chocolate cake? I promised Oku-san I'd give her cooking lessons, and I don't think I can make the above without a written guideline. Everybody likes cake, but why corned beef and cabbage? Oku-san said it's because Blondie always makes corned beef and cabbage for her husband Dagwood Bumstead! How's that for an unexpected reason?! Actually, Oku-san makes her own style of that dish, which I prefer to the American one but, if she wants to learn the American way, I'll be happy to teach her. She also wants to learn how to cook a whole chicken and how to make sweet potatoes. I knew my knowledge of cooking would come in handy even in Japan, but it's hard to figure out the centigrade scale on her oven. I hope I do it correctly.

A friend told me his mother is fond of tigers and has many statues and paintings of tigers in her home. When I asked if it was because his mother was born in a tiger year—every year is named after a zodiac animal—he replied that his mother was a monkey. He meant, of course, that she was born in a monkey year. And I am a rabbit.

I had my second *ikebana* lesson yesterday. Mrs. Kitaguni thinks I have some natural talent or feeling for the flowers. Last night's arrangement was made with yellow chrysanthemums, red leaves, and something called *hokigusan*. I've never seen anything like it in the states, but it's similar to the tall, dried grasses that grow at the side of a marsh. Unique, in any case.

I know why I'm so cold in school and needed the long underwear. A thermometer in one of my classrooms registered 48 degrees! To see Japanese people on the street, you'd think it was spring—no heavy coats, no heavy gloves, or no gloves at all. Honestly, I look downright stupid in my winter coat and leather gloves! Iwamoto-san explained it. He has an overcoat at home, but he would never wear it. Does he get cold? Yes, he freezes, but he still wouldn't wear it! I've also figured out that if I keep the gas stove in my room on all night very low, it will be warm enough for me to get dressed in the morning! It was torture to get out of bed—and this is the cold-weather kid speaking!

While walking back to the station, a man stopped me by name on the street and asked if I had been to Festival Hall. I said yes; we walked together for about a block; then we parted. I could swear I never saw the man before! But, when he called me by name, I was too embarrassed to ask who he was!!

Minō Park is quite famous in this area for a number of reasons. 1) People can walk along a river full of little waterfalls that lead to one large waterfall. 2) It is a haven for Japanese monkeys, and they wander freely throughout the park taking food from people's hands. 3) It is not a haven for wild boars, but they also roam the park and try to dodge the hunters who kill them for food and because they eat the farmers' crops. 4) The park is famous for its maple trees. At this time of year, the vivid colors take my breath away! I really went camera happy!

Because the Japanese have different food tastes and because the maple trees are so famous, it naturally follows that a big tourist seller is *momiji tempura*. Translation: fried maple leaf. Since my curiosity is always aroused, I had to try it at least once. Was I surprised to find that battered and fried maple leaves are delicious!

Mr. Nakai, head of a construction firm, took Mr. Wazaki and me out to dinner at a lovely inn in Minō Park. The view from our dining room was of the night lights of Osaka City below, framed by brightly lit golden-red maple leaves. It's amazing how many wondrous things one can find even in this seemingly ugly factory city. And, yes, I hang out in the best of circles under Mr. Wazaki's tutelage! After dinner we went to Nakai-san's home. Wow! Half his garden has 2,500 rose bushes of varying species, plus a variety of fruit trees; the other half is an oriental garden paradise. His home is very large, full of push buttons to make life easier, and loaded with souvenirs of various worldwide trips. His servants' house alone is larger than many Japanese homes!

A Japanese friend warned me that I am not seeing the true side of Japan, for I am traveling in a very wealthy circle where money flows like water. I believe it!

About the schools here: classes are larger—about 50 students per class, which makes me less of a teacher and more of a lecturer. Also, the teacher always enters the room after the students and leaves before they do. When the teacher enters, all bow. And when they meet in the halls, they bow. All high school students—and some college students— wear blue or black uniforms. All but the Christian schools have classes six days a week.

Here's another quickie before I seal the envelope. I spent the evening reminiscing with Sally Small. It was pleasant being with her and strange that we should meet in Japan. We had much to talk about, not having seen each other in 3-1/2 years. She's here with a friend.

Enclosed is my name card. Such cards are a vital part of Japanese life and every first meeting is followed by the presentation of one's card—held and presented with both hands and facing the recipient so it can be read. It was decided I should also have one.

11/18/64

I know I just wrote, but I thought I had better write again, because I have no idea when you'll get your next letter. I am about to depart on a sudden and impulsive trip. Sally Small and her friend Anne Sonntag from Salt Lake City left this morning, heading south to Kyushu. Because I have a long weekend (the 23rd is Japan's Thanksgiving Labor Day), it was decided that I would join them. I'll be traveling a total of about 1,200 miles. Friday at 6, I leave from Kobe on a night ship to Beppu by way of the Inland Sea, or Setonaikai. I'm going third class (there are only four) and will thus be sleeping with seven other men and women in one room. I arrive in Beppu early the following morning, then catch an express train to Mt. Aso, which boasts the world's largest volcanic crater and is a popular Japanese resort area. Once in Aso, I take a taxi to meet Sally and Anne at the Japanese inn where we're staying. Sunday we leave Aso, tour Unzen briefly, then head for Nagasaki where we'll be staying in a western hotel. How long I'll be in Nagasaki is the joke of the trip. I can't get reservations back to Osaka! I've tried every train that leaves in two days—local, express, stand up, sit down, and sleeper—without success. I hope to grab a cancellation tomorrow but, if necessary, I'll go without a ticket and ad lib! All things considered, it will be a great adventure! Sally and Anne will be leaving Nagasaki on Monday; how or when I leave is yet to be determined.

A word about Japan Travel Bureaus: they are all over the place and always bustling with activity. After trying to get reservations on several trains, the agent finally found one that was available. I told him immediately I'd take it but, when he went to confirm, it was already filled! You can't believe how busy they all are!

Want a good illustration of Japanese humor? There is a Japanese dish called *oyako* that is made with chicken and egg. *Oyako* means "parents and children." There is a similar dish made with beef and egg. It's called *tannin*, which means "stranger." Clever!

Since Ryonosuke will be home for his winter vacation in early December, lack of space prevents me from staying at the Wazaki's home. Nobody wants me to leave, but there just isn't enough room for their three children and me, though I will see them at least once a week—every Friday after my *ikebana* lesson next door and weekends for Oku-san's cooking lessons. I have also promised to spend New Year's Day with them as a regular family member and, since all females wear kimonos that day, I, too, have been asked to wear one. After that I just don't know, though there are certainly a number of people who have invited me to stay with them. I'm very happy here and in no hurry to leave.

I stayed late at school today to help my university students rehearse Thornton Wilder's "Our Town." Part teacher, part drama coach, jack of all trades, master of none!

Finally, after the Travel Bureau had officially closed, I was able to get hold of someone's cancellation for the Tuesday day train back home. I had to take a 1st class ticket; still only $12.50 for an approximate 500-mile trip. I'll have to spend an extra night in Nagasaki by myself, but that's okay. The boat ticket cost only $8.

One thing more before I close. I learned there's a Jewish Center in Kobe. When Iwamoto-san wrote to them to find out about one in Osaka, they told him there were only two in Japan: the one in Kobe and the other in Tokyo. I hope to go there in December for a Friday night service. When is Chanukah? I'm out of touch here.

That's it for now. I'll let you know how my adventure turns out.

11/26/64

Happy Thanksgiving!

Well, that long weekend finally convinced me I was in Japan! It's funny that it took two months for the realization to come!

Let me see if I can attempt to tell you about the trip in some picturesque fashion. On the 20th, I boarded the *Kohaku Maru* in Kobe port. Since I was headed for Beppu, the most popular year-round hot spring resort in Kyushu and a well-known spot for honeymooners, the deck of the ship was swarming with young marrieds while members of their families and friends, some still in their ceremonial wedding kimonos, waited on the dock. Each couple had several paper streamers that were held, at the other end, by their friends. As the ship pulled out, the streamers unrolled to their full length and, when they finally snapped (I likened it to the breaking of the umbilical cord), many of the young girls burst into tears. You can spot honeymooners anytime for, if they have just been married, the wife carries a small bouquet of flowers, and always wears a hat that usually covers her hair. As one new husband explained: a wife doesn't have time to fuss with her hair on a honeymoon!

My third-class room on the ship was shared by two men and three other women. We slept on mats that measured 1-1/2' x 4-1/2'. Even for the small Japanese this is a bit too short and narrow. There were only about 3" between mats. At least I had a mat, two pillows, and a blanket. In fourth class, you get only a stuffed leather block as a headrest.

The Japanese are lovers of natural beauty. It was exciting to see how many of them, despite the cold, spent the evening on deck, as I did, watching the moon casting its lights on the water. And when Shodo Island loomed suddenly out of the blackness, I thought immediately of the Titanic and its iceberg! The following morning many woke up early to watch the sunrise. The sinister-like but wispy orange mist that crept over the mountains on the horizon was one of the most splendid sights I have seen! The fishing boats that stood out black in the orange glow added to the beauty.

Arriving in Beppu early Saturday morning, I took a train to Aso. All over Kyushu the rice paddies are tiered to aid in irrigation, but they form a strange patchwork pattern. These are set off by thousands of tangerine trees and multi-colored maple trees and, every now and then, clear blue brooks with white waters breaking over the stones. It was a wonderful image.

When I joined Sally and Anne, we decided to head right up to Mt. Aso. As we went to catch the sightseeing bus, we met three young men traveling together: Dave Somebody from the states, Alan McGregor from New Zealand, and Mick Withers, the water polo goalie on the Australian Olympic team. We kept meeting them in buses, boats, restaurants, streets, and even in various towns! Anyway, the six of us headed up to Mt. Aso, the world's largest volcanic crater, measuring 50 miles in circumference. Originally five separate craters, the dividing walls have all collapsed. By bus and cable car, one can go all the way to the top, but to go to the rim of the crater, you have to pay extra. It's still huffing and puffing sulphuric gases that can be seen for miles around and, if you can avoid getting a big whiff of the strong hydrogen sulfide, it's fascinating to watch. There was, however, a tremendous whipping wind at the top and no guard rails to protect tourists, so we had to be cautious.

We spent a pleasant evening in our Japanese inn outside Aso and the next morning took train, ferry, and bus to the spectacular Unzen-Amakusa National Park, then to Nagasaki, stopping in a town enroute to see its famous hot sulphur springs and to explore the maze of winding streets down narrow back alleys—one of my favorite activities anywhere I travel.

In Nagasaki, we stayed at a western hotel with western beds—neither of which I care for anymore. But I sure did go for that big western steak! And for breakfast the following morning, I had cornflakes, bananas and cream, and cinnamon toast—with the cinnamon strong and right from the tree!

We went to visit the Peace Park, where you can't help but feel guilty by being there if you have any conscience, and to the Glover Mansion overlooking the Nagasaki port. Because of the view, it is the alleged home of Madame Butterfly (*Cho-Cho-San* in Japanese), who never existed in fact. Giacomo Puccini's opera takes place in Nagasaki and, from her home, she could see the whole port when her American lover returned to take their son. Anyway, it conjures up exciting visions!

In the afternoon I said a reluctant goodbye to Sally and Anne, then departed alone for Sasebo Naval Base, where I had been invited to spend the night by Bill Wimbush, one of the men Marty worked with in N.Y.C. and who is now a school guidance counselor there. Bill and I had a marvelous evening together: he bought me another good steak dinner, took me on a tour of the base, and introduced me to many of the King School teachers. One of them, Mel Kellman, is Jewish and, when he heard that I was Jewish, his eyes lit up and his whole attitude changed. I could only conclude that his 1-1/2 years in Japan has starved him for affection! He not only asked me if he could write to me, but he also presented me with a porcelain tea cup he had recently purchased for himself. Frankly, I thought the whole thing was kind of funny!!

> **[Note a theme is forming here: Single American Jewish Woman. It was the keystone for so many of my experiences. And if it wasn't that, it was Single American Woman. I held the golden ticket for residents of other countries, just at the time that Willy Wonka created it.]**

On the train back to Osaka, I met Joy and Mark Lemieux from Vancouver, BC. Mark, a geological engineer, was a member of the Canadian Olympic crew team. I sat next to Noriteru Hamada, guest conductor of the Tokyo Symphony Orchestra. He, of course, was also stimulating to talk to.

11/30/64

Now back in Osaka, I'm enjoying the Christmas shopping rush hours. Here, by the way, they say *Curisimasu* — (Koo-ree-see-mah-soo)! I'm also putting the finishing touches on an article for Rochester's *Democrat & Chronicle*.

My high school classes here are an absolute bug-a-boo. I gave my students a written test last week, which I now know is impossible. They just aren't learning, and one reason is because they don't listen. Having studied foreign languages myself, I can tell the difference between slow students and inattentive ones. It's a waste of their time and mine, but I haven't come up with a sufficient answer yet. I hope to discuss it with the school principal tomorrow.

12/2/64

I visited an English conversation class at the American Cultural Center. The subject under discussion was *tomokasegi*, and a rough translation of that might be the problem of both the husband and wife working. In the states the problem is created by a working wife, not by a working husband. Here, of course, a basic problem is lack of funds. One man, about 60 years old, vehemently proclaimed during the meeting that in Japan the nation is first in importance, second is the married couple, and third is the individual. My immediate reaction was shades of World War II. I was glad he stood alone in his opinion, for the younger generation in attendance was quick to state their opposing points!

After the meeting I dropped in briefly to an *Utazawa* concert, a classical song and dance, which uses as background music the *samisen*, a guitar-like instrument; a *koto*, a horizontal harp-like instrument; and a *tzuzumi*, little drum. The sound is strange and not particularly pleasant to my ears but, for a short hearing, it's entertaining.

Oku-san's aunt — *oba-san* — is 82 years old and visits from Kyoto for a few days about once a month. *Oba-san* means "aunt" but it is the only name I know her by. She is typical of many older women here—very short, with a tiny body, and slightly stooped. It was a tradition here before WWII for all women to walk behind a man with the head always bowed—thus the reason for the bent and stooped shape of older women. Her face is wrinkled with age—wrinkled in all the places that are effected when she smiles. The Japanese are a laughing people, but women's laughs are modest and moderate. When they laugh a little too much or two broadly, men and women alike cover their mouths to maintain their dignity. *Oba-san* wears her age handsomely.

Yoshihiko-san had friends for dinner on Sunday and, at Oku-san's request, I made a roast chicken. It was good and everybody liked it, though they didn't quite know how to handle the bones when eating the legs and wings. I gave them a lesson in the traditions of the wishbone!

I had my first Japanese haircut the other day at one of the department stores. I paid 84¢ for it, but Oku-san said that was expensive! She pays only 56¢ at a nearby place!

One thing I find hard to accept here is the disturbing frankness of the Japanese. If someone makes the mistake of saying something like, "I'm afraid I've overstayed my welcome," the host may reply, "Yes, you have." It's not surprising to hear phrases like, "You have an ugly nose"…"I don't like your shoes"…and so forth. It seems to be part of oriental culture. I spoke with Sally and Anne about it, and they said in the Philippines people are simply named "cripple" or "blind boy." This is only one of the many, many differences in our cultures!

The past few nights, we (I say that with a broad smile) have been making a winter *yukata* for me. "We" is Oku-san and I. And I say it with a smile, because she's doing 7/8 of the work. I did purchase the flannel material and that's about the only thing of merit I've done! What little I've sewn isn't the best handiwork, so she either sews faster and better or sews when I'm not at home. Nevertheless, it's been a fun project.

Can you believe I've been here two months already? Most of the time it all seems quite natural to me, but every so often I realize quite suddenly that I'm living in my dreams, and I get excited just walking down a crowded street! I think now that I'll stay only about a year…but, at the same time, I don't like to think of leaving. I refuse to make definite plans about anything yet. I shall never have another experience like this; I don't want to come home until I'm really ready to settle down!

Have a happy, happy Hanukkah! The Japanese have trouble pronouncing many English words, but they say "Ha-nu-ka" very well. All the sounds are in their alphabet. And while I think of it, Iwamoto-san was trying to ask me questions the other day about English "boughs" and "consulates." It took me ten minutes of utter frustration on both our parts till I realized he meant "vowels" and "consonants."

12/7/64

I'm in a significant place to commemorate Pearl Harbor Day, don't you think? It's amazing what has happened between our countries in only twenty years since the war ended!

Want to know one reason why I love Japan? (There are so many to choose from!) In New York on a Sunday afternoon, you visit museums to see ancient and historical artifacts that are out of context. Here on a Sunday afternoon, you visit the real thing! The farmer's straw raincoat of 100 years ago hangs on a hook by the door where you can see it well and imagine the farmer who wore it. It's not behind a closed glass case protected by uniformed guards! And, if you go to the countryside, you can sometimes see farmers still wearing them.

I also love Japanese illogic. In Kyoto there is a large and showy Chinese restaurant. It's name? What else but "Champs Elysées"?!

I'm moving to what I think are very satisfactory quarters in Minō City to the home of Toru Otani, a 29-year-old pre-med student, and his wife Reiko, 24, who is expecting a baby in March. They met because Toru's older brother married Reiko's older sister! They have a fairly large home, and they don't use all the rooms. They aren't particularly interested in making money, so for the use of a Japanese room that is about 11′×13′ and a western style sitting room with breakfast every day, the cost will be under $28 a month. They're a very nice couple, and I think we'll get along together well. The house is old, and the floor and my sliding doors to the outside garden are slightly warped. It has a typical non-flush Japanese toilet. I shall get used to that like everything else. The Wazakis have been good enough to let me have for my room here the gas stove, the large wardrobe, and the dressing table.

I shall be at the Otanis only until next summer sometime when they leave for Houston, Texas, for two or three years. Mr. Otani will be doing neuro-chemistry research at a hospital there. He's now at the Osaka Hospital Cancer Institute. Part of the plan, of course, is that they want me to help them improve their English.

My room at the Otani's home—the sliding door exits to the rear garden.

Some side comments:

—Japanese rooms are measured differently than ours. My room here and at the Otani's is "six-jo," which means it holds six *tatami* mats.

—Just as their birthday system is different, as I explained in a previous letter, so, too, is a women's pregnancy period. In America, it's nine months, but here it's ten months and ten days. Of course, it's the same.

My high school classes have improved considerably. I no longer dread them so! It's a terrific help having a Japanese teacher in the room. Because the system of teaching English here is so very poor, the students aren't ready for me. They need more training in basic grammar, but I'm having a hard time convincing the school of that.

Since all books in Japan are too difficult for my classes, I'm now writing my own textbook—about an American family that moves to Osaka. It's a terrible bother to write it, but it's not really a difficult problem, just time consuming. The stories are better understood, so I guess the project is a worthwhile one. When I leave Japan, I promised Tezukayama High School that I'd give them a copy of the text for use as supplementary material in the future. It's interesting writing the text and then testing it before actual classes. Then my changes are valid and proven! My S.U. teaching degree continues to come in handy, but whoever thought I'd apply my knowledge for students in another country?

I use everything in teaching, including word games and songs. You should hear my students sing "Jingle Bells"—especially when they can't pronounce the letter L! Christmas is here in all its decorative glory. The stores inside and out are decked out in *Curisumasu* lights, and the Christmas shopping rush is on in force. The most popular family gifts are food packages.

My students in the ESS at Osaka Jo-Gakuin asked me to come in during their winter break. I told them it was cheering to hear they like my lessons, but to have a good time and forget school for awhile. I need the money, but I'm looking forward to the vacation.

English tongue twisters are a fun way to teach pronunciation. Here are three Japanese tongue twisters: *Tokyo tokkyo kyoka kyoku no kyokucho* (the chief of Tokyo's Patent Approval Bureau); *sabi kugi ore kugi hikinuki nikui* (a rusty and broken nail is difficult to pull out); *nama mugi, nama gome, nama tamago* (raw wheat, raw rice, raw egg).

12/14/64

To move I rented a truck for only $2.10 per hour—a monster of a thing, particularly since I had little to move. The streets in my new neighborhood are very small, built for horses not cars. It was a laugh to see the truck maneuver around the corners. We literally scraped our way along the neighbors' bushes. *"Gomenasai"* turned out to be the laugh-provoking word of the day. It means "Excuse me!"

Last Wednesday I met a Mr. Nara from the YMCA. He acted as the go-between in getting me a job at Dai-Nippon Celluoid KKK. (Pronounced "Cerruoide," because there is no letter L in Japanese.) The translation of that is All-Japan Celluloid Company. Beginning January 6th, I'll be teaching there twice a week at $8.33 per hour. They have 5,000 employees throughout Japan and 300 in the main Osaka branch. Ninety-two of them (all male) requested English conversation lessons. They split the groups into four separate classes, each three months in length. A go-between is used in situations where a person might feel shame if he fell short of the required goals. Thus, this intermediary is used to arrange marriages, offer ones services for hire, etc. It is essential that a Japanese person does not lose face and it is, furthermore, essential to protect one's own name. It is part of that complex system of obligation.

Mrs. Eichigo, the woman in my adult group, always brings me goodies. She has a terrific sense of humor; you just never know what she's apt to say or do! I'm very fond of her. One woman in my English group is single and a university professor. Mrs. Echigo's husband owns a large trading firm. The husband of another is president of Daimaru Department Store; another was owner of a shipping firm before his retirement; and now they both are Honorary Consul Generals of Thailand. The husband of one woman, a widow for eight years, was president of the *Mainichi Newspapers*. And so it goes ...

12/15/64

Though there are modern supermarkets in Japan, the local market is more like a farmers' market. I especially like the fish stalls: row upon row of tuna, octopus, salmon, sea bream, squid, mackerel, and hundreds of fish you could never find in the states. In Mexico, I remember the markets were a confusion of ugly odors. In Japan, they are a profusion of vivid colors! Reiko goes to this market almost daily to buy what she needs—just enough meats and vegetables for the day's meals and two or three eggs, as necessary.

Plumbing here takes some getting used to. There is a strange contraption that heats the well water in the bathroom sink. First you turn on the gas pilot light, then wait for the water in the one-gallon tank to heat up. The contraption reminds me of a Rube Goldberg invention—and it makes weird noises, too!

Today I went to Nara with a friend and one of my university students. We visited the Daibutsu there, a giant statue of Buddha, housed in the largest wooden building in the world. The statue itself is 53' high. The thumb alone measures 5'! The temple, is called Todai-ji. The original was built in 752 AD but was destroyed twice by fire. The current one is from 1709. Sitka deer wander around a large park. I drew "lots" at the temple. Looks like I'll be pretty lucky the rest of my natural life if Buddha has anything to say about it! Since I was born on his birthday, I guess he's going to look out for me. He's done a good job so far!! We also walked to Nigatsu-do and Sangatsu-do. They mean "temple of the second month" and "temple of the third month." The stairs leading to these two temples are lined with stone lanterns.

I gave my university students their first test this past week. I spoke individually with each one and got some unexpected reactions. One student told me that the U.S. was a great country because President Kennedy was born there. Another told me that 1945 was the best year in history because that was the year she was born! One told me she wanted to see the "Fall of Niagara." The best response came in a discussion about the Japanese Self-Defense Force. One girl told me it was a good thing, but not in the case of war. When I asked her if that didn't make it undesirable, she said: "Well, yes, but the U.S. will defend us. We expect them to!"

Japanese television does not present programs recreating the war between Japan and the U.S., but they do televise "Combat," which shows U.S.-German encounters. Since this is Japanese television, the Americans speak Japanese. What a strange dichotomy!

My travel arrangements for January are all set. When the people at the Japan Travel Bureau told me I could get no room in Tokyo for less than $10 per night, I laughed and told them I knew darn well that Japanese people couldn't afford that much money. I'll be staying in a nice inn in central Tokyo—only $4.17 per night! The travel bureau couldn't make seat reservations for me for the six-hour train ride and told me I'd just have to stand. When you live like the Japanese, you travel like the Japanese!

12/18/64

The two most popular Christmas gifts are sugar and monosodium glutamate. Both are used with everything, so they are practical gifts. Monosodium glutamate is Aji-no-moto in Japanese. The translation of this would be "source of taste." I've been buying Christmas presents to give to friends. When I suggested to Iwamoto-san that I buy something for the Wazakis' house, he was appalled. It had to be food, so I ended up buying a tremendously large box of the best chocolate candy in Japan. I also bought a smaller box for the Hyugas. For Toru, I bought a traditional new year kite for boys; for Reiko, a traditional *hagoita* for girls. I can't translate that because we have nothing like it in the states. The style is called oshi-e (pressed picture), and it's made of cloth, wood, and paper. It can be used as a fan or for a type of badminton game played with a shuttlecock. Iwamoto-san warned me he would be mad if I bought him anything, but I wanted to give him something to show my appreciation for everything he's done for me. I decided to buy a gift for his 4-year-old son, Kazuki, and settled on a 3'-long wooden train that can be taken apart and assembled easily.

I've also received two gifts: a traditional cloth used in the tea ceremony and a pretty handmade woolen stole—good for these cold winter nights. Weeks ago, Oku-san gave me a fragrant, lacy-carved fan made of *byakudan* (sandalwood).

My university classes yesterday were informal and cozy. The groups were small, and we all sat around the gas stove and chatted.

These next few weeks will be busy. In addition to my trip to Tokyo on January 2nd, I'm going to spend the new year holidays with Hyuga-san who will be in Tokyo for a conference at the same time I'll be there. It'll be nice to spend a day with a friend.

I just returned from the Wazakis' home. Their living room was piled high with packages of food and more were arriving! One package contained American products. Included, much to our surprise, was Similac, a special powdered baby formula. I haven't a clue why someone would gift them with that! Mr. Wazaki plays an important role in the Osaka business world. As a result, they receive many gifts and, on New Year's Day, many visitors. It's the age-old tradition of exchanging greetings and requesting friendship, patronage, and guidance. As Iwamoto-san said last week, "Christmas is a frivolous, unimportant time, but New Year's Day is the most important day of the year!" The Wazakis sent out only three gifts: a joint gift to the men who work at the U.N. Association and gifts to Ryonosuke's and Mariko's teachers.

    I received a special delivery letter from Mrs. Noriteru Hamada. I previously mentioned Hamada-san, the conductor of the Tokyo Symphony, whom I met on the train back from Nagasaki. What I didn't mention was that I had helped him interpret the words and phrases in Handel's *Messiah*, which he was going to conduct in Fukuyama. I also explained to him the correct way to sing them so that they could be well understood by Japanese audiences. (Fortunately, I was familiar with the selection.) Anyway, I received a nice thank you note from Mrs. Hamada telling me that the concert was successful and they hoped I would call them when I get to Tokyo. They would be free and wanted very much to see me. I was surprised and pleased to receive the letter, for our meeting was one of those things I just never expected to hear about again. The Japanese do this to be nice. Many times there's not too much sincerity behind the request. Until I received this letter, I had no intention of calling him. Now I certainly shall.

    You asked if I would be able to save money. Yes, I think so. Come January I'll be earning about $225 a month. My living expenses come to $60-$70 per month, including lunches and dinners. Sometimes I eat at the Wazaki's; sometimes I make my own here; and sometimes I eat out. But if I eat two meals out in one day, the total bill comes to only $1.25. Food is cheap if you know the right places to go!

12/19/64

The train ride in was quick and easy—only four hours on Japan's marvelous new express line! Even without looking, I knew when Mount Fuji, or Fujiyama (Fuji Mountain) came into view because of the murmurs from the Japanese travelers. It's the bewitching, towering, iconic symbol of Japan and, because everyone loves it so, it is affectionately referred to as "Fuji-san." Snow gracefully dotted the area around the crater and fluffy white clouds hovered around to enhance its loveliness. Its exceptionally symmetrical cone, snow-capped several months of the year, makes it a perfect focus for art and photographs.

Seeing Mt. Fuji for the first time had a profound impact on me. It was a special moment in time, an *ichigo ichie*. Derived from Zen Buddhism and particularly associated with the tea ceremony, it is the concept of treasuring every encounter for it will never recur again in the same way. It's one chance in a lifetime, a rare opportunity. Every meeting—the first and the last in the same exact way with people, places, experiences. That's my life now: thousands of *ichigo ichie* to be remembered and treasured.

The most familiar of the Mt. Fuji artists is Hokusai. At a time when *ukiyo-e* artists were producing commercial works that catered to public taste, Hokusai, in 1834, brought a new depth to printmaking with the publication of his *Thirty-Six Views of Mt. Fuji*.

Ukiyo-e, or pictures of the floating world, were a unique Japanese art form developed in the Edo period, 1615-1868. They came to be associated with the momentary, worldly pleasures of Japan's rising middle class. Unable to alter their social standing and regulated in nearly every aspect of their lives from behavior and dress to the sizes of their houses, wealthy commoners found escape in licensed pleasure quarters and Kabuki theaters. There, they could watch handsome actors performing the latest plays or spend time with beautiful courtesans known for their sparkling wit, musical accomplishments, and poetry. Paintings of people from this world became a specialized form. For the first time in Japanese history, commoners had enough money to commission works that reflected their own interests and activities. They patronized artists who featured subjects wearing the most up-to-date fashions and hairstyles. These artists also created woodblock prints as inexpensive alternatives to paintings, making *ukiyo-e* available to everyone.

But I digressed! Again!

The inn where I'm staying is pleasant and relatively close to the Imperial Palace. I headed for the Ginza area, like Times Square only more so! I found a marvelous and inexpensive western restaurant, wandered in and out of exciting stores, and proceeded to walk the streets, recording various sounds as I went. I saw more Americans tonight than I've seen since I arrived! After rebuffing the advances of one Japanese man, I was standing outside a restaurant with my tape recorder trying to record a song that some men were singing inside. At Japanese get-togethers, there's always a great deal of singing, hand-clapping, and general merriment. Two young men stopped and asked what I was doing. When I told them, they literally whisked me to a little restaurant, bought me a second dinner, and took me upstairs where I could record "up close" another male get-together. After two hours and on the way to the streetcar stop, two university students insisted they take me back to the inn via subway.

That's only my first eight hours in Tokyo! Wonder what fates await me these next few days? Well, having already taken my bath—it's a ritual, y'know—and since I have a full day tomorrow... *Oyasumi nasai*. (Good night.)

12/20/64

It's now midnight and, were I not staying in an inn, I would never have returned so early. But, let me start at the beginning...

I took a terrific $7 all-day tour! For my own memory, let me jot down what I saw: Atago Hill and Shrine with 86 steep steps that a samurai climbed in 1636 on horseback...Rakan-ji Temple with about 500 gilded images of Rakan, the disciple of Buddha and where the priestess chanted a portion of the Buddhist scriptures...

Furasato Restaurant, a well-preserved 300-year-old farm house… the Japan Folkcraft Museum, appealing and well-known to foreigners but not to the Japanese. On to Toshogu Shrine's 300-year-old stone lanterns dedicated by feudal lords. I purchased a lucky key ring for my zodiac year of the rabbit. Jyomyoin Temple already has 20,000 statues of the children's god Jinzo and 64,000 more will eventually be added. These statues are paid for by the parents of children who died in infancy. Lastly, to Teppozu Inari Shrine where we saw a special Shinto ceremony. That's it in a nutshell, without the trimmings. It was a fascinating day.

Some facts I learned from our guide: salt is used to purify…a vertical tea stalk in your cup is a superstitious sign of good luck…gravestones of Buddhist monks have round tops instead of square ones…4 and 9 are unlucky numbers. The character for 4 means death; the one for 9 means agony. Thus, many hospitals skip these numbers when they assign rooms or floors. When you give presents, it's not four of anything but three or five. Dishes are sold in place settings of five.

After World War II, our guide and three other men were assigned two jeeps and living quarters for three months by General MacArthur. Their job was to judge the amount of war damage in Kyoto and Nara. As you may recall, however, these two cities were spared from bombings. There was no damage, nothing to inspect and, thus, he is grateful to MacArthur for his long expense-paid (and vehicle-provided) vacation!

By the way, I also saw today the Olympic facilities, several parks, and more. It was a good basic tour of the city. I decided that Tokyo is much more like Paris than New York, particularly the wide boulevards. Much of the city is quite lovely. I stopped at the Imperial Hotel, designed by Frank Lloyd Wright. Built of earthquake-proof *ova* stone, it has a handsome and quiet elegance.

One of my tour mates, 35-year-old Parisian Roland Henri, and I went to a little coffee shop chosen from the masses because the name of it was La Seine. Roland is now on a one-year around-the-world tour after working in N.Y.C. for three years as a mechanical engineer. Dinner was followed by a visit to one of the popular nightclubs for cocktails and dancing. We were both unhappy that tomorrow he's leaving for a five-day tour of Kyoto and Nara, and the day he comes back, I'll be on my way to Hakone. I think the appropriate phrase is something like "two ships passing in the night." That's the trouble when you meet tourists. How unfortunate for me that he's leaving Japan! "*C'est la vie*," he said. It was a wonderful, happy evening!

12/21/64

I've only time for a few words before I'm picked up, but let me start now since I'm getting up at 5 a.m. tomorrow. I started out the day with a visit to Asakusa Kannon Temple, dedicated to the goddess of mercy. The approach to the temple is famous for its many souvenir shops and is very colorful now with all the New Year decorations. Following that, I visited Kiyosumi Garden. Kiyosumi, along with Rikugien and Korakuen, are reputedly the three best gardens in Tokyo. It was elegant and serene, filled with swans, white ducks, and wild ducks. Then, since I'm me and not the usual tourist, I went to the Tokyo Zoo in Ueno Park. You know I enjoyed it!

My last stop was Korakuen Garden. As I began to walk around, the director came running after me. I thought I'd done something wrong, but he merely wanted to take me on a personal tour. I was glad he did, for I learned many things about Japanese gardens. He also showed me pictures of the 300-year-old garden before the war when so many ancient structures were destroyed. It was awkward and disturbing to see remnants of bombed trees and buildings. But, like other Japanese I've met, he spoke without malice. Nevertheless, discussions like this make me feel uncomfortable at times.

I saw a strange and ugly sight today, but I didn't understand anything that was going on. A man standing near Asakusa Temple was apparently a sidewalk preacher of the worst kind. A large crowd had gathered around him, listening to his shouts and watching as he took a long knife and slashed his arm in several places. He wore what may have been a tourniquet and was possibly preaching a lesson about the power of a spiritual mind over physical pain. I was rooted to the spot by the crowd but repelled by what I saw.

12/22/64

My evening with the Hamadas was very special. They are such a nice couple and have a precocious three-year-old son who, in addition to everything else, has a thorough knowledge of the English alphabet. In February they are going to Italy for three months where Hamada-san (remember he's conductor of the Tokyo Symphony) will do a round of concerts in various Italian cities. I hope to see them again when we both return to Tokyo.

This morning at 6 a.m. I was at Tsukiji Uogashi, Tokyo's wholesale market, the largest in the world. I was the only foreigner there and, until about 7, I was the only woman. Everyone was very friendly. I was given a front seat at the fish and fruit auctions. I shared a blazing fire with three of the fishermen; many of the people came to speak with me and explain what was going on; and a woman offered me a hot cup of tea when I paused to rest at the side of a truck. At 6 a.m., the wholesalers were getting their stalls ready, chopping or sawing the fish, and bidding for certain boatloads. By 7:15, the fishmongers began arriving, and by 8 a.m., it was bustling with activity! Then I moved over to the vegetable and fruit stands, which were just beginning to get busy. About 9:15, I wandered over to a sidewalk food bar and had a delicious bowl of *tempura* with really fresh fish!

Later I went to have my shoes fixed, and the man said, "You were at Tsukuji this morning, weren't you?" When I asked how he knew, he said my shoes smelled like fish!

I visited Tokyo Tower—taller than the Eiffel Tower and just as popular—but, because of the heavy smog, the view was limited.

Following a special trip to the Noritake China showroom and the Japan Sword Company, I went to view the Imperial Palace, wherein resides the emperor. There I met three nice girls, 16 years of age, and spent about an hour with them. They wanted to write to someone in America and, since Harv is always interested in girls, I thought he might enjoy hearing from this side of the world. One, all, or none may write to him. Harv, be prepared!

It's now 4:20 and I've already called it quits today. Besides, I woke up at 5 this morning and tomorrow I'm getting up at 6 to go to Nikko. There's a Japanese saying, "Don't say *kekko* (magnificent) till you see Nikko!" Nikko is 87 miles north of Tokyo.

Some Japanese inns offer super personalized service. Since I awoke so early this morning, they gave me an alarm clock to use. I carried my shoes with me (almost forbidden) and unlocked the front door myself to leave. Now relaxing in my *yukata*, I ordered dinner at the inn. A filling meal, a hot bath, and so to bed!

12/23/64

Well, I went to Nikko, and I'd hardly say, "*kekko*"! Toshogu Shrine, however, is far more colorful than most of the temples here because much of it is in the Chinese style. Built in 1636 by the first Tokugawa Shogun Ieyasu, it consists of 23 buildings, both Buddhist and Shinto.

When I returned to Tokyo, I joined Frank and Liz Guberlet for dinner. These two are old friends of a woman I worked with through WRVR. They have lived in various parts of the globe, though Frank is now head of the Far East Tokyo Office of Flying Tiger Lines. After dinner at the American Club, we went back to their home for nightcaps. They've invited me to join them for a "merry greaseless Christmas dinner," as Frank is on a special diet.

12/24/64

Merry Christmas Eve!

This morning I wandered over to the American Pharmacy. The smallest tube of Crest toothpaste sells for $1 in Japan. The equivalent size of Colgate, which has a branch firm here, sells for only 17¢. That's why I use Colgate!

I met Hyuga-san and his friend Tadashi ("Yoko") Yokoyama for lunch, then Hyuga-san had to catch a train back to Nagoya. Not to waste the afternoon, Yoko and I wandered in and out of stores, making a special trip to Takashimaya to see its talked-about Christmas decorations of giant moving animals in humorous settings. After going to a private collection of Impressionist paintings, we walked around the Imperial Palace Moat in a heavy but appealing fog.

While eating dinner, I felt the table shake and commented about the rumbling subways. "No subway. It was an earthquake!" A minor one, to be sure, though noticeable.

There's happy singing coming from somewhere, for tonight is the beginning of a round of *Bonen-kai,* or year-end parties. All business is completed by December 31st; debts are paid; and bonuses are received. It's a popular time of year!

RADIO BROADCAST

The New Year Holiday
"Orientation" 1965

The custom of Susuharai *began 700 years ago in the Imperial Palace and continues today in the form of a thorough house cleaning—in a sense, a purification of the house for welcoming in the god of the year on New Year's Day. Everything is dusted and cleaned; family treasures are specially cared for; the* shoji *screens and* fusuma *sliding doors are repapered.*

When Susuharai *is completed, the most joyous annual household function in the year-end season begins—*mochi-tsuki, *or making rice cakes. To the Japanese, rice cakes are an indispensable food in observing New Year holidays, somewhat like the Christmas plum pudding of England. Rice cakes are reverently offered to the deities on the household Shinto altar—a two-layer* kagami-mochi, *round and mirror-shaped, signifying spiritual purity and integrity. The two layers express the wish that good fortune may be "piled up." After seven days, they are removed from the altar and eaten, for it is believed that those who eat rice cakes will be given strength and courage.*

Making these rice cakes is not an easy task. Particularly in the cities, most people prefer to buy mochi *ready-made. The work is difficult and potentially dangerous. Glutinous rice is put in round steaming baskets that are placed one over the other upon a boiling kettle. On the floor is set a heavy stone or wooden mortar and a pail with water for wetting the hands. Nearby is a large working board. When the housewife estimates that the rice contained in the lowest basket is steamed soft enough, she takes out the basket and throws the rice into the mortar. The head of the family then pounds the rice with the help of his wife. He swings the hammer-shaped pestle up over his head and then heavily down into the mortar. Frequently wetting her hands, she turns the sticky rice dough upside down, right and left, so that her husband can pound the rice evenly. The danger is here for, should the team work out of sync, the husband might pound his wife's hand, head, or shoulder. When the rice is pounded well enough, she takes it from the mortar to the working board where the children tear off small pieces and round them with both hands.* Mochi *is made plain or with seaweed, prawns, or red beans. There are several ways to eat it. When freshly made, the cakes are good raw with sugar. But they are better in* o-zoni, *a special soy bean paste soup for the new year. They can be toasted on a hibachi and dipped in soy sauce (my personal favorite) or sprinkled with sugared bean-flour.*

Also at year's end, it is customary to send o-seibo, *gifts to those who bestowed favors during the year. It is usual to send foodstuffs, such as dried fish or sugar.*

[Now cakes, pastries, and other sweet treats have been added. Too much exposure to western culture!]

December 31st is o-misoka, *an important day to the Japanese, for it is psychologically the day before the start of a new life. Business is completed; debts are paid.*

Finally, the New Year arrives, ushered in with the pealing of the Joya-no-kane, *the large temple bells rung 108 times to dispel man's 108 errant desires, or sins, as decreed in the Buddhist religion. Contrary to the American insanity, New Year's Eve in Japan is a sober occasion on which the whole family gathers together. (The New Year holiday is one of the few occasions when this country, known for its modern technological advances, reverts back to century-old traditions.) At midnight everyone pauses for a bowl of soba, the long buckwheat noodles that signify longevity. Then to bed to await the most important day on the calendar.*

At daybreak, the mistress of each household sets about preparing the special New Year's Day breakfast. When ready, the head of the family extends greetings to all and the first cup of sake is drunk. Called o-toso, *it is a special rice wine containing medicinal herbs and spices—the first of many such cups stretching over the seven-day celebration period. Now begins the great excitement of uncovering the many lacquered or porcelain-tiered boxes revealing foods in every size, shape, color, and type--prepared days in advance. Japanese food appeals to the senses of* sight, smell, and taste, and nowhere is this more evident than during the New Year holidays. The special food eaten at this time is specifically referred to as o-sechi.

Following breakfast, the head of the family makes a round of New Year calls on his neighbors, friends, and relatives to exchange greetings and ask for future guidance, friendship, and patronage.

Some families go en masse to a local shrine for the first blessings of the year. The practice is based upon the belief that in order to start a new life with fresh determination, it is necessary to invoke divine aid. Others are more inclined to neshogatsu, or "sleeping off the New Year."

Most Japanese enjoy more activity than the last affords. For boys, in particular, kite flying is popular. For children, one of the most popular of the outdoor games is Hanetsuki played with battledore and shuttlecock, a game somewhat similar to badminton. Think of the battledore as an oversized rectangular paddle that is elaborately decorated with paintings on one side and historical figures in a fabric art collage on the reverse.

An indoor pastime during this season is a card game for adults called Hyakunin-Isshu (One Hundred Poems by One Hundred Poets). These poems were selected by thirteenth-century poet, Fujiwara-no-Sadaie. There are 200 cards in all—each of the first hundred with the complete text, while the other hundred have only the second half of a poem. The selected reader recites as much of the whole text as is necessary while the players look for the card bearing the second half of the poem—all laid out before them on the tatami mats. There is much shouting, good cheer, and even playful roughhousing. Based on the same idea is a children's game Iro-ha-karuta, which contains cards with familiar proverbs and others with illustrative pictures.

On the subject of poems, there is the New Year Imperial Poetry Contest for which Japanese throughout the world are invited to send in waka entries, according to the subject chosen by the emperor. In waka, 31 syllables are used to create a poem in five lines in a 5-7-5-7-7 form.

Throughout the New Year holidays, colorful decorations called kadomatsu adorn every door made up of pine, evergreens denoting *strength and long life; bamboo stems, which, because of their straightness, stand for constancy and virtue; and plum blossoms that bravely bloom though snow may cover the ground. With these are ropes of twisted straw symbolizing purity. Inside the house on the Shinto altar is another decoration with two large rice cakes as its central point. Their shape signifies spiritual purity and integrity. Atop these is an orange that, because of a verbal pun, suggests continuity. With the orange is a lobster representing old age for two reasons: its curved back and its name is written with the Chinese ideograph meaning "the aged of the sea." Embellishing this little fortune pile are ferns for purity and an expansion of wealth in the coming year, dried persimmons, roasted chestnuts, and dried sardines.*

Unlike the New Year holiday in the states, the Japanese celebration lasts for seven days. On the last day, some eat a rice porridge with seven herbs—yet another New Year talisman. Seven days may seem like a rather long holiday, but the fun is hardly over. In the countryside, preparations then begin for **Ko-shogatsu**, *which is celebrated on January 15th. That's the celebration of New Year's Day as it was on the ancient solar calendar. In the rural districts where entertainment establishments are few and climatic changes may prevent work in the fields, this is an especially happy occasion. In many regions, villagers gather at the local shrine and, marking a sacred plot of land, go through the actions of planting and harvesting rice. This make-believe ceremony is thought to insure good rice harvests that year, for it is done under the beneficent watch of the community deity.*

The Japanese new year is replete with significance—the beginning of a new calendar, a new life, and fresh aspirations. This conviction led to the initiation during feudal times of an unusual practice of holding an extra New Year when epidemics, famine, economic depression, or social unrest were prevalent. Five were held between 1778 and 1880. There were no formal celebrations, but customary New Year rites were observed. They symbolized fresh determination and the start of a new and better life.

The New Year holiday in Japan is a time of rest, peace, and contentment and a time for the traditional greeting: "Akemashite o-medetō gozaimasu".

This is Wendy Phillips reporting from Osaka, Japan.

Mata aimashō. Sayonara. *(We'll meet again. Goodbye.)*

12/26/64

Christmas is over for another year. In the morning I visited three of the Tokyo art museums and the National Science Museum. In the afternoon I wandered around the old bookstore area and picked up a marvelous book of black and white ink prints that depict Japanese life several centuries ago.

Last night I had dinner with the Guberlets. I bought them a little Christmas gift: a calendar. And they bought me a little Christmas gift: a calendar! We had a marvelous dinner of turkey, cranberry sauce, squash, string beans, wine, nuts, and cheeses. I felt like I was in the U.S.!

This morning I left Tokyo and went to Kamakura, stopping for a visit at the other famous Daibutsu, or Giant Statue of Buddha, as well as the Tsurugaoka Hachiman Shrine in a somewhat decrepit state of repair.

From there I came to Hakone National Park and my inn, Kowakien. What a fantastic place! There are actually three buildings: two house the Japanese inn and one, across the road, is a western hotel. There's a fairly large outdoor hot spring swimming pool. Unfortunately, I didn't know, so I didn't bring a bathing suit. There is a hot spring pool for those who like to swim in the nude, as well as a penguin pond and an extraordinary green house featuring pineapple plants, banana trees, cacti, and a wide variety of tropical flowers. To add to the scene they've created, there are also a good number of tropical birds. Nearby is a monkey house and a cage with about 12 peacocks. You just wouldn't believe this place! With two meals, it's only costing me $7 a night. My room is large and has a great view of the landscaped garden. There's a large Polynesian Bath Garden here, which I plan to use after dinner. The bath is a beaut! Women use the second level and men the first, so we don't actually bathe together, although we can easily see the men. Do I mind? Not at all! I always enjoy new experiences. It's part of my education in living as the Japanese do!

12/27/64

What a weird day this has been. I spent a leisurely morning trying to figure out what to do on such a lousy, rainy day. By noon the rain stopped and I decided to go ice skating atop Mt. Koma, about 15 minutes from the inn. The higher the bus went the foggier it got—from about 50' visibility to only about 30'. The ice rink is the only thing on top of the mountain, so to get there, you have to take a cable car. The place is quite large with indoor and outdoor rinks. The outdoor one was better, but the fog was so thick! I rented a pair of hockey skates—it was all they had—but, boy, was I floundering. The first half hour I felt and looked like it was my first time on ice!

Weather-wise this day had it all: rain, fog, snow. On my tour around Hakone, we climbed Mt. Koma by cable car. There had been a heavy snowfall overnight and it was bitter cold. The skating rink is in full view of Fuji-san, though I never saw it for, when the fog passed, clouds covered it! On the other side of Koma, I took a ferry ride on a small part of Lake Ashinoko, hopped on the bus for a trip on the Jokkoku Pass where you can get some magnificent views of Fuji on a clear day. From Atami, I took the train back to Osaka.

All in all, it was a very pleasant vacation.

12/30/64

Do you remember when I was in high school I entered a sterling silver contest and came out Second Grand National Prize Winner? Darned if I didn't do it again! *Mainichi Daily News* held a Christmas contest drawing. You had to send your name and address and what you'd like of the prizes listed. I was reading this morning's paper and almost fell off the chair (except that I was sitting on the floor as usual) when I read that I had won a pearl brooch! 542 people sent in cards; I came out in the top 5!

Last night Iwamoto-san and I went out to dinner and then went ice skating. Apparently, most rinks have figure skates, so happily I was on firm ground again, so to speak. One man asked me to teach his 13-year-old daughter how to skate. Again I went skating this afternoon. Two students joined me for several go-rounds. It was fun!

After I figured out I wear size 23.5 in Japanese shoes, I was confronted by 9-11 numbers when renting skates. After trial and error, I found out I wear a 10. Why the two numbers? The first one is centimeters; the second is an ancient measuring system still in use. They once measured with coins, now extinct, called *ichimon*. Thus, my foot measures 10 *ichimon*.

The New Year is coming quickly. People are busy with the usual equivalent of spring cleaning...*shoji* screens and the paper on *fusuma* doors is being renewed...special dishes used only at this time are readied...*kodamatsu* are hung everywhere...and *mochi* is made. Many years ago every family had a stone mortar and a heavy wooden pestle for grinding and hammering boiled rice into these special New Year rice cakes. But the work is hard and time consuming. If the timing of the hammering is off, the woman turning the dough could have her hand, shoulders, or head crushed by the heavy blows. *Mochi* is now made only by farm families or a few city folk. Most people buy it in stores. Today I watched, fascinated, a family working as a team making *mochi*. When they were through, they presented me with three freshly-made *mochi* stuffed with red beans. It is also made plain, with tiny shrimp, or with seaweed. When fresh, it can be eaten raw, served in soup, or barbecued and covered with soy sauce. The taste is somewhat like raw dough; the texture somewhat like a large mass of mozzarella cheese.

Oh, I bumped into Rick Kobayashi in the downtown crowds today. Having returned from Tokyo, he called me last weekend when I was in Hakone. Unlucky me, he accepted a job in Tokyo and will be going back there in two weeks. His dad was told that Rick's life would be more "severe if he didn't live at home." Thus, he was pressured to work away from Osaka where he'd have to eke out room, board, and other expenses on $70 a month.

Speaking of future training, I'm getting it. I do my washing in the back yard with a washboard and a wringer (tough when your fingers are numb from the cold), and my ironing is done on an old blanket while kneeling on the floor. My clothes dry in the sun, so I have to be sure they're taken in before the dew falls. It makes me appreciate what we take for granted in America!

I stopped at the Wazaki's last night and picked up a whole bunch of Christmas cards sent from the U.S. I also received by registered mail $75 in cash, my salary from Tezukayama. Sending cash through the mail is considered safe here.

1/5/65

This has been one of the nicest New Year celebrations I've ever spent. New Year's Eve I was at home with Toru and Reiko. For the past 15 years, NHK has held a song contest featuring the top singers in Japan. That ended about midnight, and then the TV camera switched to various temples throughout the nation for the *Joya-no-kane*, the ringing of a large temple bell 108 times to signify the 108 human sins of Buddhist belief and the arrival of the new year. At midnight, some people visit the shrines and temples for the first blessings of the year. Some purify themselves by bathing in icy mountain streams after imbibing a good amount of *sake*. Marathon races are held. Priests take sacrificial food offerings to the various gods in long, colorful processions. And everyone, myself included, eats a dish of *soba*, long, thin buckwheat noodles that symbolize long life.

Homes, trains, and cars are decorated with *kodamatsu* to welcome ancestral spirits, and every home and store has *kagami-mochi*, large rice cakes placed on home altars for seven days in the belief that the gods descend to earth for seven days. After that, the rice cakes are broken up and served to the whole family. This is called *kagami-biraki*. The *mochi* is believed to give spiritual power to a person and is regarded as a type of magic promising good luck.

New Year's morning I went to the Wazaki's home for a traditional breakfast that began with *o-toso*, a type of *sake*, as well as the ceremony that it's used in. *O-toso* is done only at the new year and weddings. *Sake* is drunk from cup-like saucers—only once! If you drink more *sake*, another cup is used. Then the *jubako* are brought in. These tiered boxes hold food during the new year holidays, for no cooking is done during this time and everything is eaten cold. What an array! Food is served in Japan to appeal to the olfactory and visual senses. It was a rainbow of color and a parade of shapes and arrangements—for example, potatoes that looked like roses and carrots like daisies!

After breakfast, Oku-san dressed me in my New Year kimono. I had purchased *tabi* (cotton socks) for the occasion, and Reiko had given me an *obi-hime* (kimono belt) as a New Year's present. It took 50 minutes to get it all on and only five minutes to reverse the process! Once dressed, Mariko, Ryonosuke, Iwamoto-san, his son, and I went to a shrine. The roads were jam-packed with cars. The way everyone was staring, I must have created a unique appearance as a red-headed Caucasian in full kimono dress! The rest of the afternoon was spent at Iwamoto-san's home, then I went back to the Wazaki's for coffee and chatter. It was a wonderful day!

Mariko Wazaki and I on New Year's Day

The article you read in the *Democrat & Chronicle* about my meeting with Sally sounds as if they didn't use the exact story I sent. What a way to get out of paying me a fee!

Are they really having shoe sales? Great! I can use a pair of flats and a pair or two of leather mid-heel pumps. Looks like I'll be in Japan for quite a while, and shoes don't wear well on these no-sidewalk, gravel-topped side streets. You know what I like.

How nice of you to invite Mrs. Masako Saito and her son for dinner when you don't know them. I'm indebted to Japanese people for life, and it's nice that you're helping me work off some of my *giri*. *Giri* is my duty to non-related persons due to obligations passively incurred by me. It sounds unbelievably simple, but it's part of that overly complex and important system of obligations and repayment.

1/7/65

I gave my first lesson at Dai-Nippon Celluloid. I have 22 men of varying ages, but I'm not sure how many will stick with it. They're a good group, but I can't help but feel it's something like conducting a board of directors meeting!

As of next week, I'll be busier than I'd like to be, but the thought of the money for additional travel in Southeast Asia and Europe keeps me at it. On Tuesday evenings, I'll give a senior high school student private lessons at her home—two hours with dinner for 15,000¥ per month. That's $41.67. On Thursday evenings I'll meet with Toru's 20-year-old sister and three of her friends for private lessons. Two hours with dinner for 16,000¥. It all adds up and with six employers, I've lost track of my monthly earnings. But it's good—darn good as Japanese wages go!

Today I dropped into the Wazaki's home and stayed for dinner. When I came to Japan, our conversations were in English, as much as possible. Today I noticed we were speaking Japanese. Looks like I've made some progress! And it was wonderful when I was in Nagoya to be able to talk with Hyuga-san's children at last!

Oku-san was surprised today when I told her I wore only one piece of long underwear (if I wear any). The Japanese wear two and three! Last night I broke down and bought a *yutampo*, which serves as a metal hot water bottle when it's wrapped in a cloth cover for safety. It was great in bed and was the first time my feet were warm all winter. Meanwhile, it just gets colder and colder. No snow, some rain, but, oh, the cold! It just eats clear through to the bones—and the funny thing is that the temperature is only about 30º. That's not really cold in New York, but somehow it seems like minus 30º here! It doesn't help that the Otani home is old and hole-y! Drafts are everywhere; the wind just rips through the house! As the temperature goes down, I bundle up more and somehow I've only chalked up two winter colds so far. No doubt by spring the number will triple! For someone who loves winter as much as I do, I'm forced to admit that I'm looking forward to spring as a child looks forward to Christmas.

RADIO BROADCAST

Impressions of the U.S.
NHK (Excerpt) 1965

So many questions, even from strangers! During the Olympics, interest in the U.S. was piqued. Why are there no Negroes on the American swimming team? How did I feel the day President Kennedy was assassinated? Among Mickey Mantle, Stan Musial and Willie Mays—who is the most popular in the U.S.? Which is the best city to live in: Honolulu, New York, San Francisco, or Washington? Why is the U.S. fighting in Vietnam?

When I return home, the most important question to ask me is not what were my impressions of Japan but, rather, what were my impressions of the U.S. During November elections in the U.S., the American Cultural Center showed a movie—some Gidget nonsense—that painted our elections in the most awful way, demonstrating every stupid aspect of them. What was the ACC thinking? Of course, I was asked about them and embarrassed. This was not the good type of propaganda I had expected!

Here's another great question Oku-san asked: "If Japanese roosters say 'ko kekko ko,' but American roosters say 'cock-a-doodle-do,' and Japanese babies cry 'o-gya o-gya,' how do American babies cry?" Spell that one out!

1/10/65

Friday night I went to Ohel Shlomo Synagogue in Kobe. The service was surprisingly short—about 20 minutes. Though it's all in Hebrew, it claims to be neither Orthodox nor Conservative. The sanctuary is small and plain except for a few ornate chandeliers. Eight men were present plus myself and six children. Who made up the *minyan*? Two teenaged boys, bar mitzvahed in the past four years. There is no rabbi; the men conduct the services themselves. The Tokyo congregation has a combination rabbi-cantor-*mohel*, who comes to Kobe when needed. The congregation consists of about 35 families from various parts of the world, but the largest representation is from Israel. After the service, the acting-rabbi invited me to his home for a *Shabbos* dinner. His name is Victor Moche. Originally from Bagdad, he was in Japan on business 30 years ago when the pogroms began and decided it was safer to stay here. He's about 50; his wife, about 42; and they have 7 children. They are a charming family, witty and gracious. His passport from Iraq was voided and, since he didn't like the idea of being stateless, he and his wife went to Israel long enough to establish residence. For the past 17 years, he has been on a waiting list for American immigrants and is hopeful that, when Congress revises the U.S. immigration laws, he will be able to take his family to the states. His younger brother and his family are also living in Kobe. They've been here 15 years, working as pearl exporters. Another brother lives in NY and will be coming to Kobe next week. Before dinner, there was a special *Kiddush* ceremony and then he blessed each of his children. *Shabbos* dinner was delicious and unique, particularly because it was in Japan. Every Friday, Mrs. Moche makes her own matzo, her own cheeses—cottage cheese, cream cheese, and other types. Two of the children hope to attend universities in the U.S—one this year and one in 1966. I was asked if I would help them choose an appropriate college and, of course, I said I would. Next Saturday I promised to come out again for the short morning service and then spend the day with the family. So, no doubt, in the months to come, you'll hear more about the Moche family.

Sick again! I went out and bought a heavy scarf and a thick pair of socks. With the Bufferin, Vicks VapoRub, and vitamins, maybe I can wage a successful war. Yesterday was so cold, I was wearing gloves around the house. And by the time I finished my wash, I was forced to hang my clothes out to dry (?!) in heavy wet falling snow. But what was I to do?

I'm glad you had such a pleasant evening with the Saitos. It's nice to have unpaid American ambassadors working on both sides of the Pacific! No doubt your inviting them to the square dance class was a stroke of genius! That's a real look at Americana that few Japanese would ever see. Mrs. Saito's sister is not one of my students, but even so, it's a small world. I teach at Tezukayama University and her sister is a student at Tezukayama College. It was nice that Mrs. Saito brought you some Aji-no-moto. In the states we either use it or we don't, depending on our whims. In Japan no woman would think of cooking without it. It's a typical gift.

Wazaki-san no longer invites me to any affairs. I seldom see him; once or twice a month maybe. I'm busy enough without that and it's easier not to be with him, for he is a demanding and domineering individual. He wanted me to get on my feet. Now that I've made it, he has eased off on introductory pressures. His patronage continues, however. I understand he is the one who brought me to Mr. Maeda's attention, and I gather on my visits about town he still talks with pride about me. Few people sponsor an American in Japan—and I suppose, because there's little opportunity to do so, the fact that he is doing it is a feather in his business cap!

You asked if I was sorry I didn't go to Tokyo. No. Two reasons: I'm content not to be surrounded by Americans and, more important, Osaka is close to the ancient cities of Kyoto and Nara. I'm happy here and no doubt I shall stay in Osaka for the duration of my stay in Japan.

1/13/65

I went for the first time to the Maeda's home. Their 17-year-old daughter, Sachie, is my new student. Mr. Maeda is a member of the prefectural assembly, owns a credit bureau and a cooking-*ikebana*-tea ceremony school. To say my reception was warm is almost an understatement. The Maedas have only one child. Perhaps that's the reason why they want me to think of them as my Japanese parents and Sachie-san as a sister. They have already invited me to live in their home. I was a little overwhelmed by this hospitality, as well as their immediate familiarity. They seem to be a very nice family. I shall consider their offer when the Otanis go to the states.

1/18/65

In honor of all 20-year-olds, Friday was Adult's Day, a national and school holiday. That evening I saw three plays in my first live *kabuki* performance. I didn't understand the stories, but I found them fascinating. All *kabuki* performers are men, called *oyama*, (female impersonator). They simulate feminine ways so well, it's difficult to realize that only men are acting.

Saturday I went to the Kobe synagogue and then spent the day with the Moche family. They want me to come out every Saturday, but I have too many things to do. That night I had dinner with the Wazakis. Oku-san, in one of her classic humorous observations, came out with the theory that young women look like Coke bottles and old women look like Pepsi bottles. Take another look to see what she means!

Yesterday with some students I went skiing for the first time in eight years—to Mt. Hira near Kyoto, overlooking famous Lake Biwa. You go halfway up the mountain by chair lift; the other half by ropeway. The slopes are on the other side of the ascent route. There were so many people on the mountain we had to wait three hours before we could get on a downhill cable car. But, as is usual with the Japanese, nobody complained; nobody even frowned.

During the three hours, we warmed up in the ski lodge and then made two skis into a toboggan for additional snow play. It was great fun. Any resemblance to my being their teacher was purely coincidental and much to my liking and theirs. When we finally reached the chair lift, it was almost 8:30 p.m. The moon was bright; the view was clear. The combination of the stillness of the night with the beauty of the snow-covered mountains and the lights in the towns around Lake Biwa was special. It was sad to see it disappear after the 20-minute ride down.

> **[Too detailed and boring to report, but in this letter, as in so many others, my mother and I shared recipes and wish lists. I sent her directions for making *hokonabe* and *okonomiyaki*; she sent me her wish list of purchases, like a jewelry box and pearls. I sent my wish list for warmer clothes and underwear. And then there were all the other special things I thought she'd want me to buy for her: accessories for flower arranging; unique cooking utensils; a deer horn *hera*, used to mark clothes for sewing; artwork; and on and on and on it went. There was no end to her wishlists, and they changed and increased frequently.]**

I always refer to this wonderful group of English students as "my women." They were favorites from our first meeting and taught me much more than I could ever teach them.

Today I went to a luncheon at dear Mrs. Eichigo's beautiful home. Her lunch was lovely—literally. Vegetables looked like roses, raw fish looked like herons, and a replica of Mt. Fujiyama was created in rice and seaweed. There were eggs like chickens in their shell and pressed fish cakes like daisies. If I learn nothing else while here, I'll be certain to learn these elegant tricks for serving food! Mrs. Eichigo lives in the wealthy district of Ashiya, near Kobe. Her home furnishings, her linens, and her serving dishes show her exquisite taste. There's a Japanese phrase, used derogatorily at times, that refers to "Ashiya Madames." Lovable Eichigo-san would never fit the phrase; her personality must make her stand head and shoulders above the rest.

[I always thought of this group as "my women" and refer to them as such throughout these letters.]

1/24/65

While in Kobe yesterday, I went to the American Pharmacy to pick up some stuff. I was surprised at the hard sell approach of the clerks. In Japanese stores you could practically stand on your head before anyone would pay any attention to your wants. But here, they were pushing everything. The American way in the American Pharmacy!

I went to Takurazuka with Nakamura-san, that lawyer I mentioned ages ago. Takurazuka, but for the Girls' Opera, is a nothing town. In 1919 the Hankyu Railway Company created this unique attraction for the purpose of attracting patrons to the other end of their line. Kabuki and Noh are all men; the Girls' Opera is all women. It's a spectacular and exciting musical-dance extravaganza. The park in which the theater is located has a zoo, a botanical garden, and an amusement park. We made the rounds. We were even able to play a couple games of ping pong!

Mothers in Japan carry their babies on their backs by means of a cord. The baby goes everywhere with the mother and this leaves her hands free. It's up to him to make himself comfortable. Mothers talk to the babies continually. I've been told that position is one reason why so many Japanese people grow up bowlegged. Another reason is that they're trained to sit with their legs splayed out at an early age. Here's how a child is taught to bow: when the occasion arises, the mother forces the bow with her own body. Even a baby is trained. The mother pushes his head to a lower, more respectful position.

1/27/65

Today was the New Year get-together of the Japan-Philippine Society. The students of my Wednesday class are also members of that group. Present were 14 Japanese women, myself, the wives of the two Philippine consuls, and a Mrs. Ishida, a Philippine woman who married a Japanese man. After lunch, in an old national custom, there was entertainment. Naturally, I was called on to perform. While one of the women danced, I sang an old folk song called *"Sakura"* that tells about the beautiful Japanese cherry blossoms. I was lucky they chose that particular song. It's the only one I know!!! They also had a grab bag. I got three handkerchiefs—all in purple. That's a very popular kimono color for older women. I'll be ready for it in 40 years!

I have an interesting but rather sad story about the Japan-Philippine Society. It was begun 10 years ago by Mrs. Ishida and Miss Kinoshita (one of my students). The Japanese women who are members are all from the upper class of society. Mrs. Ishida, strangely enough, is the only Filipino. Their purpose is to promote good will between the two countries. They meet monthly, if possible, and chat. Sometimes, they hold a bazaar to raise money for Japanese and Philippine charities. I commented to Mrs. Ishida that I thought it strange there should be only one Filipino representative. She told me (with a wry smile) that all members of the group are carefully screened. She has suggested several Philippine women be admitted, but somehow they never pass the rigid requirements. Even she wasn't sure what they were. Thus, the reason why there is only one Filipino woman. She told me that, since she's in the minority, she can hardly exert her influence. A perverse way to promote good will!

I came up against a problem the other day. Gorgeous embroidered blouses are sold here, and I decided I'd buy one or two. Ha! I've too much bulk in my bust! In Japanese measurements, I wear a large, and large sizes don't come with the fancy work because that size is usually worn by older women who don't wear fancy embroidery! When you travel, you never know what problems you'll run into!

In a letter I sent some time ago, I mentioned *giri*, that complex system of obligation. Japanese people don't like to "wear *giri*," and I have a story to illustrate that. When a student came for my Japanese lesson, she brought some bananas for Reiko. There was no reason for her to bring them. She has almost no interaction with Reiko, but Reiko had to accept the gift. That means she was "wearing *giri*." As a means of repayment, during my lesson

Reiko brought us some pudding she had made and topped it with banana slices. It was a means of saying thanks and showing that the gift was useful. Another example: in Japanese, "thank you" is *"domo arigato gozaimasu."* It is also *"domo sumimasen."* This means "thank you; I'm sorry." Thank you for obvious reasons. "I'm sorry" because I have incurred certain obligations.

"Giri" or *"on"* — they're almost the same — must be repaid in mathematical equivalence and within a certain time limit. Over the years, they have (fortunately) decreased in intensity — but they are still present and followed to a certain degree. It is one reason, at any rate, why Japanese thinking is so confusing and difficult to adapt to.

Having been gifted with so many amazing things during my stay in Japan, I've struggled to think about what I could gift in return so I would no longer "wear *giri.*"

The *Japan Times* newspaper has asked me to lecture to a group of senior high school students at the American Cultural Center. I can talk on anything but, since hiking and mountain climbing are such popular pastimes here, I think I'll describe outdoor recreation programs for American teenagers. My bike trip to Nova Scotia should interest them. I've also been asked to lecture at the American Cultural Center to a group of advanced adult students. I'll speak on broadcasting in America.

Reiko will be going to her mother's home on February 15th to wait out the birth of her baby, so I have to find some place to sleep until she comes home around April 1st. From pillar to post and back again! Iwamoto-san is now making arrangements, but I may stay at the Wazaki's part of the time and go to the Maeda's when Ryonosuke-san comes home for his spring vacation. I'll let you know where I'll be hanging my nightgown, but I'll be coming back here several times a week for newspapers, mail, clothes, and to do some work in quiet surroundings.

1/30/65

I opened a bank account and deposited 43,765¥, about $122. Depositing that sum caused no squeeze, but I couldn't help but recall all the newspaper articles I've read about families being robbed of 36,000¥, their life savings.

I read a provocative newspaper article the other day. Recently the Nara City government changed the color of paper used for application forms for women's holidays. The change was from white to pink and done to facilitate handling. The union claims that the employees hesitate to submit such conspicuous papers and thus abandon their right to take holidays. Investigations have begun on possible infringement of human rights. And all because a piece of paper changed color!

Iwamoto-san is no longer at the United Nations office per the orders of Wazaki-san. He's been transferred as a bookkeeper to the Osaka Keio (University) Club, directed by Wazaki-san. The job is duller but it pays a little more. Did he have any choice? Not really. One does what Wazaki-san orders!

Did you read about the football player who ran 66 yards the wrong way to give the opposing team two points? He left Minneapolis for Dallas to accept the "Boner of the Year Award" but took the wrong plane and ended up in Chicago. He's in bad shape!

2/3/65

Setsubun Day! It's a centuries-old bean-throwing exorcism rite. "In with fortune! Out with the demon!" is what they shout. Literally, *Setsubun* means the parting of the seasons. So, somewhat like our Groundhog Day, it also means the end of winter and the coming of spring.

I went with Nakamura-san to a special restaurant licensed to sell *fugu* (blowfish or swellfish). It's served raw or in *sukiyaki*. What's so special about it? The fish contains a deadly poison in its liver. One chunk and you're dead! Restaurants that serve it and dealers that sell it are carefully licensed. And all cooks that make it must, by law, attend a one-week training class. Violation of the laws may result in loss of business or imprisonment with hard labor. About a hundred years ago, people didn't know how to prepare this delicacy, and many people gave their lives for a taste of the fish. A few phrases in vogue at the time were: "I am thirsty for swellfish, but life is dear to me"..."Such a timid man who can't eat swellfish shall not see Mt. Fuji"..."How reckless, they eat swellfish when they have sea bream"..."Neither self nor Buddha, only swellfish I see on the table." Since it's somewhat of a forbidden fruit, naturally people are curious. I expected somewhat of a Lucullan taste, but it's quite bland. It does tend to give one a warm feeling—that plus several cups of *sake* wine makes one feel pretty good on a cold winter night!

After our *fugu sukiyaki*, we went to the largest dance hall in Osaka; it caters to teenagers and young men. The hostesses wear outlandish white dresses with bridal headpieces—a distinguishing mark to be sure—and the music is mostly of the twist style. As I walked in, an echo of *"gaijin"* (foreigner) followed me. On the dance floor, everyone stared to see how this American danced. One waiter took a personal interest in me and was funny the way he whispered everything to my date to translate. He even whispered "thank you" as if it were confidential information.

Sunday I'm going to the movies with Nakamura—at 9 o'clock in the morning! That's the way they do things around here! Last Sunday we went to his sister's home for a *sukiyaki* dinner. She and her family live around the corner from the Wazakis. We spent the afternoon chatting in Japanese and English and the evening playing mahjong, a popular game here.

It's a great friendship and it's amusing to see what Japanese dating is like—always with the cheery goodnight handshake! For selfish reasons, I enjoy it, too. I like being with him and I get to places I couldn't or wouldn't go to by myself.

[A few weeks after this diary entry, I found out that Nakamura would get married the following summer. Ah well, it was fun while it lasted!]

A late night walk through a train station on weekends may involve stepping over and around skis and/or skiers. Hundreds of skiers lie, stand, or sprawl in the stations waiting for night trains for the 8-hour ride to the Japanese Alps. To while away the time, they sleep, eat, or play portable chess, *go*, bridge, or mahjong. *Go* is a popular strategy game invented by the Chinese more than 2500 years ago.

Dad, I saw an amusing article in *Newsweek* called "Real Golf." What is it? In Jinja, Uganda you have a free drop for a ball that lands in hippo footprints. At Tokyo's Musashino golf course, you ride cable cars to play on the near-vertical mountainside. At one club in Nairobi, there's no penalty for a ball that lands in a snake's coil. And in Rhodesia, baboons scoop up the golf balls then run, jabbering, into the trees. As the article said, "…that's real golf!"

2/7/65

I told Tezukayama that I am leaving. The high school staff wasn't surprised. They knew all along there were many difficulties. Here's one: I take the train to get to the school, about an hour each way. The first time the problem arose, I showed up at school only to find it was closed that day. I called to remind the office staff that I speak Japanese, but I can't read *kanji* and, when school holidays are coming up, to please share that information verbally. Twice more I took the train to teach only to discover that school was closed. That was the main reason I decided to quit. As for the university, the vice president was floored. He's now checking on tax laws to see if my salary can be increased. He's offered me either freshman or sophomore classes—and at any time I want them. In short, he wants me to stay. I don't know what decision I'll eventually make, but I am definitely leaving the high school. Just the thought of it raises my spirits!

On Friday I went to the Wazaki's for dinner, as I do every week. After my *ikebana* lesson, I returned for tea and talk and then took a bath there and even washed my hair. This must sound strange to you, but it's not uncommon for such an offer to be made either in a restaurant or a home. Bathing here is not always for the purpose of being clean. It's looked on as a pleasurable indulgence. At any rate, the minute I stepped into the wooden tub I could recall everything from the minute I stepped off the plane in Tokyo. What a long way I've come since then in my understanding, appreciation, and adaptation to my surroundings.

Today Nakamura-san and I went to see the Russian version of Shakespeare's *Hamlet*. Despite the fact that it was in Russian with Japanese sub-titles, I was explaining the story to him. Japanese students don't study much about Shakespeare, but they're naturally curious. The theater was packed with students.

On my way home, I bought raw fish for dinner—tuna, the best tasting and the most expensive. Even when you buy food in the market, it's sold in style. The raw fish is garnished with grated white radish, called *daikon*, parsley, and a blob of green horseradish, called *wasabi*.

Some people go out of their way to attract my attention. They may speak English or pull out an English book and flash it around. The other day one student tried a new approach. He pulled out a French book and studied from it. Then I guess he decided I might be American, so he hummed "Home on the Range" simultaneously. Young children sometimes sneak up behind me in a sort of hide-and-seek game. I can't help but laugh when these things happen.

I've been writing scripts and recording programs for use in Milwaukee. They sent me a shipment of 12 tapes about a week ago, and I'd like to send them four programs by the end of February.

I still don't know where I'll be moving after the 15th, but I should hear in the next few days. This past week I've been alone in the house. Toru went skiing and Reiko has been too ill to come home. Since she has a good deal of pain, she's been staying at her mother's. She can't understand why I'm not afraid to be here alone, as she's terrified of being alone in the house. Most Japanese people are—particularly women. Japanese people have an anathema to privacy. In fact, there's no word for it in their language. The closest thing means "loneliness" or "selfishness." There is no privacy here. Mail is carefully perused; the houses are open to the whole outside world; the inside *shoji* screens are opaque; the walls are paper thin. Bathrooms, even in public facilities, are for both men and women; and even baths aren't taken alone. If you happen to be the only person in the tub, you can easily talk to the other members in the house. In hotels you can't always find locks on the doors. It takes some getting used to!

RADIO BROADCAST

Short Tall Tales
"Orientation" 1965

Japanese Gods and Demons

Some time ago in a small magazine for tourists in Japan, there was an article titled "Belly Up to the Bar, Boys—There'll be No Navels Nibbled Tonight!" Highly irreverent was the title, but the basis for that story is interesting and the belief not so outdated.

When the summer sky turns dark and the storm clouds roll, children playing in the nude are warned: "Come quickly—put on your clothes or Kaminari-san will come and take your belly-button!" It once was that older people would put their hands over their stomachs when they heard the approach of Kaminari.

Who is this monstrous demon? Kaminari-san lives up high in the summer clouds wearing only a loin cloth made of tiger skin. He has horns on his head, and ugly tusks protrude from his mouth. On his back he lugs about round, flat drums arranged in a semicircle; in his hands, he carries drumsticks. He has an insatiable appetite for human navels and this causes him to fall from the sky. When he beats his deep, resonant drums, thunder rolls through the sky putting fear into the hearts of the people on earth. Kaminari is the god of thunder.

Other destruction is caused by Raiju. Nobody has ever seen him, but he is believed to be similar in form to a gray-haired dog. His tail is like that of a fox and his claws are long and sharp. He's a lazy animal and always sleeps when the weather is fair. But as soon as he hears thunder, he wakes up and follows it to earth, clawing as he goes and causing damage to humans, houses, trees, and crops. Raiju? He's the god of storms and lightning

To protect temples from destruction, statues of Kaminari are sometimes placed at temple gates along with Fujin, the god of wind, who carries a big bag of air on his back.

Do you suffer from nightmares? How about a Japanese remedy? Place a piece of paper under your pillow on which the name or the image of Baku is drawn. Helpful Baku eats dreams and nightmares. According to pictures, he resembles a bear but has a small pointed head, eyes like a rhinoceros, a nose like an elephant trunk (but only half the size), legs like a tiger, and a tail like a cow. Its fur is piebald and shiny. Its teeth? No-one knows for sure, but it's believed that he eats everything. Well, everything, they say, but a really foolish dream.

Another supernatural creature is Kappa, an amphibious creature resembling a young boy — if, in fact, it can be said he resembles anything. He has a pointed face and is a bluish color. Although he has thick hair, there's a depression on top of his head that has no hair. This concavity holds water when the Kappa leaves his liquid home. When the water dries up, it is said that the Kappa dies. Its back is encased in a protective shell; its hands and feet are webbed; its nails are claw-like. It lies in muddy lakes and rivers and has a particular fondness for children. It's been a part of Japanese folklore for centuries.

Japanese folklore is not all bad and bogeyman!

Kintaro is the idol of Japanese boys or, perhaps, it's more correct to say he's the idol of their mothers. He's a plump and healthy boy about six years old who carries a hatchet on his shoulder and leads a bear on a rope. According to legend, Kintaro was a boy raised in the mountains by a witch woman. He had no other boys to play with, so he became friendly with the wild animals of the forest. Living a life of nature, he became strong and healthy. He often went into the forest and cut down huge trees with his hatchet, gathering kindling wood for the woman. He was also obedient and helped her in many ways. That's why mothers love Kintaro. He symbolizes health, strength, loyalty, and a good nature.

"Alice in Wonderland"— the oriental version

A "Kantan pillow dream" is synonymous with the emptiness of human life. Such thought developed from a Chinese legend quite similar to the story of "Alice in Wonderland."

In the ninth century, or thereabouts, a scholar visited the town of Kantan. At a local inn he met a young man in rags who complained of his failures in life and of his subsequent loss of wealth and health. The poor young man was exhausted from his many ordeals, and the kindly scholar brought him a porcelain pillow and advised him to sleep. In his sleep, the young man noticed a small hole on one side of the pillow. Intrigued, he climbed into the hole and suddenly found himself in a large, magnificent house. A beautiful girl awaited him and they married. Becoming an official, he quickly rose in rank and power until one day he was imprisoned, though innocent of the accusations his enemy had slandered him with. Several years later, he was pardoned by the emperor and given a large territory to rule. He and his wife had five children and many grandchildren. They lived happily until the man died in his eightieth year. At this point, the young man, asleep on the porcelain pillow, awoke and was greatly disappointed to find that his life of wealth and happiness had been only a dream. But the scholar comforted him telling him that human life was exactly like the dream he'd had—only emptiness.

You may be wondering why I include a Chinese legend with Japanese folklore. The explanation is simple. They are one and the same; only the names have been changed. Without the ancient influences of Chinese culture, Japan would be an entirely different nation today. Legends, arts, clothing, religion—all were imported from ancient China, most notably from the Tang Dynasty in the seventh through tenth centuries. They were received in part or whole, and many were intermixed with Japanese culture, often being improved in the process.

Japanese versions of "Cinderella"

There are two more legends I'd like to share, Japanese in origin, both similar to the tale of "Cinderella." There are numerous stories about mamako, *or stepchildren. The following is one such story.*

Once upon a time there was a mother who had two daughters; the elder one, a stepdaughter. One day the mother sent the two girls to the mountain to gather chestnuts. To the younger girl she gave a perfect bag; to the elder, a torn one. Naturally, no matter how hard the elder girl tried, she could not collect a full bag's worth of chestnuts. Seeing her plight, a sympathetic hermit gave her a good bag and a small treasure box. He gave the younger sister some roasted beans. On their way home, a devil appeared and, when he threatened the sisters, the younger one threw the beans at him and drove him away. Some time later on a festival day, the young girl, dressed in her finest clothes, went to the local celebration. The elder sister, on the other hand, was given a bamboo basket with which to fill the bath tub with water. The task was difficult and time-consuming. Before long, a priest approached and helped the girl fill the tub. Then, a kindly neighbor asked her to join the festivities. She remembered the treasure box given her by the hermit and from it she took a lovely kimono. Once at the celebration, she was noticed by the rich man of the village, who requested her for the wife of his son. As all good fairy tales end, she was married and lived happily ever after.

The other Cinderella-type story is about a young man and based on the legend of the god of love and marriage.

Okuni-nushi-no-mikoto, as he was named, was the youngest of many brothers. All of them treated him badly, yet he was always eager to please them. In the province of Inaba, east of Izumo, there lived a beautiful maiden named Yasaka-hime. Each of the brothers wanted her for his own, so they all decided to visit her and see who would be the lucky one. The brothers discounted Okuni-nushi-no-mikoto as an eligible bachelor, but he was ordered to accompany them anyway to carry the baggage. Each brother dressed in the finest clothes obtainable, but Okuni-nushi-no-mikoto wore ordinary garments. When they arrived at the home of Yasaka-hime, each of the brothers proposed marriage while the youngest stood silently in a corner. The young girl, noticing his modesty, honesty, and manliness, refused each of the brothers in turn. and then surprised them all by declaring her love for the youngest brother.

Because of his good fortune, the Great Shrine of Izumo in western Honshu was erected in his honor and people, even today, go there to pray for similar blessings of love and marriage.

"How the Earthworm Got Its White Rings"

Remember the stories about how the camel got his humps or how the leopard got his spots? Here's a Japanese one that could easily be titled "How the Earthworm Got Its Rings." In ancient times, Japanese women made hemp yarn and wove it into cloth to make kimonos. To make fine yarn and weave thin cloth required skill and patience. There once lived a woman who was careless and impatient and wove rough cloth, while her neighbor, who worked slowly, wove fine cloth. Sometimes a big market day was held in the community and, for one such day, both women began to weave cloth for new kimonos. The first woman was quick, but her kimono was coarse and poorly made. The other, being slow, had only finished winding the skeins of hemp yarn when market day arrived. The market had to be visited, so she wound the skeins around her neck and made her husband carry her in a big jar on his back. She certainly didn't want anyone to see she had no dress to wear! On the way to market, she saw the first woman and, in her anger, called out, "There goes a coarse weaver!" Hearing this insult, the woman replied, "Though coarse, I do wear a dress! Break the jar and find a naked woman!" Whereupon the husband was so ashamed of his wife, he let the jar fall to the ground. The jar broke and there, indeed, was a naked woman with only skeins of hemp around her neck. So embarrassed was this woman, she buried herself in the ground to hide. As legend has it, she became an earthworm, and the skeins became white rings around her neck.

The Good Weather Doll

Remember this rhyme?

> Rain, rain go away
> Come again another day.
> Little Johnny wants to play.

A similar and traditional Japanese nursery song goes like this—in translation, of course:

> Teruteru-bozu, teru-bozu
> Tomorrow bring a fine day true.

> Like one day's dream—a sky of blue,
> And I'll give a golden bell to you.
> *Teruteru-bozu, teru-bozu*
> Tomorrow bring a fine day true.
> Just one favor—a sky of blue,
> And much sweet *sake* I'll give to you.
> *Teruteru-bozu, teru-bozu*
> Tomorrow bring a fine day true.
> Should clouds appear, don't cry boo-hoo;
> I'll chop off your head to punish you.

Teruteru-bozu *is a good weather doll made by the children themselves and hung outside a window from the eaves or from a tree branch. This good luck charm is supposed to bring good weather or prevent a rainy day. They are a common sight in Japan. A little ball of paper or cloth is rolled and puffed up to form a head, then another sheet is placed over it. Lastly, a thin strip of paper is tied around it, separating the head from the body. It looks like the paper ghosts American children hang from trees at Halloween. It has no legs; nor are eyes, nose, or mouth marked. If their request is granted, the dolls are removed from their outdoor perches and given gifts or sweets as promised, or facial features are painted on as a reward. But if it does rain after all, the dolls are left to hang in the rain. The sorry mess that's left is the punishment fitting the crime!*

This is Wendy Phillips reporting from Osaka, Japan.

Mata aimashō. Sayonara. *(We'll meet again. Goodbye.)*

2/10/65

I gave oral English tests to Tezukayama applicants. Six years of English study and some couldn't even understand a question as simple as "Where do you live?" I can't understand why somebody doesn't realize that the whole English teaching program must be revised. Students can read and write English, but they can't speak more than a few words. Of course, it's no wonder when the majority of Japanese English teachers can't speak English either! I speak better Japanese after only four months!

Did you know that bread, sewing, and necks have sounds all their own? Oku-san is always imitating things with the sound they seem to make. I've been doing some humorous research and found that they are all standard dictionary words. Here are several examples with their meanings:

gosogoso = rustling	*gyorogyoro* = goggle one's eyes
fufu = husband and wife quarreling	*gamigami* = snap or snarl
gatagata = clattering	*gaga gaga* = croak or quack
gunyagunya = soft or flabby	*daradara* = dripping
girigiri = grinding one's teeth	*huchu* = squeak or chirp
gigi = squeaking	*patapata* = flapping
pikupiku = twitching	*pichapicha* = splashing
perapera = chatter	*paripari* = crunch
pakupaku = gasp	*pokapoka* = thrashing sound
pachipachi = crackling or applauding	*potapota* = dripping
piripiri = burning feeling	*dondon* = general noise
porapora = tears on cheeks	

One phrase might be: "He's *gudenguden*, so he feels *furafura*. No wonder he's so *gochagocha*." Translation: "He's drunk, so he feels dizzy. No wonder he's confused." Colorful way of talking!

It was all planned. I was supposed to leave on the 15th, the same day that Reiko went to her mother's. But the best laid plans... Yesterday afternoon Reiko started labor pains and by 7 o'clock last night the Otanis had a bouncy baby girl named Junko. Mother and child are both doing well. The baby was 22 days early but no incubator was necessary. Almost all Japanese women deliver by natural childbirth. Babies have to be named within two weeks and care must be taken in the name. Attention must be paid to the number of strokes it takes to write the baby's name in Japanese characters. An unlucky number may mar its future! Having just completed another radio program on Japanese superstitions, I'm in the know on that count.

Decision made—I will be living with the Matsuo family in Makiochi, close to the Otanis. I went to meet the family and check the house tonight. The Matsuos are friends of Toru's parents. The house is nice. I have my own Japanese-style room and even my own western toilet. Mr. Matsuo is in the cotton import business. They don't need my money, but I will pay them the same amount I pay the Otanis. I feel better about paying, and $30 a month isn't much of a drain on my pocketbook. But, whereas I pay extra here for dinners and phone calls, I will not pay extra for anything at the Matsuo home. The family seems nice and, at any rate, I won't be there for more than two months. I plan to move back at the beginning of April, depending on the health of Reiko and the baby. Their plans to go to Texas have been postponed till after September, so I shall probably stay here until then. I'm glad. It's a terrific arrangement, and I like both of them very much.

I gave a lecture to senior high school students about outdoor recreation programs for American teenagers at the Osaka American Cultural Center. They were excited about the bicycling hostel programs. There's nothing like that here because the roads are so bad.

You asked if the Moches in Kobe speak English. They speak fluent English, Japanese, Hebrew, Arabic—all of them, even the younger children. The younger ones don't have proficient Japanese, but they can certainly make themselves understood. It's nice of you to offer to take one of them "under your wing" if Charlie or Helena goes to the University of Rochester, but they have an uncle in Manhattan, and Mr. Moche wants them to go to a N.Y. C. school because of this. I shall certainly tell Mr. and Mrs. Moche of your offer.

Why do Japanese girls look less bundled up than me? Simple reason. Actually, Mariko is wearing as much as I am, but Japanese girls and women are all small-busted and they do not wear a bra under the garments. Thus, the reason I look so bundled up in the kimono.

2/19/65

I moved on Sunday the 14th. The move itself was uneventful (done by taxi), but my new family deserves comment. Mr. Matsuo speaks little English. Mrs. Matsuo knows about 100 words and intersperses them in our daily conversations that are almost exclusively in Japanese. They have three children. Daughter Kazumi, about 22, and Katsuichi, her 25-year-old brother, speak little English. The youngest boy, about 18, is a student at Keio University in Tokyo. I haven't met him yet. Mrs. Matsuo is very funny and unlike most Japanese women in that she doesn't like sewing, cooking, knitting, and all the other things one associates with feminine Japanese pursuits. As she admits, she's more of a tomboy. Kazumi-san, on the other hand, is expert at knitting, embroidery, sewing, etc. The family is wealthy—she doesn't have to work—and, instead, spends her days with cooking, *ikebana*, and *koto* lessons. I like the family, but I'm particularly fond of their maid, Sadako. Sada-san is a big, robust, jovial country girl. She speaks standard Japanese in her rural area dialect, so I understand only half of what she says. She also speaks quickly and laughs at everything—a big, hearty laugh.

Fifteen hours after I moved here, all the local storekeepers knew there was a foreigner in the neighborhood living at the Matsuo's. They were quick to get me into conversation to find out how long I'd been here, why I came, what I think of Japan, etc.

I made the mistake of admiring a pair of carved ivory chopsticks that Mr. Matsuo was using. Within 15 minutes, I had my own pair—despite my insistence that they were too expensive a gift. As Mr. Matsuo said, they had already begun to think about what they could give me as a gift. So now I have a pair of expensive and lovely ivory chopsticks, which will be used for display only.

An amusing aside apropos of nothing. One of my students at Japan Celluloid is Mr. Saiki. I received a written homework assignment from him signed Mr. Psyche. Don't know where that came from, but it is how his name is pronounced.

I told Tezukayama that I was definitely leaving both the high school and the university. Influenza is rampant in the schools this week. Some classes were cancelled; others were half full. The remaining students looked like masked bandits, for more than half of them wore surgical masks. They are not uncommon. The masks are worn all winter either to prevent one's cold from spreading to others or to prevent contagion from others.

Japanese wives and young girls are unhappy with their lot. All dream of someday sharing the status of an American wife—that is having a husband who is devoted and faithfully loving and enjoys spending evenings at home. (They must be reading romance novels!) Nowadays, it's still the woman who raises the children because the husbands are so rarely home. The new and exciting role of a husband wears off within a few years and so, too, does the role of being a new father. For many years, women were trained to be obedient, docile, and silent wives—good attributes but quite unexciting. And the husbands' duty was only to get married and beget heirs. Things are gradually changing, but it will be many years before a Japanese wife has an equally enviable role.

2/20/65

Last night I took Kazumi-san with me to my *ikebana* lesson. She has taken me on as a sort of Japanese sister, a role that's different from an American sister and one I'm not particularly fond of. Nonetheless, the Matsuos are very kind. Mrs. Matsuo wants me to think of her as my mother. That makes two Japanese mothers I have! Tonight they took me to dinner at a restaurant owned by Mr. Matsuo's younger brother. Before I left, I was gifted with a pair of husband-and-wife chopsticks for a few years hence when I hope to be able to use them.

This morning I went out to Kobe for the first time in three weeks. What a good day I chose! One of the congregants has just recently recovered from a heart attack, and his family gave a brunch at the synagogue. I couldn't believe what I was eating in Japan: real lox, gefilte fish, chopped herring, cheese cake, sponge cake. I was in heaven! Everything was homemade by Jewish women from all over the world, so it was even more interesting than the standard delicatessen fare in the states.

Tomorrow I'm going back out to Kobe to spend the evening with Ariela Blumenthal and her husband Tuvia, who is on an Israeli fellowship studying at Osaka University. I met them at the synagogue this morning. Everybody was in attendance, for as Mr. Moche said, "They don't come for services, but they do come for important things like really good food."

I've been so busy! One man who has been trying unsuccessfully to reach me for two weeks, finally caught me at 7:30 this morning only five minutes before I left the house. He wants me to lecture next Saturday afternoon for the *Mainichi* Readers' English Club. I can't repeat any subjects because some members are also members of the club I'll be speaking to the following week. I decided, in a final pinch, to discuss outdoor recreation programs for American adults. Have suggestions for the many lectures I'm giving? The speech on "Teenage Recreation Programs" went over so well, I decided it might not be so bad to readjust it for an adult audience.

2/27/65

Someone entered the Otani's home. He broke a wooden shutter and then a window pane and left everything in disarray—but took nothing. He wanted only money and didn't find any. My room, right off the back garden, was untouched.

Also this week, there's been a campaign by certain students on the streets of Osaka to get signatures on a petition against the U.S. nuclear submarines coming to Japan. It's the first time I've seen anything like it.

March 3rd is Hina Matsuri (Doll's Festival). The Maedas gave me a fabulous gift in honor of the upcoming festival. The dolls honored are all handmade and dressed in the style of the imperial court during the Heian period, 794-1185. They are given special food offerings on that day. Every home with a girl displays these dolls in the hope that long life will be granted to the girl. The dolls are traditionally passed down from generation to generation. All boxed, the dolls should be relatively easy to send to the states, but the large glass case may present somewhat of a problem.

Reiko, Junko, and Toru Otani

[Somewhat of a problem? I'll say it was! The glass case, shipped by an experienced exporter, shattered twice in transport. Twice it had to be replaced, but the third time was a charm! The dolls and the case have been trucked in moves to our homes in New Jersey, then again very carefully packed by me in our move to California. They are still a treasured art piece and always on display in our home—and one of Marty's favorites.]

A full set of Hina dolls consists of at least 15 dolls: emperor, empress, three ladies-in waiting, five musicians, two retainers, and three guards displayed in descending order on the shelves. They are surrounded by small pieces of furniture and serving pieces. My set also has palanquins for the Emperor and Empress and a cherry and plum tree. The case is 17" x 24-1/2".

This week I had my visa renewed for another six months. It's now good until October 1st.

I received a letter from my former instructor at Syracuse University, Dr. Hill. He's now head of WUWM in Milwaukee, the station to which I'm sending my 15-minute "Orientation" programs. The letter was written after listening to the first two in the series. He was extremely complimentary! Need I tell you of my pleasure and pride? He then asked if I would approve of submitting them to the National Educational Radio Network. They may not pass the stiff requirements for acceptance but, nevertheless, I'm happy he would even consider it. My subjects have covered wide ground: Osaka City, the problems of teaching English, *ikebana*, public baths, geishas and hostesses, the tea ceremony, a beastly law, Japanese superstitions, Buddhism and Shinto, and the Japanese people themselves. Though time consuming, I really do enjoy writing the scripts.

After my lecture today on "Outdoor Recreation Programs for American Adults" at the *Mainichi Newspaper* office, the usual question period followed. Two questions are always asked: what do I think of the status of Japanese women and what's my opinion of Japanese husbands. I'm also asked how American young women prepare for marriage—for instance, do they study *ikebana*, sewing, embroidery, cooking, knitting, crocheting? You know what my answer would be to that one!

My weekly flower arrangements usually cost 28 cents each. This week, because it was peach blossoms and camellias (special for the Doll Festival), it cost 70 cents. My teacher was most apologetic. She should only know how expensive this new hobby will be when I return to the states!

On April 1st I'm leaving for a five-day trip to Himeji, Hiroshima, Miyajima, Matsuyama, and Takamatsu—all on the island of Shikoku—and to Naruto and Fukura on the island of Awaji. Just thought I'd mention the names in case you follow my travels on a map.

Thought you might be interested to know that, when I refer to you in conversation, "my mother" becomes *haha* and "my father," *chichi*.

RADIO BROADCAST

A Festive Year
NHK "Radio Japan Journal" 1965

With a country inhabited by as many gods as Japan, and since each god has a festival day, it follows that there is hardly a day when there isn't a festival somewhere in Japan. Before television and movies, festivals were the chief pleasure of a hard-working people. Yet, today the religious fervor is lacking and the festival is more of a show. But what a show! Attending Japanese festivals is still a favorite pastime!

Setsubun: to disperse devils

In the last years of the ninth century during the reign of Emperor Uda, the god Bishamon sent a divine message to all the people saying that a pair of monstrous demons named Ramba and Sozu, who dwelt in a cave in northern Kyoto, would soon besiege the capital. The high court officials called a meeting and selected seven brave men to rout the devils. Armed only with dried beans, the men went to the cave to challenge their opponents and subdued the monsters by blinding them with the beans. The capital of Kyoto was saved and the legend remained through the years. Still, on the eve of February 3rd (or 4th during a leap year), people celebrate the annual event of Setsubun. It literally means the parting of the seasons, and it comes at the same time as our Groundhog Day.

In Japan it is the big day for exorcising the devil. "Fuku wa uchi! Oni wa soto!" "In with fortune! Out with the devil!" The highlight is "Tsuina," the night ceremony for this exorcism, when the head of the family officiates, shouting the words of command, then scattering handfuls of dried beans throughout the home. All through the night, people visit the temples and shrines. At these public celebrations, a famous actor, politician, sumo wrestler, or other notable born in the same zodiac year as that under exorcism plays the role of Toshi-Otoko, or Man of the Year. He stands atop a platform shouting the magic words and throwing the beans at the imaginary demons with red or green skin and always with horns. Those who catch the beans will have luck throughout the year.

Kodomo-no-Hi: for children

On March 3rd of every year, the home of every little girl will have on display some unique dolls. Sometimes it's just the emperor and empress, but usually there are 15 dolls in the style of an ancient imperial court. On the top will be the emperor and empress. In levels below: the ladies-in-waiting, the samurai warriors, the court musicians. Hina Matsuri, as this day is called, is the Doll Festival. The proud little girls who own these dolls invite their friends over for a kimono party, highlighted by the drinking of a cup of a special white rice wine. These dolls that express hope for a happy life are passed on from the females of one generation to the next. They are highly respected and valued and are only displayed on this one day.

On May 5th, the boys have their turn for celebration. Well, they did before World War II. The two days have been merged, so it is now called Children's Day. High above the roofs of Japanese homes fly colorful cloth carp beneath several bright streamers. These fish are powerful (a wish for all boys) and can fight their way upstream despite raging currents and other obstacles. Whereas dolls are honored on the special day for girls, this day is given over to masculine accoutrements: images of feudal generals and samurai warriors, armor, swords, helmets, drums, and halberds.

O-Bon: for departed souls

O-Bon, or Lantern Festival, is the most important Buddhist festival when, for three days each year, families are reunited with their ancestral spirits. Part of O-Bon is devoted to feasting, part to the chanting of Buddhist sutras praying for the repose of ancestral souls, and part to good old merrymaking in the form of dancing. That night, everyone wears yukata. Each year it's the same. Crowds gather and the dancers form concentric circles moving clockwise around a two-story platform, atop which sit several drummers. Lanterns hang from everywhere, and *occasional fireworks light up the sky. All night the dancing continues — circles of swaying, bobbing, weaving children, parents, and grandparents. Drums beat the rhythm; the dancers set the pace; and, when the bystander feels the beat, she, too, is requested to join the dance. And so I did!*

Tanabata: in the name of love

One summer celebration is based on the universal understanding of love. The Tanabata Star Festival is, in most places, observed on July 7th according to the lunar calendar. But some districts have stuck with the ancient solar calendar and commemorate it one month later. So it is in the city of Sendai. The story, of Chinese origin, is simple. The Milky Way is the river of Heaven and standing on the west bank is Vega, the beautiful weaver star. To the right is Altair, the handsome shepherd star. Once a year on July 7th or August 7th (according to which calendar you're using and which location you're in), Vega and Altair are permitted to meet when they cross the Milky Way over the Kakasagi Bridge. (The kakasagi *is a magpie bird symbolizing happiness and love.)*

Long green bamboo branches ornamented with bright strips of paper and other trimmings are the standard decoration for this festival. In most places they measure about two to three feet in length. In Sendai they're about eight feet! Big paper squares, balls, and triangles top multi-colored flowing streamers, flashing in the light of neon signs. Ten-foot tall dolls swing from strong cords, and plastic fish bob up and down in bubbling water tanks. It's a tangle of spice and dash and color!

Gion Matsuri: gratitude for the end of an ancient epidemic

The flashiest, biggest, longest, and most famous festival in all Japan is Kyoto's Gion Matsuri held during the entire month of July. Its origin dates back to the summer of 869 A.D. when hundreds of thousands of people died in an epidemic. The Emperor Seiwa ordered a Shinto priest to extort the devil and, thus commanded, he prayed to the deities of Yasaka Shrine. He also instructed the Kyoto citizens to make 66 halberds and parade through the streets of the capital, driving away the evil spirits with these weapons. Sixty-six were ordered, for that was the number of provinces in Japan at the time. Whether because of the success of the halberd assault or because of divine intervention, the epidemic subsided. The miracle was enough to warrant feasting and frolicking from 970 A.D. till the present time with a slight lapse during the civil wars of the fifteenth and sixteenth centuries and again from 1943 through 1947 due to greater national urgencies.

On July 1st, the parishioners of Yasaka Shrine purify themselves to prepare for the month-long observance and begin rehearsing the famous O-bayashi music of bells, flutes, and drums. On July 8th, assembly of the halberd floats, or hoko, begins in each parish neighborhood, followed two days later by the purification of the mikoshi, or portable shrines. On July 11th, a specially selected boy about ten years of age, dressed in ancient ceremonial robe, visits the shrine to receive the title of o-ochigo, or sacred page. On July 16th, the parishioners begin assembling the Yama floats, which are life-size doll representations of ancient Chinese and Japanese legends.

While all this has meaning for the parishioners, most of what has gone before is unobserved by tourists, for the first big attraction does not occur until the evening of July 16th. That night is "Yoiyama" when thousands turn out to see the Gion floats that will be used in the parade the following morning. Then there is truly sight and sound: thousands of people crowd into Kyoto's main street, many dressed in cotton summer kimonos, all complaining of the heat; policemen blast loudspeaker warnings to please not trample the little children; the kon-kon-chiki-chin-kon-chiki-chin musical rhythms animate the crowds. Homes on the street are decorated with paper lanterns, doors fully open to all guests wishing to see the families' treasured folding screens—byobu in Japanese, and thus the reason why Gion Matsuri is also called Byobu Matsuri. Matsuri, if you haven't already guessed, means "festival."

A festival eve without the moneymakers is no festival in Japan, so they are present in droves: the balloon man and the postcard merchant; the ice cream hawker and the cotton candy maker; the toy mask peddler and the dealer in trinkets; the pitchman for ball games and the vendor of cheap souvenirs; the greengrocer, the confectioner, and the bookseller; the *tobacconist, the hardware man, and the stationer; and if you happen to get through the area unscathed and unruffled, perhaps you'll consider a visit beyond to the* hoko *and the* yama *floats covered with fancy brocades and illuminated by the lights of a hundred paper lanterns. The* hoko *floats are tall, two stories high, and must, by necessity, be entered by planks from the second floor of appointed houses. If one so desires, he can enter for the price of* chimaki, *which are wrapped bamboo leaves said to have devil exorcising powers. You can try, but there is no room on the float because of its already overloaded crew of musicians. Women are forbidden to enter the floats.*

A visit that evening should be made to Yasaka Shrine, if only to see what's going on at the place that fathered it all. Nothing religious, you understand, but there are lots of swarming people being goaded by the balloon man and the cotton candy maker and vendor of cheap souvenirs and the pitchman for ball games and...their friends.

The next day, by the light of day, the festivities seem dull by comparison, yet there's plenty of action! Crowds line the street (fewer crowds on more streets) to watch the parade of slow-moving floats and to listen again to the kon-chiki-chin *music, frequently interrupted by the screams of excited spectators ready to overrun each other in pursuit of the lucky* chimaki *thrown from passing floats. The floats are drawn with thick ropes by day laborers. So heavy are they, the rope-pullers are aided by lever-operators who help move the wheels, and all are directed by two fan-carriers who shout encouragement in a yo-heave-ho rhythmic fashion. Atop every float are two or three signalmen who instruct the rope-pullers and lever-operators how to get the floats around the corners and prevent the 30-foot halberds from toppling over.*

That evening the deities of Yasaka Shrine begin a parish tour aboard three portable shrines accompanied by servants in ceremonial dress and attendants in white: warriors, pages, priests, and representatives of the parishioners. It is a tremendous honor for these people to carry or walk with the portable shrines.

The following week, there's a second festival eve, a second parade day, and a second purification of the portable shrines. On July 29th, a final ceremony is held at the actual shrine giving an accounting to the deities on what has transpired during the month-long festival. Then everyone goes home to strengthen up for the next year's observances.

Tenjin Matsuri: to cleanse oneself and have fun in the process

Tenjin Matsuri, the festival of the Temmangu Shrine in Osaka, began about a thousand years ago. Back then it was thought that dirt was a sin and a person had to cleanse his body and soul in order to welcome and honor the gods. One way to do this is called misogi, *which means washing away the filth in the sea, waterfall, or river.*

The origin of Tenjin Matsuri was an assembly like this for those who wished to get rid of diseases that were prevalent in summer. People gathered in the shrine precincts, each with a piece of paper cut in a human shape. They rubbed their bodies with the pieces of paper while Shinto priests offered prayers. Then, coming to the bank of the Yodo River, they threw the paper figures into the water, believing they would be freed of the diseases by discarding the paper figures to which their diseases had been transferred. They would go in boats and follow the figures as far as the mouth of the river. This festival on land and water is now one of the three biggest festivals in Japan, along with Kyoto's Gion Matsuri and Tokyo's Kanda Matsuri, also a shrine festival, though it is held only during odd-numbered years.

A parade is held in the afternoon: a procession of local officials in warriors' dress; dragon dances; the "wa-shoi, wa-shoi" chant of young men staggering under the weight of portable shrines; god's messenger boy and his ox-drawn cart; and the battle of the big drum when the drummers continue their beating despite efforts to unseat them. In the evening, close to a hundred pleasure boats line up along the river and thousands of tourists and merrymakers line the shore all awaiting the procession of big boats hung with tower-high frames of lanterns: boats with performing folk dancers, and musicians playing ancient imperial court music. From all the bridges and boats hang swinging paper lanterns, and the sky is illuminated with the flashing colors of fireworks. Very pretty!

Shichi-go-san: the 7-5-3 Festival

Shichi-go-san: literally the numbers 7-5-3. This is the most picturesque autumn event. November 15th is the day of Shichi-go-san, a traditional rite of passage and festival day for three- and seven-year-old girls and three- and five-year-old boys to celebrate the growth and well-being of young children. In ancient times it was marked by certain ceremonies: putting up the hair of a three-year-old girl; placing a hakama, *or pleated skirt, on a five-year-old boy of the samurai class to prepare him for introduction to his feudal lord; giving a seven-year-old girl an* obi *to wear for the first time. It meant that the children passed from infancy to childhood. At the shrines, the children underwent a purification ceremony during which a Shinto priest waved a spray of evergreen leaves over their heads. Today some receive lucky charms and sweets and presents from relatives and friends. The parents report to the deities of their children's happiness and health, express their gratitude, and invoke future blessings. The formality of the ancient ceremony is missing today, and all boys and girls aged 7, 5, and 3 come to the shrines. The girls, in particular, wear small, colorful kimonos, rouge on their cheeks, and bows in their hair—looking every inch like precious oriental dolls.*

This is only a sampling of Japanese festivals. Even the smallest shrines have their glory days and every city of size has a festival with some sort of highlight: floats, fires, lanterns, contests, parades, or dances. Their religious importance is decreasing, but each presents a fascinating, enchanting picture of what Japan and the Japanese were like before the invasion of modernization and occidental ways.

3/4/65

How can it be March already? I'm not aware that February lasted more than a few days! My, how *tempus* is *fugiting*!!

In one of your recent letters you mentioned that things always seem to work out for me. True! On the 10th I begin teaching a group of women from the United Nations Association Auxiliary. On the 18th I begin another weekly class with an adult group set up by a friend. This past month I was able to bank $190! That's more than I could ever save in the states! I figure that by October I should have around $1,500 in the bank. With that money, if I have to leave in October because of visa problems, I'll travel as far west as I can before hopping a boat that will take me back to New York harbor.

The Matsuos want me to stay with them until I leave Japan, but I prefer to go back to the Otani's. It won't be as soft a life, but I'll have more privacy and more time to study Japanese and write my scripts.

Tuesday I went with Kazumi-san to her cooking class. There were 12 students of various ages. They meet in one woman's home and the male teacher goes there every week. Two of the students are sisters, Nisei now living in Japan. What they prepared was of no value to me, for more than half the ingredients are too difficult to get in the states, but I learned some good tricks.

Yesterday was Hina Matsuri, which I explained in the last letter. For the occasion, one of "my women" (I trust you know who I mean by now) gave me a pair of wooden *kokeshi* dolls and a box of chocolate *hina* dolls.

More gifts! Embarrassing! Mr. Maeda had two coral cuff links. Each stone was a light coral color with just a trace of white and three chrysanthemum flowers carved in a delicate design. They decided to make each cuff link into a ring. So now they had two matching rings and only one daughter. Mrs. Maeda couldn't wear one, so that left one ring without an owner. They found an owner for it this week—me! After all, they said, they think of me as a daughter and they want to do for me what they would do for Sachie-san. As their gift list mounted, I protested and protested but, for every good reason I offered, they had a blind argument.

Why couldn't Mrs. Maeda wear the the coral color ring? It's too bright! Japanese women of a certain age are limited to somber dark tones. Purple and maroon are allowed and, because they have a little more "oomph" than black or gray or dark green, they are popular. There's no law that says older women can't wear bright colors, but they don't. It extends to jewelry. Pearls and diamonds are okay and the most popular. Jade is all right if it's not too large and not too bright. Emeralds, rubies, coral, et al are taboo. And they don't wear gold—silver only.

Here's the list so far of what I've received from the Maedas: a pearl necklace, a silk dress and shirt made to order in any style I pick out at a fashion show they'll take me to, and my one-way plane ticket to Hokkaido. I talked them out of a round-trip ticket. They also invited me to join them on an August trip to a resort near Mt. Fuji, but I told them I'd be in Hokkaido at that time. My first argument was expense, and they assured me that they would only give me what they could afford. Good grief! How do you say thank you for gifts like that?! You must be overwhelmed with all the gifts I've sent home. I know these people love me. And I, in turn, love them. But, living as a Japanese, I cannot tell them this. I'd do anything they asked me to. It's the same for them. It's difficult living in a society where love is never expressed.

I try to bring little food gifts to my friends. It's an acceptable way of repaying my *on* while I'm still in Japan. A gift of specially prepared sweet potatoes is good, because I'm told that all Japanese women love sweet potatoes. Sometimes I buy candy, also welcome, or American canned products. Fruit, ham, juice—I try to be a little original.

3/7/65

I found the following classic ad in this morning's paper: "Young man or girl, must read and write excellent English. English speaking not essential. Permanent position. Growing trading company.

Excellent salary." See what I mean about the Japanese being able to read and write but not speak?

Just tried to teach three friends how to play bridge at their request. And in Japanese, mind you! It was impossible! Funny thing, I vividly recalled one night seven years ago in my Paris lodgings teaching some of the guys to play bridge in French. I also seem to remember I was far more successful! We gave up on bridge, or rather I did, but I succeeded in teaching them canasta. Following that, we watched the Ed Sullivan Show on TV. It was first broadcast in Japan last week. It's in English, with a Japanese voice over Sullivan's. And when there is a guest singer, the words are sub-titled in Japanese.

RADIO BROADCAST

The Japanese People
"Orientation" 1965

I've heard it said: "Scratch a Japanese woman wearing a western dress and you'll find a kimono."

This is ORIENTATION...and I'm Wendy Phillips reporting from Japan.

I thought it might be interesting to examine the human—and most important—element of this country. The nation itself has adopted many western influences, but its people are very different from Occidentals. Let me explain.

A child born to a Japanese couple is lucky indeed. He is given tremendous opportunities to develop in a free, unrestricted world. He is carried everywhere on his mother's back. She talks to him, sings to him, or just makes noises to show she is aware of his presence. His smallest desires are granted. He may run freely over, under, and around anything in his path without a word of caution or reprimand. The child, particularly a boy, can beat his mother mercilessly to show his masculine powers—without a word of disapproval. On trains strangers will give their seats to a child, and a baby's howling at a theater performance seems to go unnoticed. The young child always has his own way amidst the happiest of surroundings. Because of this, childhood is considered the best time in the life of a Japanese.

When the child enters school, he suddenly finds that he can't dictate all situations. Certain things must be understood, and it is necessary for him to learn some social amenities. By the time he has entered middle school at the age of 12 and appropriately changed from short to long pants, he enters his difficult years. In addition to the usual pangs of adolescence, he is made increasingly aware of his role in society. Friendships developed at this time usually last throughout a lifetime. Feelings for another person are not verbally expressed, so tactile responses are the substitute. It's a common sight to see girls holding hands or walking arm-in-arm. Even boys walk arm-in-arm or with their arms around each others shoulders. These signs of attachment and affection continue throughout the adult years.

With marriage, the woman takes on certain responsibilities of home life, such as managing the finances and raising children. For years women were trained to be obedient, docile, and silent wives. All are good wifely attributes but rather unexciting. Until the present day, the husband's duty to his parents has been only to marry and beget children. He needn't shower them with attention. Home may be a dull place with a dispassionate wife and irksome children, so it's considered all right for the husband to spend most of his time away. When he is at home, much of his time may be spent on personal interests, such as music, book collections, painting, or plants. The husband is boss. If he returns at midnight, he expects a meal to be ready. In fact, he expects his wife to be prepared for everything at any time. If he visits a prostitute or gambles recklessly, his wife must pay the bills without complaint. There has to be a reason why all Japanese women, young and old, envy the status of their American counterparts. The Japanese word for one's own husband is the same as the word for "master" and "employer." I hasten to add that there are exceptions. Particularly in the younger generation, there are improvements. One reason is that young wives, though still trained to be obedient and docile, are also primed to be more stimulating.

Both men and women have a deep love of nature. They are proud of their beautiful country. Mount Fuji and the cherry blossoms are revered symbols of Japan. The four seasons are well defined; and moon-viewing, snow-viewing, and maple-viewing parties are most popular.

They love extravagance, though not all can afford it. Their homes may appear simple, yet the vertical tree beam near the tokonoma may cost as much as the furnishings of an entire room. Their outwardly plain coats may be lined in pure silk. They may spend 50 cents for a bowl of rice and chicken, then spend 60 cents more for one cup of coffee. Furthermore, they may dwindle away what little money they earn on Pachinko, a silly and time-wasting pinball game that enjoys unexplained popularity throughout the nation.

Japanese adults are acutely aware of rank and precedence. Parents speak of their first son. The boy may refer to his second sister. A pianist may be regarded as the sixth best in Japan. People are quick to mention they were the best singer or ping pong player in their school. The language itself is filled with polite forms and honorifics to be used according to the status of the person spoken to. Because each one knows his place and how he must talk to others, social intercourse is invariable. There is no aggressive determination on the part of waiters or workmen to prove their equality. Nor are there problems in seating arrangements. Everyone knows exactly who will sit at the head of the table, near the tokonoma, *or by the door. In Japan round tables are nonexistent; they would cause total confusion in the prearranged hierarchical order.*

Strict etiquette and conformity with the system must be followed at all times, with one exception. The reason why drinking parties are so popular—most particularly with men—is because with sake, *the rice wine, one can relax and forget the rigidities of the imposed conventionalisms. These wear off with the* sake *and, when the* sake *wears off, the restrictions of this etiquette are restored. By the way, friends in Japan are either drinking buddies or lady friends. In crises, a person turns to his family rather than to friends. Friends are usually former classmates. Fellow students are equals but, as one grows older, the sense of hierarchy interferes with social interaction. There is a strange nostalgia for old acquaintances. Even kindergarten classes have been known to have reunions years later. Foreigners stand outside this hierarchy. When a Japanese person entertains another Japanese, it is usually outside of his home. If he does come into the home, he rarely gets farther than the reception parlor. Yet, I have been invited into numerous homes and, usually, I get a complete tour of the house. Again, the reason is because, as a foreigner, I am not included in the hierarchical system.*

A supplement to this order is the extremely complex system of obligation and duty. There is duty to one's name, one's family, one's position, one's employer—and obligation is the same. A gift must be paid in kind and within a certain period of time. Historically, an insult, a humiliation, or a derogation must be answered even if death is that answer. The rules of this system are stiff and must be followed with no variation. To understand its complexities means to better understand the behavior of the Japanese people.

I mentioned before that the Japanese are nostalgic about their past life. Nursery songs are popular even with adults and keeping a diary or "memory book" is the pastime of young and old alike. Another book of importance to everyone is the photograph album. When you visit a Japanese home, you will be given a number of these albums that may date back 30 or 40 years. You must peruse each one carefully—oohing and aahing at every baby picture, wedding kimono, mountain scene, or whatever else has been photographed over the years.

The Japanese have an aversion to privacy. In fact, there really is no word for privacy in the language. Words close in meaning imply "selfishness" or "loneliness." There is little of it, so there is no need for such a word. It is difficult for the foreigner in Japan to realize this, but there are evidences of it everywhere. When leaving a house, one is asked about destination and hour of return. Mail will be studied and inquiry made as to who sent it. Questions we consider to be intimate and out of bounds will be asked without embarrassment. Sometimes hotel rooms and lavatories have no locks on the doors and, if they do, are seldom used. The Japanese, so they say, love contact with their fellow man. Walls in hotels and homes are paper thin so conversations can easily be heard. Large public baths are immensely popular. In many places men and women share the same public toilets. (I say toilets rather than bathrooms because here the two words have separate meanings.) In the home where there is a small bathtub, families may often bathe together. If you happen to be alone in the tub, you can clearly hear extraneous noises in the house and can usually converse with anyone in any other room. I cite only a few examples, but there are few places where one can enjoy real privacy.

Having just said that the Japanese love contact with their fellow man, it's peculiar that they react so negatively or indifferently to strangers. They are extremely courteous to acquaintances, but they can be severe with strangers in a crowded subway or train. If they step on someone's foot, they don't bother to say "excuse me." They may sneeze or pick their teeth without covering their mouths. They may strip to their long underwear *on a boat or train for comfort, but they would never appear that way in their home. Their homes are meticulously neat, but their offices may be a mess. Likewise, trains are frequently littered with disposed food and paper. Uunfortunately, this is often the only chance a foreign visitor has of observing the private life of the Japanese people. Yet the axiom—"no need for shame on a journey"—still persists.*

The Japanese have an affinity for impermanence. The paper of the shoji *screens and* fusuma *doors is changed once a year.* Tatami *mats are also easily changed. When kimonos are washed, they are unstitched and then restitched. Even disposable chopsticks, called* waribashi, *are popular. The much-loved cherry blossoms only last for three or four days. As early as the first grade of school, students memorize a short cadence which utilizes all 47 syllables of their language. In addition to the words providing verbal drill, they also teach a lesson in the Buddhist idea of impermanence.*

As each person ages, his adult restrictions are lifted. He is again allowed the freedom that was his as a child. He may omit honorifics in speech; he may use obscene language and tell bawdy jokes. Elders may indulge freely in liquor, as well. In short, they are given maximum freedom. And always, regardless of age or mental capabilities, they are accorded the respect due a sage.

I have merely scratched the surface in this analysis. One cannot possibly scrutinize a nation of people in 15 minutes. I may have painted a rather bleak picture of the Japanese. Nevertheless, I am reporting what I perceive and experience. I live with Japanese people and much of what I have said is not seen by the casual tourist. If you now have any doubts about the Japanese, let me remind you that experienced travelers claim that the Japanese are the most hospitable people in the world. As for myself, it is because of these people that I have recently renewed my visa for an additional six months. In summary, let me add only this: The Japanese have embraced practices from hundreds of years of past history and from varying cultures throughout the world. They have not always embraced them wisely or well, but whatever else can be said, one thing remains certain: they are distinctly Japanese, and they are a fascinating people to know.

This is Wendy Phillips reporting from Osaka, Japan.

Mata aimashō. Sayonara. *(See you again. Goodbye.)*

3/11/65

On Monday, I toured the Asahi Radio and TV studios. It felt good to be back in familiar surroundings. I particularly enjoyed a visit with the chief makeup artist who is equipped to do all kinds of modern and ancient hair styles. She buys real hair from northern China, then piece-by-piece weaves it into a net form and combs it into the elaborate historic styles. Each wig takes about eight hours to complete. It was fascinating to watch the process.

Saturday I'm interviewing Mr. K. Hara, manager of the Asahi stations, for my radio series. When I met him, he told me that two years ago he was lucky enough to be one of the five judges at the Miami Beach Miss Universe Contest. He explained how a winner is selected.

Tomorrow I'm touring NHK. Next Wednesday there is a program board meeting at NHK in Kyoto to audition Radio Japan programs going to the states. They wanted five Americans and managed to get four—none of whom are broadcasters. Jim Elliott, my friend at the American Cultural Center, was asked by NHK if he knew of any professionals in the Kansai area, and he gave them my name.

And Dr. Hill in Wisconsin reports that he has already submitted my series for use on the Educational Radio Network. He sent one audition tape and is waiting to hear the outcome.

I have so much fun listening to the Armed Forces Far East Network. It's the best of old radio: "Escape"…"Gunsmoke"… "Johnny Dollar" with such marvelous characters as Durango Laramie Dallhart…"The Steve Allen Show"…and TV favorites like "The Johnny Carson Tonight Show" and "Hootenanny." Also on Sunday are audio portions of Hollywood movies. I love listening!

Today I paid Mrs. Matsuo for my one-month stay, and she refused to take it. As long as I was only staying two months, she wanted me to save the money for my trip to Bangkok and points west.

Yoyo Nakamura, reknowned Sumi-e artist, designated as a Living National Treasure. Sumi-e is a monochrome art using black ink and handmade paper, but so much more—with emphasis placed on the beauty of each brush stroke!

My adult students at Dai-Nippon have been taking the lecturer's podium to practice English. So far I've heard about "The Dimensionology of Art"..."Pure Economics"..."Why Japanese People Can't Speak English"..."The Japanese School System Before the War"..."My Hobby of Writing Music"...and numerous stories from Japanese mythology. Very informative!

A friend's mother is studying *Sumi-e* from one of the most famous teachers and artists in Japan. *Sumi-e* is Chinese ink painting, and this woman has the esteemed designation of Living National Treasure, a popular term for those individuals certified as Preservers of Important Intangible Cultural Properties. She is 60-year-old Yoko Nakamura, who uses the pen name "Yoyo" and is a most interesting woman. During the afternoon, she painted and signed a picture for me of a bamboo tree with leaves. It was a thrilling afternoon!

3/13/65

I'm thrilled to report that I'll be working with NHK on various projects.

Today I went to Asahi for my interview. As for something always coming up, it has again. I started a series of lectures there on "Broadcasting in America." Each lecture is a half-hour in length and is then followed by a half-hour question period. Today's session was impromptu, but the others will be planned. I'll probably give about four or five lectures to the Planning Committee.

I laughed when you suggested I try to indulge in hot baths for my rheumatism. I indulge every night. And, I assure you, there's nothing hotter than a Japanese bath—unless it's a pot of boiling water! One doesn't take showers in Japan, baths only. And one doesn't soak in the bath, one cooks! But now I love them. I jump in with all teeth gritted so I don't scream in pain. As soon as I hit the water, every muscle is forced to relax and that's when the luxurious feeling of pleasurable indulgence takes over. Is it any wonder that some Japanese spend one hour just cooking?! If hot baths are good for rheumatism, I'm certainly in the right country!

I know you're worried about that burglar who broke into the Otani's home. It is my firm opinion that I share with every other foreigner I've ever spoken to that I'm safer here than I would be in N.Y.C. Crimes against foreign residents are almost non-existent. There are many differences between foreign residents and tourists—all of which are immediately apparent on sight. The Japanese are more cautious of us than we are of them. As they say here, "*shinpai nai.*" (Don't worry.)

Hinda reports that her mother looks forward to going to any luncheon where you'll be, Mom, because she gets to hear my letters to you. That's all well and good, but you better leave everybody with enough questions, so they'll want to purchase a copy of my book—if and when it's published, of course!

[Fifty years later and I never did write it. Life intervened. Shameful and embarrassing! I would have so loved to publicly thank all the people mentioned in this narrative.]

3/19/65

The plum tree, a little late this year, is blooming outside my window. The red buds burst into pretty pink flowers. It's a wonderful sight to see every day. Below that tree is a blooming pink camellia bush. Next to that is a white camellia bush, and next to this is yet another flower bush that will bloom in late spring. You can't really duplicate a Japanese garden in the states. You could plant trees and bushes that would blossom all year, but you couldn't reproduce the strange and wonderful tree shapes and sizes. I love Japanese gardens, especially when there is a large stone lantern in the middle.

Osaka experienced its heaviest snowfall in 19 years—all of four inches! The streets were a mess, but it was fun for the kids. Some made snowmen, or *yuki daruma* as they're called here, and some had playful snowball fights. But yesterday was warm and there wasn't a trace of snow anywhere. I can tell I'm going to like this spring season in Japan.

Sunday evening was the Purim Ball at the Kobe Regatta & Athletic Club. Actually, it was just like any country club dance that you've gone to, but with a different twist—an international social set. A floor show included a group of Israeli dancers and a little play by four men dressed in women's clothing doing a skit about the weekly bridge club. It was all in poetry and very funny. Present were synagogue members and their guests, including a number of foreign bank officials, the Belgian Consul, and an odd assortment of others. Ariela Blumenthal introduced me to an Israeli bachelor who just moved to Kobe after five years in Tokyo. He's an engineer who works for a Swiss firm and writes a weekly newspaper column for one of the Israeli papers. His name is Eli (pronounced Elly) David. Ariela and Tuvia invited me to stay overnight at their apartment, so the four of us left the party around midnight and then went back to the Blumenthals for coffee and chatter until 2 a.m. It was a pleasant evening, and I suspect you may be hearing more about Eli in the months to come.

On Tuesday the Matsuos decided they couldn't wait until my birthday, so they gave me my *haori* then. It's all silk, bright gold and red, and very pretty. This traditional hip-length jacket is worn open or is kept closed by a string that connects the lapels. Historically, they were worn over armor. During the Edo period prior to 1858, the middle class could afford the *haori,* yielding to laws against ostentatious display of wealth by all but the warrior caste. Even then, where there's a will there's a way: they wore *haori* with elaborate designs and lavishly decorated lining.

That evening I went out to dinner with the Maeda's daughter

and Mr. Maeda's private driver. They took me for *teppanyaki*, a mixture of meat and vegetables cooked on a grill that's set in the table. We also ate *okonomiyaki*, a Japanese version of Italian pizza. It's a special type of egg omelet that you order with shrimp, squid, octopus, pork, beef, or a combination of all of them. Once cooked, it's topped with soy sauce, dried fish shavings, and grated seaweed. It's very tasty. One of my favorites. Really!

On the way home from a class last night, I witnessed a fire. It wasn't very large, fortunately, but, in a country where the houses are built of wood and paper, even a small fire can turn into major destruction. Seven large fire trucks gathered at the site and were able to contain the fire in a small area.

I received a special delivery letter telling me that my Tokyo friend, Tadashi Yokoyama, will be able to come to Osaka the weekend of April 9th to help me celebrate my birthday. I'm excited about seeing him. He's the one who works at the British Embassy and the man I spent Christmas Eve with—also the night I felt my first earthquake in Tokyo. He's a friend of Hyuga-san's, so I'm hoping that he, too, will be able to come to Osaka then. Everybody wants me to celebrate with them, and I'm running out of free dates. I've already cancelled one small party that was scheduled for that weekend. It should be a memorable birthday!

Reiko is back home as of Wednesday, but I will stay at the Matsuo's until April some time. It's just as well. I can use another month of Japanese daily conversational practice and living here costs nothing.

3/20/65

I went to yesterday's Osaka Sumo Tournament. The matches were as exciting as I expected them to be. I understand the sport, but I cannot understand why the Japanese think the wrestlers are handsome.

This morning I went out to Kobe and realized that in the few months since I've been here, I've gone to synagogue more than in my three years in New York City, which has the largest Jewish population outside of Israel! Ironic? Yes!

I spent the afternoon with Rick Kobayashi and his friend, Shimizu-san. Rick's father gave him the car—a giant Cadillac, no less—so we drove about 15 miles out of the city and went for dinner at Harihan, a restaurant-inn that was written up in *Life International* last August. It's the loveliest inn I've yet seen, situated high on a mountain overlooking Osaka City and Osaka Bay. The restaurant is owned by Shimizu-san's mother. The location was once the home or the place of his grandfather's villa. The garden with its creek and waterfalls and bridges could not be duplicated today because of expense. Near the entrance is an altar to Jizo, the goddess of children. She was enshrined when the grandmother's first-born baby boy died. It is a somewhat restricted inn; guests must be introduced. What was once a good size public bath was changed into a dance hall by the Occupation Forces. No longer a dance hall, it's now a western-style meeting room. Several years ago, the emperor, empress, and crown prince stayed there. After dinner and a tour of the gardens, we drove farther up the mountain to a very old Buddhist temple. The strange yellow lights of the inside altar gave the place an enchanting, but eerie, appearance. A short walk from the main building brought us to an even more spectacular view of the surrounding area at night. It was a special afternoon and evening.

3/21/65

Dad, thanks for your suggestions of lecture topics. All four are good and usable. The one on camping, however, I've already used twice. It's an easy subject 'cause I know so much about it. Many people ask me what your business is. When I can speak in English, I can mention the various aspects of your position. But when I must speak in Japanese, impossible! One of these days, I must write a prepared answer to that question and then memorize it!

I've been here about 5-1/2 months now. I'm not quite sure when the change came, but suddenly I realized that I'm quite settled here. As I tell all who ask: *Nihon no seikatsu ni naremashita,* which means "I feel at home in Japan." It's true! I speak enough Japanese now so that even a telephone conversation doesn't make me a nervous wreck. And I know my way around Osaka so well that I even give directions to my Japanese friends. And, if they are looking up a word in the dictionary and don't know how to spell it in English, they write it down in Romaji and then I tell them how it's spelled. Kanji is still way out of my grasp and always will be, but I can now read both Katakana (printed) and Hiragana (cursive) characters. I try to study at least one hour every day, so gradually some things just have to sink in.

3/28/65

The dress designer came today with about 20 samples of material. With her help, I designed two sleeveless dresses. It was exciting! Wish I could afford to do that in the states!

Next Monday and Tuesday I've been asked to give two lectures to a specially selected group of Japanese English teachers from around Osaka Prefecture. They requested I speak on "Broadcasting in America" and "How English Should be Taught in Japanese Schools." The latter should be thought-provoking!

Today I went with a friend to Nara: first to Akishino, a famous temple loved by all the emperors because of the female spirit of its small and dainty buildings. Next to Hokke-ji, a famous nuns' temple presided over by one of the emperor's cousins. (Japanese nuns, by the way, shave their heads.) After lunch, we got involved in a lengthy discussion of Japanese writing—or, rather, its Chinese predecessor. The man whose home we were at is a Chinese language scholar and the son of a well-known calligraphy artist. They let me "play around" with their *sumi* materials and requested I paint them a picture. Can you imagine?! We all walked over to the Kompuin Temple, one of the neatest and prettiest little temples I've seen. A nun took us on a special tour, explained all that we saw, then served tea and special bean cakes. It was a terrific day!

Got your letter yesterday and the stockings. I'm so glad you sent the stockings air mail. I've been wearing the old ones—holes and all. There are no stretch stockings in Japan as yet, so women are envious of mine.

You mentioned a difficult readjustment to life in the states. The Peace Corps is always worried about cultural shock when a volunteer arrives in a strange country. Better they should worry about this shock when the person returns. I suppose the longer I live a Japanese way of life, the more difficult my homecoming will be. Having mulled the problem over many times, I have also concluded that there's not a thing in the world I can do to ease that future situation. Traveling is easy. It's coming home that's difficult!

Up until yesterday, we had beautiful spring-like weather. Then a burst of cold air and late snow fell from the skies spoiling everything. A friend told me the weather was particularly bad because it all came from Red China. Never thought about it that way.

I had better wrap this up and type up my lecture outline for tomorrow. The prefectural office wanted to make copies of my speech available, but they want me to speak for one hour. I assured them I haven't time to write out any speeches these days. I haven't written a radio script in three weeks! As it was, the whole lecture took me about seven minutes to put together. I've become very good at fast thinking!

I'm moving back to the Otani's on April 12th. It will be nice living all in one house again.

RADIO BROADCST

Spring Fever
NHK "Radio Japan Journal" 1965

The Pressures of School

The sun beats a little warmer, the birds seem to sing a sweeter song, and the first cherry blossoms appear as the prettiest harbinger of spring. A calendar isn't needed to check the date. It can be felt in the air and seen in the faces of high school students.

Patterned after that of the United States, the Japanese school system since the war has consisted of six years of primary school, three years of middle school and three years of high school. Above that, there are two-year colleges, four-year colleges, and universities, which require an additional two or four years for advanced degrees. Only the first nine years are compulsory. Here's where the first stepping stone comes.

In order to go from middle school to high school, certain examinations must be passed. They are difficult, but far from impossible. Yet, failure in these examinations can bring unwanted consequences. Loss of higher education seems to be only a minor consideration when compared to newspaper stories about 15-year-old boys and girls who couldn't qualify for high school and, in shame, committed suicide.

To succeed in life, many Japanese feel that one must attend the best middle school, the best high school, and the best university. Therefore, life for the student becomes one long series of school entrance examinations and, with this, continuous anxiety and pressure.

Entrance examinations for the universities are particularly grueling. They are supposed to eliminate the poorer students. Yet one professor at the Tokyo Institute of Technology believes differently. As they are presently administered, he feels the exams give an advantage to the unimaginative, unoriginal but careful students, while the more creative individuals are often not selected.

As the entrance examination war of competition is intensified year after year, parents must consider expenses for private tutors, reference books, and special classes for their children. Those who cannot afford these expenses usually cannot give their children a college education.

Japanese colleges are open to all who wish to enter, but there are comparatively few students from low-income families. Costs are just too exorbitant. Those who do enter often must rely on side jobs. Some don't even have enough money for proper food.

This financial problem came into the headlines in late January 1965 when Keio University students in Tokyo held a two-week boycott of classes. It was quite unprecedented. The dispute originated from an announcement by university authorities that the total sum of money, which that year's successful examinees should pay to the university would be raised from $333 to $1000. This included $277 for the expansion of facilities and an equal amount for a university bond. The increase was a tripling of past fees, and the shock was made worse by the fact that the announcement came only three months before the start of the new school year. A compromise plan was accepted, but the problems that led up to the boycott received national attention. The demonstration was favorably received by the public. The Keio affair did not involve any political entanglements. On the contrary, it was directly concerned with family livelihood and university management. For this reason, the issue was all the more serious in nature. The outlook becomes even more disturbing when the prospect arises that only children of the wealthy can go to private universities, which, up to that time, had been accommodating 70% of all university students.

Many problems surround educational policies and plans in Japan. The Education Ministry of the national government is trying to find some solutions, but its conclusions are often ill-advised and shortsighted. It is continually under attack by the Japanese press and by Japanese students and their parents. Immediate and well-thought-out reparative actions are needed.

Spring Cleaning—of Gangsters

What else is a harbinger of spring in Japan? Spring cleaning, for one. The stoves used to warm each room in the house are being turned on for fewer hours each day. In this spring cleaning atmosphere, people turn the heat on in another direction—specifically, in the direction of the Japanese gangster. Every day the press reports another crackdown on these organizations.

The gangster in Japan has a visible role. He doesn't exist underground as in the states. His whereabouts are known; his businesses provide conversational fare. Everybody knows that the first men in attendance at a public bath house may well be gangsters. The reason for this is that the hot water and the thick steam show off their tattoos to advantage! Lately, however, the gangsters have been stepping out in areas where they're not wanted. In order to raise money for their cops-and-robbers' games, they've been throwing their weight around the community and now the public is getting mad! Pachinko is the popular pinball game that offers prizes as the chief draw. Gangs buy Pachinko prizes at discounted prices from players, then sell them to the parlors with good profit. Now various federations of Pachinko parlor owners have decided to shut gangs out, thus eliminating one source of revenue.

The Yamagawa-gumi gang has its headquarters in Osaka. It's one of the five most influential hoodlum groups in the country. In 1965 it had a total of 85 branch offices and more than 1400 members. Most of its money comes from the sponsorship of theatrical performances. This seems to cause the biggest headache of all. Popular entertainers align themselves with a certain group of culture-loving hooligans. Shows are held periodically and the gang rakes in the money, giving a substantial payoff to the performer. The benefits of this system are twofold. First is the financial reward. Over and above this is the added public relations aspect of bringing top performers to out-of-the-way districts and thus getting the sympathies and support of the local townspeople. But now the gangs are running into difficulty. In some areas, the heads of wards, towns, and villages responding to a bulletin circular of the Tokyo Metropolitan Government are boycotting gang-sponsored entertainment agents by refusing their use of public halls.

On the large island of Shikoku in '65, superintendents of four prefectural police headquarters met and decided to set up a public facilities management committee to keep gangsters from using their facilities.

In the Kansai area, which includes 17 prefectures and the cities of Kobe, Osaka, Kyoto, and Nara, the Cultural Facilities Consultation Council unanimously adopted a resolution urging that public facilities not be rented to gangster groups and their associates. With this nationwide anti-gang campaign in full swing, another source of revenue is being cut off.

What's left? Well, there are always things like tax evasion, extortion, theft, or controlled gambling. Aside from these old underworld standards, a new fundraising gimmick was uncovered by Osaka police. It involved funeral services for fellow thugs killed in street fights. The police have succeeded in banning these groups from the use of public halls for entertainment shows, but there's no regulation that can ban them from using temples to hold funerals for the dead. Sponsoring groups receive money from bosses of other groups, and they receive donations of flowers and cash from shops and stores. Then, to augment the funds further, some go on a door-to-door canvass asking citizens for "condolence money."

I suppose eventually the police will find a way to crack down on this, too, but then one more unique scheme will be devised. Or, maybe, public opinion will begin to have some effect. I read in the paper that one powerful bossman—leader of a gang that was formed 100 years ago—reported to a local police station. He came to announce that he had disbanded his organization. Why? He wanted to cooperate with the nationwide campaign to rid Japan of gangsterism! Sounds like the old Lavender Hill Mob comedies, doesn't it?

Cats: A Long Story Short

The police have no rest. In Kobe and Tokyo, they have recently found another headache inducer for the spring season. It's the secretive activity of the cat hunters who leave certain box-like contraptions for capturing these animals under thick bushes or in open spaces under houses. After the cat is seized, it is sold for $10 or more to meet the increasing demand of cat hides for use on the Japanese samisen, *a traditional musical instrument.*

If I may, a digression for what we in the states would call a shaggy dog story. Here it is: "Kaze ga fukeba, okeya ga mokaru." "When the wind blows, the barrel maker gets rich." Funny, yes? No! My reaction exactly! Let me explain it, as my students did, and we'll have their example of a Japanese shaggy dog story straight out of ancient Japan when streets were unpaved and blind itinerant musicians earned money by performing on the samisen. *When the wind blows, some people will be blinded by flying dust and cinders. Those who are blinded will become* samisen *players, and thus it will be necessary to kill cats to obtain hide for the* samisen *skin. This means there will be fewer cats around, and the rat population will increase. More rats will chew more holes in the sake barrels. When more people come to the cooper for new barrels, he will get rich. Therefore, when the wind blows, the barrel maker will get rich. That's making a long story short!*

At any rate, the activity of cat killing had to be stopped, but the question was what existing police laws would apply to such a situation. After careful checking, detectives reached the conclusion that hunters of pet cats can be booked on charges of theft, while those who catch wild cats may be punished for violation of the game law!

Ah, spring! What a mantle of intrigue surrounds its approach. Intrigue and excitement. And humor.

Cherry Delirium

Cherry delirium strikes once a year, always in April, and affects men only. Induced by the sudden warmth of spring weather, the love of pink blossoms and the ancient custom of cherry-viewing, it is aggravated by the excitement of a crowd and the potency of rice wine. It is apparent in the raucous laughter, the staggering walk, the red faces, then, finally, the sullen, churlish, and strange behavior. One April a couple years back, a man under the influence of this disorder was found pacing on the left palm of the ancient and colossal statue of Buddha at the Todaiji Temple in Nara. He was, he said, tempted to see if a man could dance on the palm and walk through the nostril of the Buddha, as a tourist guide had just told a group of visitors.

In a poem written many years ago, it was said:
> "As I look down from the wooded mountain at Yoshino,
> At morn I see mist o'er the rapids of the river,
> And at nightfall hear sweet stream frogs trill.
> I am a traveler lone,
> And only wish people could behold this view."

Located near the the ancient city of Nara, Yoshino Mountain is reputedly the best place in Japan for cherry-viewing. It is covered with 75,000 cherry trees and, when they are all in full bloom, the mountain is dressed in pink. I went in search of this beauty—but on a rainy, dreary day. Because the spring season was unusually cold, the trees were only half in bloom. Nonetheless, the weather was no deterrent for the thousands who came to see. It was one of those days that's usually expected in early March, not at all a day for viewing cherry blossoms, the surest harbinger of the Japanese spring. The flowers are a symbol of the nation, and they are anticipated with breathless excitement. Daily in the newspapers budding reports are printed: Himeji-jo—nearing full bloom; Kanazawa—30% bloom; Sakuranomiya—full bloom. It's somewhat like listening to reports of skiing conditions in the states or colorful autumn leaf coverage in the northeast. Whenever spring comes around, the Japanese take immense pride in—and go to great lengths to view—the cherry blossoms for which their country is internationally famous.

One week of beauty and then it's over. The flowers die, their petals floating through the air like pink-tinted snowflakes. Streets, homes, train stations—everything is covered with a soft pink carpet. Then, there is nothing left for another year. Life is short, but it is fresh and beautiful and perfect. That analogy is drawn between the cherry blossoms and the lives of the ancient samurai warriors and those of the more recent **kamikaze** *pilots of World War II. There is a classical phrase, the translation of which goes something like this: "Ask a man what is the essence of the Japanese spirit, and he will tell you it is the wild cherry blossoms that glow in a sunrise." The enjoyment of the flowers lasts all year. They eat and drink their pleasure, as well, in the form of pickled flowers and bitter cherry leaf tea with floating petals.*

One last note about the cherry trees. The number one song on the hit parade of classics has always been the venerable "Sakura," which asks, Why don't we go to see the cherry blossoms that now appear as far as the eye can see, like mist or clouds with the fragrance of sweet cherry?

4/5/65

My lectures for the Osaka Prefectural Office were successful. They led to a contract with the Osaka City Education Office for the recording of 65 English Language Laboratory tapes by the end of August.

A funny thing happened last week. Mrs. Matsuo was at the beauty parlor. So were two of my students. All were strangers to each other. One commented that she knew a young American woman who came to Japan. Another said a young American woman was her English teacher. Another said a young American woman was living with her family. One said the teacher's name was Wendy-san. Another said it was Miss Phillips. Mrs. Matsuo informed them that it was really Wendy Phillips, and they were all talking about the same person. As they say in Japanese, "*semai sekai,*" which means, as you can probably guess, "small world."

I returned from my trip this afternoon. The best way to get it on paper is day by day, so let me begin with April 1st, a day of mass confusion. First thing in the morning, I took a train to Himeji and Himeji Castle, reputedly the most beautiful castle in Japan. I agree. Every corner holds a story from the colorful history of Japan. The castle is all white, and it is said (though I see no resemblance) that it looks like a white heron in flight. In what was either stupidity on the part of three train conductors or a successful April Fool's joke (the day is popular here), I was put on the wrong train. When I arrived back in Kobe, by my own error, I boarded a local instead of the semi-express. The man sitting next to me was also going to Hiroshima, so he offered to change trains and travel with me.

Why, you ask, do I do these things? Because he was a well-dressed man without Chinese fingernails and pointed toes! "Chinese fingernails" is my own name for the very long nails that some men grow on their pinkies related to ancient Chinese tradition. And "pointed toes" are from the ridiculous adaptation that Japanese shoe manufacturers have taken from American styles. These are real stiletto-like weapons. I steer clear of men with either, and I can tell from afar just what to expect. This man, whose name I don't know, told me a rather intriguing story of a fight with his wife, and he was traveling far to calm down. He was without luggage. I strongly suspect that his story may have been false, but he was a gentleman and an interesting travel companion. I left him in Hiroshima, and then eight hours behind schedule, I arrived on the sacred island of Miyajima. It was almost 11 p.m. by the time I reached my inn, so I was full of polite apologies—there are all kinds—and deep bows.

April 2nd: Early in the morning I toured the famous red *torii* floating shrine of Itsukushima (only at half tide, however), then took a bus and boat to Hiroshima. My first stop there was the Atom Dome, what's left of a bombed-out building, and the Atomic Memorial Museum designed to make the visitor realize how atrocious war is. There were diagrams, photographs, clothing remains, household object remains, et al. The whole thing was fairly reminiscent of the museum in Paris, the memorial to the six million Jews killed by Hitler. I suppose people go to these places because we're all somewhat masochistic and need to reinforce our opinions with substantial evidence. You certainly can't go home smiling if you're a caring human being. From there I traveled by boat to the island of Shikoku and to the city of Matsuyama. Actually, there isn't much to see in that city, but I needed a place to stop over. So it shouldn't be a total loss, I took a quick trip up a mountain in the middle of the city to Matsuyama Castle. The city has had fairly warm weather, so the beloved Japanese cherry blossoms were in full bloom around the castle, and they were delightful. While on top of the mountain, a large pipe organ repeatedly blared forth one—and only one—song. I have no idea why "Annie Laurie" had been chosen for that. I also learned on this trip that a popular gimmick at boat ports and train stations is the maudlin playing of "Auld Lang Syne" for departures.

April 3rd: Took a train from Matsuyama to Takamatsu in the morning. Takamatsu is the largest city on Shikoku and has a few well-known tourist attractions. I first went to Kashima Plateau, from which one can get a terrific view of the Inland Sea. Later, I visited Tamamo Park, which includes Takamatsu Castle. As I was walking in, a young student approached me and asked to speak with me. I said of course, so we went in together, as his two friends dropped by the way. About one minute after we began speaking in English, he asked if I could speak Japanese. He immediately excused himself and ran back for his two friends, who were happy to join us if we'd speak in Japanese. English was quickly forgotten, but they were good guides and pleasant company.

April 4th: At the inn where I was staying, all the maids wanted to speak with me and touch my soft red—or, as they call it, "golden"—hair. By morning everybody knew there was a *gaijin* (foreigner) at the inn. There were five young men staying in the room next to mine, and they requested the maid ask me if they could have my autograph. I said yes—why not?—and they all trouped in to meet and talk with me. It was amusing. In the morning I visited Ritsurin Park, one of the best examples of Japanese gardens. It was indeed lovely, and I was even treated to a band concert. I imagined that the band was made up of some members from a local company. They sounded terrible but were having a good time—and that seemed to be all that was important.

Late morning I took a train to Naruto and, from there, a boat to Fukura on the island of Awaji. The boat took a brief sightseeing detour through and around the Naruto whirlpools, but they were disappointing. I arrived at my inn about 4 p.m. and was invited to take a hot bath immediately. In the bath with me were two girls about my own age. After dinner, one came to my room. She is a teacher and was there on holiday with a group of teachers—two girls and nine men—from a Nishinomiya high school (between Osaka and Kobe). The girls had mentioned the "foreigner" to the others, and they wanted me to join them for the evening. Each of us put on a little performance of singing or dancing. (As I've previously mentioned, it's a prerequisite for any social gathering.)

As it is a standard question, they asked me what food I eat. I told them I wasn't too fond of Japanese pickles, but I did like *fukujinzuke*, a rather mild version. Three minutes later I had a gigantic plate of them in front of me—with tea and rice. You mix them all together and eat what is called *o-chazuke sala sala*. *Sala sala* is the noise you make when it's going down!

By the way, I had a bad headache yesterday, and the people at the inn gave me a roll-my-own pill—a round thin gelatin-like substance in which I was instructed to pour the medicinal powder in the middle, then roll it into a non-leaky ball and swallow it. It was an interesting exercise—and completely non-effective!

April 5th: I returned to Kobe by boat with all the teachers. It was my first time in a large harbor. Last time I was in Kobe Port it was night and too dark to see anything. This time I found it busy and exciting. After lunch with the group, I returned to Osaka. It was, in all, a very pleasant trip, as I always expected it to be.

I don't think I've ever told you about the time schedules on Japanese trains. They are accurate to the second. They leave if people are still hanging out the doors because it's too crowded to get in. They leave no matter what. I was on one train this weekend that was three minutes behind schedule. Humble apologies were announced over the PA system. They also report any and all delays—the most usual is "*Shingomachi*," which means "waiting for a signal." One friend claims they're terrific with the small favors and services; it's the big ones they forget about.

And while I'm on the subject of trains, rush-hour trains have white-gloved "pushers." That really is their job and their title. They stand outside train doors and literally push commuters to the inside so doors can close. In 1965, commuters could face any way they wanted. That was too personal—just picture it!—so a law was passed requiring passengers to face inside the car with their backs to the door!

Train stations are unlike their stateside counterparts. That's a good thing! Within their walls are temporary baggage rooms where, for little more than a nickel per parcel per day, suitcases, bags, boxes, or wrapped carry-alls of any and all sizes can be stored. It's a great way to enjoy sightseeing empty-handed. And, here's a cool idea: in summer, the stations have mounted blocks of ice to keep passengers refreshed—used for hands, face, or for a towel then applied to the neck. Other well-planned services: railway terminals are usually under, over, or next to a department store. The idea was developed by an Osaka railway executive with an eye to the returning traveler in need of last-minute gifts for family and friends. Also, bus stations are located in front of train stations, making transfer fast and easy.

Got home today and found your letter waiting and birthday cards. I also learned I got a call from America today, but the operator didn't know who it was. Hope they call again! (I subsequently received a letter from Marty telling me he and Linda, my former apartment mate, had called. He wrote about it in a funny one-act play entitled "Getting Wendy by Phone" or "Calling Japan Direct" or "The Wazakis have No Telephone? Impossible." They obviously had a deuce of a time getting through only to find out I was not at home. I was upset to hear it was their call that I missed.)

Mother, you made a statement in your last letter which needs clarification. It was about getting a job upon my return. It will probably be difficult, because I will definitely limit myself to the New York area. I love that place and, as long as I'm single, I want to live there. You also said I "should only be able to make as much money as you are making now." I hope not. What you should have said is that you only hope I can save as much as I'm saving now. Don't forget I'm earning very little on a comparative basis, though I'm averaging about 1,800,000¥ per year. **[About $5000 in 1965.]** Never thought I'd ever be a millionaire—even with yen! How I manage to save so much is a mystery even to me. It comes, I guess, to a big aversion to taking even a 28¢ taxi ride. Every time I go to buy something, I think of how intriguing it would be to visit Israel or how beautiful Germany is in the winter. That always makes me take my hand out of my pocketbook.

4/8/65

It's the birthday of two great people today—me and Buddha! It was a nice day as birthdays go, but the weather was sure no help.

It poured all day! In the morning I went to visit Nara Dreamland with Mariko Wazaki and two of her friends. Styled after Disneyland, it leaves much to be desired. In the evening I went to teach at Toru's home. His sister, who knew it was my birthday, had special little cakes and gave me a 1-1/2'-tall and beautiful *hagoita* battledore that has a Kabuki actor dressed in a lion's costume. I'll probably send it home within the next few weeks. Feel free to display it until I myself return to claim it. It will certainly be a conversation piece!

On the 7th, "my women" presented me with a hand-painted silk *furoshiki*. I don't think I've mentioned this before, so I'll explain it now. It looks like a square scarf, but it isn't. In Japan they are as indispensable as handbags, and both men and women carry them in all sizes. Instead of shopping bags, packages are tied up in a neat little bundle. It's easy, pretty, and very convenient. I've been using them since I arrived. One of the women baked a birthday cake for me; others gave me a leather-bound address book, some note pads, and a more practical *furoshiki*. It was a nice afternoon.

Please thank all the aunts and uncles for sending me cards while I'm on the other side of the world. I assumed this year I would have been thought of only, but I was pleased (not surprised, for I know them too well) to receive cards, also. Thank you one and all!

Teaching has been going smoothly. My three-month session with one group at Dai-Nippon Celluloid has ended, and I have a new batch of students. But my former students are allowed to attend my class on Tuesdays that begin at the end of the work day, so they are coming back. I'm not sure whether they come to learn English or to laugh at my jokes! In one of my all-women groups, an unusual thing happened last week. One was ill and couldn't attend. She's about 65 years old and obviously a serious student. Afraid to miss anything I might say, she sent her college-age daughter to the class to take notes!

Something happened here the other day that is typical of the type of cooperation one can get in Japan. An article appeared in the *Mainichi* paper about a William Minehart from the Voice of

America, who was in Japan seeking, among other things, people to act as stringer correspondents on a part-time basis. This is naturally up my alley, so I placed an immediate call to his Tokyo hotel, only to find out that there was no-one there by that name. Then I called *Mainichi* offices. They apologized for the misprint and then proceeded to track him down in various places in Tokyo—all by long distance and with no charge to me: hotels, the *Mainichi* Tokyo office, the American Cultural Center. They were unable to locate him, but it's a good example of Japanese service.

Yoko came down from Tokyo for the weekend, which included a visit with Hyuga-san in Nagoya. He is as interested in Israel as I was in Japan and requested that I take him to the synagogue service on Saturday morning. Following that, we went to Kyoto to visit the Imperial Palace, which is only open two weekends a year and this was one of them. He was here for much too short a time, but it was fun while it lasted. For my birthday he gave me a set of red and gold lacquer coasters.

> **[All these years later, there is still a special feeling in remembering who presented me with each of my treasures. Many of them, like these coasters, I still use today. When I broke the top of a ceramic dish a couple years ago, I was very upset because both the cover and the memories are irreplaceable.]**

I received a telephone call from NHK the other day asking me to write a 15-minute radio program about Bunraku, the famous Japanese puppet plays, for broadcast in July on their shortwave Radio Japan to all English-speaking countries. I'm flattered, of course, and I suppose it will be a rather easy assignment for me—except for the fact that I haven't yet seen Bunraku, and I'm not about to lie my way through a 15-minute broadcast. I'm hoping that the puppet troupe will be back in Osaka soon, for I must write the script in May and record it in June. There is one other American living in Osaka now and I am frequently mistaken for her. She is Edith Hanson, who is married to a Bunraku puppeteer. She is much taller than I am but has strawberry blonde hair. That must be the similarity people see.

Mom, the nightgown/bathrobe is part of your birthday present. The rice paddle, spatula, and other items are for me as reminders for years to come of the everyday things I knew and used in Japan.

[I was always responding to my mother's comments about what mysteries and surprises would arrive in Rochester after she opened each box. This was an example.]

I would like to comment on the actions of the U.S. in Vietnam if only to ask a simple question: What in God's name do they think they are doing? I'm embarrassed and tired of answering questions about the bombings in North Vietnam...and about the talk of peaceful negotiations while our planes drop yet another bomb... and about the lack of reality and the waste of money instead of spending the money in the South Vietnam territory to give the people something to fight for. I'm 9,000 miles closer to the danger area than most Americans, and I'd venture to say I know far better than most Americans how the Asian people are reacting to this potential hot war that would involve every country on the Asian continent and a good many more. It is difficult to be even an informal ambassador for my country when I find so much to criticize and question and so much that is built of confusion, seeming stupidity, and the hateful theory of "an eye for an eye..." It is a very frightening situation when one is on this side of the world!

4/11/65

Cherry blossoms are blooming... tra la, tra la! They're a little late. We've had unusual weather this year, so everyone says. But it was worth the wait. Backyard gardens, streetcar stations, tiny side streets—everything is wearing a mantle of pinkish-white. And what a charming mantle it is!

Everybody loves the cherry trees and, now, even Junko-chan (Toru and Reiko's daughter) has one. In honor of her recent birth and the "Keep Osaka Green" Campaign, the mayor of Minō gave Junko her own baby cherry tree so that the two of them can grow together.

Friends took me to Utsubo Park in the center of Osaka for a look at the cherry blossoms. We dined outside surrounded by pink and white loveliness and the laughter, singing, and dancing of other park guests—families, students, salarymen, laborers. They sat on tarps with picnic spreads of sushi, rice balls, dried fishes, *tempura*, pickled vegetables, and spicy crackers—all presented in multi-layered lacquer boxes. Tomorrow a friend is taking me to Yoshino, near Nara, reputedly the most beautiful place in all Japan for o-*hanami* (cherry viewing).

O-hanami started with the aristocracy in the eighth and ninth centuries and has evolved into extravagant ritualized excursions celebrating beauty and brevity and the haunting and glorious impermanence of life. This exposé of emotions is rare here. The once-a-year communal celebration is both social and spiritual, anticipated and planned for. Newspapers print charts so one can follow the blooming cycles for premium viewing times and positions. Long ago, cherry blossoms became the unofficial symbol of Japan; the official symbol is the chrysanthemum of the imperial family.

As of the 12th, I'm back at the Otani's. It's good to be home or, at least, all in one place. I returned with spring and, just this past week, I saw a strangely marked toad, a tiny khaki-colored snake, and I met a lizard in the road. I found a 3"-round spider in my room and was then told they get bigger as the summer wears on. I was also warned about the large, ferocious, and man-biting centipedes in this old house. Geckoes climb on my walls, but they are harmless and eat the bugs that would otherwise annoy me. Apparently a snake lives in the roof of this 40-year-old home, but it's a good thing because it eats all the rats. Good lord! This summer will be a test of my strength and endurance. I have never been bothered by these sorts of animals, but never before was I asked to live in the same house with them!

I also witnessed a strange event, but no-one has been able to provide me with a scientific explanation—a normal full moon with a halo of light around it, though it appeared to be quite far from the moon. Here it's called an umbrella moon.

Yesterday I went out to Ohel Shlomo Synagogue in Kobe for the

Seder. It was certainly a special one. There were about 140 guests, including synagogue families, tourists, and several men from one of the ZIM Line ships that had just docked in Kobe. They represented countries around the world. The tourists, all of them in their 50s and 60s, had come to Kobe especially for the Seder after seeing it advertised in the paper. I met a couple from Montreal and another from Reno, Nevada. They were traveling around the world on a flexible schedule because, as the wife told me, "it's that time," which led me to believe that every couple with grown children is supposed to take a trip around the world—it's as predictable as retirement. Sitting on my left was a Fulbright professor and his wife, an American historian and author, who is spending one year in Japan and will then return to his position as professor at The New School of Social Research in N.Y.C. On my right was a couple who proved once again that this world is indeed a small one. The husband's name is Harry Becker, an attorney from Marina City, Chicago. As conversations go, I found out he was born in Rochester and is a cousin of Phil Bernstein. "Do you know him?" he asked. **[Rabbi Philip Bernstein was at Temple B'rith Kodesh in Rochester. He officiated at my bat mitzvah, confirmation, and wedding and was a close friend of our family.]** The Beckers are nice, intelligent, and seem to be excellent travelers—adaptable, friendly, and agreeable to anything and everything (rare attributes, it seems, in elderly American tourists). The Seder itself was pleasant—conducted in Hebrew and English using the American Armed Forces *Haggadah* as a guide. We were one big happy family! There was *charosis*, *gefilte* fish, chopped liver, matzo balls, and plenty of Manischewitz wine. Three hundred pounds of matzo had been imported from Israel! After dinner there were more prayers and boisterous Hebrew songs. With everyone in high spirits and close fellowship, the Seder ended with the prophetic "next year in Jerusalem." Our last words as we parted were: "*shalom*"..."*sayonara*." I bought a box of matzo for myself and, this morning, indulged in my favorite: matzo, butter, and jam. In Japan!

4/18/65

It rained all day; the ground was wet and muddy. And this was the day I went to Yoshino to view the cherry blossoms. It was dull and dreary, and the trees were only 50% in bloom so, consequently, it didn't seem to be the best cherry-viewing place in Japan. By this time last year, the Yoshino trees were already bare, so they really are late this year. The trees by Sakurai station near my home are already beginning to lose their petals. When they fall, they float—like snowflakes—and the ground is then covered with a pastel carpet. The blossoms are truly lovely both on and off the trees.

They were a favorite of the old samurai warriors and the more modern *kamikaze* pilots of World War II. Like the warriors and pilots, the cherry blossoms have a very short life. But when they live, they are strong and beautiful. If you're wondering how a warrior can be interested in such things as flower blossoms, then let me tell you that is one thing that makes the Japanese so intriguing and such an enigma. That's the idea behind the book *The Chrysanthemum and the Sword* I recommended to you some time ago. That's why gangsters are apt to write poetry or study *ikebana*. That's why there are such gaudy movie billboards outside every theater and why so many Japanese movies are apt to be so gory. I have been trying to understand this dichotomy since I arrived, but I've yet to come up with an answer.

There are a great many advantages traveling alone, especially when you're young, single, and not too bad-looking. There are, of course, disadvantages, as I'm sure you realize and probably worry about. My rule is to "seek out adventure in any corner you can find it, but don't go asking for trouble, or you'll be sure to find it." It's a pretty sound rule I think and, so far, I've done well by it. I've learned a lot of things living in Japan, mostly about my own self. For instance, I could live alone and like it and travel alone and like it.

My friend Kay Nakano and I had an argument last week. It started out as a discussion until she couldn't see my point of view. Her school has selected a sister of a friend of mine to enter an English contest. She explained to me that it is customary for an adult, fluent in the language, to write the speech for the young girl. She merely voices it; the written work is not hers at all. To me this is a horrible idea. If it's a contest, then it seems to me that the student should be doing the work. This was taught to me growing up—probably by you—and somewhere along the line it became one of my principles. Kay said "when in Rome..." and I said that I just couldn't do it. I believed it was the wrong thing to do and, since it was my decision, I had no intention of doing it even for a friend. Not to mention the importance of this contest and what it would mean if I didn't write an award-winning speech—I being such a fluent English speaker and all that sort of thing. To further complicate it, the money I'd be getting was good, and Kay just couldn't understand why I'd turn it down. At which point I told her that if someone gave me $10,000 to kill a man, that's also good money, but I'd turn it down. She couldn't understand the matter of principles and the fact that I would stick to them so closely. It ended with my stating that I'd be willing to coach the girl's English, but I wouldn't write her speech. We left it at that. I'll be coaching her English for the same amount of money.

In answer to your question, Mom, my Kobe friend, Mrs. Moche, is only 34 with seven children. She and her husband, about 15 years her senior, were married in the old Middle Eastern way. It was all prearranged and they are, in fact, distant cousins.

Hope you had a wonderful trip or will have, as the case may be, to Kent. It is nice you can go to celebrate Harv's 21st in a gala way. I never knew about the watch Dad's Dad gave him, but I think it's wonderful to pass it on down the generations. I always loved and respected that type of continuity among family members. Sort of like that dear old samovar, isn't it?

> [That "dear old samovar" was brought to the U.S. from Russia in 1888 by my maternal grandmother...passed on to my mother...then passed on to me. It's always been a family treasure.]

4/24/65

Dear Mom and Dad and Aunts and Uncles and Cousins and Brother and Grandmother and Culture Club and Hadassah Group and Bridge Players and All the Ships at Sea—well, aren't those the people that get to read and hear these letters?!

Last night I went to see *O-sama to Watashi* (*The King and I*) in Japanese. They imitated the movie rather than the play, so the performance was 3-1/2 hours. What they imitated was good; what they originated was excellent, particularly the playlet "The Cabin of Uncle Tom." In the movie, the American children playing Siamese court children were cute; but, when they had Japanese children doing it, they were precious. Considering that the whole thing was in Japanese, I thought the classic line was "Ah-ha! You can speak English!" It was fascinating to see how Japanese audiences reacted to various scenes. After terrific renditions of songs that would have stopped the show in the states, here there was little, if any, applause.

I began my lessons in *rozashi*, a traditional embroidery using silk canvas and silk threads. My teacher is a woman of about 70, and classes are in the home of one of the students. Perhaps I mentioned at an earlier time how artistic endeavors are organized on family lines. At any rate, I was told that in the whole "family," I'm the only American who ever studied *rozashi* and only the second foreigner; the other woman was German. I went to this particular teacher because one of the students speaks English, and I didn't trust my Japanese for something as complicated as this. I knew as soon as I met Sako Allard that we would become good friends. She studied in the states for four years and is now married to an American. The lessons are somewhat like the old American sewing circles I've read about. As each woman works, she chatters and gossips, and periodically there is a break for Japanese tea, candy, bean cakes, or other delicacies.

5/1/65

This is Golden Week, as it's called, because of the many holidays. The 29th was the Emperor's Birthday; today, May Day; the 3rd, Constitution Day; the 5th, Children's Day.

I enjoyed a Claudio Arrau piano concert and saw three Noh plays—"Kantan," "Matsukaze," and "Kanawa," and a brief farcical play, or *kyogen*. All were engrossing, but Noh plays are so slow that many people were sleeping. I vowed that once was enough.

Wednesday there was a massive transportation strike throughout the nation. One train line still running had a storybook rush hour: people had to get in and out via the windows and some of the young men were riding atop the locomotive. My early morning classes were canceled but, thanks to friends, I was able to travel about without much inconvenience.

That afternoon I went to the home of one of "my women" for lunch and a tea ceremony. Before the ceremony, Mrs. Eichigo dressed me up in a kimono (somewhat like a child plays with her doll, I think) and then escorted me to the garden glen where the ceremony would be held. She behaved as my *nakuhodo* (matchmaker) so everyone was rather amused.

Mrs. Echigo and I at a tea ceremony in her garden

Yesterday I went to my *rozashi* lesson and, at the last minute decided to postpone my *ikebana* lesson till today so I could spend the evening with Frank and Sako Allard. We went to an *okonomiyake* shop for dinner, famous throughout Japan because it's the only one owned by an American. It's small, just six tables, and was in the news this week because it was robbed. Frank introduced me to Bill Humes, the owner, who at one time was a test pilot stationed in Japan. He and his Japanese wife have run this shop for a year and a half.

I got a letter from Sally Small. She recommended I visit Angkor Wat, which Frank and Sako also suggested. I had been thinking about going there, but it depends on what the military situation is like at the time. Traveling alone necessitates certain precautions.

5/6/65

Frank and Sako invited me to spend the day with them and an American guest of theirs. Blanche Lamont is a 78-year old widow, who calls herself "the old-lady tramp born with an itchy foot." Since her husband's death in '57 (and even when he was alive), she has traveled. She just keeps going around and around and around the world. She has had no permanent home in eight years and spends only about two or three months each year in the UK. She travels alone most of the time staying in hostels when she can, because she enjoys it, not because she's trying to save money. She's also an avid mountain climber—has already tackled the Swiss and Japanese Alps successfully and next month she'll try her hand at Mt. Fuji. Anyway, we all went for a drive around the Nishinomiya area. The wild azaleas were in full bloom and the mountains were covered with varying shades of purple.

Mom, I saw something today that I thought you'd love, but it's $8.33 without shipping charges. Let me tell you about it. Better yet, let me draw a picture of it first.... I have never seen anything like it in Japan in the form of a candlestick. It's a unique piece, but the question is do you want to pay for something like that? Please let me know as soon as you can, for I told the storekeeper I'd have to check with you first. Almost forgot, it's made of heavy metal and the candle holders are brass.

[I include the paragraph above because the candle piece described is sitting on my fireplace mantel 50+ years after

the diary entry. This is so typical of the type of written conversations my mother and I would have about some object my mother wanted—a piece of art; a certain dish; jewelry, especially pearls and pearl clasps; dolls; lacquer containers; decorative knotted cords with tassels; silk paintings; paper lanterns; and on and on and on. The list was endless and, as I read the diary now, it seems like almost every letter had questions or requests. I was my mother's personal on-site shopper, and she loved the opportunity to get new and unique items for their home at inexpensive prices. And, yes, I did draw a picture of the bird candle holder in my letter. In others, there were sketches of jewelry designs. My father typically cared little about all this. I'm sure he passed over all the shopping passages with exasperation, if he read them at all. Even transcribing this diary from the original hand-written or typed to the computer, I edited out pages and pages of this different version of "shop talk." They were too much even for me!]

I received a nice note from Rabbi Bernstein in answer to my letter about the Seder and meeting his cousins. Seems he had some responsibility in the publication of the Armed Forces *Haggadah*. He would like to keep up a "sporadic correspondence," which surprised me and made me feel rather honored. Despite our family's informality with the rabbi, I myself have always been in awe of him.

Mom, relevant to my studying *rozashi*, you mentioned the beautiful embroidery work that Grandma Koren did. I distinctly remember a small back room in the house on St. Paul and the many pillows there that she had embroidered. I even remember the exquisite matzo cover she made for the Seder.

Mrs. Moche is all excited about my plans to visit Israel. Her greatest pleasure lies in her undaunted belief that Israel is the place for a nice Jewish girl to land a husband—"The Promised Land" and all that sort of thing! She's really been carrying on about that point! It bothers her to think that, when she was my age, she already had six children.

RADIO BROADCAST

Faux Fair Lady
NHK (Excerpt) 1965

Months after I arrived in Japan, I finally understood what was happening, and why, and how lucky I was to be in this unique situation. Think Eliza Doolittle of "My Fair Lady" fame. Wazaki-san was my Professor Higgins; Iwamoto-san, my Colonel Pickering; and, of course, I was their willing protégée. As head of an Osaka business organization, Wazaki-san made a very good impression by sponsoring an American woman during her stay in Japan. It earned him respect among his peers.

To demonstrate the success of his "project," he took me to places where no woman would have gone before to experience things no Caucasian visitor would have ever been exposed to. The more I understood Japanese culture and the more I could communicate in the language, the better I presented myself and the more places I was taken. It was a win-win situation, an awesome privileged life I had in Japan!

It was a wonder the way things happened! In restaurants my coat and purse disappeared when I entered and were returned when I left. When a group left shoes at the door, each pair was returned to its rightful owner on departure. If I order sherry, it is remembered everywhere I go. If I order scotch and water once, next time I might get both, because it is known that I also like sherry. Though I never know where I'm headed each day—I'm only told that the Wazaki's driver will pick me up at a certain time—everyone else asks me how such-and-such was when I return.

It wasn't unusual for me to go out to a club afterwards with Wazaki-san and some of the men I'd spent the evening with at a dinner or reception. Club Ota had cocktails and dancing and hostesses. The hostesses danced with the male guests (I was always the only female guest) and plied them with drinks, which was good for the club since there is high profit in a high bar bill. I came to know the two bands there and the hostesses, but I was more of a distraction. Because I was new and different, hostesses had many questions, both personal and more random. I was often asked to teach the "Americanu Jeeterbugu" (American Jitterbug) and the "Tweest" (Twist).

One of the hostesses I met offered to introduce me to a very eligible bachelor, but another hostess commented that that would be difficult since she hadn't even been able to "capture" one herself!

Geishas, governors, ambassadors, delegates to the United Nations, government officials, presidents of well-known international corporations—yes, I hang out in the best of circles under Mr. Wazaki's tutelage! My first night in Japan I was entertained in the Wazaki's home by Kazuko Sasada, an opera singer. A few months later, she performed with the Osaka Philharmonic Orchestra. I was there for that, too. And there was a chance meeting on a train with Noriteru Hamada, guest conductor of the Tokyo Symphony Orchestra, whose home I later visited in Tokyo. I had so many rich associations with people I valued and with whom I enjoyed spending time.

5/15/65

Last Sunday I teamed up with Sako and Frank again—we've become a steady trio—and a group of people who want to preserve the ancient beauty of Kyoto. We did a leisurely tour of temples and, at each one, were offered some gift, such as a fermented *sake* drink, a bowl of eel and rice, or fortune-telling. One even offered entertainment by *maiko* (apprentice geishas). Afterwards we went with our hosts—two of Frank's students and their families—to the temples of Shisendo and Manshuin. The latter is famous for its stone and sand garden in the form of a turtle and a crane. But the former was almost the piéce de resistance of gardens for, at this time of year, it was loaded with double cherry blossoms, azalea, bougainvillea, wisteria, and purple magnolias. It was magnificent! One almost never sees cherries and azaleas at the same time but, as everyone has said, the weather is strange this year.

When the three of us travel together, you can probably guess what happens. It's assumed I'm Frank's wife and Sako, our interpreter. It can be funny at times. People are always surprised to learn the truth. Remember how I immediately predicted a close friendship with them? You can just tell about some people.

Seems like the president of one Osaka university somehow got hold of my resumé. She showed it to a graduate student at the school, who had seen me on the Toyonaka bus on several occasions. And it all led to the girl going to the Wazaki's and then calling me here. She wants me to teach her English conversation along with a friend or two and, when she came to meet me to ask this favor, she brought me the necessary gift—in this case, flowers. She is Kazuko Sugawara, a student of low energy nuclear physics, working towards her doctorate. I begin Monday. When she questioned me about salary, she excused herself so many times— "Please forgive me for speaking so frankly." Sometimes Japanese politeness is exasperating.

I saw a protest march aimed at United Nations intervention in Vietnam. I've seen plenty of students standing on street corners getting people to sign petitions, but this was different. There were about 200 men and women marchers and laborers, all shouting—no slogans just attention-getting noise—and they were carrying a varied assortment of signs. All pictured President Johnson as a monstrous caricature with bloodshot and murderous eyes sitting on a bomb, with bombs coming from his ears as he held the dove of peace. I was, at the same time, both revolted and fascinated. You can't imagine the thoughts that run pell-mell through an American patriot's mind when she sees this up close for the first time. Such demonstration activity is increasing, too; just yesterday, I saw another one.

Met some six-year-old children on the train the other day. It was a gem of an experience. We struck up a conversation, and they were full of questions. All of them were gathered around me, and the attention of everyone on the train was focused upon us. When they got to the question about my name, I told them it was Wendy and asked if they knew the story of Peter Pan. One of the little boys was carrying an umbrella with Peter Pan characters and showed it to me. I pointed out Wendy, who in this picture also had red hair, and I told them that I was the same one. They wanted me to know the extent of their English vocabulary: "Good morning, Father"…"Good morning, Mother"…"bye-bye"…and "goo-bye" (with the D omitted). Then they asked how to say thank you in English. We parted friends and with one more phrase added to their vocabulary. Speaking with children takes a bit of bravery, and it's the first time I've had the courage to attempt it on my own. There is a different way to speak to children. I was surprised at my success!

> [There is a different way of speaking directly in Japanese to show respect depending on whom one is addressing—determined by gender, age, position, or honorific. Initially, my errors would be forgiven but, once I could speak Japanese, friends and teachers corrected my words whenever they had a chance.]

Dad, I told you that I was trying to figure out how to describe your occupation in Japanese. My friends and I have dismissed the case as hopeless. There is no such equivalent in Japan and about the closest we've been able to come is that you are a district welfare commissioner, which in Japan is an unsalaried position. Couldn't you have been something less complicated like a history teacher or lawyer?!

Reiko and I were having breakfast the other day when she spied a 6-foot snake coming out of the little pond behind the house. Since we keep a couple of goldfish in there, Reiko ran out immediately and killed the snake. Her decision to kill it was impulsive but, after it was dead, she remembered the snake who lives on the roof of our house. She has never seen that snake and then began to worry that it might be the same one. If they are one and the same, superstition says that she will now have bad luck and was really worried about it. Had it been a white snake, it would have been much worse, for white snakes are worshiped as gods and enshrined. At the end of the month, Reiko was relieved to find that the snake she killed was not the one who protects our home from rats. During the season when everyone changes from winter clothes, the snake did likewise. We found the skin it shed on the roof.

When I joined your friends in Kyoto a week ago, I met two other people on their tour who told me their nephew was coming to Osaka as Odetta's manager. Do you know Odetta, the famous Negro American folk singer? They said they'd have him call me, but of course I never expected it. I was surprised when he did. He arranged to give me three tickets for last night's performance, so Sako, Frank, and I went together. One song proved a bit embarrassing for us. We were the only ones in an audience of hundreds who could understand the English and laughed! A moving finale had the Japanese audience singing "We Shall Overcome" in English. They had large cards with the English and with Japanese characters that were pronounced as the English. I sure wished I had my tape recorder with me. After the show, I went back to meet my benefactor, Charlie Rothschild, then all of us—Charlie,

Odetta, her two accompanists, Sako, Frank, and I—went to their hotel for drinks. It was an enjoyable evening. During the course of it, we met one of India's largest textile importers who cut us with his remark that he thought I must be the "boss-lady" because I was white. He told us bits about his "whole bloody palace" and his eleven servants...and then heard him arrange a sudden trip to India for Odetta and her crew, though commitments prevented them from following up at this time. Wealth and the power that seems always to go with it never fails to awe me, but my awe is rarely accompanied by respect. This case was no exception.

Earlier that day Sako, Frank and I went to a *rozashi* exhibition. Perhaps you can imagine my teacher's joy at being able to introduce me to fellow teachers as one of her students. None of the others had such a distinction!

This morning I went out to Kyoto for Aoi Matsuri, or Hollyhock Festival. It's one of the three most important Kyoto festivals each year. Period participants, dressed in eleventh-century Heian clothing, march though the streets, along with ox-drawn carts and man-carried palanquins. I was disappointed, for I compared it to the Festival of Ages I saw last October, also in Kyoto. I honestly don't know if this one today was less spectacular or whether my being an old pro at these things by now softened the glow.

The radio weather report just informed us that fallout from the second Red China A-Bomb would be in Japan in two days. Authorities don't think there will be enough measurement to endanger lives. And thank God for that!

5/22/65

Sunday bright and early I met Sako and Frank and two of their friends. First on the agenda was a drive to Hasedera, near Nara. It's a temple not at all popular with tourists because of its out-of-the-way location but is famous at this season because it's the only place in Japan that features a profusion of peonies. They were big and lovely, and the raindrops sprinkled them like fresh morning dew. Later we drove to Rokko Mountain near Kobe. It's one of the prettiest mountain ranges in Japan—a fact most Kansai people don't realize because it's in their backyard. There we went to a Kobe University Festival (Frank teaches there) and walked among several thousand students and a good many "Get Out of Vietnam" signs. One student told Sako that, as the interpreter, she ought to introduce the American couple to some real Japanese food (at his booth). His mistake in role identities is now the rule rather than the exception. From there we drove to the top of Rokko and then to a place about halfway down the mountain to go trout fishing. For 34¢ you get a bamboo rod and the chance to cast your line into a pool swarming with trout. The first two fish you get are free; each one after that costs 3¢. But these are no ordinary fish. They are skilled at slipping the bait of mud-like consistency off the hook without getting themselves hung up. But, we must have been smarter, because we ended up with 10 fish that they scaled and cleaned for us. Then we dashed home for a meal of delicious fresh *shioyaki* (salt-grilled fish).

Thursday began with my first recording session for the Osaka City High School Language Labs. The voice I use for announcing is a lower register than what is normal and, after a tough workout of 3-1/2 hours, I thought my throat would burst. The schedule calls for a recording session every week for 2-1/2 months. I suspect it will get easier as I do it.

Thursday evening may well be the culmination of all my months in Japan. At 9 p.m., I arrived at Sako and Frank's home. Bill Hume and his wife (the couple who own the *okonomiyake* shop I mentioned earlier) had just arrived, and we were busy unloading *okonomiyake* tables and dishes and *okonomiyake* ingredients and soda, liquor, and a keg of beer. Everything was set up by about 9:30 and, shortly after that, people began arriving. There were *koto* and *samisen* players, a classical dancer, and some friends. Then came Odetta, the special guest, Bruce and Leslie, her two accompanists, and Charlie Rothschild. After we ate, as always, everyone entertained. Frank sang a Japanese song; I sang the Japanese version of "Down by the Station" while everyone else hummed it in round form; Charlie did a riotous imitation of a sumo wrestler; Leslie and Bruce sang American folk songs, and then it was Odetta's turn—the moment everyone had been waiting for. It was worth it. She sang a Christmas spiritual. There wasn't a sound in the room. But the quiet didn't last long, for then the Americans broke into song—spirituals, folk songs, and popular songs. When we had run our course, the Japanese guests started. We played a baseball song game in Japanese, followed by "Musical *Zabutons*," like "Musical Chairs" only with floor cushions. There were guessing games when the Japanese would do a gesture and we'd guess what it meant. Then we'd do one. After we exhausted that, we did the same thing with sounds (as in an American dog's "bow wow" and a Japanese dog's "wan wan.") We laughed and sang and drank and had a most memorable evening. No-one is likely to forget it soon. The party finally broke up—reluctantly, to be sure—at 4 a.m.

[More than 20 years later, I went to hear Odetta perform in Piermont, New York. She absolutely remembered that night, but also quoted something I had said when we were together in Japan that stayed with her for years. It was a moral aphorism that guided her through life. I was humbled! Too bad now—some 50+ years later—I can't remember that profound precept!]

The inevitable question was finally asked. I knew it would be. In this land where the average bra size is 32A, I'm a giant among giants! I had my first dress fitting this past week and both the designer and the seamstress were at a loss as to how and what to do with the bustline darts. I wasn't much help. My knowledge of Japanese dressmaking terms is limited. One class I have of women students asked the question they've probably been wondering about for weeks: Am I true or false? Disbelief and awe was rampant, as it always is, and their reactions make me laugh. Japanese women, in particular, ask the most personal questions. Another favorite is: "What do you weigh?" One time while in a department store where sales counters are low and you can see from one side of the sales floor to the other, I was shopping for a sweater. I had no idea what size to buy for myself, so a saleswoman used a tape to measure around my bust area. She was stunned! "*Kyu-ju-hachi senchi!*," she called out over and over as the total number of centimeters echoed across the ladies department from one saleswoman to another. "*Kyu-ju-hachi senchi!*" "*Kyu-ju-hachi senchi!*" I don't know why I wasn't offended; all I could do was laugh! A Japanese beauty queen, according to a local newspaper, is lusciously endowed with the following measurements: 31-1/2"—23"—34"!!! A perfect pear!

Earlier today, I went to see the Takarazuka Girls' Review again—this time for the purposes of doing a show for Radio Japan, so I went with two people from NHK. Saw a show containing songs of the Meiji era, 1868-1912, and one based on Pushkin's "Queen of Spades." Afterwards, I interviewed some of the stars, then attended a rehearsal of the next show. It was all quite interesting, of course. I'm recording it on June 11th for broadcast on July 1st. Maybe you can hear it on shortwave. The name of the series is "Japan and I."

I expect to take Odetta and her crew to see the Takarazuka Girls' Review. She's interested in the show and the girls, in turn, are eager to meet her. Tomorrow night I'm going to see another of her shows, and then to a party afterwards.

> **[I did take Odetta to a Takarazuka rehearsal. She found it fascinating. I don't know who was happier—she because she saw it or the stars because they met her. She's a down-to-earth person, and I like her very much. She had hoped we could get together in Europe, but our schedules don't coincide. She gave me her number in N.Y.C.]**

Today a special bonus was a ride on the lake at Takarazuka in an Amphi-car—just like the old "duck" that we tooled around in at Camp Seneca. This one was a good deal more modern and streamlined. There are only two Amphi-cars in Japan: one in Tokyo and the other here.

RADIO BROADCAST

Japan: A Blended Identity
NHK (Excerpt) 1965

The best kept secret about Japan may be that it's not what you think it is. Don't fall into the trap of defining it with clichés, the way much of the overseas media does. If you think it is the land of high-tech and robots and automation everywhere, it is and it isn't. If, on the other hand, you think it's a mysterious land with the spirit of the samurai and secret ninjas and such, it isn't and it is. It is homogeneous and it isn't. It is both forward thinking and, in some ways, very backwards. Some people assume from seeing manga *or* anime *that Japanese people are incredibly perverted, but most people are actually quite prudish and conservative by western standards. It is a nation filled with people who claim to be not religious, yet every town, village, and roadside is dotted with small shrines with fresh flowers and little stone deities dressed in hand knitted caps and bibs. While it is part of Asia and parts of its culture were influenced by China and Korea, it is also distinct and unique. It's a country with a long and complicated history, and it's also a modern, messy democracy. Rather than trying to pigeonhole it, take it for what it is.*

5/30/65

I was invited to attend a ship's christening by the christener, Mrs. Macapagal, wife of the Philippine president. I had more important things to do that day, so I skipped it, but I'm always surprised at the unexpected experiences that continue to pop up.

The rainy season will begin any day now, and we had our first preview on Wednesday. I never experienced anything like it. The gods dumped water on us for 24 hours, pausing only now and then for five-minute reprieves. My boots were worse than nothing; they just enabled the water and mud to collect inside and set. The next day I promptly went out and bought a special pair of boots for the rainy season. The rain was serious, I knew that; but not until the next day did I realize how significant. It was just a small part of Typhoon Amy but, in 24 hours, 5.3" of rain fell in Osaka, three people were killed, and two are still missing. Throughout Japan there were 406 known landslides. Because of that typhoon and the ones to come in the next month and a half, the rich farming area in the north is expecting extensive crop damage. Now there's fear that this year may bring the worst famine since the 1883-87 Temmei famine, which left 4,400 persons dead from starvation and 1,800 others missing. Japan, the pearl of the Orient.

Yesterday morning I went to synagogue in Kobe, followed by a charity concert in Osaka, where one of my students performed. There were about 400 singers and a local orchestra. Afterwards, I met some people I had lectured to several months ago, and we went to dinner together. Then I raced back out to Kobe to Ariela and Tuvia's home. I haven't seen them in a couple of months. Sadly, Ariela's brother in Israel was recently killed in a factory accident.

I love coming home at night now because it sounds so pleasant. It's the wonderful summer-night country sound of a chorus of frogs. Several have adopted our little lily pond in the yard, so we hear their song all day and night.

Harv, I ordered the rest of your birthday gift. When complete, you will receive two tie tacks: one black baroque pearl and the other, a blue baroque pearl. You're free to choose whichever one you like. Dad, you did not get a pearl tie tack because I remembered your dislike for tacks and your fondness for that track shoe tie clasp!

[The end of the story: I gave the black pearl tie tack to my husband as a wedding gift. When he no longer wore it, I had it made into a ring for myself.]

I've been busy making small gifts for my Japanese friends. Mom, do you remember that several years ago I made you a dust cloth with a fancy hand? What with the nature of Japanese homes and their cleaning requirements, I thought this might be a unique and useful gift. I completed one and showed it to Reiko. She was so excited about it that the next day she made two for her church bazaar. I've been trying to think of something special I can give for gifts. Personal handiwork is especially prized and this type of thing has never been seen here. It's useful, easy, and inexpensive.

This is also what I mean about new meanings in my life. I love working with my hands in typical feminine pursuits, yet in the states I never did this. I was always too busy doing something else. I've since found the pleasures and thrills of such indulgences, and I have no intention of ending them when I return.

Friends made me abandon my plan to get a bicycle. On my next trip, I'll be getting to the youth hostels on foot and by bus, boat, and train. Of the roads in Japan, 95% are unpaved and notoriously damnable. Riding a bike would not be easy. What's more, traffic is wild and dangerous. Some hostels are very good; some aren't, but they're cheap at only 56¢ a night. Similar to the states.

Glad you like the photo album. These are as important as wedding albums in the states. One friend, after her mother died, took her mother's best *obi* and fashioned it into a set of albums. Others have embroidered theirs or have done personalized block printing. The letters on the cover mean "congratulations." As for the pictures enclosed, which I don't remember, they must have been gifts.

Japanese gardens: there are all kinds—some with flowers, some with shrubs (flowering and otherwise), and trees. The type of garden depends wholly on the amount of money the homeowner has. The most traditional garden is the one with flowering shrubs and trees with a large *ishidoro* (stone lantern), and various-sized, carefully-placed natural stones. The garden in our yard is more western style. Because no-one does their own gardening and the Otanis can't afford a gardener, it is badly overgrown in parts and rather mangy looking.

6/5/65

Saw an ad in the English *Mainichi Newspaper* about a teaching position and followed it up with a letter. That led to an interview and my ultimately getting the job. I've about seven students from the Business Department. I began this week. It's an interesting group though their abilities range from low low to high high. It's the same with my new class at the American Cultural Center. It's so difficult teaching to a group when the members are at such vastly different skill levels. I'm not sure anybody learns that way.

I was really proud to be an American the day of the Gemini spaceflight. It's been such a long time since I've had such a feeling. I've been having to make apologies and excuses for too many months. The Armed Forces Network carried the blast-off live, and I let Toru and Reiko listen to the broadcast. I myself didn't stay awake to hear it, but they reported that it was very exciting. It was the first time they'd been in on such an event. That's one way to gain supporters on this side of the Pacific.

Just before a second typhoon grazed us, one of my students drove me to the top of Satsukiyama near my home. What a view— great for moon-viewing or watching sunsets or sunrises. On a clear night, which it was, you can see Osaka, Kobe, and all points between lit up like a Brobdingnagian pinball machine. It's the best one yet, which is what I keep saying. Honest, they just keep getting better!

Last night I went out to Kobe to meet an eligible American bachelor and a friend of the Moches. He's nice, though we'll never cultivate anything. He's returning to the states as soon as he can wrap up his business here. So many people trying to make a connection for me!

This afternoon I judged an English Recitation Contest and met a fellow judge who fell in love with me! Let me explain. Eleven years ago, Akio Hayashi went to Tennessee on a Fulbright Fellowship and fell in love with America and with an American girl. He married the girl and last year became a U.S. citizen. Now he's back in Nishinomiya running a well-known English school with his brother, who has been to America and also wants to marry an American girl. That's where I come in. He saw me and within five minutes asked if I'd marry a Japanese man. He also asked if I'd teach at his school. I said yes to the latter question (during July only) and, as to the former, I told him it was highly unlikely. Undaunted, he plans to introduce us. If nothing else, he'll probably be as nice as his brother. Friendships with engaging people I like to cultivate!

I continue to see Mrs. Wazaki every week, but rarely do I see Mr. Wazaki. Their maid returned to the country, so Oku-san has been very busy lately. Now that I'm doing so well on my own, Mr. Wazaki only brags about his—er, my—accomplishments, introduces me to friends when he so desires, and signs my visa papers.

6/13/65

Last Sunday I spent a pleasant day with Eli and the Blumenthals. We drove to Kyoto's Samboin and Daigo-ji temples. Half of Daigo is atop a mountain, up a two-mile rocky mountain path. We climbed it, despite the fact we were dressed for city strolling, high heels and all. It took us two hours to get up—the temperature was also the highest to date—but it was a nice climb. The mountain temple was disappointing, but the view of the surrounding mountains covered with tall straight cedars was worth the climb.

I have a new teaching schedule with the addition of two classes a week at Toyo Kensetsu, a firm of civil engineers that specializes in harbor construction. The new routine means several early mornings, a drastic change from the schedule of the past few months. The early bird may get more money, but it also loses more sleep. I've been very tired of late.

One of my students took me to a *Biya Gaden* (beer garden) atop a downtown *depato* (department store), where we enjoyed cold *biru* (beer) and the surrounding city lights. Love the way the Japanese language incorporates foreign words and phrases!

Some of my students were asked the following question: Who is your favorite person and why? Their answers were diverse: Linus Pauling, Albert Schweitzer, Jesus, Abraham Lincoln, Buddha, and Mother. Imagine my surprise and embarrassment when two said that I was their favorite person and then proceeded to give the reasons why that was so. I turned scarlet!

I've been leading a calm and unruffled life in Japan, but on Wednesday evening, when I saw an anti-Vietnam student demonstration that turned into a scuffle with police, I uttered my first swear word in eight months. Antagonistic feelings have been increasing over the weeks egged on by the newspapers, by the numerous communist organizations, and by the plethora of movies produced about the horrors of the war in Vietnam (some factual, some filmed in Japan). There is little honest understanding of the problem, but were I in their shoes and subject to the same media, I'm sure I, too, would be caught up in the distorted facts.

Earlier today on TV I watched films that were taken by the Japanese as they bombed Pearl Harbor. I'm glad that I was alone in the house. As I watched, I became increasingly uncomfortable and, after ten minutes, I started to cry. Multiple reactions to those scenes.

The Japanese adore the western idea of beauty. Even 150 years ago, geishas painted themselves white for the idea that white skin is far lovelier than their yellow skin. Reiko frequently complains that Junko's skin is too dark and, in fact, the highest compliment you can pay to a newborn in Japan is to tell the parents that their offspring "looks just like a foreign baby." Men and women models used in product advertisements look like the western idea of beauty rather than the oriental. It's not uncommon for aspiring models and those already established to have plastic surgery on their eyes to take away the slant, on their noses to take away the breadth, and on their breasts to give them a slant and breadth. "It's always greener on the other side." In Japanese, that comes out as the other man's flower is redder!

I gave a dance lesson to Mariko Wazaki and her friend. They were invited to their first dance at Osaka University at the end of the month. They never learned how to dance or behave, which didn't surprise me so much as their panic at the idea of a "cheek dance." They're 18 years old. Mrs. Wazaki can't dance, Mariko's brothers are poor dancers and rarely at home, and for Mr. Wazaki to teach them would be out of the question. Thus, I was appointed.

The Philippine Consul and his wife invited me to a cocktail party in honor of Philippine Independence Day. I had to turn down this invitation, because I had previously arranged to spend the afternoon with friends at Horyu-ji near Nara—famous for its 1200-year-old wooden pagoda. It's in remarkable condition. Then we went to an unusual 50-year-old restaurant. Now it's located in what is the heart of the prostitute district, but somehow that idea adds to the atmosphere. It's very ornate, modeled after the elaborate Toshogu Shrine in Nikko and, in today's world, could never be rebuilt, regardless of money, because of the quality and type of handicraft within. One special aspect is the hall that contains the sleeping rooms (it's also an inn) is designed to look like a Japanese street—and does. Every room is decorated differently and follows the design of a certain profession, season, or place. Most unusual.

The Otanis are not renting or leasing this house. It belongs to a member of Toru's family who now lives in another part of Japan. They are just making use of it. When Toru and Reiko leave—and they don't know when, for there's been no word from Texas—the relative will sell the house and land. But the house is 40 years old. The practice here is to evaluate the worth of the land and to sell the land and the house accordingly. The value of the house is not taken into consideration because of its age and the belief that a new owner may just tear it down and start all over again. Home improvement doesn't have much meaning in Japan, unless a family plans to live in the home for many years.

June 1st is "Changeover Day," when everyone switches from winter to summer attire. Regardless of the high temperatures before that date, men and women still wear long underwear. But on that day, even if it's cold, they change to summer dresses and light suits. When it's real hot, the men go to work in their shirt sleeves. At the office, they change from long-sleeve gray to short-sleeve blue. (All Japanese workers wear protective jackets with company logos.) Even schoolchildren change their uniforms to the light blues of summer. It's a true clothes revolution. The same thing happens in the reverse on December 1st.

6/19/65

Department of Worthless Information:

The new fashion style these days with the younger male set is bell-bottom trousers. Here they're referred to as "trumpet trousers."

The word for "womb" in Japanese means "children's palace." I think that's nice!

I went to an exhibition this week which requires some explanation. In Japan, statues and buildings are divided into three different categories if they are important enough and old enough to be categorized at all. Most superlative is National Treasure followed by Important Cultural Asset, then Cultural Asset. This delineation gets to be confusing at times, but it becomes even more complicated when you realize that people are divided the same way—that is, intangible Important Cultural Assets and National Treasures. One of the Osaka department stores this week had an exhibition of some 100 items made by 31 persons designated as Important Cultural Assets. On display was the work of dye-weavers, metal crafters, lacquer artists, ceramicists, doll makers, and sword makers (who, during the feudal ages, had the most sacred profession in Japan). The people and their work are highly respected, and the people in attendance were silent and contemplative.

I recorded my Takarazuka show at NHK. In July I'll be writing and recording two more shows for broadcast: one on Japanese Supermarkets and the other on Japanese Leisure Time Activities. I do not, by the way, choose these subjects; they are assigned to me. I'll let you know when the other two will be broadcast, so perhaps you can hear those instead. The programs are sent to the U.S., Canada, Australia, and Europe. That is, without a doubt, the largest audience I've ever had!

I received a note from Dr. Hill. WUWM began broadcasting my programs this month and already have received a few enthusiastic calls—unusual, as most FM listeners are historically reticent. He wants me to do another series of 12 for him and is willing to pay. I had told him I could do no more without payment because of other commitments. Now I have to set a price and let him know if I'm willing. He's also trying to convince the Educational Radio Network to use the programs. They've had the audition tape for six weeks and have not yet listened to it. He also mentioned the financial factor to them and is trying to persuade them to give me a grant-in-aid. It sure would be nice.

You asked what type of work I'll do after my return. The former general manager of WRVR once told me I was the type of person who would always have one major problem when job-hunting: over-qualification. By next summer I should be qualified for everything—and nothing! I'm still in love with the broadcasting angle, but am trying to come up with something that would involve people-to-people contact, international relations, and travel (particularly in the direction of the Orient). I've come up with a few ideas though none of them have overwhelmed me.

Were you kidding about my visiting South Africa? Frankly, with the money and freedom and time I'll have, I've thought about going to a lot of strange places—even the islands of the South Pacific. Don't know if South Africa interests me but northern

Africa does. Though I'm sad about leaving Japan, I'm already looking forward to the rest of my round-the-world trip. I'll have six or nine months to play with, depending on whether or not the Japanese government renews my visa.

RADIO BROADCAST

"Ooh, la, la" à la Japonaise
NHK "Japan and I" 1965

There's no business like show business, as the song says, and there's no show business quite like the Takarazuka Girls' Opera. James Michener made the Takarazuka Girls famous in his novel Sayonara. *To call it an opera is misleading. To say operetta is more correct but still not accurate. You can draw your own conclusion.*

Japan was an isolated nation for 250 years. The country shut its doors to foreign ideas and to foreigners and even deported them from its shores as an additional measure of safety. But in the 1850s, Commodore Perry and his Black Ships ended all that. Then, under western-oriented Emperor Meiji, Japan broke away from its feudal bonds and accomplished an unparalleled turnabout in a record short time. Western fashion, etiquette, ideas, and, procedures were welcomed openly—and what's more, continue to be.

Back in 1913, a railroad was built to run between Osaka, the second largest city in Japan, and Takarazuka, a hot-spring town 16 miles to the north. In those days, there wasn't much activity there, so the question arose as to how to increase tourist travel to that area. Keeping in mind the popularity of and receptiveness to western ideas, the railroad executive decided to establish an all-girl review after the pattern of French showcase productions. Its success was immediate, and it soon became one of the focal points for all tourists visiting Osaka. Now the beginnings of this spectacular are obscured and forgotten. What's important is the simple fact that it exists for the pleasure of the masses at a price they can easily afford.

The Takarazuka Girls' Opera is a fairytale fantasy revue of stardom for the sake *of stardom, the love of bright lights, fabulous costumes, and unequalled popularity.*

When a girl turns 15, she can audition. Dancing and singing abilities are carefully judged and a personal interview is given. If she excels in all, she is enrolled for two years at the Takarazuka Music School. First-year students study academic subjects; in the second, they are permitted to appear on stage. After this training program, they may select a professional name but, during the traineeship, they use their own names and, when they perform, no individual credit is given. I wondered what happens to the girls who don't succeed during these crucial two years, but I was told that failure never presents itself. These girls want to be stars, and they work hard to achieve that status.

Of course, not all the girls can be stars and, when they realize this, their stage training becomes a matter of exceptional training for marriage. A Takarazuka girl can never marry. If she does, her ties are forever broken with the group. A Takarazuka girl begins her work at 17 years of age and retires when she pleases. Marriage or movie contracts are the most numerous reasons for departure. There is a definite spirit of camaraderie among the girls. This and the nondescript star appeal combine to keep the girls active. Not all these girls are young. Some are in their 30s and 40s; one "girl" is now over 60 years old. She began with Takarazuka only a few years after the original troupe was formed and, in keeping with regulations, never married.

Life for a Takarazuka girl is not easy, but it's a good deal easier now than it was before the Second World War. In those days in a cloistered atmosphere, a girl who wanted to go for a walk—even with her father—had to get special permission from the authorities. Today they are allowed to date. Although this seems to give them more freedom, they have little time for such pleasures.

The girls, who live in dormitories or private homes near the theater, are kept busy with rehearsals and personal training. Rehearsals are held 15 days each month, 12 hours each day. The rest of the month is a working holiday, including guest appearances on Takarazuka's own twice-weekly television show and once-a-week radio show. There are other commitments, as well. The money they earn goes back to Takarazuka, which guarantees them a certain salary each month. But it's not a big fee. Stardom here implies fame not wealth!

There is one aspect of the Takarazuka Girls' story I have purposely neglected to mention till now. The real stars of Takarazuka are the girls who are male impersonators. They are the otokoyaku, *so popular with teenagers especially. These girls are chosen for male roles during their training period. Choice is based on voice quality and height. Once selected, their hair is clipped to a short cut, characteristically called a "Takarazuka man cut." Beyond this, they prepare for their roles by watching men on television and on the movie screen, by reading books, and by daily observation. I asked one of the stars who is noted for her male leads why teenage girls idolize her so. As she explained it, she represents for them the ideal hero or sweetheart. You may disagree and counterclaim that she is, nevertheless, a woman. But that is the answer right there. Men, despite their undisputed qualities, have no real understanding of the feminine mystique. These male impersonators do understand, and very well, the complexities of a female. Consequently, they are above the normal inadequacies women attribute to men.*

The Takarazuka girls are divided into five groups. The first four get their names from the natural world: Snow, Flower, Moon, and Star. Each troupe has about 80 girls, half of whom are male impersonators. The fifth group, with no name, is made up of specialists in Japanese and western dancing, singing, and drama. The specialists are assigned to one of the four troupes, all of them working troupes. For instance, in May the Moon Troupe performs at the main theater in Takarazuka; the Flower Troupe rehearses for the next show; the Snow Troupe is on tour in the rural areas; and the Star Troupe is on a working vacation doing TV and radio guest appearances.

[In 1998, a fifth troupe was added, called Cosmos, and another theater was built in Tokyo. In 2016, the five troupes put on 900 shows a year.]

Each presentation lasts for one month. Ten writers are always at work, and they are given freedom of subject choice—adaptations of western classic musicals, operas, plays, novels, or films. The souvenir program always states that one show consists of two parts. I say three. The first has a Japanese flavor—a love story of a fisherman and a maid, for example, depicted in song and dance, or perhaps a potpourri of songs from the Meiji era. The second part begins after a 30-minute intermission. It's the non-Japanese half of the program—a story perhaps reminiscent of Puccini's "La Boheme" or an adaptation of Alexander Pushkin's romantic-tragedy "The Queen of Spades." This second play contains music and dance, as does the first, but an involved drama is embodied within. The third part, as I see it, is the extravagant finale, a show in itself with a compendium of music from the previous presentation with new stage settings, lavish costumes, and glittering performers.

The stage is large and makes use of a revolving circular platform and two movable risers. At each side, a short, narrow, extended proscenium is used for entrances and exits. Attached to these and in front of the main stage between the orchestra and the audience is a long runner used for character or situation emphasis and for the finale. In the course of the performance, the stage sets change from stark to elaborate. And with the elaborate, much emphasis is put on flowers: flower props, flower curtains, flower mock-ups. The costumes are bright and flashy, spangled with gold and silver that catch the stage lights and make them dance.

The entire show is happy, festive, and exciting. From the start, the spirit of Takarazuka has been epitomized in just three words: purity, righteousness, beauty.

Even when it's sad, it's happy. There's no true emotional involvement in this. When a person goes to a live drama or sees a movie, his empathy may make him suffer what the actors suffer. At Takarazuka, it just isn't true. The actors' problems are problems in a stage play, and they will end as soon as the curtain falls.

At every performance teenage fans sit together so their voices will unite in power. When their idol appears in a popular pose or sings a ballad, they yell the star's nickname to give encouragement and support. The same thing, by the way, is done with popular female impersonators in the ancient-style Kabuki plays.

The Takarazuka Girls' Opera is much loved, and its fame is not limited to the local scene. The girls first went abroad in 1938, visiting Germany and Italy, and have since given performances in Canada, the United States, and France.

There is the complete story of The Takarazuka Revue—updated and more factual than was Michener's novelized version. Why, in summary, is it so well liked? Because it's pure, uncomplicated, and so understandable. It's also somewhat Japanese—modern Japanese. It does not represent Japan anymore than 42nd Street and Times Square represent the United States or the Moulin Rouge represents France, but it is an integral part.

6/27/65

Let me tell you about last Sunday evening when an adventurer's dream was offered to me and I rejected it. The previous week there was an ad in the newspaper about a yacht sailing to Hawaii and the South Pacific islands and a lady crew was wanted. Journalistic curiosity (and mine, too) made me follow it up. I met the owner and his two friends. He is a South African artist from Pretoria, a man about 40. He had the boat designed and built in Japan this past year. His friends are a Danish couple. The husband, who was raised on his dad's fishing boat, has been a fisherman, sailor, and yachtsman for the past 20 years. His wife is also an accomplished yachtsman. The yacht is 43 feet long, sleeps eight and has various specially-designed conveniences. The boat's a beaut and so was the idea of sailing to the South Pacific. I made it clear from the beginning that only my curiosity made me answer the ad. I turned down the offer of actually going, but I think you should know the real reason why. It was not because of any sense of danger. That naturally was my first thought until checking the qualifications of everyone and everything. I am honestly not afraid of such a trip. It was rather a case of this was someone else's dream, and I had my own. Going with them would interfere with my own plans to visit Asia and Europe, and they are more important to me. Such an opportunity truly happens only once in a lifetime, but I doubt that I shall regret my decision.

Reiko is teaching me French embroidery, which I've long admired. When the next package gets sent out, included will be two Japanese-style aprons. The one with the roses is for you. The other, with the large flowers, is for Gram, and the large flowers are my own embroidery handiwork. I've got great plans for this new art, which is easy and cheap and pretty. You know my problem?—too many interests! I can't find sufficient time for them all. Which reminds me that I've just begun work on my *rozashi* handbag. And last night I finished all four "handy" dust-cloths. I told Reiko you'd be surprised at my work, and she suggested a *shoka shashin*—a photograph to prove it!

Yesterday afternoon I toured a supermarket and interviewed the president for another NHK broadcast I'm recording next week. The Japanese concept is far different from the American one, but listen to the program to find out! "Radio Japan Journal" will be broadcast in Rochester on July 9th at 7:20 p.m. Same frequencies.

This week or next I begin yet another English lesson. I don't want to do it, but I must. My students will be Mrs. Eichigo's son, the son of another of "my women" students, and two of his friends. I have mentioned the responsibilities of *giri* and *on*. Here's where they come in—in turn for all the things that have been done for me. I don't have the time to devote to these additional lessons but, when a person lives with the Japanese, there are certain times when it is absolutely necessary to behave like a Japanese. This is one occasion. It's not without compensation, however; I will get paid for my efforts.

In your most recent letter, you registered concern at the pace which I've set for myself and that which others have set for me. Though my pace is hectic, I am free from all the pressures of a similar pace in the states. That makes all the difference in the world!

This next week is my last session for this school year at Osaka Joshigakuen. Last week the students had an English Recitation Contest. My ESS kids had taught all the others a song I taught them—"Little Red Caboose." They like it and surprised me by having everyone sing it for me. They all gave me a fan and stand in thanks for an article I had written for the *Osaka City ESS Literary Magazine*. It was about the differences in schools in the U.S. and Japan.

RADIO BROADCAST

"Excuse me, but where can I find an orange?"
NHK "Radio Japan Journal" 1965

Irasshai-mase ... Irasshai-mase. *"Welcome ... Welcome ... please come in."* These are the first words you hear when entering any business establishment in Japan. But I invite you now to enter a supermarket. What a novel experience it will be, for the Japanese have taken this commercial concept of the western world and completely adapted it to oriental notions. It is not at all what you might picture when you conjure up your local supermarket. It's not spacious, well-lit, and sterile like so many of the supermarkets in the United States. And it's a far cry from the newest, fully-automated supermarket in West Germany.

The dictionary defines a supermarket as a store, especially a food store, operating in part on a self-service cash-and-carry basis. The definition has its shortcomings, however, for it was taken from a western dictionary describing western supermarkets. Those in Japan are more accurately explained in terms of S.S.D.D.S., which is specialized lingo for Self-Service Discount Department Store. Yet it is a supermarket and not a department store.

The distinction is important, for in addition to obvious differences, there is a regulation established by a retailers' council stating that supermarkets in the six largest cities of Japan must not exceed 4,000 square meters or, in all other cities, 1,500 square meters. If the store does exceed the limits, it is classed as a department store and, for reasons to be explained, it is best for a supermarket to stay in its category.

The idea of a self-service cash-and-carry store developed in the west. The story of American supermarkets first came to Japan via the newspapers in the late 1940s and, by 1950, the idea caught on. There were several reasons why—the convenience of one-stop shopping, cheaper prices, and the ease of self-service. What is especially interesting is the way in which it developed.

In the United States, the pattern of late has been to take the supermarket out of the city and into the suburbs, often to a shopping center, which by definition includes a variety of stores. Yet, this pattern from a nation of motorized communities could not be imitated in Japan. The automobile is still an item of luxury. The most common ways for women shoppers to get about is on foot or by bicycle or, if they come from afar, by subway or tram. Consequently, the first big difference between those in the states and those in Japan is location. Supermarkets in Japan are always located in central, well-populated areas.

Another difference is that of physical appearance. In Japan, the supermarkets are relatively small by comparison. They are crammed full of goods with no illusion of spaciousness. In order to get maximum returns from a minimum of space, shelves are narrow and aisles barely allow room for two people to move freely. Under such conditions, large, wheeled shopping carts cannot be accommodated, so buyers use little plastic baskets. Shoppers are careless with trash, and floor litter annoyingly accumulates. Because of space limitations and centralization, shopping in a Japanese supermarket is all too often analogous to a touch football game with the need for maneuvering around blonde-wigged mannequins and piles of rice and seaweed crackers.

The most curious thing about the supermarkets are the articles on sale inside. Much of the merchandise is truly of Japanese origin: fans for warm summer days, comfortable kimono-style dressing gowns, **furoshiki** *cloths used to wrap things up in carry-all bundles. In the grocery department, there are pressed fishes; candied seaweed; sliced lotus roots; dried tuna with the look and feel of driftwood; vegetables that have been pickled, soaked in brine, marinated in seaweed sauce, or dehydrated; beans that have been sugared, salted, preserved in vinegar, or steamed into jam and wrapped in bread. Housewares include chopsticks; brooms of straw and bamboo; little trays for welcome hot towels in winter and cold towels in summer; wooden cases for Japanese-style box lunches; and beaded and cloth half-curtains.*

Aside from these, an average of 10% of all the food merchandise offered in the supermarkets comes from abroad—Australian cheese; American chewing gum, dried fruits, and cereals; Brazilian coffees; Dutch chocolate; Bulgarian jams; English toffee.

There are hundreds of other products authentically "made in Japan" that correspond to the western fondness for quick meals, handy gadgets, and easy living: sausages in all shapes and sizes; canned beef, curry, hash, and hamburger; Parmesan cheese; special powdered green tea for chilling; meat sauces and white sauces; cellophane-wrapped rice hors d'oeuvres for sake *and beer; boxed dessert cookies; packaged buckwheat noodles; instant sushi mixes; canned mollusks, squid, and octopus; powdered juice mixes; ready-to-serve paper plates topped with dried jellyfish, sea urchins, and seaweed; vacuum-packed fruits in syrup in plastic bags; loaves of bread—wide, long, and uncut, or short, narrow, and sliced. There are plastic swimming tubes and beach balls, crinkly petticoats, fancy dog collars and leashes, thermos bottles—there's just no end to the list! It is true that the Japanese have adopted many western products as their own, but they are not willing to accept them all. When the supermarket idea first came to Japan, one American supermarket chain opened a branch store in Tokyo. At first it was successful as a novelty. After a time, the store lost what it had gained. There is a reason why this was so. American foods are often pre-packed, frozen, or wrapped in sanitized cellophane and cardboard, so that only a portion of the article can be seen. Japanese housewives, with a fundamental belief that cooking is an art and that food should appeal to the senses of taste, smell, and sight, prefer to select fresh meats, fish, and produce. They want to judge for themselves the value of the food to be prepared for their families. Not even eggs are divided into dozens or half-dozens and put in paper cartons. Each one is individually chosen according to size, price, and general appearance.*

Refrigerator and freezer space is often limited in a Japanese home, and it is not uncommon for the housewife to go food shopping once or even twice a day. Under the circumstances, the American supermarket could not hope to maintain its popularity. Novelty is enough to arouse interest but sustaining that interest can only be achieved by giving the consumer what she can use and what she wants.

Like all stores, the supermarkets have special bargain sales, and they keep abreast of the latest fads. For a time, the Walt Disney cartoon characters embellished a wide variety of products. In 1963, however, a Japanese character named Atom Boy appeared on national television. By 1965, it seems that he had "out-atomed" Donald Duck, Snow White, Mickey Mouse, Pinocchio, and all their comic friends. A quick look in the children's corner of the supermarket will reveal Atom Boy on toy trains; in rockets; in the shape of knock-down, pop-up plastic toys; on tee shirts, baby bibs, and bassinets; on boots; and even on mosquito nets.

[This was years before Hello Kitty came on the scene in 1974, as well as the stylized art of the *manga* **characters so popular in Japan currently.]**

The Japanese supermarket is exactly like a department store in all but size. A brief look at what department stores offer should conclusively prove the differences. They also are exceptional— originally a western concept that has been brought to Japan and improved at least a hundredfold! In addition to the usual articles of clothing, accessories, and appliances, there are cultural exhibitions, beauty parlors and barber shops, nurseries, small zoos and amusement centers, golf driving ranges, dining rooms, real estate brokers and stockbrokers, travel clinics, dentists and doctors, and photographers.

Supermarkets do not, of course, offer these services. But they make up for these deficiencies in other areas. They do provide self-service selection and one-stop shopping on a smaller scale. They are sometimes organized on a chain store system, but it is more the exception than the rule. Of utmost importance, they give the consumer the lowest possible prices.

Stores in Japan can be divided into three main categories. Department stores are highest in quality, heterogeneity, service, sanitation, and price. Neighborhood markets, a series of leased stalls located under one roof, deal in a variety of articles. Stalls are arranged on one floor, while the supermarket is often two or three stories high, and the department store seven or eight. In total square meters, the neighborhood market could be compared to the supermarket. Often it is more unsanitary than the supermarket, and it is always higher in price. So, the last category is reserved for supermarkets.

Food costs are inordinately high and it has been estimated that the average housewife spends as much as 50% of her monthly budget on food. It can thus be understood why price differences are so important, and it is in the area of cost that the supermarkets are matchless. In regard to clothing, they are an average of 20% cheaper than the department stores. Food costs on the average are 5-10% cheaper than even the neighborhood markets. Likewise, there are price variations in toys, accessories, and sundries. A middle-class 30-year-old husband with a wife and two children earns on the average about $130 per month, including his twice-a-year bonuses. It is therefore obvious that, when it comes to daily exigencies, the housewife must be budget wise. Accordingly, budget-conscious supermarkets are increasing in popularity.

Supermarkets keep up with the changes made necessary by stocking seasonal items, and most are open every day throughout the year with the exception of the four-day New Year holiday. All things considered, it's no wonder that one supermarket in Osaka not only boasts the highest sales efficiency record per square meter in all Japan, but also the fact that 18,000 shoppers enter the store each weekday and 25,000 on Saturdays and Sundays.

Supermarkets do have their problems: theft, uncleanliness, and shoppers who select the wrong article then want to return it. The problems are not unique to Japan; it is their supermarkets that are unique. There are 4,000 now in operation, half of them first-class markets in size and amount of salable items. There will be more next year and more the year after that. The convenience and ease of self-service shopping has been popular in Japan, granting adaptations and limitations. In the years to come, business is bound to increase in volume.

So, for now, excuse me, but where can I find an orange?

7/4/65

Yesterday I joined Jim Elliott from the ACC and his wife for a party in Kobe. First I went to their typical American home—the first time in nine months I've been in one. Sitting there with my shoes on and atop the wall-to-wall carpeting, I thought any minute someone would reprimand me for not removing my shoes. I can't tell you how strange the whole idea was to me. The party was at the Kobe Athletic and Regatta Club—never knew there were so many Americans in that area. There were hot dogs, beer, pop, ice cream, and plenty of fireworks. Some of them were really special, like the rocket to the moon, the Japanese flag, and the American flag, which was unfortunately and humorously mounted backwards.

Another odd happening was a goodwill gift to the Osaka mayor from New Zealand's Premier Keith Holyoake of 375 pounds of mutton. There are few foods the Japanese detest more than mutton! Somebody didn't do their homework!

The new NHK motto is taken from a Pepsi Cola commercial that asks the consumer to "Come Alive!" Since the Japanese cannot pronounce the letter L, the announcer says "Come Arive!"

I have only two more recording sessions for the City English Lab tapes. At their request, I recheck each script for English errors. So I tell them about a mistake, and they say: do it anyway 'cause that's the way they teach it. And still they ask for criticism in their English programs.

I've discovered a special problem in writing for NHK's international audience. When I measure distance, do I do it in feet or meters? Should costs be in pounds, dollars, francs, guilders, marks, or lira?

I went to visit the Matsuos this past week. Poor Yoji-san had the opportunity to visit Russia and Europe this summer with a group from his university, but the government wouldn't allow him to travel. Last December he went with his father and sister to Hong Kong, and there's a government regulation stating that students cannot go abroad more than twice in one year. And poor Mrs. Matsuo who, with the summer heat, has changed to western dresses, is having much trouble and discomfort with tight western shoes, bras, and girdles. None of these are worn with kimonos. And poor Kazumi-san who still has not had an *o-miai* because, every time the go-between gives her information about a prospective groom, her father turns the man down because he's not in the "proper" profession.

The Maedas, who never seem to tire of giving me gifts, gave me 16 freshly-laid eggs. One does get all kinds of gifts in Japan! And Mrs. Eichigo gave me a *yukata* that her mother had made for me. It's a type of dressing gown that people wear on the streets. I'm sure I've mentioned it previously.

Dad, you asked about my plans for departure. It's a good question. I've got to check with the Japanese government first to see how long they'll let me stay here. (The U.S Consulate doesn't care how long I stay as long as I behave.) They may give me only a two-month extension (even for that I'll be grateful), in which case I shall leave at the end of November. If they give me another six-month extension, I plan to leave at the end of December. If I stay that long, I'll be able to earn more money for travel. I doubt I'd stay longer than that; there's just no point to it. I still have one main goal in life: to get married and raise a family. I'm already past what the Japanese consider to be the *kekkon teki reiki* (marriageable age).

I interviewed Edith Hanson, a young American woman who came to Japan 4-1/2 years ago and ultimately married a Japanese Bunraku puppeteer. She's now a TV, stage, and movie actress and speaks fluent Osaka dialect. After the interview I went with her to her classical dance lesson. Then I left early to go to my own *ikebana* lesson.

I went to see *Kiska*, a movie about World War II. The fighting between the U.S. and Japan was tastefully done. Nevertheless, I don't think I shall ever watch a WWII movie again. Even before the title appeared, they had a battle scene and I had tears in my eyes. If Mitsuyoshi Kihara, an accountant, my student, and one of my favorite people in Japan had not been with me, I think I would have walked out. I don't know if you can understand why I get so emotional about this, but I love the Japanese so much. I'm always aware of the fact that some of my students were soldiers and killed Americans and that some close friends had homes destroyed and family killed by the Americans. I try to bury those facts in my subconscious but, when I see a movie or TV program about the actual conflict, everything wells up within me and I feel, well, I feel just awful. I can't describe in words those emotions and, frankly, I don't want to try.

I leave on the 30th, and these next few weeks are just too, too busy. I think next weekend I'll be staying in Kyoto with Hyuga-san. Though he's with the TV department of CBC, he finagled his way into a radio excursion. Friday and Saturday is also Kyoto's most elaborate festival, Gion Matsuri, and I'm going to see it with my NHK confrères. Tuesday I'm being taken to dinner by the people who handled my English recordings, which I'm completing this week. And I'm also trying to find time to write my next NHK script; attend the local festivities of O-Bon, a happy day when the dead return to earth (the Japanese believe in ancestor worship); and a performance by a Communist Chinese dance troupe. I need 36 hours in every day!!!

Mitsuyoshi Kihara, a special friend

7/11/65

These past two weeks have been particularly sultry, but I'm told it improves somewhat after the rainy season passes—within the next couple of weeks. Most annoying is that everything gets so damp—especially the bedding. And the mosquitoes! They're just awful. This week I went out and bought an electric gizmo that kills 'em dead.

On a blistering Thursday, I walked into class and said that we should forget about class and go swimming. I told them that on warm days at American colleges it is not uncommon for the teacher to hold the class session outside on the campus lawn under the cooling shade of a tree. With a quick decision we planned to hold an all-day class on the 22nd at Maiko Beach at Lake Biwa near Kyoto. I imagine it will be great fun.

July 7th was the annual observance of Tanabata Matsuri, a festival based on a romantic tale that celebrates the meeting of the deities Orihime and Hikoboshi, represented by the stars Vega and Altair respectively. According to legend, the Milky Way separates Vega, the beautiful weaver star, on the west side of the Milky Way, and Altair, the handsome shepherd star, on the right side. They only meet once a year when they cross the Milky Way over the Kakasagi Bridge—named for the *kakasagi* bird of happiness and love. Historically, it was celebrated with offerings of kimono, cloth, yarn, and decorations of long green bamboo branches ornamented with bright strips of paper and other trimmings. Poems and songs and wishes were written on these colored strips of paper and hung on the branches in prayers to the gods to become good in calligraphy. Nowadays only the decorations remain. The most delightful Tanabata Matsuri is in Sendai in northern Honshu, which celebrates it on August 7th, according to the ancient calendar. I've arranged my vacation schedule around it.

The Wazakis are having their house enlarged and remodeled beginning next week. Construction will continue until next March. During that time, they will be living in Sakurai, where I live, about 10 minutes from my home. Isn't that nice?!

Kanji, the Chinese characters used in the Japanese writing system, is not only confusing to foreigners, it apparently stumps the natives, as well. One character can be read in several ways. It's possible that the American newspapers are carrying the story of the Yoshinobu kidnapping. The kidnapper's name is Kohara. One English newspaper was calling him Ohara, then corrected it to Kohara, but another English newspaper is calling him Obara.

Also in the newspaper this week was a story from Vietnam by a Japanese correspondent held captive by the Viet Cong for three weeks. He was shown a manuscript that contained the statement that "The 71 Communist countries of the world are our friends." 71 Communist countries? Really?

7/18/65

I went to a terrific performance of a dance and musical troupe from Communist China. It was all so new to me. The dancers were less like dancers and more like fantastic acrobats. I've never seen such a display. They did one dance in western dress, or so the interpreter stated, but I can't imagine where in the west they wear such clothes! They were full, giving no illusion of sex or sexiness. The musicians, both men and women, wore gray uniforms. The hems of the girls' skirts were about mid-calf, so that, even with the legs crossed it was impossible to see anything above the ankle. The instruments were most unusual. A flute-like instrument and a one-stringed violin, due to the skilled violinist, sounded like a whole string section and then some. Their finale was done without lights. They used colored lanterns that whirled and swirled and rose and dipped and impressed me even more than the Dancing Waters at the New York World's Fair. The Chinese performers and the Japanese audience sang an Asian song at the end. As the only foreigner in the theater, I never felt more like a *gaijin*.

I went to Kyoto with Masao Tamura for the celebrations of the eve of Gion Matsuri, the largest festival in all Japan. Have I mentioned Masao before? He lives in Minō also, and we sometimes see each other on the train. After several hundred surreptitious glances, he finally spoke to me and we've been friends ever since. We still meet on the trains at least twice a week, and we decided to go together that night. It was all slightly reminiscent of New Year's Eve in Times Square. Traffic on all streets was blocked. Everything was festive: bright paper lanterns hung everywhere and many people wore their *yukata* for the occasion. The object of the whole thing was to view the *hoko* and *yama* floats that would be used in the parade the following morning. The *hoko* floats are monstrous things that carry neighborhood flute, bell, and drum bands. They're so tall they must be entered from the second floor of a house by means of ramps. And atop the main enclosure is a decorated halberd, sometimes measuring 30 feet in height! Men ride on the roofs giving directions as they move around corners to prevent them from toppling on houses, on streetcar wires, or on the crowds below. We visited one of the *hoko* floats and numerous private houses that were displaying their precious *byobu* screens. (The Gion Festival is sometimes also called "Byobu Matsuri.") The *yama* floats are not as large and depict classical Japanese and Chinese legends. The month-long festival originated in the ninth century as the result of an epidemic plague that miraculously ended after the Emperor Seiwa prayed to the deities of Yasaka Shrine. We went to visit that shrine, packed with worshippers, sightseers, corn-on-the-cob sellers, pinball concessionaires, trinket dealers, flaked-fish vendors, and the usual assortment of people who attend festivities such as these.

Hideaki Hyuga, who started off my whole adventure and opened up my world

The next morning I went back to Kyoto to meet my NHK friends. We watched and recorded the music together, which also includes the screams of the spectators as *chimaki* is thrown from the floats. These are wrapped strips of bamboo said to exorcise the devil. After the parade ended, I met Hyuga-san and, because it began to rain in buckets, we raced to a local *ryokan* and talked for many hours. I last saw him in January, so we had much to discuss.

Mom, your pearls were sent out by the owner of the pearl factory where I bought them. They were sent unstrung, and I think that the pearls for both necklaces came on one string. All the pearls for two bracelets came on another. I was told the superior ones are white with a pinkish tone. Yellow ones are not as good, but their color appeals to many people. The yellower the color, the lower the quality.

I like your idea of sending a croquet set as my gift to the Moches. The easiest thing is to send it direct to their house and you could enclose a card from that end saying: "To all the Moches with my appreciation for everything and with love—Wendy."

7/26/65

The question now is just where to begin telling you of all the things that happened this past week. Maybe by day again, otherwise you'll never make any sense of this missive.

Monday afternoon I interviewed four American Field Service students for my WUWM broadcasts and for possible use on NHK. It was a good interview; I was pleased with the results. Dr. Hill just sent me 12 more broadcast tapes, so I'm "going under" again! There's just no keeping up with the deluge!

That evening, the Maedas, the two American girls staying with them, and I went to see a performance of Bunraku, the classical puppet play originating in this area. I've never seen a dramatic art form that has excited me more. The puppets stand about 3-1/2' high, and each is operated by three men—two covered in black to make them "invisible" and the master who operates the right arm, right hand, and head. After a while you forget there are men on stage as your whole attention is concentrated on the puppets. The men move them, but it seems more believable that the puppets move the men. If you ever saw one of these puppets crying, its chest heaving, convulsed with sobs, you'd think the same thing. Many young Japanese don't like the plays because they don't understand the story and the Joruri narration that goes with it. (In Joruri one man narrates all the roles in varying tones and emotions.) I saw three plays: one was 1000 years old; the other two, only about 250 years old. I could not understand the Joruri of the thousand-year-old play, but I could understand the other two narratives very well. I was so impressed by what I saw that night that I'm going to another performance tomorrow.

Thursday was the day my ACC students and I were supposed to go swimming at Lake Biwa. Despite the fact that the rainy season officially ended a week-and-a-half ago, we were rained upon for seven straight days this past week, and only two of the students showed up at the designated meeting place. Instead, we drove to Kyoto and visited temples. Since Thursday was set aside for Mid-Summer Eel Eating Day, we searched for one hour for a good eel restaurant. We couldn't eat anything else!

Unfortunately, the weatherman that day was stronger than my *teruteru bozu*. That means "little sunshine boy" and is equivalent to our "rain, rain go away, come again another day…" The *teruteru bozu*, a paper doll that children often hang from the eaves of a house, indicates the weather on any given day. If it blows, the weather is windy; if it's dry, the weather is clear; if it's wet, it rained!

Saturday morning I reported to the Ikeda police station. There was a violation on my foreign registration (which I corrected in May), and I was called in for questioning and to sign an affidavit. I pretended not to speak any Japanese, which enhanced the situation considerably 'cause I was able to get around the direct questions after listening to the conversation between the detective and the interpreter. The interpreter from the main Osaka police office first told me I didn't have to answer any questions that would incriminate me…that I was beautiful…and then how to answer the big important question. Until that point I was going to tell the truth, but then I realized that would be folly. They asked a million-and-one questions, gave me a form that the Otanis must fill out stating they will report me if I do anything bad, and then (since I don't have an official seal, comparable to a legal signature in the states), they took my finger, pushed it into the gunky orange seal ink, then impressed it on the paper. Don't ask me why. It wasn't a fingerprint, just an orange blob, not even suitable for a Rorschach! (I found out later that my registration infraction involved a simple change in address. It has nothing to do with my visa extension.)

That ordeal took an unnecessarily long time, so I was an hour late for my NHK appointment. Our deadline was too close this time; my show is being broadcast on the 27th (your time), so you cannot hear it. I expect, however, to do others after my vacation. They've given me more tapes, which I'll send on to you.

That night I went to a well-done performance of Mozart's opera "Don Giovanni," sung in Japanese.

Yesterday was Osaka's Tenjin Matsuri, the second of the three largest festivals in Japan. Since it is common to wear *yukata*, summer kimono, on festival days, I went to the Maedas in the early morning, bringing my *yukata* with me. But the Maedas, always one step ahead of every situation, had prepared yet another gift for me: a *yukata* with all the underwear and trimmings, an *obi*, and a pair of *geta*. So I wore their gift ensemble that day; and I'm sure you can imagine the surprised looks and the amateur photographers who followed me

I'm wearing my new yukata — a gift from the Maedas in honor of the festival day.

around. It didn't much bother me; it just seemed so natural wearing it. I also wore it to a dinner party for the consular corps. Mr. Maeda, who is annually the commissioner of the whole festival, was a good person to be with yesterday. The morning began with the neighborhood festival contingent dragon-dancing to his home, racing in and out of the front door to dispel all evil spirits, then breaking up for refreshments provided by the Maeda family. It was all tremendously exciting!

Following this, we went to the sponsoring Temmangu Shrine, which was loaded with festival-goers buying lucky trinkets and enjoying the special Tenjin music. About 4 p.m. we moved on to view the parade in which Mr. Maeda rode a horse, then to the consular dinner where Mr. Maeda was host, then to the Dojima River to the boat he was using as Tenjin Matsuri commissioner. The evening was spent on the boat, zipping here and there, controlling all situations. The evening's highlights were the fireworks and the parade of boats—72 of them, all big sightseeing boats and barges—meandering down the river. Some of the boats had country music and country dancing. One had classical Japanese music from 2000 years ago. (I love that about Japan—you can't say the same for anything in the U.S.!) The boats were packed with merrymakers, tourists, and consular people; the shores were lined with about half a million others; bright lanterns swung from the bridges and the boats; fireworks lit up the sky; and the whole combined into a very happy, exciting, and memorable evening. And difficult to describe despite my efforts to do so.

My young friends at Osaka's Tenjin Matsuri

Thursday—hooray, hooray—I leave for the north country armed with one book, Mark Twain's *Innocents Abroad*, and plenty of paper and sharp pencils for additional notes for my radio scripts. I decided to take my *rozashi* along, 'cause I've no time to work on it anymore.

7/31/65

I've been on vacation for just two days and, about three hours before I left, I was tapped to do a commercial radio announcement through my contacts at ACC. I worked a total of ten minutes and walked away with about 3,000¥. It has to be the easiest money I ever earned! Here's a sample of the mixture of Japanese and English that's used these days. I quote you the two commercial messages I recorded:

1. "American-style *no* self-selection system *desu*. *Shinsaibashi Miyako no* connection sale!"

2. "Hollywood *no* Music City *to shimaiten ni narimashita. Shinsaibashi Miyako no* connection sale!"

What a way to earn eight bucks!

That night when I boarded the train, I learned that Mr. Maeda had reserved a private compartment for me. Sashie-san and the two American girls came to see me off loaded down with grapes and candy from Mrs. Maeda. Planning to get a good night's rest, I bedded down early, but the train was rather noisy so I didn't get much sleep.

I arrived in Shinagawa, a Tokyo suburb, at 7 a.m. and, from there, took a taxi to Haneda Airport. Because of foggy conditions, the flight was postponed for an hour and then, on the way to Hokkaido, they announced they could not land at Obihiro but would be forced to land at Sapporo, about 200 km to the west. There were additional delays, changed flight plans, fog issues, and bus transport. It seems to be true that no-one in these parts speaks English. Thank heavens I speak Japanese for, without it, I might never have made it through these past couple of days of confusion!

About Hokkaido. I wasn't kidding when I called it the north country. It's a wholly different world than what is found on the other islands! For one thing, there are farms. Not rice paddies, but actual farms with cows and crops and here and there a lamb or a goat. The barns and silos are reminders of a drive through New York State. When you leave the lowlands and enter the mountains, you're surrounded by lumber country and giant cedar-type trees dangling with moss, with wide and wild edible leaves large enough to use as umbrellas, and 3'-tall Queen Anne's Lace wild flowers.

The hostel here is rather elegant, sharing the same building as a resort hotel. My room last night was large, and I shared it with no-one. Tonight I've been moved into a cramped room with an American bunk bed. It's unpleasant and noisy—the dance band is almost in the same room. Most of the rooms, of course, are covered in *tatami* and, at 8 p.m., they pass around the *futon*. Dinner last night (I slept through it tonight) was half western/half Japanese, but breakfast is always strictly Japanese. The hostel is clean and pleasant and a far cry from what I had expected.

One quick look around the village yesterday, and I could see I was in Ainu territory. The Ainu are thought to be the indigenous inhabitants of northern Japan. They are almost fair in color, have thick wavy hair, and are believed to be of Caucasian descent, possibly from eastern Russia. They have full frames and deep-set eyes with a European shape—quite different from the average Japanese person. They are a curiosity and, sadly, their manner of life is terribly exploited in Hokkaido where they live.

This morning I went to Lake Mashu, a crater lake with a transparency of 41.6 meters, the world's record. There was little anyone could see because of the dense fog. I was disappointed for Japanese visitors, especially, who missed seeing Mashu because it's a much-loved symbol of Japan, and a visit there for most is usually a once-in-a-lifetime event.

Back in Akankohan this afternoon, I took a boat ride to the northern part of the lake to see the famous *marimo*, a strange, spherical green plant that surfaces for oxygen. This area of Akan National Park must be seen in summer or early autumn. Another un-Japanese thing in evidence are the snowplows. All roads in this area are closed off from December to mid-May because of the storms. I've already seen snow on the mountains.

8/1/65

The road twisted and turned through the Akan and Daisetsuzan Parks revealing raw beauty as only a wilderness area can have it. There I was surprised to find three girls in a village of about six families playing with a hula hoop! American culture stretches into every nook and cranny! Even the road signs in this wilderness are printed in English and Japanese—a leftover from the Occupation.

8/2/65

By bus, train and bus again, I went from Sounkyo to Asahikawa to Sapporo, the largest city in Hokkaido, to Jozankei Spa. I stayed in Sapporo long enough to find an English newspaper and to visit the TV Tower for a wide look around (in deference to my friends who bawled me out for not wanting to spend any time in the city) and to munch a roasted corn on the cob. The hot, delicious cobs are sold on the streets in Hokkaido. Jozankei is disappointing. Its hot spring spa is one hour outside of Sapporo and so commercialized it wasn't worth a special trip. Small compensation is my lovely room in the inn.

8/3/65

Today I took a roundabout route to travel a rather short distance. The purpose was to see two Hokkaido attractions: Lake Shikotsu, supposedly the most beautiful lake in these parts, and the town of Shiraoi, largest of the Ainu villages.

About a five-minute horse-cart ride from the train station is the *kotan*, the Ainu word for village. It's a long row of little shops selling the most popular Ainu souvenirs: dolls of white birch, products from the Japanese wych-elm, and thousands of carved wooden bears in every size—bears holding fish in their paws, bears holding whiskey bottles, and just plain bears. At the end of this double mercantile row is a *kotan* of three buildings: two huts on stilts and a modern latrine without plumbing. Inside the houses are "typical" Ainu people, who are more than willing to let you take a photo for a fee. Since it was a cold, rainy day, a group of us tourists sat around a log fire listening to one of the men explain the Ainu way of life. I find the Ainu dialect very difficult to understand and, though they were anxious to converse with me, it wasn't easy. It was all for the benefit of tourists. The Ainus these days live like any other Japanese and, because of their increasing intermarriage with them, they are losing the purity of their race. Because of their decreasing numbers, anthropologists the world over have been studying their singular culture.

By late afternoon, I arrived at the Dai-Ichi Takemoto Hotel in Noboribetsu Spa. The name is important because it contains the world's largest bath—mixed genders, of course. It actually contains four of them. The biggest consists of many pools that one can walk around. Trust me on this stereotype—especially in a steam-filled room with limited visibility—Japanese women are small-busted with dark hair and similar skin tone. In other words, they all look pretty much the same. Enter a pale, big-busted redhead. Do all eyes travel to where I'm standing? You bet they do! So you can imagine how it was when I walked into a public bath covering my privates with a skimpy towel in the hope that I wouldn't be noticed!

My million-dollar view from my room is of this public bath, and I find it funny that the chopstick holders in this hotel are in the shape and form of leering devils. Could it just be coincidence I wonder?

RADIO BROADCAST

The Bathroom Spread
NHK "Radio Japan Journal" 1965

Back in the fourteenth century, Lord Yoshimitsu Ashikaga built his magnificent Muromachi Palace in Kyoto. In it he had a bath of sumptuous Roman design and, next to the bath, a dressing room. But not so much as a knob or nail on which to hang a bit of clothing was contained therein. Since Japanese hospitality always includes an invitation to bathe, Lord Ashikaga provided accordingly. His guests were of the elite, garbed in the finest of silken kimono. To prevent the finery from being kicked about and getting wet, guests brought large square cloths to the palace, placed them upon the floor, piled their garments neatly on top and folded the four corners into the center. These cloths were called furoshiki—*literally, "bathroom spread."*

Some six centuries later, they are still called furoshiki, *but their use is not limited to the dressing room. Available today in six-inch to six-foot squares, they are made of pure silk, cotton, nylon, and plastic. Anything that can be wrapped can be carried. Dressmakers wrap up bundles of cloth to be shown at customers' homes; farmers pack their produce to be carried into city stalls; travelers tie up all the gift packages that won't fit in overstuffed carryalls. Shoppers use them instead of not-so-sturdy paper bags; students insert money before presenting one to the teacher who carefully unwraps it, accepts the money with many thanks and a gracious bow, then carefully refolds it before returning it; wedding guests wrap their nuptial gifts in silken* furoshiki *and present them along with the gift. Its uses are endless—to the limit of one's imagination—and its handiness cannot be overemphasized. Before and after usage, it is easily folded into a flat, compact handkerchief-size cloth and tucked in anywhere. Ready-made ones can be purchased in a hundred different designs, though some prefer to have theirs custom-made, handwoven, and hand-dyed with the family colors or family crest featured. They are carried by men and women alike— little ones in the hand; big ones, fully loaded, on the back.* Furoshiki *are utilitarian or beautiful and dainty, but always indispensable!*

8/4/65

This, I daresay, will be the most uneventful day of my vacation and the most restful. I had planned to journey to Lake Toya, but the weather was so foggy, so rainy, and my cold so bad, I decided to spend the day sleeping and doing my *rozashi*. I did venture out for an hour and a half when the rain stopped briefly—just long enough to visit Jigokudani, Valley of Hell, a three-minute walk from the hotel. It's the source of all the healthy sulphur water used in this spa area—and smells accordingly. Other than that excursion, I ventured only as far as the big bath!

8/6/65

After three separate soaks in the big bath, I left Noboribetsu with my head well cleared—thanks to the sulphur water, I guess. First I took the ropeway up to Mt. Shihorei for a look at Lake Kuttara, a crater lake, and at 40 bears from these parts exclusively—so advertised. I counted only 10. Others were out of my range of vision, I suppose.

In Hakodate I hoped to meet with a family of a friend—Mr. Kojima from NHK who hails from there. I had been told that his family might have time to show me around, but the red carpet was already rolled out by the time I telephoned from the station. Both night boats back to Honshu were filled and the earliest one was way too early. Despite my protestations, they insisted I stay at their home and take the boat the next morning. Once that was decided, we were off on a whirlwind tour of the city, which has a surprising number of high spots: the Trappist Monastery, the city tower, the star-shaped moat (the only thing left of the castle that was destroyed in a samurai civil war about 100 years ago), and the harbor by night from the top of Hakodate Mountain. If the Kojimas and the guidebooks are correct, it's the fourth most famous night view in the world, preceded only by Hong Kong, Rio de Janeiro, and Napoli. The view is beautiful; it reminded me of two parentheses back to back (the harbor and the Pacific) with the city squeezed between.

To the right of this is a flat-top mountain that separates hundreds of lights arranged to look like writing of some sort. But it's just coincidence; the lights belong to squid-fishing boats.

I finally did the only thing worthy of calling this a vacation—indulging in an early morning swim. Never have I anticipated a swim more; every muscle was tensed and ready for action. The lake was perfect for swimming—clear and fresh and refreshingly cool. I even remembered to shout: "It's a *mechiah*!" before hitting the water!! The only thing missing was the gold star on my forehead proclaiming my bravery!

[This was an old early morning camp activity that I did frequently with my aunt, who was a camp village leader back when I was a camp counselor. The ice cold dip in Seneca Lake earned us the right to wear a gold star to breakfast!]

Back in the hotel, I met two young men, fellow guests, who told me I was lucky I came from Hakodate yesterday. Two typhoons are expected in that area, and all connecting ferries have stopped running for the day.

I've about five minutes before the light goes out (I'm again in a youth hostel), but that's long enough to tell you about today, most of it spent traveling via bus and train to Sendai. I had two purposes in coming here. The first was to see the much talked about Tanabata Matsuri, which I mentioned before when it was celebrated in Osaka on July 7th. Here they go by the ancient calendar, which is frequently the custom in some areas when it comes to festivals. The story of Tanabata is a romantic one, if you remember, between the two stars Vega and Altair. Here they play up the romance in a big way. The streets are lined with paper streamers, paper cranes, and paper dolls in a variety of shapes and forms. Actually, they are the same in all cities, but elsewhere the streamers measure about one foot; in Sendai, they are about eight-feet long. It is almost impossible to describe their flowing, festive effect.

RADIO BROADCAST

Hokkaido to Nikko
NHK "Radio Japan Journal" 1965

My first impression of Hokkaido, Japan's second largest and northernmost island, was disappointing. Fog hung so thickly at the Obihiro airport, landing there was touch and go to the last minute and, when the decision had been made to land there as scheduled, I knew there was no hope for my flight from Obihiro to my final destination. I ended up going by bus through Akan National Park...and it was then I had my first close-up of the incredible wild, raw beauty of this naturally air-conditioned island.

Moss hangs from the leaves of the stately firs and vines cling to their limbs. At their base and along the roads are edible, umbrella-sized leaves of the coltsfoot plant, wild violet thistles, and enormous Queen Anne's Lace flowers that make their American cousins look anemic.

Akan National Park, located in eastern Hokkaido, is famous for its volcanoes and Lake Mashu, which holds the world's record for transparency to a depth of 134 feet. I saw neither. The pea-soup fog persisted and despite a three-hour journey there through the wilds, I saw nothing. I was disappointed at my failure to see this much talked about natural wonder of Japan, but I felt sorrier for the Japanese who missed the opportunity, for a trip to Hokkaido is usually a once-in-a-lifetime event. At any rate, I did see the **marimo**, *which is also famous. It's a spherical green weed in Lake Akan noted for its strange habit of surfacing for oxygen. Come to think of it, it's about the only thing I saw in that area.*

A bus trip from there to Sounkyo Gorge in Daisetsuzan National Park in the middle of Hokkaido took me through bear territory (I saw none) and over an incredibly bad road. The ride revealed forests of silver and white firs—reminding me I was in lumber country—and snowplows—reminding me how treacherous this region is in winter and why all roads are closed six months of the year.

In these back areas, it was surprising to see so many of the road signs in English. Though they do appear in other parts of Japan—a hold-over from World War II Occupation days—I didn't expect them in this forsaken place!

Imagine my additional surprise to find three little girls in a tiny mountain village playing with a hula hoop—proof that American culture extends itself into every corner of the world.

I never did see the American airbase in Chitose, but I knew it was nearby. What an array of American cars there were in a local repair garage for that side of the Pacific!

The weather was cold up there even when July turned to August. It was good to arrive at the spa town of Noboribetsu and to my hotel, not coincidentally the very same hotel that houses the world's largest integrated bath. It was not my first experience with this sort of pleasure, but it was the first time I realized how much like sport this pastime is. The children romp like they would in the ocean with goggles and flippers, beach balls and inner tubes.

A ride through the lowlands made me think of many of the states I've visited at one time or another. There are lots of farms with American-style red barns and round-topped silos, with horses and cows, goats, or lambs. There are also rice paddies, and I never tire of looking at them in the summer season with their velvety kelly green hue and well-manicured appearance. The kelly green is accented on the outside in squares or rectangles of dark green bean plants placed there to prevent the water from flowing out of the paddy. There are thousands of such farms in Hokkaido and northern Honshu, and they are presenting a serious threat to the welfare of all Japan. These farms are one of the chief suppliers of vegetables and rice, but crops have been seriously damaged by extreme weather conditions that have been building up since 1962. Measures have been taken to avert a famine, but there is no guarantee of success for it all depends upon the weather. Man still has not succeeded in controlling that unpredictable element.

In Hakodate at the southern tip of Hokkaido, I spent an evening with friends. The city has an unusual number of individual beauty spots. Highest on the list is the view of the city from Hakodate Mountain. If my friends and the guidebooks are correct, it's the fourth most famous night view in all the world, preceded only by Hong Kong, Rio de Janeiro, and Napoli. It is special—reminding me of two parentheses back to back, the harbor and the Pacific Ocean, with the city squeezed between. To the right of this sight is a squat, flat-topped mountain that separates hundreds of lights that seem to spell out something in Japanese writing. But it's an illusion; the lights only belong to hundreds of squid-fishing boats.

Before leaving Hokkaido, let me mention its most famous residents. It is believed that in Stone Age Japan, all the islands were inhabited by tribes of aborigines and, among them, were the Ainu people. The advance of civilization drove them north to the wilderness area of Hokkaido and gradually reduced their numbers. Yet, intermarriage between Ainu and Japanese is as much to blame for this as industrialization. Physically they are quite distinctive from other Japanese. Their eyes are round, not slanted; their skin is light brown, not yellow; and the men are quite hairy compared to the sleek-skinned Japanese. They have long been noted for their skills in wood carving and fur trapping. It is unfortunate that they share a common fate with the American Indian—namely, relentless exploitation in the guise of interest, importance, and education. A visit to any of the Ainu villages will reveal store after store selling wych-elm letter files and cigarette cases, white birch dolls and painted plates, and hundreds—no, thousands!—of carved bears: standing, sitting, whisky bottles between their paws or fish in their jaws—gigantic, enormous, big, large, medium, small, tiny, and even teeny! Never could you imagine such an array as is spread out before the traveler's eyes. For a price, the tourist can even don a traditional Ainu kimono and have his picture taken to prove for all time that he was there.

Travel in Japan is an institution of sorts. There are travel bureaus near every station and in the big city hotels and, in the big cities themselves, there's a travel bureau on almost every corner. When you get off the bus at resort areas, there are always men from the various inns ready to whisk you away to your destination. Often one sees a tour group, identifiable by each ostentatious tag, button, or paper flower, being shepherded around by an equally pretentious leader waving a flag or banner naming the particular group.

Of all the people that make up the institution of travel, I most like the young female guides. These girls are amateur actresses with well-memorized scripts. They sing regional songs, recite monologues of area legends, call attention to points of special interest, compare dialects, and talk about the place at other times of the year. If the guide sings off-key, her listeners may applaud only slightly, if at all. If the legend is too long, people tend to fall asleep. If the microphone is out of whack and distorting the voice beyond recognition, no-one suggests it be corrected. When the bus comes to a railroad crossing, she leaves the bus, checks for oncoming trains, motions the driver forward, then runs ahead to be picked up. It's the law. When the bus gets into a tight squeeze and the driver is wholly concerned with the right side (they drive on the right in Japan), she helps out by yelling, "Awrieee ... awriee ... awriee," which in case you can't get the connection, is their way of saying "all right." When the bus must back up, she hops out and with her shiny silver whistle in two-toot tones directs it as far back as safety allows. The one long tone that follows all the short ones means STOP!

The students who travel are easily identifiable. Most carry knapsacks instead of little overnight bags. No-one in Japan carries a suitcase; it's just not done. If it's a long trip, two or three little bags are carried, but never a suitcase. But I digress. Back to the students. All of them tote cameras; many bring along sketch pads and paints. When they return home laden down with the things that can't be stuffed into the knapsack, they carry shopping bags—colorful, plastic-covered carryalls that display names and pictures of popular tourist spots or have clever little English sayings, which I'm sure are way above the understanding of the Japanese. It seems to me that the most popular bags, strangely enough, are those printed with incomprehensible English maxims and epigrams. What's important is that it's English!

Japan is a nation of spotty beauty. It pops up where you least expect it and in the unlikeliest places. Nowhere had I found areas of continuous beauty—nowhere, that is, until I took a four-hour bus ride from Aomori on the northern tip of the Honshu mainland to Lake Towada, a large caldera lake.

From the Hakodate mountain range with its lovely panoramic scenes...to the Hachimantai plateau of rolling, well-tended lawns and stately white firs...to the Oirase River, the most splendid river I have seen in all my travels. It floats along with hardly a ripple, then suddenly crashes over stones and rocks in white, frothy turmoil. Its banks are lined with high cliffs and tall cedars and magnificent waterfalls of all shapes and sizes hide behind the trees in sylvan settings that can't be seen until one is directly opposite them. This is no guidebook lingo! The road was designed for maximum enjoyment of the scene—crossing the river back and forth, never far from its sight. The tourist, in the meantime, has no chance for rest, for his head, too, snaps back and forth, to the right and left, watching waterfalls, as one watches a ping pong game! The river branches off and branches off and branches off again until it finally flows into Lake Towada at Nenokuchi. It was there I left the bus to board a sightseeing boat to my Yasumiya destination. Lake Towada, which looks like a distended E balancing on 1-1/2 of its legs, abounds in pine-clad islets, red stone cliffs, and wooded shores. And lucky I was, for I saw it by the golden glow of the setting sun.

There's a saying in Japan (coined by the travel bureaus, I'm sure): "Don't say kekko *till you've seen Nikko."* Kekko *means "magnificent." Well, I saw Nikko, and it wasn't* kekko. *There are two attractions there. One is Toshogu Shrine, the great mausoleum for Shogun Ieyasu Tokugawa, founder of the third and last military dynasty in Japan. It was completed in 1635 and is an unusual blend of Japanese and Chinese architecture and of both the Buddhist and Shinto religions. The other tourist site is Lake Chuzenji and Kegon Waterfall. I went there in December; everything was drab and unimpressive. At that time of year I felt the trip was a waste of money—quite different than its reputation during the summer or autumn months.*

8/9/65

Now in Tokyo, I spent the day touring the new TV studios of NHK's Overseas Department. Then I wandered over to the Voice of America's offices to find out if they could use me as a stringer. The head of the Tokyo center was delighted to see me (he never did find a stringer in Japan); disappointed at my gender (Washington did not want a woman); quite sure they could use me anyway; and was ultimately crushed when I told him I would definitely be leaving Japan by December. That would give me hardly any time for work once I received government name clearance. So what it boils down to is that, if I decide to stay, I should let him know immediately. It's too bad. The once-a-month assignments (on the average) would have netted me $25 per, plus it would have been good resumé material.

8/10/65

I spent the day with a guy from Brooklyn. We visited the year-old science museum, a modern paradise for children, with push buttons that set lights flashing, gears spinning, and water moving; then took in a performance of the Taiwan and Hong Kong Circus; went for authentic (and HOT!) Indian food; and then to Tokyo Tower for a pretty night view of the city. It was hardly what I'd call a "date," but it was the first time since coming here that I've spent any time with an American bachelor. He's an exuberant personality, but he made me uncomfortable—proof of the changes in me and my discomfort in the company of presumptuous American men. I'm used to what is more of a poker-face, genteel society, and his eagerness seemed as strange to me as my enthusiasm seemed strange to the Japanese when I first arrived. Yes, it's becoming increasingly obvious that I'm going to have to go through an adjustment period upon my return.

8/11/65

By train, tram, and bus I arrived at today's destination of Shiga Heights, one of the national parks in the Japan Alps. It's cool up here and what I've seen is lovely. It's not really like the Alps except there are mountains. There's an absence of snow (they're not as high as in Switzerland), and I missed the cows grazing on the slopes. It is an area for ski slopes and lifts and is, in fact, the most popular place for skiing in Japan. That's the busy season; now it seems almost empty. One of the men from the hotel drove me around the area; it's part of the service, I was told. Lots of pretty little lakes with pretty little rowboats and happy little people. There's no city in these parts, just a lot of hamlets with one hotel and scattered bus stops or three hotels and a boathouse. Sometimes even a tennis court. Toru suggested I come here. It was a good suggestion. It's lovely; it's cool; it's far away from everything.

8/12/65

I'm now situated in a charming inn, which somehow came to be called a youth hostel. I don't understand it, but I'm content to accept it for the 69¢ I'm paying. I'm in the city of Matsumoto, still in the area of the Japan Alps. Spent most of the afternoon in and around lovely and petite Matsumoto Castle. Matsumoto City is a pretty town—15,000 residents according to a local cab driver. I think I wouldn't mind living here.

When I went to a nearby science-art-history museum, I met a painter. In the art part was a picture of several artists enjoying drink—and darned if he wasn't one of the men in the picture! An artist friend of his had painted it. I dawdled too long there leaving no time to visit a mountain plain 1-1/2 hours away by bus. I suppose it's just as well. There was a blistering sun in the sky.

8/13/65

My plans were well laid out to visit Kurobe Dam, but I changed them again. I went to Utsukushigahara—translation: "beautiful field." It is a twisty, tortuous road (that only yesterday sent four people and their auto over the side) leading to the top where there are fields of delightful wild flowers—yellows, whites, violets, and purples—daisies, black-eyed Susans, thistles, buttercups, cockle bells, and so many more whose English names I don't know. The prettiest are the orange mountain lilies with black polka dots that seem to grow everywhere in these parts. And the long distance view on the way up and from the top is wonderful! I could hardly control my camera shutter! Not in the mountains, but in the valleys and towns, it seems that hollyhocks and sunflowers enjoy far more popularity in Japan than in the states.

I've found what people for centuries tend to overlook—that things are just as lovely in one's own backyard. I found the Alps as beautiful as any region in Japan and within hours from Osaka, yet everyone sent me to Hokkaido where I wasted a week because of the weather. A shorter trip would have been sufficient. I would have liked to stay in Matsumoto, or at least nearby Kamikōchi, for another day.

I just couldn't change my plans again and at additional expense, so off I went to Kanazawa on the Japan Sea coast. I arrived at night at the youth hostel atop Mt. Utatsu, a modern structure with bunk beds and no *tatami* mats. I arrived just in time for bath and bed, and "lights out" at 10 p.m. was five minutes ago. *Oyasumi nasai.* (Good night.)

8/15/65

In Gifu. Early last evening while writing a radio program, I heard the sound of music. The rhythm of the music and my knowledge of the season instantly informed me that this was Bon O-dori. Within 20 minutes, I was part of the festivities. Bon O-dori is that wonderfully happy summer night when this nation of ancestor worshippers pays tribute to the dead who return to earth for this one night only. I quickly made friends with the children, always less shy than the adults, and four of them took charge teaching me. Everyone forms a folk dance circle and dances throughout the long night. The atmosphere is wonderful. Dancers wear *yukata*, and the children display their new *yukata* with as much pride as an American girl in her first formal dress. And the boys, too, can hardly keep from showing off. There I was in this little neighborhood, the only foreigner ever to attend their O-Bon dances, I was told—and dancing yet! You can imagine the comments and stares! The later it got, the more people came and joined in the dancing till there were four and five weaving, swaying circles going by the time I left at 9 p.m. after two happy hours.

I left because it was time to take up my position on the Nagara River to watch the cormorant fishing, which was my main purpose in visiting Gifu. My four young friends decided to join me and, after parental permission was secured at my insistence, we departed from Bon O-dori.

At 9:15 small flat-bottomed tourist boats holding about seven or eight people, took up their positions along either side of the river. By that time, excursionists were already well-polluted with *sake*, a condition which makes all things so much more enjoyable, I guess. Then came the fishing boats with long poles extended from the prows and baskets of fire hanging from the poles. Under the lights of the fires, the stars of the show were visible: cormorant birds with metal bands around their necks and cords attaching them to the trainer's control. These birds are excellent fishermen, and their favorite dish are the *ayu* (sweetfish) in the Nagara River. They catch them quickly, but their lot is not a happy one. The metal band prevents the birds from swallowing. Instead, they regurgitate the fish into a basket for the glory of the fisherman trainer, and therein lies the fame of this fishing spectacle. Fascinating!

RADIO BROADCAST

Shinto
NHK "Radio Japan Journal" (Excerpt) 1965

Part of the mythology surrounding the Shinto religion includes the Imperial Regalia: the Curved Jewels from a necklace presented to Amaterasu by her father; the Sacred Sword found in one of the eight tails of a giant serpent slain in the rescue of a maiden by Amaterasu's brother, Susano; and the Sacred Bronze Mirror used to trick the Sun Goddess and bring her out of the cave she had fled into following an argument with her brother. In the quiet little city of Ise, about three hours east of Osaka, are the Grand Shrines of Ise in which it is believed the Sacred Bronze Mirror is preserved.

The Outer Shrine "Geku" is dedicated to Toyouke-Omikami, who oversees life's fundamental necessities of food, clothing, and shelter. The Inner Shrine "Naiku" is dedicated to Amaterasu-Omikami, the Sun Goddess, who stands at the center of the Shinto pantheon. The approach to each shrine is lined with 700 modern stone lanterns donated by organizations and individuals and illuminated each New Year's Day. The precincts of both shrines are filled with tall imposing trees and small lakes. There is awesome quiet, no images, no ornaments, only the white paper cut shimenawa *strips signifying a sacred place. The buildings—in the architectural style known as "Yuitsu-shimmei-zukuri"—make use of straight lines, heavy timber, thick miscanthus roofs with overhanging eaves, and the peculiar short boards that lie across the top where the two sides meet, and the longer ones that form a V at either end. The style is distinctly Japanese, yet hard to find in Japan because of the predominance of the Chinese architectural style. In the Grand Shrines of Ise, the stillness, the simplicity, the suggestion of the past, and the veiled innermost shrine compel awe, fascination, and respect. Until modern times, every Japanese was expected to visit Ise at least once in his lifetime (or send a deputy), and the history books and novels are full of stories of these pilgrimages. In recent times the intense feelings of obligation and duty are missing but still they come by the thousands—the devout, the curious, independently, and in families.*

8/22/65

Let me first finish off my trip. The last day I visited Ise Jingu, the holiest ground in all Japan, for the shrine is dedicated to Amaterasu, the Sun Goddess and the great-grandmother of the founder of Japan. No-one but the emperor can enter its sanctuaries. You remember that until January 1, 1946, the Japanese believed that the emperor was descended from Amaterasu in the longest unbroken line of divine rulers. All imperial births, marriages, and accessions are recorded there. All new emperors visit the shrine to pay their respects to Amaterasu's spirit within. The town about it is small and inactive. And the road leading to the Inner Shrine (there's also an Outer Shrine) is lined with 700 stone lanterns, donated by various people and groups, that are lit on New Year's Day. Both shrines are quiet, awesome, and pretty.

Waiting for me when I returned were your letters and a big box from Michi Suma, the Japanese Vice Consul who was in N.Y.C. and is now stationed in The Hague. It was full of Dutch chocolate, biscuits, and cookies. He knows me well!

Back home is hot. Real hot. But now that the rainy season has long since ended, there's very little humidity. My Japanese friends are convinced that Osaka is the hottest place in the world—it is supposedly the hottest place in Japan. They use fans even in air-conditioned rooms.

The high school baseball championships are now in progress, and radio and TVs blast forth their coverage to eager ears who follow the games with almost as much interest as a Yankee fan follows the World Series.

Last night I went to visit the Wazaki's new temporary home only ten minutes from where I live now. It took me an hour-and-ten-minutes to find it! Finally, with the help of two men who had joined me in the complicated search, we located the Sakuragaoka Kaikan, a key place in Oku-san's directions. I asked if they knew where number 308 was. They asked the name of the householder. I said Wazaki, but it was a new family. And then one man, whom

I swear I have never seen before, turned to me and said, "Are you Wendy Phillips?" Haven't the foggiest notion who the man is, but I suspect that Mr. Wazaki was talking about me at one point and this man happened to be there. I can explain it no other way! He knew, by the way, where the house was and my long search ended.

It has been decided that when I leave the Otani's, I shall move to the Maeda's home in Kita-ku, Osaka for as long as I stay in Japan. I'll be moving there on September 11th to give Reiko and Toru an opportunity to put the house in order. The house, or rather, the 130-*tsubo* plot was sold for $20,000.

Typhoon Lucy assured that my schedule this weekend remained uncluttered. Prior to Lucy and her hourly storm warnings, I had planned to spend yesterday and today on the island of Shikoku in the city of Tokushima, the festival site of the largest and most famous Awa-Odori (Fools' Dance). Some of my students from Toyo Kensetsu invited me to join them but, when we realized that Lucy might hit the area and we had to make such dramatic and uncertain alternate travel plans, I dropped out of the excursion. Instead, I stayed home and wrote three radio programs.

8/28/65

I received the package with the shoes but, for some reason, they were held at the central post office until I either paid an import tax or proved they were a gift. Either for sentiment or foresight I have been saving your letters and, since you mentioned you'd be sending shoes to me, it was easy to prove they were a gift.

I don't know if you've read in the papers about the serious, but not epidemic, proportions of encephalitis cases in Japan. If so, I'm sure you thought of me and worried. Don't. Though the disease has now spread to this area, I have already received the first of two shots necessary and the second one will be given in a few days, so I shall be quite safe from harm. I write this not to worry you but to reassure you. I was myself enough concerned about it to take necessary precautions.

9/4/65

A comment on the differences between bowling and tennis in Japan and the U.S. In the states, bowling alleys are filled with the noise of falling pins, rolling balls, swear words, and yelling—right? In Japan, even if bowlers wanted to swear, it would be impossible. There are no swear words in Japanese. And nobody yells at successful strikes or spares—they clap. On the tennis courts in the states, if you miss my lob, I cheer or, at the very least, I feel great about my increased score. In Japan, if you miss my good lob, I apologize. Quite a difference!

Mrs. Maeda showed me some jewelry the other day, which always puts me in an awkward situation. I said nothing about them, which is unforgivably impolite. But when I comment that they're pretty or appealing, she gives them to me. Silence is the only way I've come up with to cope with her generosity. She asked me directly what I thought about them. I told her, and now I have a set of German yellow opal jewelry. Have you ever in your life heard of a family like this?

I spent all Wednesday morning with Mr. Maeda, who was busy pulling strings for my visa renewal. Then he wrote a letter to Mr. Wazaki telling him he would take over full responsibilities and financial care of me for as long as I stayed in Japan. I kept telling him I wanted only a two-month extension, but he wants me to stay longer, and I think has asked that I be given a six-month renewal. Did I tell you they want me to call them "Mama" and "Papa" when I move into their home? Mr. Maeda also told me that, if I so desire, I can get a free ride by freighter from here non-stop to Saudi Arabia. A friend of his runs Caltex Oil. I thought about the fantastic opportunity for only a minute. I'm just not willing to skip over the whole Asian continent to save a few hundred bucks.

I did a ten-minute recording for NHK on Japanese superstitions for incorporation into a longer weekly show they air. My illegal working status has raised a possible bug-a-boo with them, because they are government-owned. So, from now on I'm using the name of a girl I know who teaches in Japan legally. She most graciously allowed me the use of her name.

Just last week I wrote about my speculation on jobs after I return home. And today I received a letter from Dr. Hill with his thought that "we should begin to talk about whether and when you might be interested in a midwest position." Milwaukee is as appealing as anywhere, but I certainly never considered an academic position (not since I turned down the offer at the University of California's Riverside campus). It's something to consider, but I don't know...

Dr. Hill is still fighting for the distribution of my "Orientation" series on the national network and, if nothing comes of it, is thinking of syndicating them himself with the help of WUWM. They will, at any rate, be broadcast this fall on my old alumnus, WAER in Syracuse.

I have been sending out packages of late in an effort to clean out my room before the move to the Maeda's. You can't imagine how much stuff I've managed to accumulate! Most of it is literature that I've been saving for possible use in my writing. Moving—whether from a five-room apartment in N.Y.C. or an eight-*tatami* room in Minō—is a pain!

On the 6th, I'm going to check out my visa renewal, for I finally have all the necessary papers. I shall know definitely that day what's what, but renewal is almost certain what with all the influential help I've had. And the 6th is a fitting day. It marks my eleventh month to the day that I've been in Japan. And still it seems incredible!!!

9/10/65

It is not the lull before the storm. It is the storm, and in two hours it will reach its fury. I'm now sitting in my room watching a typhoon increase in intensity. Most of them by-pass Osaka. This one is coming straight toward us. And because it is, my classes today were canceled.

We fared well. We say, "the lull before the storm." The Japanese say, "the calm after a storm." Someone's gutter flew into our backyard, and we were without electricity and water for five hours (the water pump is electric). Osaka City was lucky that the bay and the Yodo River that flows through the city were at low tide. Elsewhere there were floods and destruction. 36 people were killed and 12 are missing.

I haven't remembered to tell you the best news. Namely, my visa was renewed until March 30, 1966. I feel like I've been given a reprieve! Though I can stay until next March, and I would love to stay until next March, I'm quite sure I shall leave in December, only because I promised to return by next June and I do want some time for leisurely travel. I'm sure you realize that were Harvey not graduating next June, I would not return by then.

9/11/65

I moved today and am now relaxing in my large and lovely room at the Maeda's. It seems almost strange to be living again in a house with western flush toilets. I am disappointed to find that so close to the center of Osaka (three minutes by train), I am unable to receive the Armed Forces Far East Network which, until now, I have listened to religiously. It's radio at its best, and I am unable to understand most of Japanese radio. Living so close to the city center now, tall buildings and/or electrical interference is a problem for good reception. But I can get Radio Moscow. What a fascinating listening experience that is! But how aggravating to hear a perfectly straight newscast with just a bit of a twist to make the U.S. the heavy. One analysis about what the U.S. was doing to undermine the United Nations made me so angry, I wanted to punch my radio!

Thanks for inviting Mr. Yagi to your home to introduce him to the Saitos. Nice that your house has become a meeting place for Japanese people! I got us all involved, didn't I?!

In answer to your question: Mr. Yagi calls me "Miss Wendy" for a reason. Phillips is a difficult name for most Japanese to pronounce, because of the double L and without a vowel after the S consonant at the end. It sort of comes out as Fu-ee-ree-pu-su! To make it easier to say and more pleasant to hear, I tell students and friends to call me Wendy. Most, however, consider just my first name to be impolite. So, what would be "Wendy-san" in Japanese becomes "Miss Wendy" in English.

RADIO BROADCAST

Baths, Geishas, *Ikebana*, and *Chanoyu*
"Orientation" 1965

A foreigner in a public bath house is something of a rarity, but not a phenomenon. And, as one foreigner stated, "In a public bath you look, but you are not supposed to see."

This is ORIENTATION ... and I'm Wendy Phillips reporting from Japan.

There are many time-honored customs in this oriental country, but there are four, in particular, that excite my interest. Two are for fun; two are classified as arts.

To know the first tradition, you need a small towel, 23 yen (about 7 cents) and knowledge of where the nearest bath house is located. It's the best way of seeing people—and of being seen.

The Japanese are pretty blasé about going to the public bath; for the foreign initiate, it's filled with suspense! Many questions arise about this new experience. Does one enter the bath house with hesitation or as though it were an everyday thing? Do you greet your fellow bathers with a cheery hello or with silence? Does everyone stare or does your presence go unnoticed? Bathing is a normal human function, but bathing in public takes a bit of practice!

Public bathing in Japan began as a religious obligation about 800 years ago. Baths were taken at the temples once or twice a month as part of a purification ceremony. The first real public bath is recorded in the sixteenth century in Kyoto. That bath, too, was on temple grounds, but a small fee was charged. No soap was used in the old days—instead, a bag filled with rice bran. The rice is reputedly better than soap, for it smoothes the skin. It wasn't until the 1870s that immersing one's self became standard practice. Before that time, a bucket or a gourd filled with water and tossed over the head was considered sufficient. In the nineteenth century, mixed bathing was forbidden, but the law even today isn't carefully observed. Still, in local bath houses and rural communities where everybody knows everybody, mixed bathing continues. But with the modern generation, which is a bit more self-conscious than the older, the custom is gradually dying out.

The routine for bathing at a public bath is simple. Pay your money, put your clothes in the basket or lockers provided, and go to the bath area. There will be a large tub or, perhaps, two tubs—one hot; the other, devilishly hot! Near them will be a number of hot and cold faucets where you squat, kneel, or sit and wash. Rinse the dust off before getting into the tub. After getting out, rinse again, wash yourself with soap, rinse and, if you wish, return to the tub. You may remain there as long as you like— or as long as you're able to tolerate the heat! When you finally get out, dry yourself with the small towel, dress, then return home.

In most places, the bath is plain in appearance and has a partition between the men's and women's sides. You can hear what's going on, but you can't see. I went to one bath house decorated in a Polynesian style. Filled with palm trees and tropical plants, it includes in its decor spouting fountains and an elegant waterfall. There you have your choice of bathing with women only or bathing with men. Frankly, it was all rather luxurious and dégagé!

Present bath fees have become the subject of detailed economic analysis and public debate. The question is whether or not to raise the fee another 2-1/2 cents. A recent Tokyo survey showed that only 51% of Japanese families have baths in their homes. This means that most urban dwellers in the middle- and low-income brackets go regularly to public baths. A rise in bath fees, even of 2-1/2 cents, would greatly add to their financial burden. One opposing argument of interest is that years ago the bath fee was the same as the price of a bowl of buckwheat noodles. Now, a bowl of buckwheat noodles costs 14 cents, while the bath fee stands at 7 cents.

Another tradition of interest, particularly to men, is the geishas and hostesses. I've been collecting various nightclub advertisements. To give you an idea, here's one printed in an English-language newspaper in December. I quote: "Needless to say, Christmas is the holy occasion for Christians to celebrate the birth of Jesus Christ with pious prayers. Manners and customs, however, differ by countries and places as to how Christmas is celebrated. The way the Japanese greet Christmas may look strange to the eyes of Westerners. In greeting Christmas Eve and Christmas, most Japanese men prefer places where they can drink surrounded by cuties and hearing nice music. Here are nightclubs where you are assured of a really good time during the Christmas season." Unquote. What do these clubs feature? Just listen to this list! I quote again: "well-mannered hostesses will make you feel relaxed"..."a bevy of beauties will wait on you with rich topics of conversation"..."one thousand hostesses with their Japanese charms offer comfortable service"..."visits with refined hostesses will make you forget the passing of time"..."enjoy the flattering remarks of hostesses"...and on and on, each club trying to outdo the other in gracious surroundings. How can you resist? The hostesses serve as waitresses, personal assistants, nurses, playmates, dancing partners, confidantes, and, sometimes, for an extra fee, bedmates. These fees may range from $2.75 per evening to $2.75 per hour—depending, of course, on the quality of the club and the quality of the women.

These hostesses are the modern version of the classically-trained geisha. Geisha girls, wearing kimonos and stylized wigs, are far more refined and feminine. They are meticulously trained from childhood for this profession. Contrary to American opinion, they are not courtly prostitutes. Not these days, anyway. They entertain their guests with music, dances, games, and light stories. The variations of their music, their gestures, and their pleasantries are designed to be expressive and suggestive. They offer a man what a wife cannot. An evening with a geisha is an expensive affair. Not many can afford it but, for the wealthy Japanese man, it is a usual occurrence.

I should add that the geishas' duty is to entertain all guests who are paying for their services. Usually, only men are present but, when women are in attendance, they receive the same elegant treatment. I have been to a number of these parties where geishas have showered me with attention, danced and sang for me, played simple games with me, and even scratched my back!

In Japan it's the wife who handles the purse-strings. Thus, the bill for an evening with a geisha is sent to the man's wife. She's the one who totals his expenses and pays for his pleasures.

Wait! Before you raise your eyebrows and cry "shocking," let me explain that in Japan, love and marriage are not always the ideal. In the states, we insist you can't have one without the other. As the song says, they "go together like a horse and carriage." But remember that, until recent years, marriages were arranged for political or financial gains. Love was seldom involved. To older Japanese, love is one thing and marriage is quite another. For the younger generation, marriages are still arranged by a go-between but with one essential difference. As one of my friends told me, "The boy's mother proposed to my mother." In this case, as in many others, love was not involved, so nothing came of the proposal. Present-day go-betweens arrange introductory meetings, but resulting marriages are not guaranteed.

There are two other ancient traditions that deserve mention. Both are popular now. Without adequate training in these arts, the average Japanese girl is considered unsuitable for marriage.

The first is ikebana, *or flower arrangement. To understand the importance of flowers in Japan you must realize that they represent the nation itself. The Japanese verbal calendar is based not on months, but on flowers. When is Spring? "When the cherry blossoms bloom." When does the weather turn hot? "When the wisteria's on the vine." What is the nicest time of year? "The chrysanthemum season. And wait till you see the plum blossoms!" They know what month it is by the flowers in their gardens. Flowers symbolize love and beauty!*

Once you've seen ikebana *arrangements, you will never again want to throw a bunch of flowers in an upright vase. As my* ikebana *teacher keeps telling me, natural talent is not essential. It's the nondescript feeling one has for the flowers. One can create varying styles and moods by simply altering colors, shapes, forms, and types of plants and flowers. Unlike American flower styles, Japanese designs use a variety of materials—stems, leaves, gracefully bent twigs, water reeds, pine needles, cattails, even peacock feathers. Another big difference is that here the arranger seeks out flowers with buds. The excitement and anticipation of the flower that will blossom has as much beauty as those already in bloom. Each arrangement in the classic style stresses simplicity, but now modern schools are coming out with all kinds of show techniques. If you like modern abstract art, no doubt these strange flower forms will appeal to you. I myself prefer the classic styles, and I'm happy to say that most Japanese people do, as well.*

Flower arrangements are everywhere in Japan—subway stations, restaurants, washrooms, museums, department stores, and always in the home, artfully displayed in the tokonoma, *the room alcove devoted to the exhibition of fine arts. For a long time,* ikebana *has captured the interest of foreigners. There are schools throughout the world anxious to train all flower lovers in this beautiful art form. There is also an organization called Ikebana International that keeps Japanese and foreign enthusiasts in touch with each other.*

Like the art of ikebana, *the* chanoyu, *or tea ceremony, developed from the custom of making offerings to the gods. Powdered green tea was first brought from China in the thirteenth century by a Zen Buddhist priest. By the fifteenth century, the ritual ceremony had spread from the Zen sect to the warrior aristocracy. The form of the tea ceremony practiced today originated in the sixteenth century from the tea master Sen-Rikyu, who simplified the practices.*

The house or special room used for the tea ceremony is bare except for a simple flower arrangement. The beauty is in the structural balance and natural materials of the room, as well as in the utensils used in the preparation. In its true practice, the tea ceremony is designed to cultivate the mind and elevate it from mundane thoughts. The choreographed rituals of preparing and serving the thick and powdery green tea, called matcha, *are strict; the ceremony, long and arduous; and there is a standard conversation among the participants. Traditional Japanese sweets are served to balance the bitter taste of the tea. It is seldom that a tea ceremony is performed in modern-day homes. Why, then, must every girl master this ancient art? Because it trains a young woman in the skills of grace, beauty, harmony, and self-discipline—all of which are considered important attributes in a wife.*

Somewhat like Ikebana International, there is an organization called Chanoyu International, which promotes the study of the tea ceremony among foreigners. Notwithstanding, because of the difficulties in its inherent nature, few non-Japanese develop an interest in learning this art form.

The tea ceremony, flower arranging, geisha girls, and public baths—four traditions out of ancient Japan that are still practiced today. The old struggle with nature continues with the new struggle of industrial development. Japan as a nation has changed radically in this mid-twentieth century, but the soul of the people remains quite unchanged. The Japanese must, because of their very nature, pause to reflect, to enlighten, and to enrich their own life experiences by continuing the practices of their ancestors—even in this hectic, noisy, and machine-powered world of today.

This is Wendy Phillips reporting from Osaka, Japan.

Mata aimashō. Sayonara. *(We'll meet again. Goodbye.)*

9/17/65

It is not the lull before the storm. It is the storm. Does that sound a bit familiar? Like the beginning of one of my last letters, maybe? But what's so is so. We're now in the midst of yet another typhoon, only this time I'm in Osaka City rather than Minō. Last Friday I spent the entire day at home because the typhoon came in the afternoon. This time I went out as usual and came back only thirty minutes before all trains stopped running. Naturally, I was wet; umbrellas in a typhoon are useless. Funny thing, I was watching TV news earlier and saw myself on the TV screen. My face wasn't visible but I recognized my flapping sweater, the wind-blown flowers hanging from my big bag (I had just returned from my *ikebana* lesson), and my flashy umbrella that was flying out of control. Coming home when I did, I saw many workers going home from their offices dripping wet and running to catch their commuter trains before they stopped. I feel sorry for the tourists that may now be in Japan and didn't know that September is the typhoon season.

I have a typewriter again. Mr. Maeda has given me the use of his whenever I want it. I've lived here just short of a week, and I can't begin to tell you how perfect it is. There are five of us here: the Maedas, myself, and Suzuko Nagamoto, the live-in maid who studies bookkeeping three nights a week. There's a 70-year-old man who comes to do light cleaning every day; the masseur, who I see on occasion; a full-time driver; a driver-secretary; and another male secretary. Of course, I knew all of them from before, but now that I'm a member of the family, I see them all the time. The Maedas have given me freedom of the house, and Mrs. Maeda and I spend much time talking about life in the United States—a subject that interests her greatly. They are everything I could want in a family and, perhaps, a little bit more because they are Japanese, our life is Japanese, and we speak in Japanese. But I do not call them "Mama" and "Papa" as they requested. They call me by the formal *sensei* (teacher) and so I stick to name formalities, as well. In Japanese there are so many ways of saying one thing—ranging from very polite to very impolite. Before I came to live here, their language to me and mine to them was always polite. Well, at least it was as polite as I could remember to make it. It's difficult enough to learn the Japanese language without having the extra burden of learning the myriad ways to say just one sentence. Many is the time I forget to use the honorific form and substitute the familiar form. Fortunately, because I'm a foreigner, my mistakes are always forgiven, but I do like to be correct (when I remember). At any rate, both the Maedas and I dropped all the formalities when I moved into their home, making it infinitely easier for me and far more friendly.

The Maeda family.

Animals live here, too: Sanpei, a ten-year-old Ainu dog; Ryu, a three-year-old Akita dog, who cries continuously until Wakabayashi-san, the young male secretary, comes to the office; and Charko, a lovable and loving cat. Tchombei, another cat, suddenly disappeared about two weeks ago. It's a big and very happy family.

The neighborhood is way above a slum but lower class by our standards. And quite safe. This large house is highly incongruous. It is next to the intra-city loop train, about a 30-second walk across an open road to the station. Between the house and the station entrance is the home of one family that lives under the elevated tracks. It's naturally noisy here, but one gets used to it after a while. Across the tracks is a fifth-class strip theater, and nearby is a typical city neighborhood full of food stores, coffee houses, and pachinko parlors.

Last Sunday Mr. Kihara and I went to Fushimi-Inari Shrine in Kyoto, dedicated to the gods whose messenger is in the form of a fox. The shrine is the most unusual one I've visited in Japan. The deities of agriculture and business are enshrined here, and there are 10,000 red *torii* gates forming a long path up the side of Inari Mountain. Yes, you read that right: ten thousand! There are many separate shrines, always crowded with people praying unintelligible prayers and leaving candles and food offerings at every little shrine that is of special interest or has special meaning. Half-way down the other side of the mountain shrine, we took a little woodland path past a rippling brook, a redirected waterfall under which you can shower and pray to the waterfall god, through a bean field and a lovely bamboo grove to Tofuku-ji Temple, which has the only toilet designated as a National Treasure. The toilet is twice as long and one-and-a-half times as wide as your house, so, despite the fact that it's 729 years old, it has absolutely no resemblance to any toilet I'm familiar with.

It would be a crime to live in Japan and not take advantage of every minute to learn something about this nation and its culture. In the year I've been here, I've had time to develop into the person I always wanted to be and to explore everything that arouses my interest. I've had the inclination and the time to study *ikebana, rozashi* and French embroidery. Now I've added yet another course of study in light of the fact that I'm in the greatest pottery producing country of the world. This past week I began studying the art of Japanese pottery-making in Kyoto—twice weekly, about six hours each day. I study at the Kyoto Municipal Research Institute of Industry, or Kogei Shidosho. Most of the students are full-timers and serious artists. It's an intriguing atmosphere to work in, but I've a long way to go before I become even half-competent in the Japanese vocabulary of pottery-making. I have the freedom to create anything I desire, which is part of the thrill of pottery—that is, shaping and creating a piece of art from an ugly, formless lump of clay.

Mom, I should have known better than to tell you that the *kapomaikake* aprons with their practical 3/4-length sleeves don't come in dark colors. I forget about the crazy seasonal system. Now that winter's on its way, they're reappearing in the stores. Want one?

9/19/65

I spent a perfect seven hours with the Hondas at their home. They are indeed nice people, and we had a very pleasant time together. We spoke of many things—in Japanese. They called it "getting even." In America they had to speak in English, so here, I had to speak in Japanese. "Getting even" included a barbecue (which is what you had for them) with plenty of good food. It was my first barbecue since coming here. The Hondas thought that Rochester was the prettiest city they visited...you the kindest people they met (but the steaks were so big and there was too much good food)...home lawns very impressive...strange that people walked barefoot (like at Cape Cod, for instance)... and amusing that, when Mr. Honda requested a restaurant bill, he received more beer. (He pronounced it "bee-ru" because the Japanese can't say the letter L.)

9/26/65

I began teaching English at Dentsu Advertising. They wanted two lessons a week but, because of my pottery lessons, I could only handle one.

Autumn has come to Japan as it always does after the typhoon season. The days are warm but clear; the early mornings and evenings, crisp. The maples on the mountains are beginning to turn, and *matsutake* mushrooms are in the markets and on the tables, which is the surest and most edible sign of autumn. *Matsutake* are only available in autumn (frozen foods are very unpopular), and the first ones on the market may fetch as much as $10 for four ounces! They're worth it, too—big, meaty, and very tasty. One autumn sport is *matsutake* hunting.

I'm so happy to be able to spend another autumn in Japan but painfully aware that this is my last. The American Consul General would disagree with that last statement. After a recent discussion we had, he was convinced I wouldn't leave Japan or else would soon return. Because my time is running out, everything has taken on new importance. My senses have become more alert. Even my friends seem to want to spend more time with me. Time's running out for all of us. We all know our time together is limited and are acting accordingly, but no-one really talks about it. Most of my friends, as you probably long ago concluded, are men and our friendship is something very different from what could be possible in the states.

On Thursday, Autumnal Equinox Day and a national religious holiday, a group of us went for a picnic atop Mt. Rokko. Then Mr. Kihara invited me back to the Toyo Kensetsu Dormitory to see how most salarymen live in Japan. It was a revealing visit and helped fill in some of the empty cracks in my knowledge. Mr. Kihara plays the guitar, so several of us sat in his room singing American and Japanese folk songs. It was a wonderful jam session, and one man even served green tea, having learned the ritual from his grandfather.

Last night two other friends and private students—all my students are now good friends—took me to a baseball game between Osaka's Nankai Hawks and Tokyo's Toei Flyers. The Hawks lost, but we had a winning time, anyway. After the game, we went to a wonderful New York-style supper club. It's the first time I've been in a place like that; and, indeed, I hadn't even known such a thing existed in Osaka. The clientele was older, "upper class," but the prices were surprisingly cheap!

This evening I went to the Kobe synagogue for a brief, half-hour Rosh Hashanah service and then to the Moche's home for dinner. Mr. Moche's sister-in-law invited me to her home, but my going there would have involved me in a little family feud that's been brewing for a few months, so I politely declined. The croquet set arrived and is even more of a success than I had envisioned. Helena never plays and that leaves six kids to match the six mallets and balls. Perfect. Mr. Moche won't let them put the wickets in the lawn, but they've made up their own game and rules and have managed to play croquet every day since the set arrived. Thanks for the good gift idea.

I can't say I really enjoyed spending Rosh Hashanah there. The service was short, dull, and incomprehensible. One point of interest is that, before we ate dinner, there was a mini Seder where different food was spoken of in Hebrew and then eaten. It's a Middle Eastern custom, I'm told. Because Jews there have been surrounded by hostile nations for thousands of years, these special foods call for God to smite their enemies. This ritual is done at every important holiday. For instance, the Hebrew word for dates is a homophone for a word meaning "to smite" and the Hebrew word for pomegranate seeds is a homophone for "kill," or something similar. They take the double meanings and use them accordingly.

Did I tell you, Mom, that Mrs. Maeda said you must be a very nice person. When I asked why, she said that any mother who sends shoes to her daughter in a foreign country must be a wonderful person!

As for your sending more clothes, Lord knows I need them, but I don't want to carry them. I'll send some home before I leave Japan. As for others, well, wearing thin summer dresses day after day tends to produce holes and bad wear. Those I'll throw in the nearest wastebasket. My clothes have worn well, but now they are well worn!

RADIO BROADCAST

"Kampai!"
NHK (Excerpt) 1965

One reason for the popularity of drinking (and it is still almost exclusively indulged in by males) is the lack of social gatherings as Americans know them and the need to be relaxed and uninhibited with others. Surely, Japanese men become uninhibited. Sake *is drunk warm in little cups and that may contribute to its potency. Warm alcohol is said to enter the blood stream more quickly than if cooled on ice. At a party in New York City a couple years ago, a friend was challenged to a rather humorous and unusual drinking contest, which called for nothing more than downing one can of ordinary beer. A simple feat it would seem, but the beer had to be drunk from a shot glass, one glassful every 30 seconds. The theory was that small amounts of alcohol consumed between breaths have a more lingering and powerful effect than that which is gulped or chugged. My friend, a sturdy and proven drinker, suffered no ill consequences, but the challenger insisted it is true and that he had seen it work on lesser men. If, indeed, it is true, then the Japanese habit of small cups of* sake *accounts for the rapidly rising spirits (no pun intended) and the flushed faces — the ruddy glow, an indisputable way of telling who has been drinking.*

A Shinto priest in Japan waves a sacred staff over the heads of a bridal couple, thus purifying them. This is followed by a special prayer suitable for the occasion. The male matchmaker approaches the altar and reads the contract of marriage. At this point, ancient court music begins as a background to the rite which unites the couple in matrimony. A set of three saucer-shaped cups in graduated sizes are placed before the bride. She takes the top cup in her hands, and a serving girl pours sake *into it in three pouring motions. The bride drinks the* sake *in three sips, then the same cup is given to the groom and filled in a like manner. He also drinks the* sake *in three sips. The second cup is offered first to the groom and then to the bride. The third cup is again drunk first by the bride, then* by the groom. Since the three cups are filled three times and the sake is drunk each time in three sips, the ritual is called san-san-kudo (3-3-9 times). By this rite, the marriage is solemnized.

Indispensable in Shinto religious rites, sake is used in celebrating New Year's Day and seasonal holidays when offerings are made to the guardian deity and shared by all. Sake dispels grief at the end of funeral services and brings an appreciation of the flowering of cherry blossoms. The departure and arrival of friends calls for a drink, as does the completion of a building. Indeed, drinking is almost a national sport. A bit of imbibing before returning home makes the journey that much more pleasant; and a heavy quantity helps lift the restrictions of daily courtesies and self-control. With the belief that alcohol is conducive to unobstructed business negotiations, some men spend most of every evening in pursuit of alcohol and contracts.

Sake *drinking is traditional, so it is no disgrace in Japan to become fully drunk. On the contrary, on many occasions persons who don't get thoroughly drunk are sometimes regarded as unsociable. Since the state of intoxication can naturally be expected to follow drinking, words and actions of a drunk are never held against him. Petty misdeeds committed under the influence of alcohol are always excused. There's quite a difference in the treatment of a drunk on either side of the Pacific. American restaurants heave him out the door with a shove and a "Don't come back here until you learn how to hold your liquor!" Japanese restaurants bring a pillow for his head and lay him down to sleep.*

Made from rice by fermentation, sake *is the product of a brewing art refined over the course of 2,000 years. Its origin dates back to the age of mythology; no-one is sure just how old it is. Taste, flavor, and color are the most important factors in rice wine. About 4,000 brands are produced throughout Japan—sweet, dry, or medium in taste, ranging in color from crystal clear to pale gold. Its flavor has been described as resembling madeira or sherry, but it is more delicate.*

As storage life is limited, a fresh supply is brewed every year. It has an alcohol content of about 15 percent. Intoxication comes slowly and endures. Sake *is usually served from small porcelain pitchers, called* tokkuri, *one to a customer, that have been warmed in hot water.* Sake *of inferior grades tastes better when heated to a certain temperature. Also, warming the liquid kills the alcohol aroma and accents the almost imperceptible flavor. The serving temperature is at body warmth or, in yet other terms, when the neck of the pitcher feels warm, not hot. The* sake *is then poured into the small* sakazuki *cups that are usually refilled about a dozen times during a meal.*

Sake *can be taken in larger quantities and cold, when the effect is more noticeable—but never underestimate the power of this wine! It remains longer in the body than our accustomed spirits, and one may not be aware of the actual point of satiety until it has long been passed.*

There was a restaurant in Osaka, called Shusembō, which roughly translated from old Japanese is "Much Wine Restaurant." A large sakebayashi *cedar ball hung from the ceiling, the identifying sign of a bar many, many years ago. The first rule of etiquette was not to bother others. But guests were forewarned that to drink is to forget the etiquette, that wine is the best medicine, and that drinking will make one "comfortable." A list was given of the effects of* sake.

One tokkuri, *or beaker, will give you a taste for* sake...

two will quench your thirst...

three will settle in the chest...

four will provoke a belly laugh...

five will cause you to sing...

six will eliminate your troubles...

seven will make you comfortable...

eight will make you most comfortable...

nine will induce bravery...

ten will compel heroism.

That's as high as it goes, but no-one ever makes it to the eleventh one, anyway! "Kampai!"

10/3/65

I went to NHK on three different occasions this week: first, to get my assignments and record several renditions of "Peter Piper picked a peck of pickled peppers..." for local broadcast on a program about tongue magic. Then, to do some special recording for a two-part series on Kyoto. And again last night to edit and rewrite an English script about fish farming. We finished late and then Mr. Sakamoto, the man who goes with me on most field recordings, and Mr. Kojima and I went to that great Yodo supper club. We ate good Chinese food, danced, and had a pleasant American-style evening.

It seems incredible that Wednesday, October 6th, marks my year anniversary in Japan. Less than two years ago, I would never have dreamed it possible. And yet, when I try to review all that has happened in the past twelve months, my mind gets bogged down in muddled confusion. Surely, it has been the most satisfying, the most complete, and the happiest year of my life. So with recommendations like that, I could hardly understate the experience. What it has meant in terms of my values in life and in my future life is incalculable. It's an important anniversary, and I have tentative plans to celebrate with my NHK colleagues.

I spent a very pleasant day with Mr. Kashiwara, the man from the Osaka City Planning Office whom Dad met in March, along with his wife, baby daughter, brother-in-law, and sister-in-law. He just received an excellent promotion placing him in charge of one aspect of the much-anticipated Osaka World's Fair in 1970. Plans for sprucing up the city are already well under way. Just two days ago, a new and sleek subway began operation. So popular is the idea of working for the Fair office that 5,000 applications were sent in for the relatively dull job title of "office girl." Only ten girls were needed and subsequently hired.

I've heard nothing about payment for my "Orientation" series. I continue to do it for the experience and my great desire to get the facts out about Japan to the American people. But where did you get the idea that I'm not working now? Yes, I've been dropping some classes, but I still teach 18-1/2 hours each week and, last month, managed to earn close to $400. Still planning carefully for my world jaunt, I banked about $325. If I weren't working, I'd be in a panic about travel expenses!

Were you able to renew my driver's license? A friend with a recently expired International Drivers' License just took the first of three parts in the Japanese Drivers' Test—and flunked! That is surely "losing face"!

10/9/65

Well, it's been a year. Incredible, in every way. I called Iwamoto-san the morning of the 6th to remind him that he's known me a year. I could recall that first day as vividly as if it happened yesterday. I even remember the flight from Los Angeles and the Turkish journalist sitting next to me. That's how significant was the culmination of a five-year dream! I celebrated with my NHK friends as planned.

Last night I was with Sako and Frank for the first time in about three months. They recently moved into a new and lovely home in Takarazuka City and I went out to see it. It's on a mountain overlooking Kobe, so you can imagine what a spectacular view they have, especially at night.

This morning I went to Kobe to visit a dentist for the first time in almost a year. I chose Dr. Yamamoto, in particular, because he advertises in the English Daily and he did graduate work at the University of Rochester in 1955.

RADIO BROADCAST

"The Sky is High and the Horses Plump"
NHK "Radio Japan Journal" 1965

"Ten takaku, uma koyu." "The sky is high and the horses plump," according to a Japanese proverb describing autumn. The sky is clear and blue; the horses plump from the profits of the harvest. It's a rich time of year, more than a prelude to winter. The searing heat has ended and the typhoons have passed or will soon pass. Thoughts turn inward to romance, sentiment, and the beauty of the harvest moon.

Uninitiated foreigners are often puzzled when invited to a moon-viewing party. "You mean you just sit and watch the moon?" they ask. Yes, that's partly it. The custom of tsukimi, *or moon-viewing, dates far back in Japanese history. The unrivaled night of the entire year is Jugoya, which literally means "fifteenth night"—the fifteenth night of the ninth month according to the ancient calendar. What a day for a celebration! An ugly typhoon lashed the Japanese islands for hours leaving death and destruction in its wake. But, by evening, it was over, and the full moon shone brightly and peacefully through puffy clouds, each with a silver lining. Despite the typhoon, Jugoya passed in all its glory.*

The essentials of moon-viewing include the presentation of offerings to the gods; eating little rice cakes covered with bean paste; drinking sake, *an indispensable custom at any time; and, sometimes, composing poetry expressing the beauty of the scene. Often, to get the best view of the moon, the Japanese will climb to the top of a hill or go to the seashore or river.*

As in the states, "O-tsuki-sama" (Honorable Mr. Moon) is a beautiful sight, but no Japanese would go along with the story of a man in the moon. Ask anyone, and he'll tell you there's a big rabbit in the moon pounding away at glutinous rice in a wooden mortar. He's making rice cakes, "mochitsuki" in Japanese. Mochitsuki can also be translated as "full moon"—thus, it's the probable reason for the legend. Others may tell you that the dark craters on the moon form the outline of a Judas tree. According to a Chinese legend, there's a woodchopper up there, as well. His name is Wu Kang, one-time master alchemist and magician who misused his powers and was sent to the moon as punishment. His Sisyphean task is to continually chop away at the Judas tree, which remains smooth and undamaged regardless of Kang's strength or the amount of flying chips. But I digress. Again!

There are several sure-fire signs that autumn has approached. One results from the unpopularity of frozen foods in Japan, which means that all foods are not available throughout the year; rather, they are highly seasonal. Highest on the list of seasonal delicacies are the large, meaty **matsutake** mushrooms. One September day I joined 16 adults and 3 young children on a **matsutake** hunt on a nearby mountain known for its abundance of such mushrooms. We were first guided to a clearing on the mountain, spread with straw matting and covered with canvas "roofs" to shield hunters from the sun. When our group's turn came, we were guided to our hunting territory and left to ferret for ourselves. Under red pine trees and over clinging vines, through berry bushes and prickly plants, I wandered. I heard nothing but the crisp crackling of dry leaves beneath my feet and the rising waters of a mountain river in the chasm below. The sky was clear and the sun beat warmly. It was perfect—that is, until we rejoined our group and each reported his unsuccessful hunt. Somewhat dejectedly we returned to our assigned tent to enjoy a meal of chicken **sukiyaki**, prepared over tiny charcoal stoves. Our **matsutake** hunt had a pleasant ending, anyway, but to make it complete, the host and hostess presented each guest with a basket of **matsutake** mushrooms—purchased the previous day in a downtown department store!

Though the Greeks named the flower, no-one has cultivated the chrysanthemum better than the Japanese. Originally introduced from China more than a thousand years ago, it has been tended by generations of horticulturists and today is the national flower, recognized around the world as a beautiful symbol of Japan. This is strengthened by the fact that, since the twelfth century, the 16-petalled chrysanthemum—representing peace, nobility, and long life—has been used as the personal crest of the imperial family.

An ancient Chinese legend gave sanctity and the quality of longevity to the flower. When Emperor Mu of the Chou Dynasty went to India to obtain the secret of Buddhism, he took along a young man named Tzu Tung. Quite by accident one day this young retainer kicked the emperor's cushion. Because of the prevailing law, he was banished to a remote mountain area for his crime but was requested to repeat daily a certain Buddhist prayer in the hope of salvation. One morning he wrote the sacred words on a chrysanthemum leaf that hung over a mountain stream. The morning dew from the lettered leaf dripped into the stream and, suddenly, appearing before him was a paradise of singing birds, fragrant blossoms, and angels. Tzu Tung was given a golden goblet of stream water now sweetened with the dew from the chrysanthemum and, from it, he received the gift of life for 800 years.

There are 5,000 types of varicolored chrysanthemums that bloom throughout the year in Japan, yet the autumn flowers are the most famous. They can be roughly divided into two specific groups: those of large, individual flowers and those having hundreds of small blossoms. One of the unique features of chrysanthemum cultivation here is in the training of these multi-flowered plants to grow in the shapes of animals, people, and other easily recognizable forms. The creation of these chrysanthemum dolls led to public shows in which blossoms of different colors are used to form settings and costumes for historical or dramatic tableaux. Every city of size has a Chrysanthemum Doll Festival in October and November. Each one is unique and draws thousands of dedicated fans.

As a footnote, chrysanthemums, like cherry blossoms, are also eaten: the leaves fried and served in tempura *or in a bowl of hot soup and buckwheat noodles; the petals, delicately seasoned in soy sauce.*

At one time, farmers made up the bulk of the labor force. Considering Japan's 250 years of self-imposed isolation and its great population, it seems reasonable that the farmers, who provided for the nutritional needs of the nation, would occupy an important position. Indeed, the Tokugawa rulers listed the four important classes of people and farmers were second, preceded only by samurai warriors. Rice has long been Japan's chief crop and its nutritional backbone. Yearly, the success of its growth is dependent upon a sufficient rainy season and an ability to withstand insects, disease, and the fury of the typhoon season. When successful, rice harvesting is marked with feasts of joy and rites of thanksgiving; the gods are given offerings in gratitude for their divine protection of the rice crop. Farmers place the first grains of rice on the family shrine and, sometimes, even scarecrows and farm implements receive offerings in thanks for their service. In appreciation to the gods, villagers march to the local shrine beating drums to attract the attention of the deities and there indulge in various forms of merriment for their amusement. Today in local neighborhoods, even in cities, autumn festivals are held; their origins dating back to the festivals of thanksgiving for the rice harvest. These can be seen in October and November at neighborhood shrines and in farming villages. Once, I even saw a large group at a gas station after closing, the paved surface providing a suitable floor for dancing as neighbors circled the gas pumps! A festival is a festival regardless of location, and everyone loves an excuse for rejoicing and imbibing.

Autumn is also the time for life's happiest occasion: a wedding. Shinto shrines on auspicious days for marriages are analogous to factory assembly lines. One Osaka shrine married 49 couples on one November day—and that wasn't even a record!

The four seasons of the year clearly marked the life and habits of people generations ago. Many of the practices have disappeared over the years, but one remaining is that of "koromagaye." And what a strange one it is! With four seasons in each year, there are four major "koromagaye," or clothes-changing days. A definite date is fixed for each change; in autumn it is October 1st. On that date—not a day before nor a day later and regardless of the weather—people change to winter clothing. School children and policemen don their cold weather uniforms; office girls change from thin, light-colored work jackets to heavier dark-colored jackets; men put on their long underwear. Because of the unheated homes in winter, both men and women may wear long-johns and undershirts. Even I found them indispensable! Yet, in the hot days of an October Indian summer, I've worn light blouses and sweltered, while all around me the Japanese were comfortably attired (or so it seemed) in warm garments and long *underwear. By the end of November, when the cold winds are stiff and I've donned my winter coat, the Japanese freeze in their business suits. Why no coats? The day for donning overcoats comes December 1st and, until that time, it's rare to see a brave lone wolf who's warm!*

That is autumn in Japan—an exciting blend of colors in maple trees and chrysanthemums, a combination of beauty in a bride and a harvest moon, and the pleasures of a mushroom hunt and a harvest festival. It's my favorite season here!

10/11/65

Yesterday was much fun! I went on a hunt with the Otani family—16 adults and three children. They rented a microbus for the day and we drove to a mountain near Takarazuka. For $2.78 per person, we were entitled to hunt for these special mushrooms on the mountain and enjoy a good chicken *sukiyaki* dinner and beer or *sake*. The hunt was less than successful; only 11 mushrooms were found and none of them by me! But it didn't lessen the enjoyment of the hunt.

After that, we went to a new place in Minō called Spa Garden, ("Su-pa Gaden" in Japanese!), a hotel and amusement center in one. Before a sushi dinner, some of us went fishing. This is nothing like the fishing you know. These man-made pools—there are hundreds in Japan—are stocked with goldfish or trout. For about 30¢, you rent a pole and bait and then take home what you catch—usually a limit of three are free; the rest you pay extra for. A big 10" goldfish got away with my hook as so often happens, 'cause the line is so thin and weak. But I caught four little goldfish and now have four pets I named *ippiki, nihiki, sanbiki, and yonhiki*. The translations, respectively, are: one animal, two animals, three animals, four animals!

10/12/65

Know what *karushum* is? Neither did I! Mrs. Maeda was talking about bones and *karushum* this evening, and I just couldn't understand what she was trying to say. I went to look it up in the dictionary, at which point she told me it was an English word. English? Sure enough! *Karushum* is "calcium"! Two weeks ago I was trying to figure out how to say "toilet paper" in Japanese. I tried every combination of words for "toilet" and "paper." Nothing worked. Then I thought of the toilet paper core. As soon as Mrs. Maeda saw it, she recognized what I was trying to ask for: *toi-re paipa*! And in my pottery class, I learned that "sandpaper" is simply *sando-paipa*! Oh, and one more: *torori busu* is "trolley bus."

It seems that the anti-America-in-Vietnam campaigns have been eclipsed. The new bandwagon protestors are collecting petitions for is in opposition to the Japan-Korea Treaty. One thing seems clear to me: the U.S. has really missed the boat in propaganda, at least as far as Japan is concerned. The Japanese people have more freedom now than in 2,000 years of past history, but still the U.S. keeps screaming "freedom...freedom...freedom." That's fine for you and me, and I'd fight for it till death, but the Japanese are fanatic about "peace...peace...peace." That's what the communists scream and, unfortunately, that's what's getting increasing support.

10/16/65

Your letter to the Maedas was received and much appreciated. They expressed their pleasure and informed me of its contents. It was sent first to a similar address. The office girl couldn't read your Romaji (it's not called English) and opened the letter by mistake. It was re-mailed and re-delivered with humble apologies from both the office girl and the postman. As to the letter you sent them, I must assume that you typed it and that your English presented no problems, for, when a letter is written by hand, I am asked to translate it for them. Mr. Maeda, who speaks in words only, no phrases or sentences, has an amazing facility for writing letters in English. With a dictionary by his side and years of experience, he turns out very impressive letters, which I am sometimes asked to correct. I suppose he files all the corrected ones for future reference, but he told me that he writes all English letters himself.

One of the teachers I met during my April visit to Shikoku sent me a six-page letter in Japanese. Mrs. Maeda did me the favor of reading it to me, which was all that was necessary—spoken Japanese. But six pages? We all laughed when I opened the letter!

This afternoon I was a judge for the *Yomiuri* newspaper English Oratorical Contest. They paid well, plus gifts, for three hours of work. But imagine my surprise to see Miss Sumiyama's young sister as a contestant. It was her speech that broke the friendship between Mrs. Nakano and me, and it was her speech, the first few paragraphs of which I so long ago corrected. I explained this to the *Yomiuri* staff so, while I did score her on delivery and pronunciation, I did not score the content. She was, however, very good and won third prize.

My first effort at pottery-making is now sitting in my room filled with unusual leaves. Crude though it may be, it's exciting to see one's first efforts completed, glaze and all. If I make anything good enough, I shall give my work to friends as personal gifts. I am also now hard at work on my *rozashi* pièce de resistance—two children dressed in the apparel of about 200 years ago. When completed, I shall frame them and present them as a gift to the Maedas. I can think of no other way—and, in fact, nothing better—to express my deep thanks for everything than to give them this labor of love.

You asked about drivers' tests in Japan. The system is quite different here in that every potential driver must attend a driving school. There are special practice courses all over Japan, but the amount of time spent in real traffic differs according to prefecture. The test consists of three parts: driving, rules and regulations, and the mechanics of a car. A friend has flunked two out of the three and will try again a third time next week. He's getting pretty anxious about the whole thing 'cause he recently bought a used car. I promised him I'd go for a drive but not before he gets his license. Up to now, he's been driving illegally and keeping his fingers crossed.

10/24/65

I just returned from my two-day trip with eight of my students from the American Cultural Center. We first went to Akame 48 Waterfalls. The largest and prettiest fall splits in two with a rock in the center. We climbed onto this rock and sang, hootenanny fashion. We had fun, but I'm sure our efforts weren't appreciated by those who wanted to take unblemished pictures of the falls. From there we hiked to Kochidani, attractive in its autumn foliage. Last night we stayed at the Tōnomine Youth Hostel and today we hiked up to Aoyama Heights. I saw for the first time soy bean plants, a staple food in Japan; tea bushes, another staple; and mulberry trees whose leaves are the food on which the precious silkworms feed. We played card games and group games. I behaved like a student and not like a teacher, so I had a heck of a good time. Even did some shenanigans on parallel bars to the amazement of my students. In all, we hiked about 18 miles, half of which were up!

On a last-minute rush job, I went to NHK to edit an English script. The department for which I recorded the tongue twisters for local broadcast presented me with a very nice butane lighter in lieu of money. It's not customary to receive a gift instead of money when working for a radio station, but the work I did for them consisted of about two minutes of concentrated effort. That doesn't fit into a wage scale, though I would have been happy to do it gratis in return for all the things NHK does for me gratis. I suppose NHK felt that it would be nicer to give me the butane lighter with "NHK" on it than to give me some insignificant amount of money.

Friday evening, I went to the Otani's home for the last time to say goodbye. I have become very fond of Reiko, Toru and Junko, and we're all hoping that we can meet again in the states sometime within the next two years.

[Sadly, it didn't happen.]

Mom, that evening jacket is a *haori*, given to me by the Matsuos for my birthday. It is a simple every day jacket worn over a kimono. In the states, silks and satins are worn for appearance. Here they are worn for the "feel." A man's suit may be lined in silk because it feels especially good and not because people can see it. I had wondered how to wear my *haori* in the states. Never thought of an evening jacket. Good idea!

Gram wrote that Steve avoided the draft, and I hope Harvey will, too. It's enough that one of the Phillips family is overseas—and on a peaceful mission, at that. Better they should come as I did—with a heart full of good will and love.

10/30/65

I'm so busy these days my head is in a spin! I'm trying to make reservations on a boat leaving for Taiwan and Hong Kong on January 8th. With departure only two months away, there's much to do and see before I close the book on my life in Japan.

I have a new student at *Mainichi Newspaper*—an 18-year-old messenger boy who speaks rather good English in an intensely humorous didactic tone. He comes from a very poor family, goes to high school at night, and has long aspired to attend Kyoto University, one of the two most prestigious universities in Japan. He realizes he could never go there and has resigned himself to it. He talks of his broken dreams and hand-me-down clothes in a very matter-of-fact way and is self-conscious when speaking English, though he speaks better than some of the other students. He has such a robotic manner about him that others in the class are forever stifling laughter.

That explanation calls to mind a 73-year-old man I met in Aoyama Heights, who climbs the mountain two or three times a year—and has done so all his life—to pray at the small shrine at the very top. He claims that his physical fitness is due to his piety; it's God's way of rewarding him. Seeing old people on strenuous hikes is nothing surprising in Japan; they do it for religious reasons or to test their character. I've climbed up many strenuous mountain trails in Japan only to get to the top and find an old woman selling tea. Though I may have struggled to the top, she got to the top carrying a heavy cask on her back filled with hot water!

A new member joined our family. Someone dropped a month-old puppy over the back wall into the garden. He's a mutt, but what a beauty with light brown, silken hair. We all adore him and, although the other animals tolerate him, they are suffering from extreme pangs of jealousy.

This week I went to the Hirakata Chrysanthemum Doll Festival, nicer than the one I saw a couple weeks ago. This one related the story of Sankichi, an Osakan and *shogi* (chess) king.

I visited the Kyoto Museum of Modern Art to see a painting exhibition, then the Kyoto Municipal Art Museum, as well, to see a once-in-a-lifetime exhibition of 45 relics found in the tomb of the young Egyptian King Tutankhamen. His treasures had been extremely well preserved. It seems incredible that such works of art were designed and created 3,000 years ago—gold, lapis lazuli, silver, alabaster, and wood. But the feature attraction—one that is considered by many to be the most valuable artistic relic in the world—is the massive gold mask that covered the head of King Tut's mummy. The mask shows the appearance of the pharaoh in his formal attire and is decorated with obsidian, carnelian, feldspar, and other stones. It is magnificent. This is the first time these priceless treasures have been taken out of Egypt.

In response to your question, I seem to be the only one who realizes that the reason for all the TV and radio English programs and the after-hours English lessons at companies is due to the basic problem that English classes in high schools, especially, are loaded with poor and insufficient teaching methods and teachers who have very, very little knowledge of English conversation!

I have purposely saved for last an idea that you proposed in your most recent letter, Mom—an absolute genius of an idea that was broached so innocently that I wanted to laugh and cry with joy at the same time. I'm referring to the idea you're "playing around with" to meet me in Israel. That's brilliant! I can't begin to tell you how excited I am about the idea!

RADIO BROADCAST

Families
"Orientation" 1965

During the feudal reign of Ieyasu Tokugawa some three hundred years ago, people (like boats and dogs) were divided into official classes. The most important was the samurai, the class that controlled land, strengthened the learned professions, and administered the government. Next were the farmers, then the artisans and, last, the merchants, who were relegated to that low position because they dealt with money, thought to be a tainted commodity at the time. These were the four official classes, but there were yet two more groups—so low, so despicable, so derelict as to be unnamed and ignored. One was the Eta, a hereditary caste forced into menial occupations that were taboo to orthodox Buddhists. Included were animal slaughterers, executioners, and those involved in the manufacture and sale of footwear. The other group of outcasts was the Hinin, literally translated as "non-humans," a non-hereditary group composed of those who had their caste distinctions withdrawn, such as beggars and criminals, street performers and street cleaners. Six classes, two of them pariah, and from that point the family as we know it today evolved.

This is ORIENTATION... and I'm Wendy Phillips reporting from Japan.

The system of division was legally abolished by the ever-wise Emperor Meiji in the 1850s. But allowing for the absence of samurai and a shift in status for the farmers and merchants, the class system still exists today. And despite what the books may say, Japan still has not freed itself from the impositions of aristocracy.

During the Tokugawa shogunate, rules were specifically stated as to how all family members must react and interact with each other. There had to be absolute conformity with the father's will and uncompromising identity with one's group. There could be no variations in the pattern. Amazingly, most continued till the end of World War II. They exist today, as well, but in considerably mitigated form.

In the past, a married couple and their children were part of a larger group—specifically, a family of related males, their wives, and children. The senior male patriarch could, if he so desired, control the lives and fortunes of all the individual members, who were not equal in either privileges or responsibilities. Each had a rank and status dependent on age, sex, and relationship to the family head. Primogeniture was the custom until it was legally abolished by the Occupation Forces. The head of the household was usually the highest wage earner, and this position entitled him to the first bath, the first portion of food, and every consideration for his comfort and well-being. A girl born into the large family left it at marriage and became submerged in her husband's group. She had no control over matters but was slave to the whims of her mother-in-law. And if you think the mother-in-law image is bad in the states, well, the stories they tell here might curl your hair! At the time, women were thought of as mothers, wives, sisters, or daughters, rather than as individuals in their own right. But that was a good many years ago. Emperor Meiji saw to it that they gained the right to own property and initiate divorce actions. As recently as 1946, they were given voting privileges. Women, as mothers, were indispensable; but men, as heirs, were imperative. If a family had no male heirs to carry on the line of continuity, it was the practice to adopt one, a sticky procedure and one that is almost non-existent today.

Relationships within the family developed from the attributes of duty, obedience, and loyalty. Groups outside the real family were frequently organized along formal family lines with the same qualities at the core. Many true families used the apprenticeship system, for it was the way in which the children could be trained to carry on the family traditions. And here, again, if there were no talented progeny, adoption served as a suitable substitute. To this day, such a family order (minus adoption practices) exists among artists and craftsmen, racketeers and prostitutes.

The three basic familial virtues of duty, obedience, and loyalty were glorified as the source of the nation's strength and unity during the first half of this century and was a major part of State Shinto, which was so infamous at the time.

Defeat at the end of the war terminated legal subordination of the individual to his family and the right of those in authority to demand unquestioned obedience. The absence of absolute powers allowed the father to act more freely and to enter into an informal and more effective relationship with his family. These past 20 years a family setting has evolved in which the husband and wife are emerging as equals in the business of raising children.

Other changes have occurred, as well. A law was passed in the last 60 years stating that young people cannot be forced into marriage against their wishes, But it wasn't until 1948 that a married couple and their off-spring were made legally capable of managing their own affairs independently of a larger circle of relatives.

This matter of marriage needs some explanation. For centuries it was based on nothing more than a political, social, or economic arrangement. If love was involved, it was by accident. Marriage has always been taken for granted, and spinsters and bachelors have always been thought of as curiosities.

Young people expect marriage in the natural order of things, but they are beginning to exercise their own initiative and choice. There still is an upper class distrust of romance as a primary consideration of marriage, because of the importance of preserving the family property, business, or social standing. This is what I meant before when I referred to the still present aristocratic society. The usual procedure is to select a go-between—preferably one of eminence for optimum status advantage, but a professional matchmaker will do. The importance of the matchmaker is that, in case of dissatisfaction, loss of face is avoided. The course is as follows: girls and boys seeking mates submit their pictures and resumés to the nakōdō, *or go-between. From his hopefully handsome file, he selects pictures and resumés to be inspected by the marriage-minded. If the picture is good and the resumé satisfactory, a first meeting is arranged. This* o-miai *may take place anywhere, but the families of both young people are always present. If, after the first meeting, courtship doesn't seem worth the pursuit, both parties start again from the beginning. If it does, the young people begin dating and the parents begin discreet inquiry into the other family's social standing, genealogy, and the suitability of the other partner's character, personality, and health. If everything and everyone meets with approval, negotiations then begin. Financial matters create the biggest problem, but that sounds so familiar, doesn't it?! The size of the bridegroom's family gift must be decided, as well as the size of the bride's trousseau (usually paid for out of that gift). Also, the type and size of the wedding feast to be given by the family of the bridegroom, not bride, as in the states.*

In middle and lower class families, it is becoming increasingly common for young people to get engaged through their own means and choice. (It is so, perhaps, because of the increasing opportunities for them to meet the opposite sex in offices, at dances, or on trains.) Nevertheless, they still go through the arrangements in the traditional way.

In the lowest classes, common law marriages are prevalent. Neither religious nor secular nuptials are required or recognized by the state; the validity of a marriage being based only on its registration with the local authorities. Because of this, some people neglect registration until just prior to a baby's birth.

Despite common law unions, Japan is a nation where marriage and the family are sacrosanct, and it logically follows that divorce is unacceptable and, as yet, unusual. Even to this day, it is not easy for a divorcée to remarry. Last October the new phrase **Orimpiku rikon** *was coined. And though I'm sure it was coined as a joke, the translation is "Olympic divorce"—said to be caused by the influx of strong, virile athletes who made local husbands appear less so.*

The family is, even now, the fundamental political, economic, and social unit, albeit in moderated form. Rationing to households rather than individuals and family registration (as in voting) are what remain of the days when the family was a self-contained, omnipotent, duty-bound group.

In feudal days, when an individual committed a crime, the whole family shared the responsibility for it. Today, farm communities and city neighborhoods assume group responsibility for those who have met with ruinous circumstances. The lack of facilities for the aged, sick, and destitute point up this total family and group responsibility.

Children are raised as children until they marry. They are coddled, caressed, amused, and flattered till they are well into their adult years. With few restraints and prohibitions and sheltered from all adult problems, they live relatively free and easy but always dependent upon their parents.

In a nation where approval is tantamount to performance, the child is often left to himself. An intramural high school sword-fighting tournament was attended by hundreds of students and six parents. A child's award-winning painting hung in an exhibition is often not seen by the parents till it is brought home several weeks or months later. Likewise, a school exposition displaying the finest of the students' work is largely visited by students and teachers.

Japanese young adults do not break away from home at 20 or 21. Indeed, they receive no preparations for adulthood as we know them. Recently I met a 16-year-old American girl, here for the summer with the American Field Service program. She told me her most difficult personal adjustment was the realization that her 16-year-old Japanese "sister" behaved exactly like her real 13-year-old American sister. I myself have noticed that 25-year-old Japanese bachelors have as much social poise as 20-year-old American men.

In the states, a young girl preparing for marriage may learn everything from her mother—everything but how to care for the baby she hopes to have some day. For that she may attend classes at a baby clinic. In ancient Japan, all things were passed from mother to daughter. But these days, the reverse situation from that in the United States exists. A girl learns nothing from her mother except how to care for a baby. For lessons in cooking, sewing, flower arrangement, and whatever else is deemed essential, she goes to a number of specialty schools. As for the son, he's pretty much on his own, though his mother may well give him advice on how to please a woman both emotionally and physically.

If in a family there is an older brother and a younger sister, but only a few years apart in age, it is judged a necessity for the younger sister to marry first to avoid any bitter feelings between her and a sister-in-law. When the marriageable age, the **kekkon teki-reiki,** *comes around, it is decided by the parents when the children shall begin looking for a spouse,* as well as what type of spouse they shall have. Parental disapproval is usually enough of a threat to keep an errant child in line whether it be in his behavior as a teenager or in his selection of a life partner.

For all the faults I could find with the system, one predominant factor remains obvious—close and satisfying relationships between mothers and children, brothers and sisters. Between wives and husbands, affairs are not always as they should be, yet nowhere have I seen such gift of tact for living in peaceful coexistence. Their problems are rarely exposed to the children, never disclosed to guests, and calmly spoken of between the couple themselves. It is an interesting difference that, while in the states the wife is the sentimental, excitable partner and the husband the pragmatic, imperturbable one, the exact opposite is true in Japan.

Those who remember say that things were better before the war. The loss of unquestioned loyalty and duty and the increased adoption of western practices has produced uneasiness within many families. The father who has studied the Chinese classics cannot understand his son's modern lingo. The daughter, who has had a better education than her mother, is at times impatient with her mother's lack of knowledge in certain areas. Both parents lament their children's disinterest in Japan's cultural heritage. Both daughter and son want more freedom than their parents ever dreamed of having. And they insist on a "love marriage," meaning they are not interested in a politically- or financially-beneficial match.

Families are undergoing drastic changes these days, changes that began during the industrialization and urbanization of the Meiji era when many family groups were separated. They may never emulate the American family system, but there is no need of that. Their unrestrained, unembarrassed relationships with each other are worthy of praise. Would that I could take back this newfound knowledge and respect for such meaningful relationships to my own family in the states.

This is Wendy Phillips reporting from Osaka, Japan.

Mata aimashō. Sayonara. (We'll meet again. Goodbye.)

11/6/65

I spent an evening with the recently arrived American vice consul in Kobe. He just came from his last assignment in Cameroon. It's funny how I met him. I telephoned the American Consulate about Cambodian travel. After speaking with the visa officer, he asked my name and phone number. Within a week, the new vice consul telephoned me. Why? It seems he has bachelor seniority now, so he gets first crack at the young females! We spent a lovely evening at his apartment. It was strictly American right down to the baked potato and homemade apple pie (cooked and served by his Japanese maid). Unfortunately, because of his position and my position, we spent most of the evening discussing American foreign policy. As pleasant as the evening was, I was very happy to get back to my Japanese surroundings in which I must admit I feel much more at ease. Though he's a very nice guy, I don't much care if I see him again.

Wednesday was Culture Day and a national holiday. I spent it with some people at Asahi Broadcasting who took me sightseeing in Nara—first to Horyuji, where I met with a Buddhist scholar; to the home of a man who raises chrysanthemums as a hobby; then to Kasuga Shrine, where I interviewed the High Priest. It was a pleasant day, and I learned a great many things.

Thursday I skipped my pottery lesson to visit Nara again. This time to go to the Kofukuji Museum and the Shosoin Exhibition. In the eighth century when Nara became the capital of Japan, Emperor Shōmu had the Great Daibutsu constructed. Then, when he died, Empress Kōmyō had the Shosoin Treasure House constructed to preserve her husband's belongings. Such was the nature of Shosoin, built without a single nail, that the contraction and expansion of the wood in varying seasons ably preserved the treasures within. These are put on display twice a year. The clothes and the tapestries are lovely and quite Chinese in design. Just as the Japanese assume western dress today, they assumed Chinese dress at that time. During this same era was the Tang Period in

China and the Silla Period in Korea, and both cultures are strongly reflected in the clothes and design when Nara was capital.

11/13/65

It's definite ...

I'm leaving Japan on January 8th aboard E&A Line's SS *Aramac*, arriving in Keelung, Taiwan on the 10th, leaving the 11th, arriving in Hong Kong on January 12th. I wish I could tell you how happy I am to be going home but, if I said that, it would be an out-and-out lie. I knew I'd be returning to the U.S., so I am not extremely unhappy about leaving. But I'm not so sure about returning to Japan. The thought is terribly sad. And I'm a little bit afraid of going back to American life. Ah well, it has to be.

> **[I went to Japan with a six-month visa that was renewed once—legally. Through Mr. Maeda's standing on the Osaka City Council and his influence with the authorities, I was given an extension for six additional months. At the end of that period, I would have had to leave the country before I could get another visa. That being the case, it seemed the timing was right for me to leave the country and start my round-the-world journey on the long way home.]**

This is the month for weddings in Japan, though this year there are fewer because next year is a *hinoeuma* year—a horse year that comes every 60 years. It's said that a girl born in a *hinoeuma* year will kill her husband. Since nobody wants to have a baby girl born next year, many young couples are waiting till next April. Figure it out. Nine months later will be 1967 and the danger will have passed!

Odds and ends:

It's an established fact that when the deer who wander freely about Nara are in their mating season, they are known to attack tourists. Signs in Nara warn tourists, therefore, "beware of deers in the puberty season"!

The other day Mrs. Maeda gave me a skin ointment good for a whole variety of ailments, including "fruncle" and "acne vulgaris." I can't even imagine what "fruncle" is, but no-one can dispute the fact that acne is certainly "vulgaris"!

Guess I've been in Japan a long time. I'm repeating taxi drivers! Had one the other day, and we were gabbing away about nothing in particular. As I left the car, he told me that I had been in his taxi about a year ago and, at that time, I couldn't speak a word of Japanese. Funny he remembered me!

I went to the American Consulate this week with a strange request. I was looking for a pretty, photogenic, young American woman to work as a photographic model at NHK for two days. The bachelors didn't know one, but they had such a good time thinking about it!

Saw a poignant exhibition of paintings and poetry by Jewish children from Czechoslovakia who were imprisoned in a German concentration camp. All, without exception, were memories of happy lives outside the camps.

While doing research, I had an exciting idea and can't imagine why I never thought about it before. I want to explore going back to school to study oriental history—specifically, Chinese and Japanese history. And even more specifically, the role of Chinese history in the development of Japan as it was 12 centuries ago and as it still is, in part, today. Without China, Japan would be an entirely different country. Full-time study is financially out of the question, but part-time. I must look into it when I return.

11/14/65

It was a most pleasant Sunday after a long rainy night. By 10 a.m. the sun was shining—as it always does in Japan. Most rainstorms are only at night; the Japanese say it is because they are good and devoted and this is their reward. My NHK buddies had to cancel our planned weekend trip to a Buddhist mountain retreat because of a too-busy schedule. Instead Yoshiko Otani and I went to Kurashiki, famous for its white-walled houses and museums. Both were wonderful. We toured the Ohara Art Gallery built by an Osaka philanthropist to house his collection of western paintings by Picasso, Klee, Kandinsky, Monet, Degas, Lautrec, Van Gogh, Gauguin, and many others. Two folk craft museums built in old white-walled granaries were exciting, as well, and included bamboo ware, pottery, woodblock prints, carved wooden bowls, and textiles.

The Archaeological Museum, while interesting, was a hodgepodge of relics from Japan, China, and the Inca civilizations. The Historical Museum was an even greater hodgepodge—Japanese relics piled one on top of the other in no particular order, all located in a two-story home that we were guided through by a woman and her talkative four-year-old son. In a sub-division of the Ohara Gallery, we saw relics from Egypt, Persia, and Turkey. Each museum was a cultural festival. Combined they are the most exciting museums I've been to in all Japan.

Mom, I really can't say when I'll be in Israel at this point. The boat to Iran has no published schedules because of the Indian-Pakistani War and I won't be able to learn the schedule until I arrive in Calcutta. It seems that I'll have to go to Turkey or Cyprus first in order to get entry into Israel. I estimate that I'll be there at Passover on April 4th. Or thereabouts.

Winter's on its way. My room was so cold today that Wakabayashi-san made a special trip to buy me a gas stove. I'm warm again. And Thursday in Kyoto it was so cold that my hands—or, rather, my fingers—lost their sensitive touch so essential when working with clay. Every time that happened, I'd have to stand over the stove and thaw them out. Winter was bound to come sooner or later, and the weather this past month was so exceptionally beautiful that I can hardly be angry about such a natural occurrence.

11/19/65

I suppose it was inevitable once I set a departure date for the calendar to fly from me. I cannot say that the past 13-1/2 months have flown by. They have not. And in retrospect, it seems like a great deal longer since I've been in the United States. But suddenly time is flying now and, with my schedule the busiest ever, I need at least

36 hours in every day. Frankly, I could have used them all along!

My friends have taken the word of my departure date with mixed reactions: "It's so soon!"..."I'll be so sad after you leave."... "You'll be here long enough to see *Mary Poppins* before you leave."..."How soon will you be coming back?"... and so on. It's so depressing for me. Because of family ties, life in the U.S. is without a doubt more precious to me. But in terms of my personal and meaningful existence, life in Japan is far more cherished. Is it any wonder I'm reluctant to return?

Since *Mary Poppins* will be coming to Japan shortly, an ad appeared in the English paper requesting a brunette with blue eyes to assist in the promotion of the movie. Further qualifications were: "a cheery disposition, kind and witty, very sweet and very pretty, rosy cheeks and no warts." And this wart-free young lady must even speak some Japanese!

How can I help but love the Japanese? Mr. Umesaki, a friend and student, showed up in class today for the first time in about six weeks. As a routine conversational question, I asked him how long it had been since he had seen me. Perfectly straight-faced and serious he replied in English: "I haven't seen you in a long time, but I always thought of you in my heart."

My unique student at *Mainichi*, whom I have mentioned before, informed me that he is going to Tokyo's Waseda University next April to be a politician. (Waseda has been known as a training school for politicians for the past 60 years or so.) He's confident he'll pass the entrance examination. Why a politician? He wants to make a better life for the Japanese. He's so filled with innocent idealism. It's refreshing to find it in a Japanese person; they are normally so fatalistic.

On Monday I went to see the Japanese garden that represents the highest achievement in landscape gardening. Katsura Imperial Villa in Kyoto is not open to the public. Permission for visiting is granted by the Imperial Household Agency. It is beautiful, elegant, and refined with the utmost simplicity. I also went to the Shugakuin Imperial Villa; permission must be granted the same as for Katsura. Both are in Kyoto and represent landscaping achievements. I wanted to express my thoughts to the English-speaking guide. I tried in English, but I couldn't do it. I reverted to Japanese and was able to express myself fully. There are some things that cannot be translated—either from English to Japanese or Japanese to English. This was one such case when I could speak about the enormity of this garden only in Japanese.

11/20/65

I earned 7,000¥ today judging a particularly dull English contest sponsored by the Osaka Commercial High School Federation. It's the money that counts.

I read in the newspapers about the blackout in the northeast. At the time, New York City was alarmed by shouts of "the Russians are coming; the Russians are coming!" I shared this with friends and students, who were both shocked and fascinated by that.

11/21/65

I attended a delightful dance recital with 3-, 4-, and 5-year-olds all dolled up in elegant kimono and high *geta* (wooden clogs), and with the simpering look assumed by all classical dancers. One of the little ones went into a backward pose with the *geta* facing up, and her top-heavy kimono caused her to flop on her bottom. A second of discomposure and all was well, but how precious that moment seemed. All the performers were skillful, but the the little ones won the hearts of the audience.

Takashi Aoki is head of the Kansai branch of Servas, a worldwide cooperative cultural exchange with a network of travelers and hosts working together to foster peace, goodwill, and mutual respect. I had read about it in the newspaper and wrote him a letter. I'm extremely enthusiastic about the program and plan to join before leaving Japan. He invited me to his home this evening to discuss Servas, to meet a couple of Servas people, and Dave Horner, as well, who finished a Peace Corps assignment in Thailand in May. Because he's been traveling through Southeast

Asia as I will be, Mr. Aoki thought it would be nice for me to meet him. It was. Dave is a special person with a fine sense of humor and a wonderful understanding of people. He gave me several tips and the names of two of his friends in Bangkok, whom I will certainly contact. It was very pleasant being able to shoot the proverbial breeze in an American English that I've almost forgotten. For example, I said "goodnight." He said "sleep tight." And we both chimed in with "don't let the bedbugs bite." That brought quizzical looks from the Japanese while we dissolved in laughter. It was a wonderful evening

11/27/65

On Labor Thanksgiving Day and a national holiday, I went to a wedding at which the Maedas played the role of go-betweens. The difference between Japanese and American weddings is the difference between black and white. It was fascinating and my being there enabled me to understand just one more aspect of the Japanese character.

As guests of the U.S. Information Service, Romney Brent, playwright, and Helen Hayes, whom you well know, were in Osaka. Mr. Brent gave a lecture on the development of the American theater and Miss Hayes performed excerpts from Shakespeare, Wilder, O'Neill, and Albee. What a joy it was to see her in such an informal, intimate setting. She's like a young woman

Japanese bride and groom. The bride's head covering is called a Tsunokakushi, or "horn-hiding." It is worn by brides in Shinto wedding ceremonies to hide the bride's horns of jealousy, ego, and selfishness, as told in traditional folk tales. The ceremony relies on Shinto themes of purification and includes drinking three cups of sake three times.

when performing. Afterwards, when I met her, I was surprised to see how really old she looks.

I met a Mr. Nakagawa, Time Salesman at Mainichi Broadcasting, who was in the U.S. for three months this year. He called tonight; I'm having dinner with him next week. And last night I spent the evening with a Mr. Yamamoto, a druggist who lived in Indonesia for a year. He speaks no English, however, so it was a rather unusual date.

I received an interview-by-mail from the *Democrat & Chronicle,* which is planning a series on Rochester women not working in Rochester. Since the problem of contacting a local newspaper photographer to take my picture would be great, I suggested that, if they want a shot of me, they should call you. Maybe there's a suitable one from among those I've sent home.

This afternoon I recorded a program at NHK on "Working Women in Japan." For the first time, I stepped on the men's toes and, though factual, my friends made me change a few words to soften the impressions. I was amused. Wish I had copies of all my NHK scripts!

Hope your Thanksgiving was pleasant. Mine was a typical Thursday and nothing more. Daytime at my pottery class in Kyoto; evening teaching English conversation. And not a turkey in kilometers!

RADIO BROADCAST

**The Enigma of the Japanese Language and Smile
"Orientation" 1965**

If you hear a dog gami-gami, *a frog* gaga-gaga, *or an insect* bun-bun...*a* goso-goso *of leaves,* gata-gata *of chairs, or* pisha-pisha *of water...a* bara-bara *of glass,* picha-picha *of rain, or* pota-pota *of a faucet...you're living in the Orient; and you're probably trying to learn the Japanese language!*

This is ORIENTATION ... and I'm Wendy Phillips reporting from Japan.

I have often heard mention of a language barrier, but not until I came to Japan did I realize the truth in that phrase. I studied French and Latin in high school, and I don't recall ever having insurmountable difficulties with either. Reading Latin was fairly easy; it was the spoken portion that was troublesome. With French, the reverse was true. Conversation was easy (after all, you could use short sentences), but the literature was perplexing. With Japanese, one is licked before the fight!

There are three different forms of writing: Kanji, an adaptation of Chinese characters; Hiragana, a cursive style; and Katakana, a shorthand, printed type used for foreign names, words, and phrases. Signs, movie subtitles, newspapers, and other matter are written in a mixture of all three. In addition, Hiragana and Katakana have the same sound system. Sometimes a system of Romaji is used. Take for instance, the word "kimono." You spell it k-i-m-o-n-o. Consequently, you may say that's English, in which case you'd be mistaken. For, in fact, it is made up of the sounds of three Japanese symbols: ki-mo-no. That's Romaji, though it really looks like English. You see the confusion? Many times I have asked why there is a necessity for all these different forms. Their detailed answers aren't exactly clear to me, but it is, after all, their language. They can handle it; so should I.

I have found it very helpful to know both Katakana and Hiragana. It makes it easier to get around, and each one with its 48 symbols is easier to memorize than the thousands of Chinese Kanji characters. Although I can recognize a few of the more complex ones, they are the essential characters needed for life in Japan—important words like subway, toilet, woman, entrance, exit.

So much for written Japanese. What is perhaps more difficult and certainly far more intricate and confusing is spoken Japanese. The first thing one learns is that there is one language for men and another for women. Women, being the softer, more feminine sex, use a softer, more feminine mode of expression. The foreigner is expected to abide by this, depending, of course, on which sex the foreigner happens to be.

Then, because this island nation is divided by mountains and water, there are many local dialects—surprising when one considers that the whole of Japan is smaller than the state of California. Tokyo Japanese is fairly standard Japanese, but I live in Osaka. Friends told me not to learn Osaka-ben, as it's called, because it's impractical and not particularly pretty. But local Osakans speak their dialect to me, so I had to learn both forms, an additional handicap.

The most difficult lesson to learn is that there are various ways of expressing the same thing ranging from polite and very polite to impolite and very impolite. A speaker's role and status must be closely identifiable to the individual or group to whom he's speaking. He must adjust his words to suit the relative status level of the person he's addressing. One cannot correctly talk to a professor in the same language used when speaking to classmates. It is interesting to watch a company president, for instance, speaking to a department head and a secretary at the same time. His body posture, movement, and facial expressions vary, in addition to his language as he changes his addressees.

There are many forms of pronouns available for use. Reportedly more than fifteen forms of the first person "I" exist and about the same for the second person "you." To speak Japanese correctly, you must identify yourself in terms of whom you are addressing and choose the right type of language and honorifics. Perhaps this is why at introductions the exchange of name cards, which immediately establishes relative social positions, is so common in Japan.

One must become accustomed to such vague words (or, perhaps, sounds is more appropriate) as "ne," which is like the equivalent of "isn't it," as in "Samui desu ne?" "It's cold, isn't it?" The long emphatic saaa, which means "I say." The broad prolonged eeeah, which denotes surprise and approval. The "o" sound has several meanings depending on which way it's pronounced. How many ways can "o" be pronounced? Several! But the source of real confusion is the "o" as an honorific. The word hime means "princess," but o-hime shows a respect for royalty. Such usage is fairly logical until you come across words like o-sushi and o-benjo, signifying esteem for raw fish and the toilet respectively. This "o" is used before many words, though usually not before foreign imports. One would never say o-masaji (massage) or o-depato sutowa (department store), although nowadays some do speak about o-toire (toilet).

A nation's language is what the natives speak, not what one finds in most books, not what an author thinks they should say. I tried at first to study Japanese from special textbooks but, except for the fundamentals, none of them seemed to agree. I finally gave up that idea and concentrated entirely on listening to and learning from the people themselves.

Difficulties in language are further complicated by a difference in mores and semantics. Ambiguity in speech is considered polite and respectful. In Japanese one gives thanks for just "a gift." In English we name the gift; to do otherwise would be rude. But the reverse is true in Japanese. To specifically name the item is thought to be discourteous.

There are other cultural differences. The simple phrase "thank you" takes on a whole variety of nuances, and it is best to learn who deserves what style of phrase. Domo is a nondescript word that literally translated means "very" but between friends conveys the idea of thanks. Domo arigato, or the more polite domo arigato gozaimasu declares "thank you very much." Domo, meaning "I apologize" or "I'm sorry to trouble you," is often used to show gratitude and indebtedness. But the deeper meaning, the explanation of which goes way back in history is "I'm sorry to have received an obligation from you, for I can never repay you and I am sorry to be placed in such a position." This is said, for instance, by a storekeeper to his customer, by a person who is given a seat in a crowded train, or by a housewife to the man who delivers the laundry.

Lafcadio Hearn, Greek-Irish writer who spent his last 14 years of life in this country, was revered by all for his devotion to Japan and for the books he authored which, for the first time, presented a completely accurate picture of life at the turn of the nineteenth century. He once wrote: "The ideas of this people are not our ideas; their sentiments are not our sentiments; their ethical life represents for us regions of thought and emotion yet unexplored, or perhaps long forgotten. Any one of their ordinary phrases, translated into western speech, makes hopeless nonsense; and the literal rendering into Japanese of the simplest English sentence would scarcely be comprehended by any Japanese who had never studied a European tongue. Could you learn all the words in a Japanese dictionary, your acquisition would not help you in the least to make yourself understood in speaking, unless you had learned also to think like a Japanese — that is to say, to think backwards, to think upside-down, and inside-out, to think in directions totally foreign to Aryan habit. Experience in the acquisition of European languages can help you to learn Japanese about as much as it could help you to acquire the language spoken by the inhabitants of Mars. To be able to use the Japanese tongue as a Japanese uses it, one would need to be born again, and to have one's mind completely reconstructed, from the foundation upwards."

Having revealed the many intricacies of the language, let me expose yet another enigma for foreigners — the smile. You will notice with older Japanese that facial lines of age have become heavily etched around the eyes, the mouth, and on the forehead — the lines and wrinkles that form with a smile or with laughter. The salient features of such a face are penetrating yet soft, gentle, serene.

One can't fail to notice the generally cheerful disposition of the people. At first, the smile and the laughter seem charming. But then this same emotional response is seen in moments of pain, embarrassment, humiliation, and disillusionment. Occasionally, with strangers, its apparent ill-timing arouses feelings of distrust and anger. Why does a reprimand cause the recipient to smile? What provokes laughter when a person makes a simple mistake? What induces a person, pushed to the ground in a moving crowd, to laugh? For what reason does the story of a recent funeral cause laughter on the part of one we would expect to be bereaved?

The answers lie in self-restraint and self-sacrifice. "He is the greatest conqueror who has conquered himself." And even deeper, in the undeniable belief that one's happiness in life is dependent upon the happiness of those around us. "He is truly happy who makes others happy." Further, it is what on some occasions is flippantly termed "face-saving." It is what compelled the starving samurai warrior to walk about smiling and picking his teeth as if he had just finished a large meal. It is what causes the individual who fell in the crowd to laugh, as if to say, "I am not angry at what has happened. Do not let yourself become upset on my account." The recipient of the reprimand is saying, "I was wrong. I deserve this, yet I have no animosity towards you." The person who makes an embarrassing mistake says, "It was a foolish error of no consequence. Do not think I am upset by it." Even in Japanese this is called a bitter or forced smile. The person suffering from the death of a loved one is expressing still another idea—the ultimate in selfless courtesy. Referring again to a Lafcadio Hearn explanation, the bereaved is stating, "This you might honorably think to be an unhappy event; pray do not suffer Your Superiority to feel concern about so inferior a matter, and pardon the necessity which causes us to outrage politeness by speaking about such an affair at all." Such was the case of the misunderstood smile when ex-Prime Minister Ikeda attended the funeral of President John F. Kennedy. Finally, there is the unaffected, innocent smile that illuminates all conversations. And, as with the language, there is a laughter for men and another for women. One is a loud, boisterous bellow, while the other is a refined, restrained giggle always done with one hand over the mouth in an act of naiveté and embarrassment. One is contagious; the other, charming.

The smile unfolds the mysteries of the heart; the language holds the keys to understanding.

This is Wendy Phillips reporting from Osaka, Japan.

Mata aimashō. Sayonara. *(We'll meet again. Goodbye.)*

11/28/65

Toyo Kensetsu had a Cultural Festival. That's Mr. Kihara's company where I teach twice a week. Everyone contributed—even the English class. I rewrote the last three stanzas of "This Land is Your Land." For the record (mine not yours), here are the words:

I've roamed and rambled and I've followed the footsteps

Of a thousand pilgrims to the Ise Shrines,

'Long the modern Tokkaido by majestic Fuji—

This land was made for you and me.

And when I leave it, there'll be great sadness.

I don't know when I'll return again.

I've found in your land a life of wonder—

This land was made for you and me.

This land is your land; this land is my land

From wild Hokkaido to Kyushu island,

Through busy cities, green velvet rice fields—

This land was made for you and me.

12/5/65

Monday during the day, "my women" entertained me at a lovely inn in Kyoto. Mrs. Echigo gave me a gift of a wall-hanging with two tiny fans and the women, as a group, gave me a pretty silver and pearl brooch.

That evening, Mr. Kihara and I went out to celebrate his 25th birthday. I gave him one of my pottery masterpieces (if you'll forgive the use of the word). It was a stylized bird I designed and created especially for him. We met after my last class at 8:30, had a quickie dinner, went dancing, then went to a semi-private strip show. We were in a private room with the stripper, and he had me under strict orders not to let on that I spoke Japanese. During her act as expected, she directed all her attention to Mr. Kihara. She talked as she performed but, when she told a funny joke and I laughed, she knew immediately that I understood Japanese. From that point on, her attention and her patter were directed to me, not to Mr. Kihara. It was really funny!

Tuesday, I went to NHK to rewrite programs about working handicapped people that Mr. Sakamoto had written and translated himself. Thursday, my *rozashi* teacher had an exhibition in Shukugawa, where I saw for the first time my finished handbag and my framed *Edokko* that I embroidered for the Maedas. I am unabashedly proud of them; I can't tell you how nice it was to hear people oohing and aahing over them. Visitors had no way of knowing I did them, but I was sitting at a nearby table eavesdropping.

Yesterday, nine of my American Cultural Center students and I went to Nachi Waterfall. It's ever so much lovelier than the more famous Kegon Waterfall in Nikko. Later, armed with bamboo poles, we walked down to the Pacific Ocean to fish. We used sweetfish for bait and caught a few grotesque mullets, which the hostel cooks prepared for us, and a blowfish, which we didn't eat because the poisonous liver is deadly if not removed. When the tide came in, the waters churned angrily. The rocks were wet and slippery and everyone fell at least once. On the way back to the hostel, we looked like Japanese Huck Finns—barefoot boys with bamboo poles, lugging the fish in a pair of rubber boots, walking carefully in the lanes of terraced rice paddies. At one point, we were crossing over the tracks literally seconds before a super express train barreled around a curve and tooted at us. We ran for our lives! Nothing like a little excitement!

Last night I taught the kids some American games, including the Hokey Pokey, Round-Robin Ping Pong, the Mexican Hat Dance, and Cat and Dog, as well as the song "One Finger, One Thumb" and the Limbo. They loved it, and I've never seen it played in such earnest and with as much laughter. Two girls staying in the Nacho Youth Hostel were invited to join our fun, and they had such a good time that, before they left this morning, they gave us boxes of candy and a thank-you message for me.

Today we went to the resort area of Shirahama and viewed a place called "the thousand-*tatami* rock," 'cause that's how many should cover it. There weren't any *tatami*, but generations of tourists had carved their names and pictures on it. Graffiti—just like in the states. We also visited the aquarium there, which is operated by Kyoto University. What a multitude of unusual sea life can be found in these parts!

About Israel. I'm also beginning to get excited about meeting you, Mom. Try not to go as late as the 18th of April. The earlier in April the better 'cause I don't know how long I'm going to want to spend in the Middle East. I don't mind arriving in Israel before you, but it would be nonsense to travel there then. I'd rather wait and see Israel with you. Though I would like to work on a kibbutz, I won't know the possibilities for that until my arrival. As for the invitation to be your guest, I'm sure you know how happy that makes me. Every cent counts, and I'd like to have a little left over for some European travel after Israel. It seems to be getting more definite that you'll be able to meet me. Instead of your worrying about my schedule, let me worry about yours and prepare to meet it.

This brings me to the problem of mail while I'm traveling. There are no American Express offices in the Middle East, but I can probably use the American Embassy offices. I'll check into it. I want to consult the Consul General this week, anyway, to get his advice and counsel about oriental study centers in the U.S. I'll give you a list of addresses as soon as I can; dates I'll give you as I go; but there are going to be a lot of blank areas where I get no mail from home.

Less than five weeks to go. I'm torn between my sadness at leaving and the excitement of this once-in-a-lifetime trip.

12/12/65

I went to Daisen-in in Kyoto to do an interview with a Zen priest. It turned out, however, that he didn't speak English, so we chatted in Japanese. Sōen Ozaki is a young man, about 33, candid, and sociable. But damned if he didn't propose to me at the end of the interview! He was so complimentary and so pressing for an answer that I was very happy to leave. He dropped all traditional barriers of formalities between us. I was extremely flustered both by his manner and my loss at what to say. The first thing I could think of was that I couldn't marry him because I was Jewish. He said, "So?" He commented that one reason he was endeared to me was because of the pimple on the right side of my forehead. The location, by Japanese superstition, means that someone loves me and he assured me it was he! He's an expressive and amusing man; the experience was a most unusual one! (Yes, Buddhist monks in Japan can marry.)

The Japanese are so preoccupied with trivia. For fear of making a minute error in grammar, students say nothing. For the most insignificant questions, they apologize in advance. One individual, in true Japanese style, went to the states and was first impressed by the great number of "cripples" there. And, then, there was that pimple on my forehead. A writer once remarked that the Japanese are good in small things and small in good things. There's some truth to that.

Your package arrived. I tried on the suit, which I don't remember, and started to laugh. It fit and the shock of it was too much. It's been months since I've worn a straight skirt without a permanent bulge in the backside!

Friday afternoon, I went to my *ikebana* class for the last time (I can no longer spare that afternoon) and received my certificate and two books—in Japanese, of course. A lot of good they'll do me! I promised my teacher I'd visit her once more before I leave, but still the parting was a sad one. For a woman trained to mask her emotions, she did a poor job of it. That night I went to the Wazaki's for the last time before the New Year holiday (I can no longer spare that night either). Mrs. Wazaki gave me a lacquered jewelry box that plays the folk song, "Rakudan." That morning I interviewed a Japanese woman, who for the past 10 years has been on a private campaign to further relationships between Americans and Japanese by cultural art exchange programs between the children of both countries.

Saturday morning, I went to Houn-ji Temple in Sakai City, a suburb of Osaka, for a festival in honor of the famed Buddhist scholar, Takuan, who founded the temple several hundred years ago. The Sumiyamas and I were guests of Nakamura-sensei, the sumi-e artist whom I interviewed many moons ago. *(Sensei* is teacher). Her paintings are at the Zen temple. I'll never forget it. First, I had to participate in a tea ceremony, then sit through a 45-minute memorial service, and then the particular style Zen lunch. Not that it wasn't interesting; it was. But I was required to sit in a formal sitting position for more than two hours—45 minutes at the longest stretch. First came the creeping pain in my legs and then the numbness in my feet. By lunch, I was in agony. Ordinarily I'm a bundle of curiosity about such things and filled with a thousand questions. But my mind couldn't seem to concentrate on anything but the pain in my legs! After the formalities, the present priest Takuan brushed a calligraphy picture for me, part of which was a copy of something the first Takuan had done. Then everyone received Takuan *tsukemono* (pickled radish), named for the scholar who first ate it.

Last night, I went out to dinner with Misters Kojima and Sakamoto from NHK. I'll really miss those two after my departure. We had some incredible and memorable experiences together while doing the radio programs.

This afternoon, I went out to the Morio home in Sakai. Mrs. Morio invited Mrs. Umegaki (both from the class of "my women") ... and her son invited his friend, Mr. Kunisada (both private students of mine on Monday evenings). I was entertained in typical Japanese style. First, a tea ceremony, then a tea ceremony-type of dinner in the tea room, then pleasant talk. It was a most enjoyable afternoon and evening. Mrs. Morio presented me with a fan and a *fukasa* (used in the tea ceremony to wipe the utensils). Mrs. Umegaki gave me a pretty orange and gold covered bowl, which in Japan is used for pickles but can be used for anything. A point of interest: Mrs. Morio changed the calligraphy scroll in her tea room before I arrived in keeping with my upcoming departure from Japan. The new one that hung there held special sentiments for me. The translation in very rough form was something like "When you travel, go with a sound mind and a sound heart."

In the next two weeks, I have at least six farewell parties and too many sad goodbyes. My life in Japan has never seemed so precious to me as at this time, and every day I pray for a financial miracle to bring me back within the next five years. Parting is not sweet sorrow. The fool who said it—I believe it's Shakespeare that I dare to call a fool—could never have had Japanese friends!

From my students at Toyo Kensetsu, the following comments were written on gold-edged boards in calligraphy:

I never forget your teaching but I could not understand your freedom. -Takuji Katayama

From Japan With Love. -S. Iwasa

This land is your land. -Y Kodera

Toyo Kensetsu will be better company in the world. Take care of yourself. -M. Kihara

Be young and charming forever. -K. Suzuki

My list of people to contact around the world is growing: Dave Horner's friends in Bangkok…a client in Baghdad of one of my students…the Rosenzweig's niece and nephew in Tehran…Marty's brother and sister-in-law in Germany, whom I met in New York just before I left. As for Norway where Sue Balter and Nancy Berger live, even in the wildest stretches of my imagination I can't see how my money will last that long. But it sure would be nice if it did!

This is now the season to be jolly. Especially in Japan. Drunks are the order of the night, and I've doubled my precautions. Christmas and the cherry blossom season are the worst for that sort of nonsense, especially now 'cause this is also bonus season—three months' salary—and they blow it in whiskey! It gets worse as Christmas approaches, but already one drunk came to the Maeda's at 4 a.m. this week to complain of his troubles. After the incessant buzzing succeeded in waking up the household, Mr. Maeda, who is a pearl at diplomacy, listened attentively for three minutes through the speaker system, then advised the drunk to telephone him the next day. I don't think he did.

RADIO BROADCAST

Friendship
NHK "Japan and I" 1965

My favorite quote by a writer whose name has long ago been forgotten is, "Though we may travel the world over, we have not really budged a step until we take up residence in someone else's point of view." One purpose in coming to Japan 15 months ago was the desire to take a "giant step." I believe I have.

I have because I can—with an open mind ready to accept every new idea... with an eagerness to live as much as possible like a Japanese person...and with enthusiasm for learning the Japanese language, so I can speak with everyone I meet. As Caesar said it, so might I: "I came, I saw, I conquered." I have come to love this nation a very great deal, so much so that I think of it as my adopted homeland. Without a doubt, home is where the heart is and half my heart is here.

Regretfully, I am leaving Japan soon. I know the difficulty of my parting is in direct ratio to the wonderful friendships that have developed. For me, this final chapter of "Japan and I" is a summing up of emotions, an explanation, an interpretation of my friendships in Japan.

I have many friends here, most of whom speak conversational English: A Tokyo high school student, whom I met in the Ginza, and who adopted me as a pen pal...a broadcaster whom I'd met in the states and who was the driving force behind my coming to Japan before he himself returned...an accountant friend who is always providing me with new experiences and new adventures so that I may learn more about this nation...a businessman who has been acting as my problem-solver, business manager, and walking dictionary...a husband and wife who have been like parents to me...several university students who have been my traveling companions...a young couple whose home I lived in for eight months and with whom were spent endless hours of explanatory question-and-answer periods. There are more. But to mention them requires much time, for the list is long.

Like the song says, "friendship, what a perfect blend-ship!" It is so, and yet friendship in Japan is not the same as friendship in my native United States. I teach English conversation, and most of my students are businessmen, my age or older. My classes are conducted informally and, for that reason, strong relationships have developed between the students and myself. Many of them are personal friends whom I see after hours. What has resulted is that all my close friends are men. In a way, it's an ideal situation, but it was a difficult adjustment to make. In the beginning, I so missed sitting down with a female friend for just plain "girl-talk." But at this point, I no longer miss it, nor do I feel deprived of anything by the absence of female friendship.

In the states, it is possible to meet a person, realize you have certain things in common, graduate from a casual relationship to one of depth, and develop a lasting friendship. In Japan that is not so easily achievable. For one thing, the closest friendships develop not late in life but in elementary or high school. There is a strange nostalgia for old acquaintances. Even kindergarten classes have been known to hold reunions years later. Fellow students are equals, and it is with them that relaxation is possible. With business colleagues and others, a strong sense of hierarchy often interferes with social interaction. The Japanese are much aware of rank and precedence—an awareness that evolved from the system of primogeniture and the historical grouping of the people into five classes according to their importance to feudal Japan.

Here, a person who is both a friend and confidant is rare. Families are close-knit, and the members are dependent upon each other. In crises a person turns to his family for advice rather than to a friend. Therefore, friendships are not as binding nor as intense as in other countries. This is especially true when a foreigner is involved. Regardless of language ability or shared interests, there is a conscious awareness of difference. With red hair and fair skin, I attract attention and comments wherever I go, so that anonymity is impossible. In most cases, I have more travel experience and more money—both of which set me apart. I am fluent in English and familiar with the American way of life—qualities to which so many Japanese aspire.

All these in combination hinder a natural relationship. The Japanese, obsessed with the belief that the grass is always greener on the other side, mistakenly believe that a foreigner is somewhat superior...and this consciousness of a ghostly gap inhibits normalcy.

Despite these factors, I have close friends. I am inclined to agree with an American who once commented that there is nothing so dear, so worthy of being treasured as a Japanese friend. Let me try to explain why.

Because confidential problems seldom pass between friends, a relationship is rarely weighted down with an onus of responsibility. The Japanese are artistic champions at masking emotions, so there is almost no opportunity for empathetic responses. When friends are upset by something, there is no way of knowing it, which puts a false rosy glow on everything. One day a friend came to visit me, and I noticed that he was bothered by something. I mentioned my sorrow at seeing his distress. But, when he realized I was aware of his feelings, he apologized immediately and asked me to forgive him for bringing his troubles into my home.

The ability to hide unpleasantries gives rise to the belief that the Japanese are at peace with themselves and others. This is not exactly true, however, because controlled sentiments smolder and somewhere they erupt. It is a known fact that the Japanese are afflicted with high blood pressure, a consequence of this emotional self-control. Even so, I think there is a certain peace of mind that exists here — to a greater degree than in ...well...my country, for instance. Here, there is no such stereotype as the animated clubwoman, for, both by nature and tradition, the housewife spends most of her time at home. Before the industrial revolution, women wove their own cloth and converted it into wearing apparel and useful objects. While this is no longer necessary, they continue to pursue home handicrafts. Housewives of all ages spend hours crocheting, knitting, sewing. Most study the tea ceremony, which, by its very nature, teaches grace, beauty, harmony, and self-discipline. Japanese men spend most of their time away from home but, despite this, may have private interests, such as guitar playing, oil painting, writing, 12-syllable haiku *poems, calligraphy, or researching Buddhist sculpture. Until coming to Japan I had never seen so many hobbies pursued so actively by so many people!*

All Japanese have a passion for and a deep understanding of the natural world around them. It's a wonder that this is so, for they have been ravaged by nature for centuries. Typhoons batter their homes; rains swell rivers and flood their farms; the earth trembles and buildings are reduced to rubble or consumed by fire; the ocean on all sides wreaks havoc with monstrous tidal waves; and the mountains, which form the backbone of the islands, erupt and cover surrounding areas with deadly lava. Perhaps for this reason, they have turned toward other, more kindly natural wonders: the harvest moon shining through the branches of a pine tree, polished stones in a dish of water, bamboo trees casting flickering shadows through paper screens, small home gardens representing idealized and personalized nature. Beauty is found in simple diminutive forms—a budding rose, a spread fern, a dew-wet peony, raindrops splashing in a stone basin, a miniaturized ancient tree in their beloved art of **bonsai***. There is another factor linking the Japanese and the natural world about them. It is referred to as* **mono no aware***, and it is a quality that most foreigners can neither appreciate nor acquire. It is an instinctive ability in each person to sympathize with nature according to one's own personal viewpoint and depth of compassion. A Japanese looks at a pine tree, its branches weighted down with snow, and subconsciously thinks: how wonderful that the tree can endure such a burden. Mt. Fuji, the towering symbol of Japan, is loved by all. It is beautiful, yes, but it is more—strong and solitary, and its distinguished eminence represents the heights to which all men aspire.*

The love of nature is only one aspect of the Japanese personality. Men are diligent workers and surprisingly emotional and visionary. Throughout life they retain a certain amount of naiveté and childishness—the latter, perhaps due to their dependency on female family members for basic needs. The women, before marriage, desire independence but don't quite know what to make of it. They, even more than men, depend on their family's support and guidance. They are far less serious about life than their counterparts abroad, and this is true in their attitudes towards higher education and personal fulfillment after graduation. Women, especially, are highly attuned to a person's wants. Many times I have been awed by the clairvoyant powers of those who anticipate my needs—no matter how small—when I myself have only just thought of them. The Japanese are a very sensitive people. This correlates with their emotional ardor—a faculty which too often is responsible for their thinking from the heart rather than with the mind. Among adults, sexual embarrassment and modesty don't exist; questions and comments considered somewhat taboo in other societies are advanced without constraint. This, however, is true only with friends. Mere acquaintances sometimes astound me when they beg my forgiveness in asking a personal question and then, forthwith, ask an ordinary and casual question, such as the name of my hometown or my reason for coming to Japan.

There is a wide gap between the attitudes toward friends and strangers. If strangers step on your toes in a crowded train or accidentally knock a package from your hands, there is not even a sign of apology. But if a friend does the same thing, expressions of regret are so lengthy and so intense, it can be exasperating. Such contrary manners require a certain amount of getting used to, though I have never really been able to reconcile myself to those standards of conduct.

I consider myself fortunate in having developed friendships with Japanese people of all ages, because I have been able to know Japan through the eyes of different generations. And there is a difference! My relationships with older Japanese abound in formalities, unstated emotions, and acute awareness of duties and responsibilities. Men and women my own age are more inclined toward informality, frankness, and emotional expression. It is only in small part due to the difference in ages. Essentially, the determinant was World War II. It was the before and after of a nation still operating under a modulated feudal system, then the sudden influences of up-to-date American ideologies and those who experienced both orders. In many respects, the two generations have widely differing viewpoints and habits. World War II halved Japan with more thoroughness than an act of **hara-kiri**. What's more, older Japanese friends never discuss the war willingly, while my younger friends are anxious to get answers to ease their own painful doubts.

*There is one quality in Japanese people that is common to all—conformity. No-one is really a free-thinker, a pioneer, an original. A character trait may stand out, but an individual doesn't. The phrase that allows the Japanese themselves to define this quality is "*Deru kugi wa utareru.*" "The nail that sticks out is hammered down." Non-conformity is frowned upon, and all through life there are forces that suppress it.*

I wish there was more time in which to delineate the Japanese character. In a subject area such as this, it isn't fair to have a time limit. But I do. And while there is much more I wish to speak of, the best thing is for each of you to know the Japanese.

In summary, there are not words enough in any language to express the many kindnesses and the thoughtfulness of the Japanese people I've known. Friendship and love that stemmed from their hearts and flowed out to me without restraint will always be treasured. The Japanese are among the richest of all people in loving, giving, sharing, and in friendship.

12/20/65

To express my emotions at this time is impossible. I have less than three weeks left in Japan and each day brings more sadness. Once upon a time, when my friends asked if I'd return to Japan, I said honestly that I didn't know if I could, though I wanted to. Now I answer with an unequivocal YES. I don't know when, but I will. I must. If I didn't think I could come back, I'm not so sure I could leave. I love the United States for many reasons, but I love Japan in ways that I could never love my own nation.

Well, what have I done this past week? Plenty! Last Wednesday afternoon, the *rozashi* class had a farewell party for me and presented me with something they knew I wanted but couldn't afford—a large "*o-Hime-san*," a princess from the Heian Era. They gave me the thread and the frame, and I will embroider it myself after I return to the states.

Friday night, I stayed overnight at the Allard's. God bless Frank. He has offered to solve my problem after all else has failed. He's giving me U.S. $1000 from his California bank account in exchange for my yen. That means I do not have to smuggle out 360,000¥ in cash. It was a tremendous problem, and I'm grateful to him. My friend at the Osaka First National City Bank has been providing me with all sorts of illegal advice (I'm grateful for his confidence, too) but no-one, not even Mr. Maeda who owns eight banks, could get me dollars. As an advance the night I went there, Sako and Frank gave me a bag of gold coins—all chocolate!

Saturday morning I went to synagogue to say goodbye to everyone and discovered that Chanukah began that night. In the afternoon the woman I interviewed last week, invited me to her students' Christmas Party. What a joy it was to hear 4-year-old Japanese children speaking English. What a priceless recording I made of their conversations. I taught them the Hokey-Pokey; they especially loved the part with "your backside in"! That evening Mr. Kihara and I went to see *Love is a Many Splendored Thing*. Following the movie, he took me for sushi, then to a bar where there were nude dancers and to another that's popular with the men at Toyo Kensetsu. By the end of the evening, both of us were comfortably warm with *sake*—and he had managed to show me more of Japan that I had never seen before. His personal campaign is to introduce me to "real" Japan. And what a good job he's been doing!

Yesterday was the Christmas Dance Party at the Maedas' Cooking School. I invited Mr. Kihara. At one point, we were partaking in a tea ceremony (which, by tradition, is conducted in an atmosphere of complete silence), but we could hear the band music loud and clear. Mr. Kihara didn't know the manners for tea ceremony, and I was busy instructing him. Suddenly, from the next room, I heard the strains of the Charleston. "Hurry," I said, "I'll teach you the Charleston." I did, too, but attracted the attention of others who wanted to learn that "crazy American dance."

This morning my pottery teacher was trying to get me to finish up a large vase I was glazing so he could put it in the kiln. "Hubba hubba," said he. "Do you know what that means?" I asked. His answer: "Hurry up! Hurry up!" Of course, I started to laugh and asked him where he learned that meaning. When he was a POW during the Occupation, American soldiers would regularly and quickly repeat "hubba hubba, hubba hubba" to the prisoners in an effort to step up the speed of a march. I set him straight on the meaning, but the story was so good that I translated it for the Israeli woman with whom I study. Since I speak in Japanese all the time, I don't usually translate for her, but this was too funny not to repeat.

Last week I met with John Stegmaier, the American Consul General in Osaka. He gave me much good advice and a great deal of encouragement. He also asked me to use his name for a reference when seeking a fellowship.

Also last week, I went to Kobe to get my visas for India and Thailand. After filling out the Thai forms and getting my photo taken for them, I was surprised—and the Japan Travel Bureau representative was embarrassed—to find after I went there, that

Americans do not need a visa for travel in Thailand. Did I tell you the irony in my travel arrangements? I did not want to go to the Japan Travel Bureau for my arrangements, nor did I want to make any arrangements in Japanese for fear I'd make a mistake. But Mr. Iwamoto had an English-speaking friend who works at JTB, so I decided I should meet with him. But he's never there when I go, so what resulted is that I'm not only making all my arrangements at JTB but also that I'm making all of them in Japanese. They have arranged my flight from Hong Kong to Phnom Penh and from Bangkok to Calcutta and secured my visas.

Japanese radio offers the listener everything! The other day I heard a Mickey Katz parody of "Where is My Heart" with such unintelligible phrases to the Japanese as "blintzes I'm making" and "where are my gatkes" (long underwear).

Last week Mrs. Maeda presented me with a dozen-and-a-half tangerines to eat "tonight and tomorrow morning"! Unrelated, Mr. Maeda bought himself a Chrysler Imperial for his personal use. His wife's not too happy about it, because the attention it will attract embarrasses her. He paid $16,000 for it!

12/25/65

Merry Christmas! I wonder—is yours a white one? I've been singing the song for days to no avail. The ground is as brown and bare as any unpaved surface can be!

This morning on my way to the hospital—I've been getting shot up with typhoid and cholera injections—I paused to enjoy a Christmas Band Concert. The 30 bandsmen were university students. They brought back nostalgic memories of Syracuse University's "100 Men and a Girl."

It's been another full week. Wednesday I went to NHK to record a program about my friendships in Japan. We had planned that night to have a farewell party, but Mr. Sakamoto had gone home early with stomach cramps—his wife is expecting their first baby this week!—so Mr. Kojima and I went out to dinner. As a thank you for what they've done for me, I gave them samples of my pottery "masterpieces." They called it Japanese folk craft handmade by an American Japanese. An "American Japanese"—that's what they've nicknamed me! I love that!

That day was *Susuharai* in the Maeda home. It's the Japanese version of spring cleaning, but its purpose is to purify the house for the new year. It was a busy time.

Thursday my students at Toyo Kensetsu had a farewell party for me at the company and presented me with a painted plate of Kiyomizu Temple in Kyoto. The oldest student in the class, Mr. Hamada, about 63-years-old, gave me on his own a coral pendant. He told me that in his life he had three benefactors: a disciple of the founder of Keio University, a disciple of the founder of Doshisha University, and me. The men taught him English for 15 years, but I was the only one who taught him how to speak English. I was pleased, of course, but embarrassed by his compliment, for I did no more than any English teacher should do for her students. Mr. Hamada enjoys English books—he's read more of Shakespeare than I have—and from time to time I gave him books for his personal collection, books that I had already read and didn't want to send to the U.S. After the party ended, Mr. Yamaguchi invited Messrs. Suzuki, Inoue, and Kihara and I for a *Bonenkai* (year-forgetting) party. Everyone attends *Bonenkai* at this time of year, though I assured my friends this was one year I never want to forget. We went to a small bar and spent the rest of the evening singing Japanese songs.

I attended a party last night given by my students at Dai Nippon Celluloid. Earlier I was informed that the president of DNC, in thanks for my teaching there for one year, wanted to present me with a special gift—and what did I want? I tossed out a few ideas and Monday two of the students and I are going gift-shopping in Kyoto. After the party, one of my DNC students, his wife, and I went to the Christmas Eve Dance party at the company. We came late and I left early to go to a similar party at the Osaka Kigyo Club. That's Mr. Wazaki's new nightclub venture. I think he set up his mistress in the business. Yeah, that's the way it works here. It's a long story …

In honor of Christmas Eve, free champagne flowed like water. I did the "tweest" for everyone by popular request and, when it was learned that I spoke Japanese, I was swamped with requests to just sit and talk "for three minutes." Japanese people love foreigners and, when they find one with whom they can communicate, it's a once-a-year event—sort of like Christmas Eve!

This week I was invited by NHK Tokyo to come up there for an overnight trip—all expenses paid—for one more program evaluation meeting before I leave. Regrettably, I haven't any free days. And the five-day New Year holiday cuts a big chunk of time out of my last two weeks. Mr. Kihara and I are trying to spend as much time together as possible before I depart. Leaving Japan is difficult, but leaving Mr. Kihara is far more difficult than I'd like it to be.

I received a delightful letter from Toru and Reiko the other day. Toru lamented the fact that Americans don't understand his English half as well as I did. And Reiko apologized for not writing sooner because speaking with all her neighbors has made her tired of using English. She further commented: "…washing machine in America moves with one button, as you said, cooking is very simple, and dust is much less." The ease of living amazes her. The washing machine in their home was the old-fashioned wringer washer with a washboard. Just to get hot water to wash up in the morning first required my turning the pilot light on under the small tank, then waiting for the water to heat up.

Earlier the Maedas had a farewell party for me. The eleven people that make up this happy family (drivers, secretaries, and others) went to the International Hotel for dinner. Afterwards, Mr. Maeda, Wakabayashi-san, Sachie-san, and I went to watch a karate lesson. It was fascinating. On Tuesday evening, I'm going for a lesson of my own. Karate is extremely effective self-defense, and there is no reason why women shouldn't know it.

12/28/65

On the 26th, my handbag was "removed" by a purse snatcher creating a great deal of inconvenience. He didn't get much money, but he did get my glasses, my alien registration, my proof of vaccination (I already got another vaccination) and worst of all things, my precious, irreplaceable, invaluable address book. That upsets me far more than anything else! But the saying here is: *Shikata ga nai:* "That's life!"

Yesterday I said goodbye to my pottery teacher and picked up the last of my things. That afternoon, two of my students met me in Kyoto, and we went *byobu* shopping. Wait till you see the gorgeous screen given to me by Dai Nippon Celluloid! It's 3'x6', an autumn scene painted on gold paper and covered with double silk. It's an original; the artist is Shizui Maruyama. It's lovely, and I'm so pleased to have it.

> **[There is definitely more to the story. The store shipped the screen to my parents' home in Rochester, so I never saw it till I returned from my travels a year later. In shipment, a small tear occurred in one of the screen's inside edges. I contacted the Kyoto store a year after they had shipped it. They told me to take a photo of the torn panel and of the whole screen. I did, and the artist painted me another whole screen, same design, at no additional charge. That much-loved screen hung over our living room couches in every home we had in New Jersey and now in San Jose, CA. My mother repaired the damaged one and it hung in the dining area of her home for several years.]**

There were many farewell parties. At Kagaku Gijutsu Center, Mr. Kanagae invited his *shamisen* teacher who, some 30 years ago, had been a *geisha*. He also wrote the following note and *haiku*:

"Thank you very much for your joyful chattering with us spending your precious time in Japan. We say 'Sayonara, Wendy' with a sorrow too deep for tears. But tonight with our last get-together, we would like to sing some songs, hoping your happy future, your health, and meeting with you again some where in this world by chance.

> *The year is going*
> *Our beauty is leaving*
> *Nothing remains*
> *but only a drizzling rain.*"

I had my last class at Toyo Kensetsu. It was most difficult saying goodbye to that particular group, because a very special bond has developed between us. I'll see Mr. Kihara again before I leave, but the others... I'll have to wait until my next trip to Japan.

This week I received a note from Dr. Hill saying that WUWM in Milwaukee has already gone through my "Orientation" series twice, WAER in Syracuse has played it once, and WRVR has not yet broadcast it. He just couldn't get anywhere with the national network.

1/2/66

It's the start of a new year...and a bitter end.

In answer to the question: "How long have you been in Japan?" — there's a phrase in Japanese *"Ashikake ni nen ni narimasu."* The translation could be: "Stretching it a bit, two years!" One of my students, knowing how sad I am about my too-short stay, came up with the following idea. According to the old Japanese calendar, it could be said: "Stretching it a bit, three years," because I came in 1964 (Showa 39 in the Japanese calendar) and am leaving in 1966 (Showa 41). But that's really s-t-r-e-t-c-h-i-n-g it a bit!

I had my first karate lesson. It was only two hours, but I'm amazed at the self-defense tips I learned. The teacher, far more serious about the whole thing than I was, brought me a karate suit, a karate organization pin to wear in my lapel, and a membership card in the Japanese karate organization—all of which I'm sending home.

Apropos of nothing, I finally bought you a larger damascene disc which you requested so long ago. It's about 4-1/2" tall and comes with a stand. The gold-etched design is bamboo. Please add $6.95 to the money you owe me.

[I haven't included the pages and pages and pages of notes about what I bought for my mother, her friends, and the family. I was her personal counselor to a shopper's paradise, and she made full use of it. There were even drawings in the letters I sent, so she would know what something looked like in advance to see if that's what she wanted. My father kept the tally for repayment.]

One of my students from Toyo Kensetsu stopped by my home and left me the English translation of Soseki's *Kokoro*. The word *kokoro* means "heart." The book was given to me in thanks for my lessons—he has also come to my home for private discussions—with an inscription I shall always treasure about my comprehensive understanding of the Japanese heart and soul.

[That book and this diary were the inspiration for the title of this memoir.]

The railway station is a laugh during the New Year holiday with extra guards, big circus tents to hold those waiting for trains and to keep them dry in case of rain, and thousands of people milling about. Last year I was able to avoid the station with ease, but now I must go to the station every day. What a mad-house!

Friday, I delivered a bowl I'd made to my *rozashi* teacher, some plates to the woman in whose home we have the lessons, and a large vase to my *ikebana* teacher (who gave me a purse, in return). One dividend of studying pottery is that it has given me an opportunity to give personalized presents at minimal cost. Good for my budget!

I couldn't have asked for a quieter New Year's Eve. I stayed home and did a bit of typing and sewing. At midnight, I joined the family for a bowl of long *soba* noodles, traditional at this time and symbolic of long life.

The morning of the 1st, I had the special New Year's breakfast with the Maedas, at which time I thanked Mr. Maeda for his kindnesses and presented them with my framed embroidered dolls. Then I went to the Wazaki's home and spent the entire day there—eating, talking, and playing cards.

The special food eaten during the New Year holidays is called *o-sechi*—and how I love it! So many varieties are arranged in lacquered boxes; you select what you want. It's all excellent food, the finest of the entire year—all laid out as if on an elegant buffet table.

Today I'm staying home. I finished up typing some notes, did some packing, wrapped some packages. There are so many to send home! The house has been full—every year about 100 people come each day—and I briefly paid my respects to a few of the guests. They come to say thank you and ask for continued patronage. The guests included young couples married the past year at whose weddings the Maedas were the formal go-betweens.

Mr. Kihara, in answer to your question, is not married. He's quite single. Our time together is too quickly running out, a fact which we are wise enough to realize is unfortunate and, perhaps, also fortunate for reasons that are probably obvious. I do date married men on occasion, but I would not date them with as much consistency. Nor is dating here related to dating back home. Since I do not discuss my dates with women (all my friends are men), they have no opportunity to know that I date married men. But, since that is the custom, there would be little comment. My being a foreigner sets me apart from jealousies, and the fact that I'm "unusual" is one reason why I've made so many friends. Curiosity, which initiated relationships, was quickly and happily replaced by endearing friendships.

1/5/66

The trip to Shikoku with the Sumiyama family was pleasant. Driving down, we stopped near Okayama to see Suizutani Gakko, a school built in 1666 for Chinese studies. It's in a remote area and, because few people go there, it's in remarkable condition— hard to believe it was built in the Tokugawa Era. From there to Kompira, where we stayed in a relative's inn. The following morning we all went to the local cemetery for *Hakka-mairi*, which means paying respects to the ancestors' tombs by throwing dippers of water over the gravestones. The water, when reaching the bones of the interred, is believed to help in salvation. After that, we girls went to Kompira Shrine and, at my encouragement, climbed all 1,368 stone stairs to the top of the mountain. Coming back we crossed Awaji Island, where the roads are as bad as anything you can imagine. Automobile travel in Japan is a reminder of automobile travel in the U.S. a good many years ago. On one of the ferries, the pitching and rolling was a preview of what it's going to be like from Japan to Hong Kong if I'm not lucky.

This morning I raced about the city wildly—settling down only when I got to NHK to do my last recording (on Japanese weddings). Then back home where I'm now awaiting Mr. Kihara's return from Shikoku.

So more anon.

1/6/66 — Anon

To my great pleasure, Hyuga-san came to Osaka to spend a few final hours with me. Our contact has been continuous since October 1963, first in the U.S. and then in Japan. It's sad not knowing when we shall meet again. I owe this special friend a great deal, not the least of which is my wonderful and amazing experience living in Japan.

After 5 p.m., I had a final farewell party hosted by Mr. Wazaki. Present were Mr. and Mrs. Wazaki and Mariko, Mr. and Mrs. Maeda and Sachie, and Iwamoto-san.

Soon I will take my last, luxurious Japanese bath and sleep on the *tatami* floor and *futon* a final time. I don't know if I will sleep much tonight, for there is so much to think about. The end of this phase of my life is too close to the finish, and it saddens me more than words can express. Leaving means dying a little.

This is all from Japan, dear people. I'm off to see the world...

Part 2

ASIA AND EUROPE

The purpose of life is to live it, to taste it, to experience to the utmost, to reach out eagerly and without fear for newer and richer experiences.
    ~Eleanor Roosevelt, political figure, diplomat, activist

Not all those who wander are lost.
    ~J.R.R. Tolkien, author

You will travel in a land of marvels.
    ~Jules Verne, author

There are no wrong turns, only unexpected paths.
    ~Mark Nepo, poet, philosopher

Travel is fatal to prejudice, bigotry, and narrow-mindedness.
    ~Mark Twain, humorist, author

Things turn out best for the people who make the best out of the way things turn out.
    ~Art Linkletter, radio-TV personality

The shortest distance between two people is a smile.
    ~Victor Borge, comedian, pianist, conductor

Making one person smile can change the world—maybe not the whole world, but their world.
    ~Anonymous

You receive from the world what you give to the world.
    ~Oprah Winfrey, media owner, commentator, actress, producer

Oh, the places you'll go!
    ~Dr. Seuss, author, artist, political cartoonist

One's destination is never a place, but always a new way of seeing things.
    ~Henry Miller, author

So much of who we are is where we have been.
    ~William Langewiesche, author and journalist

1/9/66

From somewhere in the Pacific and, according to the *Bridge News*, seven hours away from Okinawa.

The last full day was so sad. 28 people came to see me off. Miss Kinoshita gave me violets; Messsrs. Ono, Oda, and Oshima from Dai-Nippon Celluloid gave me a cloisonné dish, which developed from a private joke I long ago forgot; and Mr. Kihara gave me a pearl and silver brooch and a letter. I was so strong. I never cried once all day; I was so proud of myself. But at 11 after Mr. Kihara left, I went to the lounge and read his letter and lost my self-control. And I lost it again when I got into my berth and cried myself to sleep.

I just can't believe that Japan is behind me. I'm at the start of a 'round-the-world tour, and I should be deliriously excited and filled with happiness and anticipation. I'm not. I feel like I'm going to a funeral. I just can't work up enthusiasm about anything. It is only the second day and I do realize that, but I wish I could snap out of the doldrums.

The *Aramac* left at 2 a.m. on the 8th. I never knew it; I was sleeping. Pressures the last month have exhausted me, and I'm delighted that this ship is so deliciously dull. I share a room with five women, all Australians. There are 305 passengers on board and all but about 15 are Australians or New Zealanders. I'm told there's another American girl and there are some Chinese people. According to the chief officer who shares my dinner table, the average age group on this ship is usually 60 but now, because of the summer vacation down under, the average age is 32. It seems to be a friendly group.

I talked with the girl at the writing desk opposite mine and it turned out she is the other American—Nancy Nash, age 22, from Kansas City, Missouri. She was living in Japan for four months and, just prior to her departure, wrote and illustrated a children's book, *Ii-chan*, which will be published by Tuttle next spring. We're so obviously tuned in on the same things. Nancy is as much of a travel bum as I am. We're going to "do" Taiwan together when we land tomorrow and, since she will be living in Hong Kong for at least a month, has asked me to consider it. I'll decide what I want to do after I get there. And it's a small world. Nancy was given my name in Tokyo by Dave Horner, but she never got to Osaka to call me.

This is so obviously an English ship. The steward wakes us up each morning with tea and a biscuit at 6:45. Breakfast is at 9; beef tea at 10:30; lunch at 11:30; and tea at 4. Dinner is at 7, then tea again at 10 p.m. No tea or coffee with lunch or dinner, but it's available in the lounges. With our wake-up tea comes a "Good Morning Sheet" that lists the day's activities, the ship's whereabouts, instructions for turning the clocks back, and a morning thought. Yesterday's was: "The secret of patience is to do something else in the meantime," which was interpreted by one of the girls to mean "try not to get too bored on the ship." It's possible.

1/12/66

Taiwan is only hours away. The trip has been uneventful. The cabin was a sweatbox for a few days despite air conditioning. As the refrigeration engineer so kindly explained the problem to us: "You've got the room over the engine room—what else do you expect?" Last night, while all made merry at the ship's dance, I suffered in my berth with piercing stomach pains. Whatever it was, it wasn't sea-sickness. It might have been something I ate at lunch or the recurring ovary infection. I took medicine for both and feel considerably better this morning.

Taiwan was interesting, though I would have preferred getting out of the cities and into the rural areas. The houses are brick and strong; poverty is everywhere. Not many Taiwanese speak English, but a large number speak Japanese because of the Occupation from 1895-1945. That enabled me to get around, though most probably preferred not to hear that language again, loaded as it is with painful memories. The first day Nancy and I took a bus from the port of Keelung to Taipei. I contacted Mr. Tomoto, Director of the Japan Consulting Engineers Office and a friend of a friend. By luck his office happened to be opposite the bus terminal and, again with luck, he was in. He gave us a marvelous tour of temples, parks, the beautiful Grand Hotel, and the museums. To my regret, the museums were all closed on Monday. I wanted so to see the Chinese treasures. But we saw Chiang Kai-Shek's home from the road and a bicycle procession of goods being transported to a bride's new home. He took us to dinner and drove us back to the ship. It was a good tour, and I enjoyed speaking Japanese again, but Taipei is not much of a city to look at. I'm not unhappy we were there only a day. The next morning, on Mr. Tomoto's advice, Nancy and I took a pedicab to a mountain cave to see the temple within and the natural stone bed, table, and oven that formed the central area of a bunker. The road passed many mountain cliffs near the harbor and each had row after row of bunkers.

Taiwan's city streets are crowded with pedicabs, taxis, cars, buses, and carts drawn by water buffalo. Oh, yes, and bicycles, too. And lots of American servicemen. I'm sure Taiwan has things to interest me, but I couldn't find it in the cities nor in one day.

I bought three books here at greatly reduced rates, as there are no copyright laws in Taiwan. Two I've already resold to an Australian. I urge you to buy Dan Greenburg's *How to Be a Jewish Mother*. Its humor is attributed to its positive truths!

1/14/66

Hong Kong! The emerald city. A shopper's paradise or a shopper's hell, depending on your point of view! The approach in the harbor at sunset is beyond words—so lovely. But on the surface, it could be anywhere. Signs in English; bright neon lights; white skyscrapers climbing up the mountains on the Hong Kong side, some of them sticking out like chimneys for the mountainous island. Only scattered junks and sampans give the scene a bit of reality, a stamp of China.

Nancy and I were waiting at the Sea Terminal on the Kowloon mainland when a dressmaker approached with his spiel. He, Jimmy Kwok, was a joy. His assistant drove us back to the hotel, then bundled us off to his shop. And, since then, we've sort of used Jimmy's shop as a meeting place. He's given us advice; introduced Nancy to people who might be able to give her a job; and he's given us special prices. Has he ever! Since arriving, I've been shopping and spending. The prices are fantastic but one must bargain viciously and never, for a minute, let your defenses down! Because my glasses were stolen with my purse in Japan, I also had two pairs of glasses made. But the two pairs of handcrafted shoes fitted to my feet were my personal favorites. Jade was exquisite but untouchable. Americans can't bring it into the U.S. 'cause it comes from Red China. There is so much here, and it is so painfully easy to lose one's sense of balance. Were I rich I'd come home the best-dressed, best-bejeweled, best-shoed woman in Rochester! Mother, you must never come here—you would never leave!

Which reminds me that I'll be here until the 20th, anyway, for letters. I've cancelled my flight on the 23rd and will stay till after the Chinese New Year. There are some interesting possibilities that may be coming up after then. Leaving after two weeks works out well because Nancy and I have rented a room by the week, which is cheaper. It comes out to $1.75 a day!

Last night we and four Australian women from the *Aramac* went up to Victoria Peak, from which one can see the world's most beautiful night view. That's not just my opinion; that's on international travel lists. As I said, Hong Kong Colony is the Emerald City. Tonight we're going out with one of Nancy's contacts— Stephen Fong of the Siberian Fur Company (and Hong Kong's first furrier to the rich and famous). He is reputedly one of the world's richest men. He owns a great deal of Hong Kong island and has five palatial homes scattered around the world.

1/15/66

Last night we went to dinner at the Golden Crown Nightclub with Peter Chang, one of Mr. Fong's assistants whom we had met two days ago. We met Mr. Fong, also, but he was too ill to join us last night. We had a delicious Cantonese meal—there's nothing quite like real Chinese food—and enjoyed 15 minutes of firecrackers that preceded a wedding dinner. The Chinese New Year will be on the 21st and 22nd; won't it be fun to be in Hong Kong for it?! But, I was talking about Peter. He's a pleasant person, sharp, and good-humored. We did delve into politics and, according to Peter, things are not as they seem. There's a side of Hong Kong, the communist side, that tourists are never aware of. There's a wealth of journalistic copy here, but I still don't know if I want to stay more than two weeks. I'm now trying to line up job interviews, but working anywhere for a month of part-time work might be difficult. Ah well, by the time you receive the next letter, I will definitely know what's happening.

This afternoon, Nancy, Jane Hayes, an Australian from the *Aramac*, and I went on a yacht with Philip Chin, another of Mr. Fong's assistants. We walked up to the Kowloon Pier and Philip, with a wave of his hand, summoned the yacht waiting for us in the middle of the harbor. Was that a kick living *la dolce vita*?! We made our way to Aberdeen, past the refugees' squatter huts on the cliff sides, to the Sea Palace, one of the two floating restaurants. Aberdeen is the mooring place for the 140,000 who make up Hong Kong's floating population. The place is a bustling thoroughfare inhabited by people who rarely leave their boats. Weaving among them are flat boats guided by young girls, babies hanging on their backs; old men and young boys; floating grocery stores and vegetable markets; and, anchored nearby, a red fire boat. We stopped at the Sea Palace, ordered lunch, took a quick ride on a sampan, re-boarded the *May Flower,* and then ate our lunch leisurely while cruising on Deep Water Bay, where *Love is a Many Splendored Thing* was filmed. Then on to the lovely beach area at Repulse Bay. I was offered a chance to swim from the yacht—they carry bathing suits on board for just such pleasurable emergencies—but the air was cold and I declined the invitation. It was, in every way, a perfect afternoon. We saw so much more from the yacht than had we been on land.

1/16/66

Nothing much to report except that we returned to Repulse Bay Beach today—this time by bus. It was a warm sunny day and, though I'm not much of a sun worshipper, it was a joy just swimming and lying on the sand—especially so because Repulse Bay Beach is the most beautiful I've seen.

1/17/66

Poor Nancy. She's the one who's really looking for a job, and I was offered one today if I stay for three months.

[Wish I could remember what that job was!]

I visited the Cat Street area, a jumble of food and bric-a-brac shops. Then I went to Tiger Balm Garden, created by the man who became rich from Tiger Balm Ointment. It's bizarre and, seeing it is not believing it. It's a monster's nightmare; indeed, the world's greatest monstrosity. Stairs wind up, over, and around—going everywhere and nowhere. A large funhouse mural depicts everything and nothing. Wild boars challenge wild dogs. An impish warrior pops out of a conch shell. Women ride sea serpents. A tiger prepares to pounce. Walruses cavort and bridges connect. People watch strippers in wide-eyed wonderment. And it's all in papier-mâché and plaster. Colors scream from every direction; there's not one inch of sobriety. There is a series of pictures in relief depicting life. Life?—maybe as the Marquis de Sade sees it: a bloody man beneath the heavy wheel of a truck carrying men; a man against a post, his bloody intestines being cut from his body; a man being thrown into a fire while another fans the flames; women impaled on a bed of nails; a woman lying on the ground, dismembered by two hungry dogs; the seven-storied Tiger Pagoda; two women being crushed beneath stones, a man atop them for added weight with a heavy mallet in his hand; rams locked in combat. And I've left things out! It must be a sheer delight for connoisseurs of bad taste! Are these grotesqueries social comment, or the product of the mind of a sick man? The garden surrounds the mansion and overlooks the swimming pool. It's awful. All of it. The man couldn't have been serious or well in his head!

[Many years later I learned that the statues and dioramas at Tiger Balm Garden depict scenes from Chinese folklore, legends, history, and illustrations of various aspects of Confucianism. Wow!]

I saw Man Mo Temple, the oldest in Hong Kong, bustling with New Year preparations. It's dedicated to the gods of literacy and martial valor. Nearby was a man sitting at a sidewalk stall. His business was reading and writing letters for the illiterate.

Hong Kong parking lot!

1/19/66

I struck out on my own into the New Territories into Un Long, the biggest market town, then to the walled village of Kim Tin, occupied by members of the Teng family, who have lived there for a thousand years. It's a tiny ghetto with houses of gray brick surrounded by a stagnant moat. The women wear distinctive clothing: black pants and jacket and a reed hat with a center-cut hole and the outer edge fringed with black cloth. The only color in their costume is provided by gold earrings, jade rings and bracelets, and the tie that's used to hold the hat in place. Kim Tin provides a good look into the past. The New Territories are the closest I can get as an American to viewing life in China. From Kim Tin I went to Tai Po, which, like every other train station these days, was jammed with people returning to Red China for the New Year. Just this morning 10,000 left from Kowloon's main station, and each person is loaded down with baskets of wrapped bundles of gifts and fresh vegetables. One man at the Tai Po station was wrapping up 10-cent coins in old newspaper. La Wu is the last stop in Free China, and I would have liked to go there, but it's a restricted area. From Tai Po I went to She Tin and from there home. Much of the bus drive around the New Territories is lovely, especially the Castle Peak and Plover Cove areas.

But there are squatters' huts everywhere. Mostly, they are built of scrap timber, cardboard, old newspapers, flour sacks, and rusting, corrugated iron sheets—shared by as many as can cram in, plus pigs, chickens, and Chow dogs. When the Hong Kong rooftops and tenements are full, the refugees move to the fringes of the urban areas and build their shanties on the hillsides. Usually the families sleep in one room—sometimes on beds, more often on straw matting. Some of the tenements are so crowded that a rotation system is used for sleeping. Those who are lucky enough live on junks or sampans, but even that's no great improvement. In one month alone, 1,700 boat squatters were removed from 200 boats and resettled. It's a grim life. In the hillside communities the government has built communal latrines. Water for cooking or other purposes is drawn from a well and carried in buckets that hang from a bamboo pole slung across the shoulders. Poverty is everywhere and dirty, barefoot children reach out begging hands to a foreigner in what seems to be an intuitive, reflex action. The refugee problem is a big one, and it's extremely important. They need all the help they can get.

1/22/66

I somehow lost a few days here. I've been busy, though. Two days ago I went to dinner at the Kowloon Cricket Club with Nancy and Alex Mendoza, who has spent most of her life in Hong Kong. (Alex— Alexandrina is her real name—is the product of a Portuguese-Filipino marriage and grew up on Macau.) There we met some of the members of the Malayan Sikh field hockey team who are in Hong Kong now. We also spent the evening with several Ceylonese who have been here for years—most notably Gerry Delilkhan, Managing Editor of *The Asia Magazine*. Five years ago when Mrs. Bandaranaike came to power in Ceylon, Gerry had to get out. He had been a political writer for Time-Life and had antagonized the new regime. He came to Hong Kong and has been here since.

Yesterday Alex and I picnicked at Victoria Peak Gardens with some Ceylonese friends of hers. We went for dinner at the home of another of her friends, and there I met the woman's son, Tony Myatt, who took me to a nightclub that evening. Tony is a DJ and local pop singer, has some recordings to his credit, and was called on to entertain. When I went to his radio station, we saw each other there. How could we have imagined that just two days later we'd meet at his home?

The 20th was the Chinese New Year's Eve, so *"Kung hei fat choy"* to you! That's "happy and prosperous new year." I was told that in Red China they leave out "prosperous." It's nice having two new year holidays within one month. The Chinese love climbing mountains on holidays, and the Peak Tram had an incredibly long queue. And they do love firecrackers! The more crackers the more luck for the new year. They don't sweep away the red cracker paper the next day, either, 'cause that would sweep away the year's luck. They hang red crackers in long 200-foot chains from the tops of buildings, then let 'em rip! Sleep is impossible and, in fact, so is walking on the streets. Kids light all manner of things, throw them at cars and people, drop them from windows. Homes have gone up in smoke, and children blinded by overzealous merrymakers.

Names in China are virtuous. and meaningful. Really! Pollyanna Wu, Cinderella Wong, August Liu, Novina Chan, Scholastic Lee, Sincere Company, Decency Industrial Company.

A Chinese store in Hong Kong has issued a new "ten commandments" for its employees, which reveals most tellingly the shrewd, straightforward, and economy-conscious mind of most Hong Kong merchants:

1. *Don't lie. It wastes my time and yours. I'm sure to catch you in the end.*

2. *Watch your work and not the clock. A long day's work makes a long day short, and a short day's work makes my face long.*

3. *Give me more than I expect, and I'll pay you more than you expect. I can afford to increase your pay if you can increase my profits.*

4. *Keep out of debt. You owe so much to yourself that you cannot afford to owe anybody else.*

5. *Dishonesty is never an accident.*

6. *Mind your own business and in time you will have a business of your own to mind.*

7. *Don't do anything here that hurts your self-respect. The employee who is willing to steal for me is capable of stealing from me.*

8. *It's none of my business what you do at night, but if dissipation affects what you do next day, you will last half as long as you hoped.*

9. *Don't tell me what I'd like to hear, but what I ought to hear. I don't want a valet for my vanity, but I need one for my money.*

10. *Don't kick if I kick. If you are worth correcting, you are worth keeping.*

1/24/66

I woke up early to watch shadow boxing in the park. It's a slow-motion, isometric-type of exercise, which includes a bit of karate, boxing, and judo.

This afternoon I went back out to Aberdeen, this time by bus. It's so different when seen from land. There's nothing enchanting, quaint, or captivating about it. The filth of Hong Kong is centered here with the members of the floating population. The smell of rotting garbage rises up at the visitor; children of all ages beg; and women plead for visitors to take a half-hour ride in their sampans. They swarm like the area flies. From land, Aberdeen is more real, more frightening, more unbelievable. Their crowded slum conditions are far worse than anything I've ever seen before. How do they live there? How do they love there? How did I not see this when I came here a few days ago on a rich man's yacht?!

1/25/66

After pressures and encouragement from all sides, I have decided to visit Malaysia. I now have friends in Penang and Kuala Lumpur on the Malayan Sikh field hockey team and, since I would like to see Malaysia anyway, I decided now was a good time to go. Indeed, it's probably the only time! As you may recall, I said long ago that I didn't know where my travels would take me nor how long I'd stay in each place; it depended on the people I met. And so it has. I extended my stay in Hong Kong and have now decided to visit Malaysia.

Dinner tonight with Alex and then a Chinese Opera. I had a lukewarm reaction about the Chiu Chow Opera and stayed for only an hour-and-a-half of it. I'm glad I had the experience, but once was enough.

> **[Alex and I remained friends for many years until her death about 2004. She and I exchanged newsy letters every Christmas, and Marty and I spent time with her on our 1999 trip to Australia. She was living in Sydney at the time.]**

Adieu from the Crown Colony. I leave for Cambodia in two hours. When I left Japan, I didn't really feel like I was going on a journey. It seems to begin today and, finally, I'm excited about it!

1/28/66

I left Hong Kong, not by Air France as expected, but by Royal Air Cambodia. Never have I had such luxury service on an economy flight—champagne included. Before boarding the plane, I met Chris Malloch, who had been living on the same floor as I at Chungking House. We decided to travel throughout Cambodia together. Chris is 30 and from Riverside, California, an internist who just completed duty with the U.S. Navy in July and promptly set off on a one year round-the-world tour. He joined the navy to see the world but was assigned to the Long Beach Naval Station, not far from home. Now he's touring on his own money.

I have mixed reactions about the flight. It was smooth; the champagne was good; and Chris was pleasant to talk to. But flying over Vietnam gave much food for thought and most of it was unpleasant. We flew over Da Nang, then into the golden setting sun. The deeper blue of the night sky surrounded the moon, then faded into a lighter blue and turquoise near the horizon. The blue was pierced with ascending pink rays of a tropical sun and blended into an orange gold. The earth was black below, but the strings of golden napalm fires burned as a frightening counterpoint to the golden sun. Can this war be realistic when commercial airliners carry travel-happy passengers over territory where too many people are being killed each day? I was told that such flights must fly low enough over Vietnam so they can easily be identified as commercial, rather than enemy planes. That's unsettling!

Once we landed at Phnom Penh, I was eyed suspiciously by Customs because I had marked my profession as journalist, and they are suspicious of my profession. After a few questions, I was permitted entry, then Chris and I met Kirsteen Landall and Dave Edwards from Scotland and England, respectively, who had also formed a travel team. The four of us decided to share rooms to make it cheaper, and we've been together ever since.

Yesterday, while Kirsteen and Dave flew up here to Siem Reap, Chris and I took a local bus for all of 6-1/2 hours, but it was fun. Many of the homes are built on stilts, and the poorer ones are made of thatching. Some are painted to cover the weather-beaten gray; more often, only the front porch is painted. Water buffaloes bathe in the muddy waters—and so do men, women, and children. The young ones run barefoot and often in the nude. Pictures of King Sihanouk and his wife hang everywhere to such an extent that I'm inclined to believe it's dictated. We watched two nuns mix chewed betel nuts with their saliva to create the stimulant high. The fragrance of frangipani, oleander, and hibiscus filled the air. Lunch consisted of delicious tropical bananas; dinner included papayas. Kapok hung from tall trees in this land of intense heat, where kapok-filled sleeping bags need never be used.

Phnom Penh is a lovely, quiet city of tree-lined streets, while Siem Reap is a tourist center because of its proximity to Angkor Wat and Angkor Thom. Still, there is none of the hustle-bustle one might associate with other such towns. The four of us bicycled to Angkor Thom and spent so much time there we had to put off Angkor Wat till tomorrow. It's an incredible place. Westminster Abbey is only slightly younger and so much better preserved—one cannot draw comparisons. The simple fact of its having been buried in the jungle for so many years makes it impressive. The monuments to the Khmer god kings are massive stone and some, even today, are overrun with trees and roots (and playful, screeching monkeys). It is amazing how destructive nature can be as its living plants creep and crawl and smother and crack. We loved Angkor Thom, and traveling together here is so much more fun than traveling alone!

The Cambodian people are a handsome group and genuinely friendly. Few speak English, and my French is not what it used to be. *C'est terrible! Mon Dieu!*

2/1/66

On the 29th, the four of us cycled out to Angkor Wat and spent the entire day there. It certainly is the most magnificent of all the temples and obviously its reputation is based on that. In the evening we rented pedicabs and again went there to watch a performance of classical Cambodian dancing. At its close, we wandered again through the largest of the buildings aided by young boys carrying flashlights, and it was more awesome than ever. And eerier, too, I might add.

To sleep at 12:30 a.m. and awake at 3 a.m. to catch the bus to the border at Poipet. A 100-yard walk across No Man's Land, registration in Thailand, a bus to Aran Pradet, and from there a train to Bangkok, where we arrived at 7:30 p.m. on the 30th. The Thai people are so friendly, and the young ones smile with ease. Unlike in Hong Kong and Cambodia, they do not demand money for having their pictures taken. The countryside is barren and flat, except for occasional oases of houses. The houses, as in Cambodia, are built on stilts, and there are a number of small villages linked by muddy canals where the people bathe, fish, crap, and more. Despite this, their clothes are "sunshine bright." They are washed in the dirty canals, called *klongs*, but rinsed with three-day old canal water stored in jugs in which the dirt has settled to the bottom. Though dishes are washed in the same canal water, foreigners have taught them to dip the dishes in boiled water before eating from them and, thus, diseases have been reduced. In the countryside, boys ride atop water buffaloes that thresh the rice as they walk in circles. There are an abundance of coconut and banana trees. Chris and I have had a diet of bananas for days! Scattered are the sweet fragrances of frangipani and jasmine.

While at the deluxe Erawan Hotel making plane reservations, I met Kumnon Sutabtr, who works there in the evenings and is a private tour guide by day. He invited me to a birthday party for a man who opened a new silk store and celebrated both occasions by holding this party for about 300 travel agents. It was a delight, especially so, since I was the only foreigner in attendance. We went to the party by boat along the Chao Phya River, starting at sunset and arriving 75 minutes later after dark. There was plenty of good Thai food (of course!) and entertainment with classical folk dances of Thailand, Laos, and Malaysia. Instrumental music was provided by alto and bass xylophones made of bamboo hung on oblong sound boxes; a set of gongs hung on a semi-circular frame; a set of drums; and a Thai violin with an ivory neck, a beautifully carved coconut shell, strings made of buffalo hide, and a bow of ivory and horse hairs. A popular TV singer also performed. It was, indeed, a unique and enjoyable experience.

Homes along the Chao Phya River use electricity, but charcoal is used for cooking because it's cheaper. Here are three good quotes from Kumnon:

1. "Where there's a willage, there's a *wat*." Thais cannot pronounce the letter V, as in village; and a *wat* is a temple.

2. "There aren't so many children now that there are radios and televisions." True. The birthrate dropped dramatically when TVs were introduced into the country.

3. There's not much of a brain drain in Thailand from students who study abroad, because "they return home to 'the happy kingdom.'"

Today I visited the Temple of the Reclining Buddha, Wat Po, the most extensive monastery in Bangkok. The Buddha, cement-covered brick with gold leaf, is 160' long and 39.3' high. Its position represents Buddha attaining nirvana. The soles of the feet are exquisite—inlaid mother-of-pearl with the 108 signs, marks, and qualities by which a true Buddha is recognized. Then on to the splendid Royal Palace, a fantasy land of pavilions, frescoes, porcelain-studded towers, mythical figures, golden stupas, and demons. All glimmer and gleam in the bright sun. It is truly a combination of masterpieces. Among them is also Wat Phra Keo, Chapel of the Emerald Buddha, the most sacred Buddha image in the country. It is a solid piece of jade 2' high and has three changes of gold-embroidered clothing for the hot, cold, and rainy seasons. In Thai, the word "emerald" refers to the dark green color and not the specific emerald stone.

Then I went to the National Museum, which was extremely interesting, but I couldn't concentrate on the artifacts there. The heat was weakening me, and this is the cold season! I came back to the hotel at 3, collapsed, and have been here ever since.

Department of Bits of Useless Information:

There are different taxicab prices for Thais and foreigners.

Four years ago there was a taxicab scandal when meters were installed but never used. A three-wheeled motorized pedicab is called a *samlor* or *tuk-tuk*. They're fun!

2/3/66

I visited the beautiful Marble Monastery of Italian Carrara marble—Wat Benchamabopit and Wat Trimitr, a pure gold-covered Buddha discovered in 1953 after a heavy rainstorm caused a crack in the plaster. Beneath the plaster, glittering metal was found. The Buddha, cast in the fourteenth century, had at some point been covered with plaster to protect it from invading armies. It was forgotten over the years.

In the afternoon, long after I thought he had returned to Hong Kong, I contacted Gerry Delilkhan. We spent the afternoon and evening with an Asia Magazine photographer here on assignment with Gerry. Also with the Southeast Asia Bureau Chief for the Associated Press. I may meet up with Gerry in the Middle East, as he's expecting to be there about the same time I am.

I'll never forget this morning—unfortunately. I went to the Pasteur Institute Snake Farm to watch them feed the Banded Kraits and King Cobras and to see how they extract venom from cobras for the production of antivenin serum. As part of the process, they inject the venom into horses, and I wandered over to see how the horses were enclosed for the injection. One horse was badly spotted where his hair had been shaved at the points of injection. I remember thinking he was pretty ugly. Then, while watching another horse, the one I mentally insulted thrust his head out of the stall and took a walloping bite out of the back of my arm! I was immediately treated at the hospital—fortunately the institute is located at one—and was provided with pills and dressings for one week. The pain the first three hours was excruciating, but it has considerably subsided now to my great relief.

Tonight Kumnon took me to see Thai boxing. Everything is allowed in that sport but biting and wrestling. Fighters box to non-melodic and percussive music, and there is a good deal of fancy footwork. One guy was carried out on a stretcher after being kicked in the chin, and last year, Kumnon told me, 14 people were killed throughout Thailand after being excessively kneed in the stomach. We had ringside seats. The man next to me was overly enthusiastic when he punched his arm up in the air, whacking me right where the horse had bitten me. I saw stars in every color!

2/5/66

Yesterday morning I went on the Floating Market tour, which was disappointing but nonetheless interesting. Then back to the hotel to say good-by to Chris. Dinner with friends of Dave Horner's, and a late date with Kumnon who took me to a nightclub. I'm waiting now for him to take me to lunch and then a too-long and too-tiring 27-hour train ride to Penang, Malaysia.

Summing up Bangkok, I had a good time, but three or four days would have sufficed. I stayed here a week because the train to the Malaysian border only runs two days a week. I missed out on going to the seaside resort of Bangsaen with Gerry because I couldn't contact him earlier. And Mu, a friend of Dave Horner's, had invited me up to her school in Cholburi, but her student who was to have mailed the letter forgot to put a stamp on it, and I never received it. A comedy of errors. Fortunately, I do get to see southern Thailand on the two train trips, for Bangkok is hardly representative of the whole country.

2/7/66

Penang, Malaysia. I was pleasantly surprised to find Pretty Paul waiting for me when I arrived. I should explain that the name Pretty Paul is in no way meant to reflect on his degree of masculinity. That's a self-styled nickname to make it easy for his non-Sikh friends. His real name is Triptipal. I'm sure you hear the similarity. He met me with his brother Baldev and a Tamil friend, Naga. Tamils originate from southern India; they are one of the ethnic groups that make up the racial jigsaw of Malaysia. After washing off 27 hours of dirt at the hotel, we went out to dinner and then did a bit of sightseeing.

There was nothing particularly special about the train trip, nor was much of the countryside en route picturesque except for the tropical sunset, which is always a source of wonder to me—coconut palms silhouetted against the deepening glow of a burning sun. I enjoyed watching a flock of geese being herded home. As the twice-weekly train goes through each little station, people gather to catch the excitement of it—standing, sitting, squatting, staring, awaiting no-one, awaiting nothing but a streaking flash of train or, if lucky, a full three-minute stop. They gather and wait as if nothing else ever happens in their tiny hamlets; and, indeed, it's highly possible that nothing ever does.

Malaysian Customs has been the most demanding so far. It was the first to require a suitcase opened (I left my heavy one with a friend in Bangkok since I must return there, anyway). Some Chinese women behind me were loaded down with cardboard cartons. Each had to be opened and inspected. The poor dears were carrying packets of powdered soap. Each one—and there were hundreds!—had to be removed and smelled to make sure they did not contain opium.

The Snake Temple is a haven for pit vipers. How disappointing it was that there were less than 25 snakes! Today was the birthday of the deity Chor Soo Kong and the annual festival when the temple is supposed to be loaded with snakes. Two days ago there was a large Hindu festival when men walk around pierced with nails, but I couldn't come here in time. That would be hard to see.

Apropos of nothing, I realized how grateful I should be that I'm not a school teacher for, if I were a conscientious one, I would need an extra large suitcase on this journey to carry the wonders of the world, the likes of which no American Customs officer or student had ever seen: tea flowers, mulberry leaves, rubber tree nuts, a banana palm frond, a carved water buffalo horn, the husk of a durian fruit (after deodorization), a devil tile, a piece of thatched roof; and endless other samples to decorate my classroom and enhance my social studies lessons! Good thing I decided to go into broadcasting!

Penang is about the size of Rochester without its suburbs. And a hodgepodge of architecture, vehicles, people, and clothing—sarongs, *samfoos*, *saris*, and western dress. And languages and letters. The official language is English, but next year it will be changed to Malayan. There's also the Punjabi of the Sikhs, Tamil, Chinese, and Mandarin. The alphabets are English, Arabic, which is what the Malayans use, Chinese, and others. I am told there are no racial problems, or none to speak of in Malaysia—an attitude which is far afield from what I've read in the newspapers. It needs more investigation, for it's a point of both interest and import.

2/9/66

Naga, chairman of the Malaysian Youth Clubs in Penang, invited me to an afternoon tea yesterday for a visiting group of 12 from Japan. Their leader is at the Osaka YMCA and, coincidentally, an acquaintance of both Mr. Maeda and Mr. Wazaki. One of the young men, after kindly presenting me with a fan, said in a voice too loud—but fortunately in Japanese—that if I really loved Japan and the U.S., I must go back home and convince my fellow Americans that they must end the war in Vietnam and they must never, never drop an atom bomb there as they did in Japan. The only footnote I'll add to this is that the young man lives only two hours outside of Nagasaki.

I took the night train from Penang to Kuala Lumpur with Colin Alexander, an Englishman with a great sense of humor. Actually, I met him on the train to Penang, and we agreed to take the same train to KL.

Colin and I were driven to the Batu Caves that are both incredible and dangerous. There we met a man on assignment from the U.S. State Department Ministry of Health who catches and bands the bats to study their diseases as they relate to humans. Thousands upon thousands of bats flew out of the caves as darkness set in. It was a stirring sight!

I visited the new national monument sculpted by Felix de Weldon, who did the Iwo Jima Monument. It was just unveiled yesterday during President Park Chung Hee's visit to Kuala Lumpur. The streets are lined with the flags of Malaysia and Korea. Had lunch with Arthur Jacobs of the American Embassy and an Indian man who spent 5-1/2 years in jail on charges of publishing seditious newspapers. His story is a fascinating one from anti-communist to communist to socialist, but too long to relate here.

As you probably have gathered, things are working out well for me. My friends here have tried to convince me to stay two extra days but I am concerned about the hotel costs. One offered to take care of my bill, but I refused. Tonight I contacted Ananda Sivaram, a friend of Alex's (from Hong Kong). Poor Ananda has been waiting for me for days and has gone to meet every plane arriving from Hong Kong. At any rate, tomorrow I'm moving into Ananda's home, and so I shall see about changing my reservations to Bangkok and Calcutta. Even when I make my flight reservations on short notice, I end up canceling them!

I shall get this in tomorrow's mail and, in the next letter, you'll find out if the Air India elephant has an extra howdah so that Uncle Wiggily can get to Calcutta after all!

[Some readers may be too young to know Uncle Wiggily Longears, a gentleman rabbit who always set things right. His amusing stories were among my favorites as a child. Every chapter ended with a cliffhanger like the one at the end of the previous diary entry.]

2/11/66

I'm now staying in Petaling Jaya, a suburb of Kuala Lumpur, with two bachelors: Ananda Sivaram, an industrial chemist, and MP Gopalan, writer for *Asia Magazine*.

Another of my friends, Amar Singh of the Criminal Investigation Department of the Police Force, invited me to a spur-of-the-moment luncheon with friends. Then I was taken to see Sungei Besi, a nearby tin mine and site of the world's largest man-made hole.

This morning Ananda was up early, went to the Hindu temple to pray, and returned home by the time I got up. He had laid out breakfast for me, the morning paper, and a good-morning note. He is a rare host but somewhat like an overindulgent husband. He drives me everywhere and refuses to let me take a taxi from the suburb where the house is. I spent a quiet day writing letters to friends who think I'm still in Japan. Ananda came home during his lunch hour and had coffee with me, but I refused lunch while waiting to hear from the others. When he realized I would not be going out for lunch, he was back home within 20 minutes—hamburger and french fries in hand. I promised I'd write him a letter of recommendation when he decides to marry!

2/13/66

What a perfect day this has been! Early this morning, Amar, Ananda, and I drove down to Bentong, about 50 miles outside of Kuala Lumpur. Amar took me to one of his rubber estates, showed me how they tap the trees, what happens with the latex after collection, and gave me a good general background of the whys and whats of the rubber industry. Then we went for lunch at the home of Jock Reid, a Scotsman, now a citizen of Malaysia and manager of a large rubber estate. Among the 12 of us, 6 nationalities were represented, and guests included a garage repairman, a multi-millionaire banker, a rubber planter, and one foreign visitor—me! I learned a great deal about the past and present, for all the men have been here about 20 years and thus experienced the Emergency. And what gruesome stories they had to tell! Jock entertained us on his bagpipes, for he was at one time captain in the Scottish Highlanders and piped his way through World War II.

[The Malayan Emergency was a guerrilla war fought in the pre- and post-independence Federation of Malaya from 1948 until 1960. It was a British victory won against an attempted communist revolution in Malaya. The rubber plantations and tin-mining industries had pushed for the use of the term "emergency" since their losses would not have been covered by Lloyd's insurers if it had been termed a "war."]

I've had too few hours of sleep in KL, the consequence of friends over-entertaining, but I'm happy I came down to Malaysia—all because I was fortunate to have met the Malayan Sikh field hockey team in Hong Kong.

2/15/66

Namaste from India.

I flew Japan Air Lines to Calcutta after refusing a hundred requests to stay in Bangkok at Kumnon's expense. There were only 10 passengers on the jet, and I was furious at myself 'cause I had to pay overweight charges. I shall send a package home from India and avoid this nonsense! And I was angry again when the only hotel accommodations I could get was in a first-class hotel at appropriate rates!

This was not the ideal way to form first impressions of an entire country but so it was as I traveled from east to west. India is not a place for the faint of heart. Bony, bitten cows (sacred to the Hindus) wander the streets causing traffic accidents and are scraped up upon death by government workers. Starving and diseased men, women, and children beg for anything to keep them alive. In Calcutta **[the name was changed to Kolkata in 2001 to lose its colonial identity]**, one million people sleep on the streets each night and, in Mother Theresa's Home, a man may go to die—but, if he does not die within a few days, he is put back in the streets to make room for another.

There is so much misery to be seen—the beggars, the derelicts, and all those who queue up for their rations of rice, wheat, and sugar. There's an overload for the eyes, the nose, and the ears.

People in every direction, a clamor of noise and color and smells, of action and motion. I see no reason for dilly-dallying in India. I am ready to leave Calcutta tomorrow and head down to Bombay. My route has changed. I shall be business-like about this visit, see what I came to see, then move on without further delay.

This morning I contacted a friend of a friend in the Japan Consulting Engineer's Office who assigned an Indian engineer to show me around. At the entrances to the Victoria Memorial dedicated to Queen Victoria are sandbag barriers, placed there to prevent destruction by bomb splinters. They are at all such places throughout India—products of the Chinese emergency in '62, the Pakistan emergency in '65, and an uncertain future.

Then on to Dakshineswar Temple where Ramkrishna saw and felt the presence of god in the nineteenth century. Across the Ganges River, his disciple Swami Vivekananda founded the Ramkrishna Mission in 1899. You may know there are Ramkrishna missions in some U.S. cities. From there to the Parasnath Jain Temple with its magic mirrors, mosaics, and jewels. The Jain religion, over 2,800 years old, is characterized by a refusal to deprive any living creature of life.

I have found two things to be true in Southeast Asia—a blatant distrust of journalists on the part of immigration officials and a fear of letting anyone in who has no immediate address to proceed to. Oh yes, and one more: a profusion of hotels that "are not fit for ladies," as in the Bangkok hotel I almost stayed in that offered double rooms to single men and a girl to go with them!

For Indian Customs one must register all that you bring in, including money. I brought 1,000 illegal rupees into the country, which may yet cause me some trouble, but they were double the rate of exchange in Malaysia, and I needed that extra $100 worth. At the hotel, the desk man—also a black market operator—warmed up to me.

2/16/66

I did not leave Calcutta today as I hoped. In my wish to see no more of troubled India than necessary, I cut Benares, the Hindus' pilgrimage city, from my plans. I don't like myself in India. I want to be an ostrich and bury my head in the ground. I don't want to see the grotesqueries that walk about the streets. I don't want to feel the touch of those who stroke my feet then place their palms together and to their foreheads as a sign of respect but more a plea for money. I don't want to see men jump to retrieve a dropped cigarette butt. I do have compassion, but a human being reaches a saturation point—and I am already approaching it. I have seen so little of India, but it seems that the world does not care enough for the Indians. And the rottenest thing I could say, but I shall, is that in this dying nation there seems little to care about. God, it needs help! Seeing it makes it believable in an unbelievable sort of way.

The country is struggling with an exploding population and a shortage of wheat to feed them. To deal with the former, the government promotes one-child families. To help with the latter, the government has outlawed serving breads in restaurants on Monday nights. This is such a minimal effort for such a serious problem—like a bad joke.

I have moved into the home of Balmukund Adalja, a Servas host and a merchant by profession. The apartment is small and is shared with his wife and six-year-old son. The Adaljas are in the process of moving to Bombay, and their four other children (a sixth is due next month) are already there. Their bath consists of a large earthenware jug that is kept filled with water and used for wetting and rinsing. Their small kitchen is similar with a type of hot-plate for cooking and the jug water for washing dishes upon the cement floor. There's a small dining area and a larger room with one bed. It is the family's living room and bedroom, for all sleep in one room: the parents on the bed and the children upon mats on the stone floor. During my stay, they are kindhearted enough to give me the bed, and everyone else sleeps on the floor around me. Their one luxury is a 14-year-old jalopy, and the way it's driven, I'm amazed it has lasted this long!

I asked the Adaljas about their part-time servant and learned that their home and neighborhood could be considered lower upper class. You can see the tremendous difference in the standards of living. It must be difficult to live in such a home when all are present. They have, by the way, made sure I eat all types of food, most of it good but spicy. And I enjoy the informality of eating with my fingers! I even tried chewing betel nuts, but I had to spit them out—much too unpleasant for my taste!

I'm traveling with a tape recorder for broadcast purposes, and the family had never seen a tape recorder before. They were entertained for hours talking and listening and touching and watching the tapes go round. Even the neighbors came in to enjoy the fun!

RADIO BROADCAST

Servas
U.S. Educational Radio Network (Excerpt) 1966

Though Servas was founded in 1949, I first hard of it in the fall of 1965 with an article in a Japanese English-language newspaper. I was already dreaming of my round-the-world adventures, and this organization seemed to go right along with my wanting to meet people as I traveled—I mean, really meet people—and understand their different cultures. Servas, from the Esperanto word meaning "to serve," is an international hospitality social network of hosts and travelers committed to building understanding and peace by putting together people from different cultures. Its members are either hosts who want to meet international travelers or travelers who want to connect with people in the countries they are traveling through. In 1965, the rule was that you were interviewed and approved in your home country. Since I was living in Japan, an exception was made. I was interviewed, approved, and given host lists from many countries. The procedure assumed that while the traveler was still in her home country, she would write to the hosts, give the dates she would be traveling there, then wait for a reply of approval. Since I would be traveling through Asia and Europe like a moving target, this was impossible for me. I picked my hosts by profession and languages spoken. Journalists and teachers were high on my list, and French speakers were sought out so I could practice speaking French again. I never expected to find anyone who spoke Japanese—and I never did!

One could stay three nights with a host, longer if invited. I wrote ahead to tell hosts my expected dates of arrival—not even a sure thing because of the unplanned and impulsive manner of my travels—then I called once I arrived in their community. My experiences were priceless! I showed up at one home in India where the man had died five years earlier. (The lists were imprecise in so many ways!) I slept on the only bed in an Indian home while everyone in the family slept on the floor around me. I attended an Indian wedding. In Norway a home was located in a courtyard of a square of buildings, its hidden location never found by the Nazis. I stayed in homes where the owners gave me the key, then left for vacation, or left a note that instructed me to pick up a key elsewhere, and I would be the only one there. In one town, there were two of us Servas travelers and no host. Adventurous? Yes! Crazy? Yes! Crazy fun!

2/19/66

I'm now waiting at Manmad station. The city, in the state of Maharashtra, is somewhere within 24 hours of Bombay. The train ride down was pleasant, though long. I spent most of the time discussing the India-Pakistan situation with a stranger on the train. A drawback in world travel is that one must be completely knowledgeable about the past and present of each nation—and that is a difficult task! I booked a third class sleeper, which is far from the best but suitable for my few needs. Seated around me were a group of Indian Mohammedans on their way to Mecca for a once-in-a-lifetime pilgrimage. I smiled to see they were wearing sneakers!

According to the Indian Tourist Office, I had to change trains here for Aurangabad. But, when I arrived, I found I was misdirected. To go to the Caves of Ajanta, where I am headed, I had to get off at Jalgoan, which the train passed through earlier this morning. So now I'm awaiting a train back to Jalgoan.

Do you know the following?

"If you will be a traveler, have always the eyes of a falcon, the ears of an ass, the face of an ape, the mouth of a hog, the shoulder of a camel, the legs of a stag, and see that you never want two bags very full—that is one of patience and another of money." It was written by John Florio, a linguist and lexicographer, in 1591.

In the Indian countryside I saw boys herding goats and sheep, women bearing jugs atop their heads, villages of mud-plaster walls, and water buffalo dairy farms.

The Adaljas had given me some food to carry on the train. When I offered it to some people in exchange for what they offered me, they had never seen it before. They were Bengalis, and it was Gujarati food. That's like saying they were New Yorkers and it was Ohioan food. Such differences in one nation only add to the problems of understanding and unification.

I'm now at Jalgoan—only to find that I cannot go to Ajanta today but must stay here the night and take an early bus on the morrow. I am only about 60 miles or so from the Caves of Ellora, but going there means another day, and another day in India. I'm ready to head north and out.

2/20/66

I spent a restful night in the Railway Retiring Rooms, as they're called. It's a two-hour ride to Ajanta past villages and parched land, and a few farms being tilled with archaic wooden tools pulled by cows. There are no cars out there because no-one could afford such luxury; all transportation is by bus or bullock cart. In one village I saw a sleeping camel and ten tapirs. I can't imagine what tapirs would be used for unless their milk or meat is edible. I've already tasted sweets made from buffalo milk and goat milk curd. I am not overly cautious about food, for when people share their foods with me, I feel it would be an insult not to accept. I shall trust to luck that I don't get sick and, anyway, I like everything!

The Caves of Ajanta date back to about 200 B.C. For about a thousand years after that, Buddhist monks chipped away the side of a valley rock fashioning shrines and monasteries. Painting, sculpture, and architecture are all there. The approach is impressive seeing all these halls cut out in the valley wall. The sculpture, too, is done on a grand scale, but Ajanta is particularly famous for its frescoes, which represent themes from Buddhist folklore and relate legends of the life of Buddha (563 B.C.-483 B.C.).

2/22/66

After saying only two days ago that I'm trusting to luck, last night I got the "Delhi Belly" in Bombay—though it was nearly as intense as my bout with "Montezuma's Revenge" in Mexico a few years ago. I'm feeling human again after the medicine and the fact that I've had nothing to eat in 30 hours!

Somehow I made it to the Elephanta Caves this morning, located on an island about 10 miles out in the Arabian Sea. The caves were built in the eighth century and have stone tableaus depicting the life of Siva as Brahma, the Hindu lord of creation. But he is also shown as Rudra, the god of destruction, and Vishnu, the god of preservation. Several of them show marital scenes, including the wedding of Siva as Brahma and Parvati, his wife. Because Hindu deities change form, they are confusing.

(I know you can't possibly follow or remember these details, nor are they important to you. I write of them so I can remember where I've been, what I've done, and what I've learned. It's all a part of my global education as citizen of the world. I don't want to forget anything!)

I saw a protest march against automation with signs that read: "Don't buy American machines—employ Indians."

I don't know if I'm leaving tonight. You see how this freedom of movement can do one in? Finally made contact with friend Amar Singh from Kuala Lumpur, whom I had hoped to meet here, and now I am expecting him to pick me up shortly.

The Prince of Wales Museum here has some marvelous paintings of India's glorious past. In one portrait gallery of Englishmen and the wealthy Tata family, there was a portrait of Abraham Lincoln, the one and only American in this museum. It was purchased in the U.S. by a Parsee merchant from Bombay at the time of Lincoln's assassination. (Parsees are descendants of Persian Zoroastrians who emigrated to India in the seventh century to avoid religious persecution by Muslims.)

About that *sari* I said I bought for you, Mom—I didn't. What I bought instead is gold silk with a touch of pink and blouse material attached in a solid golden color. The silk is accented with raised gold thread. I think it's stunning, and I'm sure you will, too. I have never seen material like it in the states, which means it should make a unique cocktail dress.

[There's a wonderful finish to this. My mother had that material made into a mother-of-the-bride dress for my wedding and, indeed, both she and the dress looked gorgeous!]

Permit me an introspective comment. As is more than obvious, I am now on an around-the-world tour that is almost anybody's dream of a lifetime. I'm doing it with a great amount of freedom and very little planning. I go where I'm moved to go and stay until I decide to leave. Every so often I realize what I'm doing and, when that happens, as in the Jalgoan station late at night, the thought occurs to me: "Wendy, what's a nice girl like you doing in a remote place like this?!" And then I laugh and think for a minute and realize exactly what I'm doing in that remote place, and I'm grateful for it. I'm grateful to my parents who are courageous enough to put up with the shenanigans of a nomadic daughter. But I'm more grateful for the fact that they raised me to be the adult I am. So on that basis, dear mother and father, I thank you.

2/24/66

I'm beginning to feel like the man who came to dinner in all these widely scattered cities. It's hard even for me to believe that I am still in Bombay four days after I had originally intended to leave.

[Bombay's name was changed to Mumbai in 1995. Like Calcutta, the city name was an unwanted legacy of British colonial rule.]

The other night I was with Randhir Singh Gentle, the only man in India ever to win three consecutive Summer Olympic gold medals in field hockey, 1948-1956. Gentle comes from a family of four boys, and his Sikh father wanted them to have more than the usual surname of Singh. So he named them Gentle, Able, Humble, and Noble. Something else I meant to tell you: a Malayan Sikh friend is one of 16 children! His mother barely stands 5′ tall.

Only an hour-and-a-half before my train left for Jaipur, Amar convinced me to stay longer. We have flight reservations to Delhi tonight. I will visit Jaipur and Agra when Amar visits his mother in their village in the Punjab.

2/28/66

On the plane to Delhi I met Dave Edwards, who had been one of my companions in Cambodia. I was also approached by an

American girl who remembered seeing me five years earlier at Syracuse University! Do I have a face no-one can forget? Or is it the red hair again?!

A word about red hair in India: horrible! The dye is made from mehandy leaves and ground into a paste, then rubbed onto the hair—a russet orange hue that lasts about 15 days. We know it as henna. It's used to color hair and decorate the body.

Last night I took a train to Jaipur, the Pink City, so called because the buildings in the old city, circa eighteenth century, were constructed of pink sandstone. I arrived at 5 a.m. Since I had almost no sleep on the train, I wrapped myself up in an army blanket that a friend gave me, and sacked out on the waiting room floor for three hours. I decided that tonight I would travel in first class luxury and damn the expense for a few hours of sleep!

On my own this morning, I visited the City Palace, which is a marvel of architecture and design. There are three museums. The art gallery, in particular, was amusing. A male guard pointed out with special emphasis all the erotic pictures. It was hard to keep a poker face! I was treated to another bonus at the Palace, for a movie was being filmed there. Earlier today I met a man from the Rajasthan State Travel Office. I never found out his name, so I shall call him "X." He had a motor scooter and a free afternoon, so I spent the better part of the day in transit on the back of the scooter while we covered about 30 miles. Monkeys in the trees above were screaming at us! In one day I managed to see all of Jaipur and then some!

I am thrilled with Jaipur. The city is surrounded by hills atop which are walls and watch towers. It's an alive city and the traffic itself is enough to keep one alert: taxis; pedicabs; scooter cabs; horse-drawn carriages called *tonga*; bullock carts; bicycles; camels carrying farm products to market; and, yes, even elephants. Visiting the City Palace and the Amber Palace (actually a palatial fort) is exciting if one can imagine what they must have been like three centuries ago—especially the richly-dressed ladies of the maharajahs' courts, chattering and tittering as they watched through elaborately sculptured marble grilles the action in the courtyards below.

The 11-mile ride to the temple of Galta was a joy. The road is lined on either side with old city walls. Some of their turrets and doorways were like Hollywood sets—one-dimensional buildings that open up to a desert wasteland and blue sky beyond. People live in these old ruins, and they are poor. But it seems that the people are trying and that Jaipur, anyway, is not dying with the rest of the nation. In Jaipur, if in no other place in India, I can believe that humanity, at worst, is a beautiful thing and, at best, it is sacred.

Two signs caught my attention here.

"A small family is a happy family." One-child families are encouraged, as India tries to reduce its population. (I bought a matryoshka nesting doll with a father, mother, and one child.)

"Spitting in the pool is quite a bad habit."

Tomorrow Agra ... and then? I had wanted to leave Thursday for Kabul. But before leaving India, I have to get my visas for the Middle East, and I must have another *sari* blouse and petticoat made for a *sari* Amar gave me as a gift. I don't have reservations on the Kabul flight and that alone may keep me here another week. Amar invited me up to Amritsar, and Inder Grewal wants to take his family and me on a short trip. Bal, Inder's brother and a doctor in the Indian Army, has invited me up to Jalandhar where his Army post is located. I have learned my lesson. All plans are now made on a daily basis, and I will not even consider anything that is more than four days hence!

3/3/66

On the 28th, I took a night train to Agra. After arriving, I went directly to the home of P.N. Mittal, a Servas host. He lives in a comfortable home with his wife and three children. The family sleeps in two connected rooms, but each has a bed made of rope straw. It was pleasant staying there overnight.

The first afternoon I went about town on the back of a motorcycle owned by a friend of a friend—down one road where peacocks wandered freely and another where monkeys were swinging from the trees in such a way that we often had to duck.

I've seen many Mughal Muslim monuments, but one stands out above all others—indeed, above all other structures in the world. That, of course, is the Taj Mahal. I first saw it in the afternoon sunlight and, when I did, my heart stopped for a second. It is a vision in marble. There is nothing I could add to the miles of words that have previously been written about it. It is not only a tribute to love but also a tribute to architecture. I saw it again at night under a shiny half moon as it appeared in splendor from the smoky night air. As I approached it, I was hypnotized, moving like an automaton. The Taj creates an emotion within the heart and mind of each individual and, therefore, it will always remain uniquely special. To each individual the Taj Mahal becomes a private personal joy. I went back a third time to see it at sunrise; I was still mesmerized.

A friend took me to Fatehpur Sikri, a ghost town about 23 miles from Agra. The palatial fort was built in the sixteenth century by Akbar, the third Mughal emperor, but abandoned after 11 years for insufficient water supply.

My favorite building in all the world! The exquisite Taj Mahal was elegant and perfect—at dawn, by the light of day, and once again by moonlight. Note the lack of crowds in 1966. I had it all to myself!

I am now back in Delhi at the Grewals. It is already March and that gives me only a month and a half in the Middle East. I think it is perhaps wiser for me to forget Amritsar, Pakistan, and/or Afghanistan and hightail it over to Tehran via BOAC on Sunday, the 6th. After making my reservations, I received a note from Amar telling me a visit to Amritsar would be a waste of time: bad hotels, dirt, et al. By the time I leave India, I will have been here three weeks, which is ten days longer than I had originally intended. But, like everything else on this trip, it has worked out well, and I'm not sorry I stayed.

Today I got my Iraqi visa—marked invalid if I get an Israeli visa, though Americans don't need one. I listed my religion on the visa application as Protestant-Methodist. (Borrowing from a former S.U. roommate.) It was the only way!

3/4/66

This morning I met up with Hubert Lall, my Delhi guide, and went with him to the beautiful Mughal Gardens behind the president's home. Beautiful from a western standpoint, that is. I shall always think Japanese stroll gardens are the ultimate in form and beauty.

I'm now back home getting organized, adjusting my suitcases for winter weather again. This evening I am having dinner with Balbinder Singh, a medical student at Delhi University and brother of Baldev and Triptipal, my friends in Penang.

I had an amusing experience this morning at the Iranian Embassy. I walked in and asked for a visa application form.

"What nationality are you?"

"American."

"In that case you don't need to fill out a form. Just give me your passport."

A pause while the gentleman perused it.

"What is your profession?"

"Freelance radio journalist."

"In that case, you need to fill out three application forms."

This is relevant to what I mentioned several letters ago.

RADIO BROADCAST

Fabled India?
U.S. Educational Radio Network (Excerpt) 1966

So this is the fabled land of flying carpets; turbaned maharajahs upon fully-caparisoned elephants; harem girls in lush silk saris; and glittering palaces that reflect the sun. No! No! No! No! This is the land of rickshaws, tongas, autos, bullock carts, and hackney coaches; of bony, bitten cows that belong to no-one, cause traffic accidents and are scraped up upon death by government workers; of starving, diseased men, women and children who descend upon a person who looks moneyed and plead for a paise *or two to keep them alive; and of plaited bamboo shacks and concrete hovels. Where has the glory of India gone? In Calcutta one million people sleep on the streets each night and, in Mother Theresa's Home, a man may go to die—but if he does not die within a few days, he is put back in the streets to make room for another. There is so much misery here.*

I don't like myself in India. I want to be an ostrich and bury my head in the ground. I don't want to see the grotesqueries that walk about the streets, that follow me about like flies. I don't want to feel the touch of those who stroke my feet then place their palms together and to their foreheads as a sign of respect that is a plea for money. I don't want to see men and boys jump to retrieve a dropped cigarette butt. I'm repulsed by the spotted red sidewalks stained by those who chew the leaves of the betel pepper plant then spit out the juice. I do have compassion, but a human being reaches a saturation point—and I am approaching it now. I have seen so little of India, but it seems that the world does not care enough for the Indians. God, it needs help! Seeing it makes it believable—in an unbelievable sort of way.

Because the British Crown ruled India for almost 100 years till India declared independence in 1947, English is taught in the schools. And because customs and languages here change every 100 miles or so, English is often the common language.

When I offered part of my lunch to some passengers in exchange for what they had offered me, they had never seen it before. They were Bengalis and it was Gujarati food. That's like saying they were New Yorkers and it was food from Ohio. Such differences in one nation only add to the problems of understanding and unification.

I've seen many Mughal Muslim monuments, but one stands out above all others—indeed, above all other structures in the world. That, of course, is the Taj Mahal. I first saw it in the afternoon sunlight and when I did, I swear my heart stopped for a second. It is a vision in marble, and there is nothing I could add to the miles of words that have previously been written about it. It is not only a tribute to love but also a tribute to architecture. I saw it again under a shiny half moon when it rose in splendor from the smoky night air. Yet again at sunrise as I approached it, I was hypnotized, moving like an automaton. The Taj creates an emotion within the heart and mind of each man and woman. The Taj creates an emotion within the heart and mind of each man and woman who sees it. To each it becomes a private, personal joy.

> [After saying for so many years that I would never again return to India, I returned in December 2014—this time with my husband on a first-class tour, staying in fine hotels, eating at excellent restaurants. We avoided Calcutta, or Kolkatta, as it's called now. Yes, we did see sacred cows wandering freely in the smaller towns, as well as turbaned guests at a fancy Rajasthani wedding we were spontaneously invited to. At this same wedding at New Delhi's finest hotel, female guests wore bejeweled saris, while women on construction crews worked in inexpensive cotton saris. We saw the magnificent Taj rising through the mist of a rainy day through the window in our elegant hotel room. This time I was able to take India in, not be overwhelmed or repelled by it. This time and from a different and privileged perspective, I welcomed the crush of colors, the busy streets, and sidewalk vendors. There were too many people still and the population is growing. There was no end to the chaos, traffic noise, smells, and the cacophony of constant horn blowing though there are laws against it. This time I was at peace with pressed palms to my forehead in the prayer position, but also with open arms.]

3/7/66

Salaam from Iran.

We flew into Tehran over brown landscapes barren of color, though the Alberz Mountains that rise behind the city are a counterpoint. In the distance is Mount Damavand, a 19,000-foot-high volcanic peak. But for the snow-capped mountains visible from every part of the city, Tehran would be depressingly dull.

I was delayed through Customs because of my tape recorder, but a final concession was made, and I was allowed to take it in without payment. At the airport I met a representative from the Ministry of Information on the lookout for visiting journalists. I was sent off to the Ministry office and loaded down with pamphlets and tea. It all worked out in the end and, when the Frankels returned from a day of skiing, I was at their home to greet them.

Jack and Judy Frankel are warm and welcoming. You may remember, Jack is head of the Peace Corps program in Iran. Their son, David, is in high school here and their daughter, Sara, is a junior at Syracuse University. Currently there is a Peace Corps volunteer on recuperation leave staying with them in their comfortable home in the outskirts of Tehran. I don't know how long I shall stay here before moving south to Isfahan and Shiraz, but I've been invited to stay as long as I like. **[The Frankels were niece and nephew of my parents' friends.]**

Today I visited the Ethnological Museum and its wax figures depicting various phases of Iranian life and tribes. With my letter of introduction from the Ministry of Information, I did not pay the admission charge and was given a private guide, who spoke his own style of abbreviated English. "This ... gun." "Afghanistan?" "No, Kurdistan. This ... BOOM! This ... blood." We move on. "This ... wedding." "Caspian Sea?" "No." "Afghanistan?" "No. Isfahan. This ... husband. This ... mrs. husband. This ... marriage contract." "Islam?" "No. Jewish." "I ... Jewish."

The last sentence, if that's what it can be called, was mine. Why does one always revert to pidgin English in these situations?

"Oh! You Jew? Good. See ... charcoal. This ... pipe. This ... opium. This ... water. See ... hubble-bubble." (Understand? A hubble-bubble is an opium water pipe.) "This ... Reza Shah," and he pointed to a six-foot picture on the wall. Then he pointed to an adjacent picture while taking out a box from an inside pocket, upon which was written the word MINISTER. "Minister," I said, very willing to help the poor man out. "This ... Turkoman. This ... landlord. This ... mrs. landlord." And so it went for a full hour!

Tomorrow the Ministry of Information has arranged for me to visit a kindergarten at my request, and I'm told that, if I want a job here, they will help me find one.

3/10/66

Well, let's see what's been happening these last two days. I've been to the Golestan Palace, the Archaeological Museum, and a kindergarten. With Bill Roche, a Peace Corps volunteer who works in cooperation with the American Joint Distribution Committee, I visited the *mahaleh*, the old Jewish ghetto now inhabited by both Jews and Muslims. It is impossible to tell the difference between the two, except for the fact that Jewish women never wear a black *chador*, a cloth wrap-around in Tehran. Bill is doing a survey there about the number of people on relief, their problems, and their needs. Included in the visit was a look at the Jewish Youth Club, run by Bill, and one of the six synagogues. The Jews greet Bill with "*Shalom*" and, instead of responding with "*Salaam*," he also replies "*Shalom*." This confuses them. They don't understand why he uses Hebrew if he is not Jewish. He is Catholic.

In the *mahaleh* I saw a man standing and twirling on a large metal platter to scour it. Wouldn't that be fun to try?!

Judy took me to see a performance of "Pahlavan-Katchal" ("The Bald-Headed Hero"), a classic puppet play adapted for human actors and presented for the American Women's Club at the Iran-American Society. It was enjoyable despite its performance in Farsi and my limited understanding.

I saw the crown jewels so beautifully displayed in the vault at Bank Melli Iran. They are to Iran what Fort Knox is to the U.S.A. Surely there is no collection in the world like this: a globe of sapphires, emeralds and diamonds, a jeweled throne, diamond- and ruby-studded sword cases, tassels of seed pearls, bejeweled epaulets, glittering hubble-bubbles, and women's jewelry that is incredible even when standing in front of it. The Central Bank of Iran has issued currency worth 7,922 billion *rials* on the strength of the crown jewels instead of gold reserves.

Then I went to a *zurkaneh*, a House of Strength. They are physical fitness gyms for men, but the exercises are unique—push-ups and push-downs with boards; twirling weighted wooden clubs; heavy metal chains swung back and forth over the head—and all to the rhythm of a drum and the chanting of a drummer.

Iranians are a very handsome people, but it is unfortunate for me that so few speak English. My sign language is improving rapidly! I'm constantly pursued by lottery ticket sellers, and now one can see a few *Haji Firouz* roaming the streets. They are men who, at the time of the New Year on March 21st, go around in crazy costumes, painted faces, and carry musical instruments to entertain anyone who'll offer them *baksheesh*. In Iran, I'm spending extra *rials* on pistachio nuts. They're so delicious here!

I am now thinking of ways to get out of Iran. I had thought of going up to Moscow and then back down to Turkey, but traveling with Intourist, as one must, would limit me to dull buildings and offer no opportunity for exploration on my own. Thus, I eliminated that. I had also thought of going up to Trabzon, Turkey, then taking a ship through the Black Sea to Istanbul, but I think I shall eliminate that plan, too, for varied reasons. I'm going to the Syrian Embassy today to try to get a visa. I'm not stopping there but the train passes through. The trouble is that the governments in Iraq and Syria are so unstable now one never knows what may ultimately happen. I shall, at any rate, probably leave Iran next Wednesday, the 16th, or thereabouts. Tomorrow I'm heading south for about four days to Isfahan, Shiraz, and the 4,000-year-old ruins of Persepolis.

3/11/66

I feel I must get today's experiences down on paper before they fade from memory. It was a seven-hour bus ride down to Isfahan through barren desert backed by snow-capped mountains and various geological formations in shades of russet, brown, green, and white; past small villages built of mud bricks, where shepherds and their flocks roamed; and where long stretches of desert were colorfully broken up by flowering almond trees.

I checked into the hotel then wandered up to the Chaharbagh Madrasah (theological school), completed in 1706 and the last of the mosque buildings built by the Safavid kings. The Safavid kings ruled in Isfahan and the kaleidoscopically beautiful buildings here in colorfully ornate tiles are to their credit. Then over to Chehel Sotoon—Hall of 40 Columns, 20 real ones and 20 in a reflective pool—which was originally a summer pavilion for Shah Abbas and is now just a bad museum. From there to the Joobareh, the old ghetto of Isfahan, where I had decided to attend Friday night services.

I walked into the synagogue, the largest of 20 in the Joobareh, and was greeted by one woman, Chouchana Javedanfar, with whom I communicated in French. I had been told that going to the Joobareh alone was not wise and not encouraged, but what resulted in my decision to do so was contrary to everything I had anticipated. Mrs. Javedanfar, a woman of 65, invited me to her home for dinner and assured me that her son, Isaac, a 25-year-old pharmacy student, spoke English. Once I accepted, she interrupted the service to introduce me to one of the worshipers and leaders—Nedjatollah Saparzadeh, a 26-year-old gynecology student, who also spoke some English. It was previously established, I should add, that I was a *mademoiselle*. I was taken to see the Torahs and the other two chapels in the synagogue, where Mrs. Javedanfar had to explain to all the worshipers that I was a Miss American Jewess. In embarrassment, I insisted that the service continue, and I took my place again with the women until its conclusion. Nedjatollah invited me to dinner, but Mrs. Javedanfar quickly invited him to join us at her home, where her son waited. We three walked to her home in another part of the Joobareh.

I can only imagine the surprise her husband and son had when they saw an American woman in their home for the first time ever. Mr. and Mrs. Javedanfar have been married for 53 years. Meir is 75. They have four children—two boys and two girls. All but Isaac are married. The ghetto area is built of mud brick homes and ovens for making bread three times daily, but the Javedanfar home is made of cement. Their two-and-a-half rooms are quite bare save for the Persian carpets on the floor and the pictures on one wall—scenes from Israel; drawings of Herzl, Moses, and Abraham; a wedding photograph of one son and his wife; and a painting of Shah Reza Pahlavi, his wife, and the Crown Prince. Ten years ago, it was explained, there were 10,000 Jews in the Joobareh, but 8,000 have since moved to Tehran and Israel—to the latter with the help of American Joint Distribution Committee and Alliance, a French organization. Dinner was served and Isaac proposed marriage (I turned him down, of course). Since I had my tape recorder, Mr. and Mrs. Javendanfar both sang Farsi songs for me. The family shofar was pulled out and blown, and then we spoke of Passover and how they celebrated it with the aid of the American Armed Forces *Haggadah* in English and Hebrew. I read the Four Questions—they wanted a demonstration of my ability to read Hebrew—and, at their request, sang "Addir Hu," "Dayenu," and "Had Gadyoh." It was getting late and despite requests to spend the night in their home, I excused myself with heartfelt thanks. I was given a bag of halvah (I had already tasted their homemade wine), then walked back to the hotel accompanied by Isaac and Nedjatollah—but not before Mrs. Javedanfar had kissed me warmly on both cheeks. Once out of the home, Nedjatollah proposed marriage. That's a record—two proposals in as many hours! It was a wonderful evening with a warm and loving family.

RADIO BROADCAST

An Isfahan Welcome
U.S. Educational Radio Network (Excerpt) 1966

It was only a coincidence that I was in Isfahan, Iran, on a Friday, but it was a good opportunity to attend a local synagogue service that evening. I chose one in the Joobareh, the Jewish quarter, despite warnings to the contrary.

The Joobareh—the correct term for it since there is no longer a ghetto as such—is a network of twisted, dusty alleys with cement and mud-brick walls rising on either side. Homes, well hidden behind the walls, are situated around a courtyard, perhaps three or four in each group. I had no idea where I was till a stranger suddenly stopped me and pointed into a dark and narrow passageway. At that moment, I heard the rhythmic intonations of Sabbath prayer and I entered the building from which they came.

Synagogues I have visited in Asia and Europe often relate in physical style and spiritual practice to the architectural forms and principal religion of each country. So it was in Iran. This particular synagogue in Isfahan was a large hall with a side altar reaching to the center. It faced west to Mecca and Jerusalem. Benches placed against the walls were decorated with faded blue tiles similar to those found in Persian mosques. Windows, open on the north and blind on other sides, formed recesses in the walls—an architectural design that has been used in Persian homes for centuries. On the floor lay a large number of overlapping Persian carpets, worn and faded. As in Islamic mosques, I slipped off my shoes as I entered.

I walked over to a wide tiled pillar behind which six women sat cross-legged on the floor, looking quite bored.

"Shabbat shalom."

"Shabbat shalom," *all six replied, suddenly animated.*

Their overtures in the Farsi language brought no response. Nor did Hebrew.

"Parlez-vous Français?" asked one woman.

"Oui, je parle un peu Français."

One French-speaking sexagenarian was wrapped in heavy, mismatched clothing, a sheitel *(wig) on her head and a* chador *(a full-body-length semicircle of fabric with no hand holes that was worn over her head and shoulders). The direction of the conversation was almost predictable. Within two minutes she found out I was an unmarried Jewish American tourist in Isfahan for one night. In the next minute I found out she had a bachelor son studying to be a pharmacist...and would I please come home with her that evening for a Sabbath meal. I said yes, smiling at the earlier warning not to enter the Joobareh alone and that women are never welcomed into homes there.*

Once certain I would come, she stood up and, with great commotion (and my total embarrassment), called to the young man leading the prayers.

"Nedjatollah...Nedjatollah! See who's here! An American tourist! She is unmarried!" That much of the conversation yelled across the sanctuary was obvious; the rest was beyond my understanding. I was led to the front of the altar, introduced to the men present, and welcomed warmly by them all. Nedjatollah, who spoke a smattering of English, was pleased to meet me...and would I wait for him until the finish of the service. I did not reply to his request but begged him to continue worship and quietly retreated back to the corner.

My dinner hostess had other ideas. I was led outside to probe deeper into the dark passageway from which I had entered. In the back were two smaller synagogues. I was taken into both, generally introduced to all present, and the same story was related each time: "an unmarried American Jewess in Isfahan for one night."

By the time we returned to the first synagogue, the service had ended and my new friend began leading me to her home. Nedjatollah was right behind us with a dinner invitation for me. I explained to him that I already had plans, but the problem resolved itself when he came with us to the home of Meir and Chouchana Javedanfar and their son, Isaac.

I have often wondered what a great shock it must have been for Mr. Javedanfar and Isaac to see "what" was brought home from the synagogue that Friday evening. It was the first time a foreigner had entered their home, and they had no advance warning of the visit. Their hospitality attested to the family's warmth and loving kindness.

Their two-room home was situated on one side of a courtyard. As in the synagogue, the windows were recessed on all sides and open to the north only. Faded Persian carpets covered the floor. On the wall opposite the entrance were pictures of Moses, Abraham, the present Shah Mohammad Reza Pahlavi and his wife, and an elder son and daughter of the Javedanfars. In one corner on the floor were some pots, pans, a small kerosene stove for cooking, and a samovar, indispensable in Iranian homes for heating and boiling water. Mr. Javedanfar, who was smoking a hubble-bubble pipe while reclining against a pile of quilts, stood when I entered and vigorously shook my hand.

Nedjatollah and Isaac, both medical students, were obviously pleased with my presence. They were full of questions about my family, my unmarried status, my profession, my unmarried status, my travels, my unmarried status…and would I marry someone who wasn't American? Dinner was ready and the kiddush *was made with wine prepared in the Javedanfar home. Conversation was somewhat confusing: I spoke to the two young men in English, to Mrs. Javedanfar in French, and to her husband not at all, since there was no common language between us. I managed to turn the subject away from me and to their families, to schooling, to life in the Joobareh, and to the Javedanfars' desire to join their eldest daughter in Israel. Dinner ended and, while drinking a social glass of tea, the first of two major questions was asked by Isaac: "Will you marry me?" My answer, for reasons right and absolute, was no. Still, it was difficult to state such a refusal politely and without hurting his feelings.*

At this point, Mrs. Javedanfar brought out the family treasures—a silver menorah and a shofar. Isaac blew the shofar as he does each Rosh Hashanah and, simultaneously, everyone decided they must entertain me. Mrs. Javedanfar gave a brief fashion show with instructions for wearing the chador. *She and Nedjatollah each sang a song in Farsi. Then*

Isaac again blew his shofar, while Mr. Javedanfar became impatient for his turn. "Meir, Meir, Meir," he chanted, a broad smile on his bearded face, and everyone laughed at his gaiety. After his song, tea was served, and I was invited to stay at their home for the night. In fact, I was invited to stay for several days, but I declined their generous offer in the light of Isaac's proposal of marriage during dinner and my determination not to offend in any way this wonderful family.

I left the home accompanied by Isaac and Nedjatollah, who were to walk me to my hotel, and Mrs. Javedanfar, who escorted me to the exit of the Joobareh. There she hugged me warmly and kissed both my cheeks. I was surprised to find we both had tears in our eyes as we parted with "shalom."

Now that we were away from the Javedanfar's home and, since I had rejected Isaac's marriage proposal, Nedjatollah took his chances—despite Isaac's presence. It's a strange and sardonic discovery for a single girl to realize she has turned down two matrimonial opportunities in as many hours! How often do these things present themselves?!

The next day, Isaac came to my hotel to say goodbye and, since there was a full hour before my bus left, I asked him if we could return to his home so that I might take photographs of his family. My second unexpected appearance in their home sent the Javedanfars into a flurry of activity. Quickly the beans for Passover cooking were removed from the veranda where they lay drying in the sun. Three chairs appeared and, in a matter of minutes, Mr. and Mrs. Javedanfar had changed into their Sabbath-best clothing. Isaac, already dressed in an almost-fashionable suit, sat between his mother, who had removed her sheitel and chador but had substituted a kerchief, and his father, who wore a three-piece pinstripe suit and smiled with all the charm befitting Shah Pahlavi greeting visiting royalty.

Before my second and final departure, Isaac again proposed marriage and gave me his photo. His mother gave me a scarf and a peacock pin, both dear to my heart for the sentiments involved. His father waved and called, "bye-bye, bye-bye," in a childishly endearing way. These are all warm and cherished memories of a family I had known less than 24 hours, that shared their home and their love with a foreign stranger, and who shall always occupy a warm place in my heart.

[My experience in Isfahan was a true story of adventure, trust, hospitality, friendship, happenstance, intrigue, surprise, the passage of time, and a "Holy Moses"! Hear me out!

Let me set the stage. In 1966, Iran was ruled by Shah Reza Pahlavi, who instituted land reforms and social and economic modernization but had to rely increasingly on the secret police to control opposition forces of his reforms. By 1978, the political situation had deteriorated and martial law was imposed. In 1979, the shah and his family were forced into exile. That's when the Islamic fundamentalist Ayatollah Khomeini returned to Iran and the Islamic Republic was proclaimed.

That same year, 52 Americans were taken hostage inside the U.S. Embassy in Tehran. That period of time did not bode well for the Jews of Iran. Emigration accelerated after the 1979 Islamic Revolution. The Jewish population dropped from 100,000 to about 40,000 as they emigrated to Israel, the United States, and Western Europe. In 1979, also, the honorary leader of the Jewish community was arrested and sentenced to death on charges that included economic imperialism and contact with Israel and Zionism. Since the revolution, more have been executed as spies. Today there are fewer than 9,000 Jews in Iran, the majority in Tehran.]

[Here's the rest of the story...

For many years I thought of the Javedanfars, wondering if they were safe and if they had been able to get out of Iran.

And then, somehow, in December 2015, by way of an email newsletter from Israel or a story in an Israeli newspaper sent over the Internet, I saw a byline from Meir Javedanfar with an email address. Might this be the grandson of the Meir Javedanfar I met in the Joobareh? I was excited by the possibility. Armed with his name and email I wrote to him:

"In 1966 while traveling in Iran, I had the privilege of sharing a Sabbath meal in the home of Chouchana and Meir Javedanfar in Isfahan's Joobareh. I met their son Isaac and know that there was an older son and daughter, as well. Because of your name, might you be the grandson of Chouchana and Meir and the son of Isaac or his older brother? I wandered into the Joobareh to attend Friday night services in a synagogue where Chouchana "picked me up," so to speak. The spontaneity and joy of that wonderful visit has been imbedded in my memory ever since. I was a journalist at the time and had written a short report on the welcome reception I received. I read it again last night, which prompts my note to you. If, indeed, there is a family connection, I would be happy to send you what I wrote. You would find it an interesting and unknown anecdote of your grandparents. It is also possible that Javedanfar is a common name among Jews in Iran and there is no connection at all—but wouldn't it be fun if there is?!"

There was no answer to that email, and I thought for certain there was no connection, that he thought I was a crank, or that he wasn't interested in responding. Until mid-April 2016.

"Please forgive my tardy response. This email somehow got lost. Yes, you have the right Javedanfar. My father Isaac still remembers you. What a small world. Do you still have the newspaper clip from your interview? I would love to see it. Thanks for getting in touch."

There were more emails, then I sent him the story above about my visit to his grandparents' home in Isfahan.

"Holy Moses!," Meir responded. "This is amazing family history." I sent a photo of his grandparents and his father—a poor photo but a photo nonetheless—several of the Joobareh, and one of the colorful peacock enameled pin his grandmother had given me. He sent an update of the family's journey from Isfahan to Tehran to the UK and finally to Israel. His father had become a pharmacist. Both grandparents had passed away, but his grandmother—smiling Chouchana, the instigator and my warm and welcoming hostess, lived to 100. How true that strangers are only friends we haven't met. "You have made me very happy," wrote Meir. I felt the same way.

This Meir Javedanfar is the owner and editor of *The Iran-Israel Observer*, an author, lecturer, radio and TV commentator, and a frequently quoted Israeli expert on Iranian affairs.

To think that 50 years later I would reconnect with the Javedanfar family is both astonishing and extraordinary! This wonderful random adventure of mine really has come full circle!

And from Meir himself: "Thank you…You have breathed life into an important part of our past."

The sweet coda, the icing on the cake, and the cherry on top:

Late one night just a few days after an exchange of emails with Meir, the phone rang. His father was calling from Tel Aviv! We were both so excited! Words came tumbling out! Isaac and I chatted about my long ago visit, his parents, and our families today. At one point he gave the phone to his wife, Sarah, who speaks English more easily than he does. Of course, we each hope for a future visit in Israel.

3/13/66

I spent yesterday morning with a rep from the Ministry of Information, who took me to the School of Fine Arts; another synagogue; the Shah Mosque (for ladies of the harem); and the Khajoo Bridge, where Persian carpets are washed after they've been laid out on the road. Cars pass over the carpets to make them look aged and to beat out the dust and dirt. We also went to the Lotfollah Mosque, one of the architectural masterpieces of Iranian architecture. The vivid blue and turquoise tiles at the mosques in Iran are exquisite.

A 7-hour bus ride down to Shiraz took me again past long stretches of desert, sagebrush, and mountains that get their beauty from the pattern of sun and shadows playing upon rocks and crevices.

This is an example of the exquisite mosaic-tiled buildings in Isfahan, Iran. Mosques and palaces are covered in intricate geometric patterns, swirling calligraphy of the texts of the Koran, and the graceful arabesques of Islamic art—all with an emphasis on turquoise and cobalt blue colors.

There I was met by another rep from the Ministry of Information, who promptly took me to the Ministry's offices at Radio Shiraz and introduced me to the bachelor director, Assdollape Mondmanpeure. We visited the tombs of Hafiz and Saadi, Persian poets of world renown, and the bazaar—in some ways more exciting than that in Isfahan for nomadic desert tribes, in clothing both unique and colorful, come to the bazaar for their needs. Then lunch with Mr. Mondmanpeure, who proposed marriage! It seems to be the current fad in Iran!

The manager of this hotel I'm now in is typical of the men one meets throughout Asia. Actually, I suppose the women are the same, but most of my time is spent with men. You know the type—they exist in Europe, as well. He thinks he speaks English, and you think he does, too. He has a good beginning: "Where are you from?" "Do you want breakfast?" And even "What about Persepolis?" So you relax, confident in the security of his knowing English and his perpetual smile. You ask him a question: "What time is the bus to Persepolis?" Perpetual smile. "May I have my bill, please?" Perpetual smile. "Can you wake me at 5:30?" Perpetual smile. And your confidence collapses for want of a common tongue!

Questions I'm asked here: Are you with the Peace Corps? Are you a missionary? Are you traveling alone? Don't you have any friends?

3/15/66

Early yesterday morning I went to Persepolis to see the 4,000-year-old ruins created by Darius the Great in 500 B.C. and completed by his successors. It was well worth the visit. When it began to rain, I spent half-an-hour in the mountain tomb of Artaxerxes, but I couldn't stay there forever, so I tramped around in the wet and the cold weighted down by the heavy mud that clung to my shoes. The visit had an unfortunate after-effect. My rheumatism did not leave me when I left Japan as I had hoped it would, and I was awake all night on the bus to Tehran with a throbbing pain in my left knee. It is still with me now, though I've taken some medicine to relieve the pain.

Sorry about the mess this letter is now in. Apparently my suitcase wasn't well covered on the top of the bus. The rain leaked through and, now back in Tehran at the Frankel's, I'm drying everything out on the line.

3/18/66

I left Tehran by bus to Baghdad on the 16th. When we stopped for lunch, I saw a Japanese man from another bus. I can only imagine the shock he had when a Caucasian redhead approached him in a small town in Iran speaking Japanese. It was most amusing, and I have to admit I spoke to him only for the effect it would create!

In Kermanshah, we stopped for the night at the TBT Rest House, owned by the bus company. What a scene that was! The manager's assistant approached me babbling away in Farsi. A helpful elderly Pakistani on a pilgrimage with his wife came to the rescue to translate. I was put in a room of my own, which was later to cause such chaos, and then went out in search of food. There wasn't a restaurant in the area and again the Pakistani man came to my rescue. He asked me to join his group—some older men on pilgrimage, some younger men on their way to Frankfurt in the hope of finding work with the U.S. Army. On my bus there was one American, two Iranians, three Afghans, and all the rest, Pakistani. I joined them, and they quickly provided me with tea, biscuits, and apples. Then they asked me to sleep in their room—for two reasons: 1) they felt it was safer than to stay alone and 2) that way I would be charged only for a bed and not a room. But the manager wouldn't hear of it, nor would he allow me to sleep in the same room with the Pakistani's wife while her husband stayed with the men. An argument ensued and then a minor tussle, at which point the manager's assistant was locked out of the room. An unfortunate incident because he started banging on the door, so that everyone in the rest house was aware of a disturbance. I ended up staying alone at only a little more than the cost of a bed (40¢) after the bus driver marched in and pulled me out! Then I found out there was more to it. The men should not have offered tea to a lady—that's forbidden with Iranian men—and, further, they were Pakistani and a bit of prejudice was evident in the grimaces and hand signals of the driver who escorted me upstairs.

The road from there to the border took us up into snow-capped mountains, past shepherds and their flocks and their mud-hut hamlets. Do people in these situations and locations realize the beauty of their surroundings? That they are rich in nature if not money? Or is it only the wealthier that can concentrate on extraneous things when there is no need to worry about the very basics in life of food and shelter?

In this area are a great many Kurdish people—distinguishable by their dress, their black fringed turbans, and their dark features. When three of them boarded our bus to cross the border, they entertained us with folk songs.

My traveling companions—Iran to Iraq

After all the trouble I had getting my tape recorder into Iran, I left it in my suitcase on top of the bus. But the Customs officers did not make us unload the bus as I had feared. My honest face, no doubt. Nevertheless, getting everybody through Customs in both Iran and Iraq took a dull total of five hours!

And then to the unhappy country of Iraq—3-1/2 hours from the border to Kadhimiya, a suburb of Baghdad. During those 3-1/2 hours, the bus was boarded seven times by military police! Twice my passport was demanded and once the book I was reading was grabbed from my hand, and the plain white paper bookmark was examined. For what?! Incriminating notes? Disappearing inked messages? When no "evidence" was found, both were thrown back at me.

Once settled in a hotel, I went out for tourist information and wound up at a travel agency called Baghdad Tours, owned in part by Nuri Salmu, an Iraqi-born Catholic and a bachelor, who is emigrating to the states on the 31st with his sisters and mother to join his brothers already there. Nuri took me out to dinner and then to a nightclub. It was there I told him, only after a revealing comment he made, that I was Jewish. He warned me never to tell another person, but I'm glad I told him for I learned a great deal. There were once 100,000 Jews in Baghdad; there are now 2,500. I asked him what would happen if it were found out that I was Jewish. "They'd throw you in jail as an Israeli spy and prosecute everyone who had contact with you here."

Today we called a Jewish business contact of a friend in Japan. We were told he was too ill to answer the phone. The man who did answer the exporter's phone quickly stated that they were no longer in business, though he acknowledged Mr. Nakamura after quite some time and with a good deal of caution. He may have been protecting himself. The exporter had already sent a note to Mr. Nakamura that he was awaiting my visit.

This morning I met Sabih Dawood, Nuri's accountant but a graduate in civil engineering. He's Jewish, a bachelor, and extremely likable. The three of us spent the morning together. I later learned that Nuri asked Sabih if he'd like to spend some time alone with me. His answer was no. "She's nice and I like her, but I'm scared. I can't take the risk."

Yes, the Jews are scared. Since President Abdul Salam Mohamed Arif took over, things have gone from bad to worse. Jobs are denied them, export licenses are not forthcoming, property is confiscated, and passports are not allowed for them. Sabih is desperate to leave but, unless he smuggles himself into Iran, there is no way for him to go.

The three of us drove out to Ctesiphon on the left bank of the Tigris. The building that remains dates from about the third century A.D. Its Sassanian hall is the widest single span built of bricks in the world. On the way, we were waved past by military police at several checkpoints and general points of interest were noted: the military camps; the cannons and tanks; Parliament House, which is used for government offices since there is no longer an elected Parliament; and the building in which Karim Qasim was killed by a bomb in the revolution of '63. (Qasim was a nationalist Iraqi Army brigadier who seized power in a 1958 *coup d'état* when the Iraqi monarchy was eliminated.) We passed by monuments "to the revolution" and the inevitable question was asked each time, "Which revolution? 1958 or 1963?" We drove past Unity Park, once Opera Park, built by Qasim but renamed by Arif, then to the Unknown Soldier's Mosque near the monument to the Unknown Soldier in any revolution, which has never been completed because of continual government changes. It is hard to say who hates Iraq more, Nuri or Sabih. From the comments they made, I said they'd both be thrown out of the country, and Sabih, with all emotion possible, wished for that. Nuri is leaving in two weeks. Inside the car, we spoke freely; outside, in whispered tones.

The car we were in, a Muscovitch made in Russia, was owned by Nuri's cousin—good looking (the car, that is), smooth running, a dashboard of hard plastic. Cost in Iran: $2,240. Another of Nuri's cousins owns the hotel I'm staying in. And another owns the Baghdad Hotel, the plushest in Iraq.

The countryside is not much to look at aside from the date palms and the groups of Arabs passing the time of day. Baghdad, cut through by the Tigris River, is surprisingly modern, though not in the least attractive. Its political situation makes it positively ugly. I've heard disappointing things from tourists who've been here and even travel agent Nuri tells me, as a friend, that there is really nothing to see and my desire to visit Nineveh—assuming I get police permission, for there is a war up there now between the Iraqis and Kurds—he considers a waste of time, though I must go there anyway enroute to Turkey.

To complete the picture of Iraq, the women, as in Iran, wear long black cloaks—*chador* in Farsi, *abaya* in Arabic. Many of the men and children wear *dishdasha*, which look exactly like long cotton or flannel nightshirts. (You should see the boys play soccer in these long shirts!) Those that wear the Arab headdress, wear *kufia* and *agal*.

3/19/66

I shall add a bit each day, but I shall not mail this until I reach Turkey. Mail is sometimes passed through censors and were that to happen, Nuri, Sabih and I would all be in dire trouble. I cannot take that risk.

Spent the morning getting permission to visit Mosul, for which I stated my occupation as teacher. It took 1-1/2 hours to get it, but it would have been longer had not Nuri's friend, Zuhair, himself a military officer, accompanied me. I saw eight different officers there, some of them twice, and when the chief officer asked Zuhair's name, even he was scared. He gave Nuri's name, but the chief officer demanded to know his (he was in civvies) and what his relationship was to me.

Zuhair is a close friend of Nuri's, but even he can't be trusted. At lunch, Nuri told him I would be in Turkey a month and was meeting my mother in Istanbul. Everyone is on edge here!

We were going to drive down to Babylon today, but it has been raining heavily and it's nonsense to traipse around in the mud. Instead, I am spending part of the afternoon working on the flowers I'm embroidering for you. I had hoped to finish them by the time we meet but the work is time-consuming, and I so rarely have time for it while traveling.

> [As the time got close to meeting my mother in Israel, these letters were filled with requests for dresses, stockings, shoes, underwear, mascara, bandages, and bleach tablets. I even asked her to pack light, so she could return to Rochester with a full suitcase filled with clothing I no longer needed. There also was much confusion about my mailing addresses since I wasn't sticking to an itinerary or a calendar.]

3/23/66

I am free to write again, no longer responsible for the safety of others. You have read the first three pages of this letter, and I'm sure you realize how I would have implicated Nuri, Sabih, Zuhair, and myself. For fear that I might be searched, I rolled up the letter in an empty Tampax tube and packed the dummy tube with a hundred others. All notes after that were written in unintelligible (except to me) cryptic form, even including some Pitman shorthand.

[My mother had always encouraged me to study shorthand because it would be so valuable if I had a secretarial job. It certainly did prove to be valuable, though not the way she intended!]

The morning of the 20th, I visited the Iraqi Museum, thought-provoking but frustrating 'cause nothing was labeled. In the afternoon, I finished the embroidery for you and, in the evening, Zuhair picked me up to drive me to the train station. He is reticent in his answers to my questions, but you find that in everyone. All seem afraid and nervous—and military officers are no exception. He was a guard at the Presidential Palace for a time. Every day was hell, he said, for in a revolution (and people seem to think there will be another before too long), he would be the first killed. He's now in a special training program only because that allowed him to be free of the other, more onerous and dangerous assignment. It is unfortunate that he likes me as a friend, for I don't feel I can be his friend. Being with him, or writing to him as he wishes, is living a lie and remembering that lie. It makes me uncomfortable. Had I met him under any other circumstances, I would have ignored or avoided him. But because he is Nuri's friend, I treated him kindly. Perhaps that was a mistake.

I took a night train to Mosul on the main line to Turkey. It was a simple passenger train but looked more like a troop train. Mosul is an old town 268 miles north of Baghdad. It is not a pretty city—mud houses and treeless dirt streets. It is not as urban or advanced as the capital city and, thus, a great many of the women still walk about veiled. One also sees armed pro-government Kurdish soldiers in baggy-pant suits and colorful sashes. There are few outward signs of a nearby rebel war, except for the hundreds of government troops and the one armored tank moving about town.

I went out to see Nineveh. As Nuri tried to tell me, nothing was there. An empty field. Nothing remains of the Assyrian Empire and Sennacherib's city between 705-681 B.C.

Yesterday morning I boarded the Turkish train passing out of Iraq, in and out of Syria in an hour, and into Turkey, where we were welcomed by thin-legged storks standing in their nests on the chimney tops and a fat-legged woman with a fat hypodermic needle ready to give cholera shots to those who had not yet had them. What a reaction they had after she "shot" them! So glad I planned ahead!

Fun and games—someone just lobbed a rock through a train compartment window.

RADIO BROADCAST

Trouble in Iraq
U.S. Educational Radio Network (Excerpt) 1966

[Names changed for the broadcast.]

"Don't ever tell that to another person while you're here! Don't you realize you could be thrown in jail as an Israeli spy?"

I hadn't realized—or, perhaps, refused to realize—that the atmosphere of the place in which it was whispered in frightened tones was hardly suggestive of danger. The music was gay and the guests animated as I sat with a Christian acquaintance in a large nightclub in Baghdad. I had just told a new Iraqi friend, named Ahmed, that I was Jewish. It was at that moment he grabbed my arm and wildly looked about to make sure no-one was listening.

Looking back on my week in Iraq, I suppose I was foolhardy in going there, but my overriding sense of adventure never stops me from exploring new territories and learning about new cultures. I had been attracted to Baghdad and the biblical sights of Iraq, never once foreseeing danger. I had lied about my religion to get into the country and only revealed the truth after Ahmed spoke openly about his Jewish friends and their insurmountable problems.

When I was there in March 1966, President Abdul Salam Arif was serving as the second president of Iraq, having been part of the bloody coup that overthrew the Hashemite monarchy eight years earlier. In April and after I left the country, he was killed in an airplane crash, believed to have been sabotaged. But while I was there, Arif and the military were still very much in control of things. During the 3½-hour ride from the Iranian border to the capital city, the bus was boarded seven times by the military. Though the bus was filled with foreigners, I was the only non-Asian. Twice I was singled out and my passport demanded—once by a young man in civilian clothes.

"Give me your passport."

"Where is your uniform?" I asked, never knowing at what times to obey quietly.

"Passport!" he demanded more emphatically.

"Are you police?"

"Shut up and give me your passport!" he yelled.

I did, of course. Another time a uniformed soldier boarded the bus, grabbed from my hands the book I was reading; thoroughly examined the plain, white paper bookmark in the light; then threw both the book and the paper back at me with anger and disappointment in finding no secret writing nor anything incriminating.

Baghdad was not a very attractive city except at night. Along the date palm-lined banks of the Tigris River that slices the city in two, neon lights from new, modern buildings flashed in the dark waters. Orange flames from the oil refinery lit up the dark sky, while reflections of the smaller, flickering lights of the fish stalls danced in the river. At each stall, large fish, cleft in two, were speared on sticks and roasted in a circle around open fires.

Men paraded aimlessly in their western-style clothes, military uniforms, or in an Arab **dishdasha** with **kaffiyeh**, *a white or checked square scarf folded into a triangle and sometimes worn over a small white cap with the* **agal**, *a circular black rope or plaited-cord to hold the* **kaffiyeh** *in place. The* **dishdasha**, *the traditional dress of Iraqi men, is a loose-fitting, ankle-length caftan that looks like a long flannel nightgown. In cooler weather, a long tan cloak, called an* **aba**, *covers the kaftan, but it may also be wrapped loosely around the neck, across the ears and lower face to protect against the elements. Think Lawrence of Arabia. Underneath, the men also wear trousers and a coat. Iraqi women do not walk about at night. When seen during the day, they wear western-style clothes or an* **abaya**, *a long, black semi-circular-cut outer cloak that is thrown over their head and shoulders and covers the body from head to ankle. Under the* **abaya**, *they wear brightly colored dresses. Veils are only removed at home or in female-only groups.*

Most of the centuries-old ruins for which Iraq was famous were in a bad state of repair or inaccessible by standard transportation because they lie so near Kurdish rebel territory. Truly, there was not much to excite a visitor in Iraq...and few conveniences...and few really happy people.

In Baghdad and the northern city of Mosul in 1966, tanks and armed soldiers patrolled the streets. There were numerous monuments "to the revolution" and the inevitable question was always asked: "To which revolution?"

Walking in Mosul, my Assyrian guide explained: "This old bridge was built by the English; that new one was built by the Germans."

"When will the Iraqis build one?" I asked.

And then his voice dropped to a whisper and he moved closer to me. "That won't be for another thousand years or more."

In Baghdad, someone pointed out the Parliament House on the banks of the Tigris River and quietly sighed, "... but, of course, we no longer have an elected government here—only a dictator." That's how it was with citizens who dared to have dissenting opinions, who lacked faith in whatever Iraqi power was in control. In normally audible conversations, voices suddenly dropped to a bare decibel, and the speaker glanced nervously over his shoulders.

Ahmed introduced me to his friend, a military officer and a Muslim who had served for some time as a presidential palace guard. Knowing that he would be the first killed in a quick revolution (which was expected at the time), he had lived in constant fear of death. But he was luckier than most; he somehow had managed to get a transfer of duty. Despite his status and rank, he was reluctant to give his name to the commanding officer who, after eight subordinate officers had reviewed my request over two hours, finally issued the military police permit allowing me to visit northern Iraq. And, despite his close friendship with Ahmed, he could not be trusted with the information that I was Jewish. Ahmed went overboard to protect me. At lunch one day he suddenly announced, quite out of context, that I was meeting my mother in Istanbul. (In fact, I was meeting her in Israel.) And when I later asked casually, "How do you spell Karim Qasim?" (the presidential dictator before Arif), the officer snapped at me immediately. "Why do you want that information?" I was also questioned when I commented upon Iraq's refusal to recognize the State of Israel as such in all printed materials in English. It was referred to merely as "Israel" in quote marks—an important distinction at that time—in other words, that so-called nation of Israel.

Ahmed introduced me to a young Jew in Baghdad, a university graduate with a degree in a highly technical subject, but who was forced to work in an unrelated and unskilled area.

"It wasn't so bad before," he explained. "My family has always lived in Iraq and my parents just didn't want to move anywhere else. There were no hardships before; life was not unpleasant. Before 1948, there were 100,000 Jews in Baghdad; in 1966, there are 2,500. Things are terrible under Arif. Everyday we pray for the future, and I am not a religious Jew. We are denied jobs and business licenses; our property is confiscated; and worst of all, now we're refused passports and can't leave here unless we somehow manage to escape into Iran." Then he quickly switched to an innocuous conversation on Ctesiphon and Babylon, and thereafter pointedly avoided all reference to Judaism.

The next day, Ahmed asked him if he'd like to spend some time alone with me. His answer: "No, no! It's too dangerous. I can't take the risk." And he couldn't, for had I been discovered in his company, I was told he would have been implicated for treason.

I called a Jewish importer with regards from a Japanese business associate. The importer himself had been ill in bed for more than ten days, I was told, when an assistant answered his phone.

"We don't do business anymore," he said.

"I have regards from Mr. Hirano in Osaka to ..."

"We don't do any business."

"Yes, but I only want to tell you ..."

It was five minutes before the voice at the other end reluctantly acknowledged Mr. Hirano but disavowed any business liaison.

A not-so-amusing part of this story was later revealed in a letter from Mr. Hirano when he sent me copies of the correspondence written by this Jewish importer just eight days before my arrival. (Was it possible, then, that he had really been bed-ridden for more than ten days?!) In his letter, he told Mr. Hirano how he was looking forward to meeting me and showing me around the city of Baghdad. What is more enigmatic, he enclosed a purchase order for U.S.$100,000 worth of Japanese goods. (Could he have been doing business without a license? And did I really talk to an assistant or to the Iraqi importer pretending to be someone else?) I had plenty of questions, but no answers then or now.

When it was time for me to leave Iraq, Ahmed was nervous. I had written a too-honest letter to my parents about conditions in Iraq and had endless notes on file giving names and places and facts of life in the country. Ahmed wanted me to destroy everything, but I refused. Instead, I did the next best thing—took all the papers and rolled them up in a little cardboard tube and buried it deep in my suitcase, where I thought it would be safe. It was.

3/24/66

The train arrived in Ankara at 7:45 a.m., and I asked a taxi driver to drive me to the YWCA. He didn't know where it was, so I found a Turkish man who spoke English and gave directions to the driver, who then understood perfectly. We stopped at TUSLOG (Turkish-U.S. Logistical Command) Headquarters. A man came out and asked if he could help me, then he, too, gave directions to the driver, who then understood perfectly. We drove on and stopped at a TUSLOG Detachment. A man came out and asked if he could help me. Then an American airman came out and asked the same question. At that point, I started to laugh—mild hysteria, no doubt! I asked if I could use the TUSLOG phone. Then the driver started worrying about his money. I told him I'd pay him what was initially agreed upon and refused to pay more for his having dragged me around. He refused to take me for that amount, so I removed my suitcases and dismissed him. I moved into the TUSLOG offices just long enough to get a room reservation in a "cheap but respectable" hotel. While waiting for a taxi, an amused bystander, Herman Fields, offered to drive me down since he was going that way. He has been overseas with the U.S. government for the past 20 years, the last three in Turkey. We drove by the embassy, where he stopped long enough for me to pick up your letter, then drove me to the Hotel Pinar. I'm having dinner with him this evening.

3/26/66

My first day in Ankara, the 24th, I walked and walked for hours. I saw a good deal on foot, but the countries of the Middle East don't hold the same charm and fascination for me as the countries of Southeast Asia. I'm not quite sure why. Perhaps I still feel deeply rooted in Asia.

Some observations:

I saw a horse going down a steep hill while traffic was stopped by the police. The driver kept tightening the reins, but that horse just slid all the way down leaving streaks in the pavement from his metal shoes. Totally unrelated, superstitious Turks pin evil eyes—blue, black and white stones—on their children's clothing. And Turkish men have small feet and "brushtaches." (That's what I call their big thick mustaches that look like brushes.)

Yesterday I whiled away time at the American Library, had lunch with Herman at the Officers' Club, then met him again for cocktails in the evening. He introduced me to some wonderful associates there, and I enjoyed our conversation. I wanted to stay in Ankara in the worst way, but I knew that, if I had to fly to Tel Aviv on the 28th, I should get to Istanbul so I could see a bit of that city.

The train trip to Istanbul was quite comfortable. The seats in second class become bunks, so I was able to stretch out. Once off the train, I caught a ferry across the Bosphorus and went straight to the El Al office, where I was able to cancel my reservation on the 28th and make another one for the 4th, arriving in Tel Aviv only a few hours before the first Seder. I was almost ready to hop the first train back to Ankara. But what's done is done. I expect to meet Herman again in Israel or Athens; the latter will be his new assignment after May. And a whole new world of adventure awaits me in Istanbul.

El Al fixed me up at a perfect hotel in old Istanbul on the other side of the Golden Horn and in a cobblestone square near the famous Blue Mosque. It's about $2.25 a night. But I haven't budged since arriving 'cause it's another dreary, rainy Turkish day.

Now that I'll be here till the 4th, I think I'll investigate buses to Izmir and then to the ruins of Ephesus. While I can't see all of Turkey in nine days, I'd like to see as much as possible.

3/27/66

Yesterday afternoon was spent at the covered bazaar, the world's most perfect maze. It's a fascinating jungle of meerschaum and alabaster and brass and embroidery and nuts and carpets and jewelry and antiques and leather and socks and…a hundred thousand other things! It's high pressure, too, but in a humorous sort of way. One merchant invited me into his shop, asked if I'd been in Israel, then in Iran, and finally came to the point—"Are you Jewish?" The merchant, David Musazade, offered me tea and conversation. He was born in Russia but grew up in Meshed, Iran. He likes to have foreign guests in his home on Friday night and was most disturbed that I didn't come a day earlier. Also at the bazaar I met a part-time merchant and full-time student, Daniel Sengül. Last night he took me to a nightclub to see authentic Turkish belly dancers.

Today was bitter, through-to-the-bone-kind-of-cold, and rainy. I was out in it anyway—to the St. Sophia Mosque (first a church, then a mosque, and now a museum) and to Topkapi Palace and Museum. There I met Murat, a friendly 20-year-old Turkish university freshman, and a German chemist, Mr. Thomashevske, traveling alone for six weeks in a Volkswagen minibus. I was invited to join them. Since it was so cold and we all felt it, we returned to the minibus, drank tea, and ate a sugared French toast delicacy made especially by the Turkish student's mother. The three of us went on to the Archeological Museum; the Hippodrome (the little that's left of it from 325 A.D.); the Obelisk of Theodosius in perfect condition with excellent hieroglyphic inscriptions; the Sultan Ahmet Mosque, more familiarly called the Blue Mosque because of the bluish reflection on the blue-green tiles inside. It was built in 1616 and is the only mosque with six minarets. Then on to Süleymaniye Mosque, 1557; the Eyup Mosque outside the old city walls; and a fortress overlooking the Marmara Sea. There is much to excite the senses in old Istanbul!

In old Istanbul I am once again in Europe—it becomes Asia across the Bosphorus—and that is sad and frightening. While not exactly "close" to home, I am closer now than I've been in many months. I am still emotionally rooted to Asia and, forgive the harshness of truth, I am still in no way willing to return to life in the U.S.A. The hour I reach NY may be the hardest I've had to face.

3/28/66

I had dreamed of having a real Turkish bath in Turkey. But where to find one? I was instructed to go to a particular courtyard and yell out the caretaker's name several times—very loudly—till he heard my call and came to fetch me. And that was my introduction to Cagaloglu Hamam, a bath built in 1741. Any relationship to what you think of as a Turkish bath and an authentic Turkish bath is purely coincidental. Let me describe it. In the center of the front room is an octagonal marble fountain long out of use, with drying towels hung over its side. Money collectors sit to the right amidst fresh towels slung over a couch and chairs. To either side of the door are wooden enclosures for those who prefer privacy. On three sides are steps leading from the marble floor to the tiled floor and nine leather couches on which clothes are placed. Around a central platform are little alcoves, each with a floral-patterned marble fountain, hot water gushing from modern spigots. It was steamy, but not too steamy. Five rays from the sun pierced the steam, shining through star-shaped holes, now covered with glass, in the high domed ceiling. Women smoke, eat lunch (and throw their orange peels about), nurse babies, and relax. Women who are massaged, as I was, sprawl out in the nude on the central platform. It is an experience and a method few foreigners might submit to. A standard massage is designed to stimulate tired muscles, but this one is done with one hand and a rough fabric. It is a milder scrub and does nothing more than scrape out the dirt from pores opened by the steam. When my masseuse, with pendulous breasts and dressed only in cotton underpants rolled down over her big belly, saw how many little twists of dirt were rolling around, she was delighted and made sure I understood the success of her efforts. Total cost was 53¢! Being in there made me realize what a harem might have been like. I imagine that in its early days, this marble bath must have been really elegant. Today, only a suggestion of past luxury remains.

Once refreshed, I walked up to the Eminönü area to the Misir Çaşisi, the old bazaar where foreign traders historically came to purchase spices. Today, though, it's not quite as exotic, nor even that intriguing, except for the Yeni Square where Turks mount their "soapboxes" and discourse. I visited the Museum of Islamic and Turkish Art, which may have the best collection of Korans and Koran holders and the goriest miniatures. Then to the Byzantine aqueducts under which modern traffic passes and to a nearby mosque that is not on any map. Meandering leads to priceless discoveries! Finally to the Yerebatan Basilica Cistern and Binberdirek Cistern built by the Byzantines with its 224 columns, though the name means "thousand and one columns."

In India I remember being amused to see a Brazilian and a Japanese girl conversing in Italian. In Turkey, I converse with the natives in French. It's taught in Turkish primary schools; English comes later in high school and university study; and not everyone makes it past the first stage.

3/31/66

Yesterday Murat and I went to the zoo (perhaps the world's worst!); to the bazaar again; then to Kariye Mosque, which has the most glorious Byzantine mosaics. "Glorious" is the word from the guidebooks and, while I never depend on their inflated descriptions, this is one case where even "glorious" understates the facts!

Then a 15-hour bus ride here—to Izmir, once Smyrna, in western Anatolia, the port on the Aegean Sea. I'll explore the city briefly on Saturday, for I didn't come here to see Izmir itself. It is the starting point for visits to Ephesus and Pergamon.

And today in the rain, which is getting to be as natural in Turkey as the rain in Spain's plains, I wandered around Ephesus, about 52 miles south of Izmir. In order to see Ephesus and the House and Chapel of Virgin Mary on top of Mt. Aladag, it is necessary to walk about 10 miles in all. Luckily, I hitched a ride with a restaurateur and his food up to the mountain—walking only about three miles in all.

In St. John's Gospel, there is biblical and historical truth that claims to make this the actual home of the Virgin Mary, her last home before death. It was easy to visualize Mary living in this tiny home, fetching spring water, enjoying the panoramic view below her mountain, and relishing the beauty of spring daisies that grow on the hillsides as abundantly as grass.

The deity of Ephesus was Artemis (Diana), mother of the gods, and it was here that the Temple of Diana, one of the 7 Wonders of the Ancient World, was located. Ephesus dates back prior to the eleventh century B.C. Once one of the world's greatest cities, in the sixth century B.C., it fell to Croesus of Lydia and then to Cyrus, the Persian. In 334 B.C., Alexander the Great established his democratic government here. Later it became the first port of the Roman province of Asia. In 55 A.D., St. Paul came and spent three years founding the first Christian community. In other words, Ephesus is rich in history. Its streets are paved with marble; there is a large amphitheater; a gymnasium; a small concert hall; the Library of Celsus (he was governor of the province of Asia in the second century A.D.); and numerous other remains of what once was. In the town of Selçuk two miles away, I visited the Basilica of St. John, built in the sixth century A.D. Beneath it is the tomb of St. John and the Archaeological Museum. Then I headed back to Izmir for a good night's sleep to prepare for tomorrow's exploration of Pergamon.

> [I am not surprised years later to read this bland and edited report of my Ephesus visit, but must note that the worst experience of all my travels took place at Ephesus. I was alone and presumed the man walking well behind me was no threat—until he caught up with me and tried to throw me to the ground. Fortunately, I had been gifted with a few karate lessons before leaving Japan in the event I might need them. I must have learned something, for I left my attacker groaning and writhing on the road, his hands pressed between his legs. Since I was writing this diary to my parents, I left out anything that would be of great concern to them. Indeed, I never shared with them this attempted rape, but it is as clear in my mind now as it was when it happened so long ago. Suffice it to say that I was shaken but not harmed, and I left that Turk in agony on the roadway as I ran down the hill to safety.]

4/1/66

Hello April! It's hard to believe that it's here already. Traveling around like this I hit summer weather in February, winter in March. I go for so many days without sight of an English newspaper I never know what's happening in the world. Although I do know about boxing. The waiter in my Istanbul hotel informed me with elation that "Chuwalo...(George Chuvalo—V's are pronounced as W's in Turkish)...finished... Clay...good!" He had to show me Clay's picture in the Turkish paper before I could figure out why he was so happy! And each time I begin a letter home, I have to figure out what day I'm on.

Pergamon reached its real state of importance during the Hellenistic period with the arrival of Lysimachus, one of the generals under Alexander the Great. Like Ephesus, it was later handed over to the Romans and became one of the principal cities of the Roman Empire. There are two sections to it, 5-1/2 miles apart. The first is the Aesculapium, built in the name of the god of medicine. Here the sick came for cures by means of sun, water, baths, drugs, dreams, and therapeutic play. The other is the Acropolis where the altar to Zeus was located and the library, from which Mark Antony took the entire collection of 200,000 volumes and sent them as a gift to Cleopatra in Egypt. It is rather nice, I think, to imagine the great Mark Antony walking up the ancient road past the Temples of Hera, Demeter, and Athena, up to the King's Palace and the nearby bibliothèque. Ruins are, after all, nothing more than broken pieces of stone and marble, often lying about but sometimes held together with modern man's invention of cement and plaster. It is the imagination that brings these bits to life and assembles them as a visionary whole. And what stories they tell!

After visiting the Archaeological Museum and the little amusement park in town crowded with people because Friday is the Islamic Sabbath, I still had some time to kill before the bus left for Izmir. I decided quite impulsively to see half of a Turkish movie for all of 9¢! It was a modern comedy with a western plot. At one point, the film stopped. There were deafening catcalls and whistles. Windows at the top of the theater were immediately pulled open, and I could think only that it was to prevent a sudden riot in the increasing heat.

Tonight I'm devoting to the study of German, which I'm quite sure I'll need but which is stymying me completely. Something else you can bring me that I haven't been able to find: a Berlitz French book. It won't take long to brush up my French, and I can always fall back on that. And, if Berlitz puts out a Hebrew conversation guide, bring that, too. It will help both of us.

Yesterday I walked around Izmir to an old Roman street, the Agora; the ruins of a market built by the Romans; to the Archaeological Museum; and to Kültürpark, which is exactly what you think it is. Here the Izmir International Trade Exposition is held each year. It's a well-kept modern park; 2-1/2¢ admission is charged; and guards stand about to make sure no-one violates the flowers and fountains.

Another night bus brought me back to Istanbul, and I spent today with Murat. We took a boat ride up the Bosphorus to as near the Black Sea as one can go without permission, then we wandered about Rumeli Castle in the narrowest section of the Bosphorus Strait on the European side. It was built in 1452 by Sultan Mehmet II for the final attack on Constantinople, which led to the downfall of the Byzantine Empire. (As the song says, "Istanbul was Constantinople. Now it's Istanbul, not Constantinople. Been a long time gone, oh, Constantinople—Why did Constantinople get the works? That's nobody's business but the Turks!") From there we went into the center of new Istanbul. I felt I had to see it at least once.

Murat's English, by the way, is far from perfect, but that's what's so wonderfully funny about it. He gets ecstatic over the musical sounds of some words—like "satisfaction"…"stranger"…"Stewart Granger"—and repeats them over and over again.

He really is a gem. So wish you could meet him!

[All these names and dates enable me to keep track of and remember places and details. I didn't want to lose what had been so important. To spare readers, however, I've left out abundant facts and figures of information! Really, I have!]

4/6/66

Shalom!

For someone who never had any particular interest in coming to Israel, I certainly was excited as the plane flew into Lod Airport. I felt almost as if I were coming home. It was most strange.

The Whiteson's Seder was very enjoyable. There were 14 people in all with Joe and Sophie's two sons, Theo and Harry, and their families. What a wonderful family it is and how happy I am to be a part of it! In a bit of speechmaking prior to the Seder, Joe expressed his disappointment that you, too, Mom, were not with us.

Yesterday morning I was up early and took a long walk around Ganei Yehuda, a pleasant suburban community. Then I drove about 30 miles up the Mediterranean coast to Netanya with Rima and Danielle, Harry's wife and daughter, to pick up Rima's Great-Aunt Polly visiting from South Africa. In the evening I played bridge with Joe and Sophie and two of their friends.

To think there was nothing here 15 years ago, not even a tree, and now there is so much. And the orange blossoms—oh, Mom, just wait till you smell how they perfume the countryside! It's such a joy to sleep with the windows open!

It's warm here now, definitely spring. Bring transitional clothing that can be worn in the evenings with a jacket and in warm days without a jacket. Don't bring any hats, for women just don't wear them in Israel. And you might want to bring a swimsuit, for it's warm enough to swim in the Dead Sea, and we may well be in that area.

4/10/66

My mind is filled with new impressions! I've been living on a kibbutz for two days. On the night of the 8th, I quite suddenly came up to Kibbutz Yizre'el, four kilometers from the Jordanian border, with Keith Greenberg, a cousin of the Whiteson's daughter-in-law. The kibbutz is located in the Valley of Jezreel. There are about 120 official kibbutzniks here—70 children and 50 adults, whose average age is 25. It's an agricultural kibbutz, mainly fruit trees, but they raise milking cows, milking sheep, and eating hens. A kibbutz is only half of what American Jews think it is. My first shock was the hashish smokers. I'll spare you the other "truths." I never thought I was cut out for permanent kibbutz life, but I wanted to try it for a few days. I don't like it. I don't like making 136 hamburgers (I'm on early kitchen duty now from 6:30-noon) for unappreciative workers with their minds on more important things like cotton planting. I don't like seeing 50 adults with the exact same plaid boots. I don't like the idea of children sleeping in homes away from their parents, only to be seen at certain hours. I don't think I'd like the lack of intimacy in family life. I don't like the communal dining. It takes a special type of person to be able to live in such a close, dependent, and static society; I'm obviously not that special person. The whole thing to me seems like spending one's entire life at Camp Seneca, including the walks to the showers and the walks to the mess hall for food and evening entertainment. To look at a kibbutz from the outside only is a different matter. In terms of end result, the work is gratifying—that type of society seems to be just perfect for those who've accepted it. The kibbutzniks are happy and sing all the time and somewhat pity the poor unfortunates on the outside. Minor irritations pass and big problems, like medical bills and clothing expenses, are all provided for.

Some residents, both men and women, are soldiers serving their time in kibbutz service. No other military is in evidence but, because this kibbutz is so close to the border, two armed guards, members of this kibbutz, patrol the premises all night. The rest of us are responsible for checking for bombs or anything else suspicious under our cabins each night. Strange as it may seem, it's as routine as brushing one's teeth before bedtime.

Kibbutz Yizre'el was established by demobilized Palmach soldiers in 1948 next to the abandoned Arab village of Zi'rin. I'm told that the biblical Jezebel lived in that village at one time. The people here now are predominantly South African, Australian, and Israeli. Two Dutch girls are here for four months of service, and visitors come and go.

4/14/66

I left the kibbutz yesterday and went to Nazareth. While living in N.Y.C., I had an Arab friend, Zahi Muammar, whom I thought might now be in Israel. But when I telephoned his family, I learned that Zahi is still in New York. His family invited me to visit them. They live in a comfortable home overlooking old Nazareth. Only two of the seven children are left at home and they, too, are leaving. Rita, the youngest daughter, named after Rita Hayworth, is getting married this summer. And Ramzi, the youngest son, is leaving for Denmark next month. Last night Ramzi and I went into Haifa. A highlight of that visit was the view of the harbor from Mt. Carmel. I spent the night at the Muammar's home, woke up to the aroma of Turkish coffee and was treated to an unusually large Arab breakfast. Rita showed me some things she's purchased for her marriage, then Ramzi took me for a brief tour of Nazareth. There are two Churches of the Annunciation, one Roman Catholic and one Greek Orthodox. Both claim to be the real site; take your pick. The Greek Orthodox, however, offers a bit more—the stairs by which Angel Gabriel entered Mary's cave. And I always thought angels flew! We visited the marketplace and an old synagogue in which Jesus is said to have worshipped. And Mary's Well, which seems to be in every ancient biblical city!

Yesterday I stated that the Iraqis expect a revolution any day. And today, Abdul Salman Arif, Iraq's second president, is dead and a fight for power is on.

4/16/66

Mom arrived in Israel!...and already she's climbed and crawled through a barbed wire fence to visit a 2,000-year-old Roman mausoleum. And, at a ruined castle now used part-time by Bedouins and their animals, she saw her first camel outside a zoo and was all excited.

Your letter, while welcome, made me uncomfortable, Dad. And now I don't know how to explain my position. For some reason I assumed that everyone realized I would not be home for Harv's graduation. Obviously, they did not, so I must apologize and beg understanding. As you surely must know from all my letters, I am thriving on my experiences! Though fleeting, life is extremely meaningful at this time. Everything but family is here: Japan, Malaysia, Iran, the world. I have no job to return to in the states, no definite idea of what I want to do, and no idea where in the states I want to work. I suppose I am undecided about everything because I just don't feel ready to return. The best of everything, the least of problems—is to enjoy my life as it is now and live it to the fullest, relishing every moment for now and forevermore. I know that when I left the states I aimed my return for Harv's graduation. While I'd like to be with the family to share the glory of the moment, please try to understand why I will not be. I'm sure Harv will forgive me. I do not know when I'll be back in the states, but there's always time to take that family vacation after I return. I hope you can feel what I'm trying to express.

If Harv should be drafted and sent to Vietnam, I assure you that nothing will keep me from returning before his departure. But his graduation doesn't seem to justify a return when I balance it with all other factors.

I will be applying for a job with U.S.I.S. (United States Information Service), which would be government work in some country of this wide world. If I get such a job—the embassy doesn't even have exam dates yet—I shall, of course, return to the U.S. before going to my post. Were I in the Peace Corps, I would be away for two years, and I see that my own private peace mission will stretch out as long.

4/20/66

Yesterday Mom and I went by bus down to Eilat, the southernmost tip of Israel, within easy sight of the Jordanian city of Aqaba and the mountains of Saudi Arabia and only a few miles from Egypt. But it is Israel's quietest border. Egypt learned its lesson during the Sinai campaign in '57, and Jordan is wise enough not to arouse trouble in its only port. But I am digressing.

The ride down to Eilat at the northern tip of the Red Sea was long but rewarding. Through Beersheba, past Bedouin encampments, and a stop at Avdat to visit the remains of a Nabatean-Roman-Byzantine castle, below which is an experimental farm where a professor at Jerusalem University is trying to cultivate lands using the same canal techniques employed by the early Nabateans. From there to the Negev, into the Mitzpe Ramon depression with its raw beauty and multi-colored sands, then to the alluvial plains of Meyshar and through the Arava Valley.

In 1948 the Arabs tried to limit the Jews to all areas north of Beersheba, but an old Turkish law stated that, if the roof of a house is put up overnight, the inhabitants within cannot be displaced. So on Yom Kippur night 1948, Jews from all over Israel came into the Negev and overnight, after a day of fasting, built roofs on the homes of 11 villages in the Negev. These kibbutzim, now grown considerably, enabled Israel to stretch as far south as the Red Sea. Today their green and fertile fields rise out of the desert like a vision, but they are an even more awesome sight from a plane. It is unimaginable to see what can be accomplished in a barren land, but it is also incredible to see how beautiful the valleys, deep craters, and ochre mountains are in a still tortured desert.

Into Eilat after a quick tour of the Timna Copper Mines and Solomon's Pillar, a natural rock formation. In the evening I went out with Miron Galia, our tour courier. He's a fascinating character—ex-member of the Irgun, twice-divorced, and with a quick sense of humor. He's had a checkerboard career.

This morning we toured Eilat by bus and visited an Eilat stone factory where they make jewelry. Imagine my embarrassment when I walked up to Miron and jokingly asked: "So, what did you buy me?" And he handed me a pretty pair of earrings. I don't think I'll ever ask that question again—even in jest! We went for a ride on the Red Sea in a glass-bottomed boat, then went swimming. After lunch, Mom and I flew back to Tel Aviv via Arkia ("up to heaven"), Israel's inland airline.

4/22/66

Just returned to the Whitesons from Jerusalem. It's an impressive looking city. The highway corridor leading there is strewn with armored vehicles, grim memorial tombstones to those who were ambushed and killed during the siege of the city in '48. Jerusalem is in many places only spitting distance from Jordan and/or No Man's Land. Walls are built up high to prevent injury from trigger-happy Jordanian snipers. Signs scream border warnings.

New Jerusalem is unquestionably new and modern. And what is consistent throughout is the good taste in construction and design. Hebrew University is so modern it's distracting, and its ultra out-of-the-world modern synagogue is so cold and barren I couldn't bear to be there for even five minutes. We visited the Shrine of the Book; Herzl's tomb, the Israeli equivalent of Arlington Cemetery; the incredible Hadassah Medical Center and its synagogue with the colorful Marc Chagall stained-glass windows; the Mandlebaum Gate; Mt. Zion; David's Tomb—"light a candle for the dead, for the living, for the sick, for the healthy"; the Mea Shearim district where Chasidic Jews stone passing cars on Shabbat; and Yad Vashem, a powerful memorial to the memory of the six million Jews— "Forgetfulness prolongs the exile; Remembrance is the secret of redemption" from the Baal Shem-Tov.

Today there was a mixed synagogue tour: Yemenite, Sephardic, Persian, and Middle Eastern. Prior to the walking tour the guide gave examples of how various Jewish sects worshipped with imitative chanting and jokes in Yiddish and English. What a rabbi he'd be; I would enjoy his sermons!

4/25/66

Hag sameach! Happy 18th Independence Day! *Chai*! To life!

Mom and I went to an entertaining show last night at the Yad Eliahu Stadium in celebration of Independence Day. Following that we walked over to Dizengoff Circle in the center of town. Loudspeakers piped music into the streets; people danced; colored lights gave the scene a Christmas flavor (excuse the analogy); people chatted in sidewalk cafes; and holiday revelers bopped passing strangers on the head with colored plastic noisemakers. Sidewalk peddlers hawked candies and soda and crazy hats. Joy was pervasive!

This morning, we went to the Independence Day Military Parade in Haifa. I dislike such displays, but I was impressed to see what has been accomplished and acquired in 18 years. Jews have always been peace-loving; I felt most uncomfortable at seeing bombs emblazoned with a *Magen David*. The best I can wish for the Israeli Army is that their armaments should rust with disuse. May they never need to use them.

Incidentally, Israel has no Red Cross. It's the Red *Magen David*, or *Magen David Adom*. Also, the plus signs in school are not "+" but "T." Or, to be more specific, not a cross.

4/27/66

Mom and I are now on a three-day tour of the Galilee. Time is flying so quickly—she leaves the day after tomorrow.

First, we went to the ruins of Megiddo, a strategic point on the north-south caravan routes of old and, thus, the site of a Roman town, an Egyptian town, and those of King Solomon, the Canaanites, and others. We had lunch in Afula, only 10 minutes away from the kibbutz where I'll be staying but impossible to get to while on a tour. We stopped briefly at an olive wood art production center and an observation point overlooking Canna, where Jesus turned water into wine. We drove up and around new Nazareth, which is predominantly Jewish and, in old Nazareth, visited Mary's Well and the Greek Orthodox Church of the Annunciation—both of which I saw on my first visit to Nazareth and mentioned in a previous letter. From there to Deganya, Israel's first kibbutz founded in 1909 and located in the fertile Jordan Valley bordering Lake Tiberias. Fertile now, yes, but, when it was founded, this same area was a malaria-infested swampland. The panoramic view of Lake Tiberias is not only lovely but, conversely, frightening. Rising above the kibbutzim in this region are the hills of Jordan and Syria, and perched on these hills are Jordanian and Syrian military border outposts.

Last night while Mom wrote letters, I went out with our bus driver, Chagi Bry, who came to Israel seven years ago from Czechoslovakia and speaks about eight languages. I lost count!

Today, by boat, we crossed Lake Tiberias, from the town of Tiberias to Kfar Nahum (in Hebrew) or Capernaum (in Latin), then visited a second-century synagogue and the Tabgha Church of the Multiplication of Loaves and Bread. There Jesus allegedly took five loaves of bread and two fishes and satisfied the appetites of more than 5,000 people. Kfar Nahum was also the place of the Sermon on the Mount and the site where Jesus met Simon and Andrew and made them "fishers of men." In Safed (Tzfat in Hebrew), we visited the synagogue of Yosef Caro, writer of the Shulchan Aruch, and, finally, the local gallery for this artists' colony. In the old crusader town of Acre (Akko in Hebrew), we saw a caravanserai, the marketplace, the Mosque of Ahmet Jazzar, and a bonus performance of a Hebrew skywriter.

RADIO BROADCAST

The Galilee: Gemütlichkeit and History
U.S. Educational Radio Network (Excerpt) 1966

"*Shalom. Welcome.*" *It was obvious from the beginning that our three-day bus tour of the Galilee was going to be enjoyable. It was the* gemütlichkeit *of our group that was special, but what we saw—the history, the development of northern Israel, and the beauty of the region— was filled with vitality and wonder and excitement.*

First stop was Megiddo, an archaeologist's dream! Situated on the north-south caravan route from Mesopotamia and Syria to Egypt and overlooking the Valley of Jezreel, it was long a strategic outpost and the site of countless battles. Excavations that began in 1903 have revealed no less than 20 cities dating from 4,000 to 400 B.C.! To some people, ruins are nothing more than dislocated or broken pieces of outdated civilizations. Others, with more imagination, assemble them as whole and give them life. Megiddo can start a person on an incredible see-saw journey through past ages! It was frequently mentioned in the Old and New Testaments—"a place called in the Hebrew tongue Armageddon"—and more recently, in 1918, was the site of the Allied Armies offensive against the Turkish forces. When the British commander was later raised to the peerage, he took as his title Viscount Allenby of Megiddo.

Israel is so steeped in biblical history! On the hillsides of Mount Tabor, Deborah and Barak achieved victory, and Jesus was transfigured. In Nazareth the Angel Gabriel told Mary she would "bring forth a son and shalt call his name Jesus." It was here, too, that Jesus spent his youth. In Kafr Canna, six miles northeast, Jesus performed his first miracle: the transformation of water into wine at a wedding feast. In each place we relived these historical moments so well known to all.

Past half-ruined Arab villages our bus climbed up to Mitzpe-Kinnroth observation point and suddenly there was the impressive but fearful panorama of the Jordan Valley—the calm, blue water of the Lake of Tiberias/

Sea of Galilee/Sea of Kinneret—call it what you will; they are one and the same. There are the kibbutzim that created such lovely, green, fertile settlements out of what once was a malaria-infested swampland, as well as border outposts that perch dangerously overhead on the slopes of the Syrian and Jordanian hills. We then made the descent to Kibbutz Deganya Beit and its underground shelter for children, used whenever border clashes threaten.

The town of Tiberius, built by Herod in honor of the Roman Emperor Tiberius, is now a leading winter resort. Several hundred years ago, it was a center for Jewish intellectuals. The Tomb of Maimonides at the edge of town is a reminder of that period. In fact, little remains of old Tiberius; an 1837 earthquake reduced much of it to rubble.

The boat ride across the Sea of Galilee was not particularly interesting, but it was considerably better than cramped space on a bus! On the lake shores, Jesus met Simon and Andrew and made them "fishers of men" and Jesus multiplied five loaves of bread and two fishes and satisfied the appetites of 5,000 men. The Benedictine monastery at Tabgha has well-preserved mosaics representing this miracle and depicting the wild life that once thrived in the area. Nearby Arbel Valley where, according to Hebrew legend, the Messiah will be revealed, is the town of Magdal, birthplace of Mary Magdalene, the Mount of the Beatitudes where the 12 disciples were chosen and Jesus preached the Sermon on the Mount ("Blessed are the peacemakers for they shall be called the children of God"), and Capernaum, the Greek spelling for the Hebrew Kfar Nahum ("village of Nahum"), where Jesus preached. In Capernaum we visited a partially-restored second-century synagogue with its sculptured stone of a seven-branched menorah, the Ark of the Covenant, and a shofar on which the Messiah would announce Israel's redemption.

We drove up to the Palmach Memorial atop the Hill of the Twenty-eight with its commanding view of fertile Hula Valley and there heard the story of the 1947 attack upon this hill. It was an assault by determined and courageous members of the kibbutzim in the valley below and was told to us by our guide, who had participated in the fighting. It was narrated without passion, but silence followed his story as each person wrestled with unsettling thoughts.

Safed—or Safad, Svat, Tsevat, Tzfas, Tzfat, S'fath—is Israel's highest town and to Safed came the Sephardic Jews in the sixteenth century following their expulsion from Spain. Here they developed the mystical interpretations of the Old Testament called Cabal. Now known as much today for the artists as the Cabalists, Safed boasts an old artists' quarter and winding cobblestone lanes. We visited the museum to see works of local artists and the synagogue of Yosef Caro, author of the Shulchan Aruch, a codification of Jewish religious practices in all phases of life. We drove past the tomb of Rabbi Shimon bar Yochai, second-century Talmudic scholar and reputed author of the Zohar, the Book of Splendor, a mystical documentary on the Five Books of Moses and basis for the Cabalist beliefs.

Acre, Akko, or Ptolemais is one of the oldest cities in the world and today recalls, in particular, the Ottoman empire. A walk past the ancient port, Crusader sea walls, and through the noisy bazaar and Turkish caravanserai of Khan-el-Umdan brought us to the Mosque of Ahmet Jazzar Pasha, who built it in 1781 as part of a grand design to restore Acre as a commercial center and to remodel it on the plan of Constantinople (now Istanbul). It was Jazzar, by the way, who defeated Napoleon at Acre in 1799. How incongruous it was to look over the walls of the old Turkish city and see a Hebrew skywriter!

Haifa is the most beautiful of Israel's cities as it climbs the slopes of Mount Carmel and overlooks the Mediterranean. A visit to the clean and bustling port area revealed the fact that Jewish longshoremen look no different than all other longshoremen. A visit to Technion City disclosed an impressive university complex—perhaps the most modern technical university anywhere in the world. How pleasant it was, too, in Haifa to wander through the formal gardens of the Baha'i Temple and dream comfortable thoughts of a brotherhood of man!

Since I have a particular interest in ruins and potsherds, I was thrilled with our visit to Caesarea, the port city of Herod the Great, home of Pontius Pilate, a Crusader fortress, and source of countless graceful Roman columns removed by the Arabs and scattered about the Middle East. The long Roman aqueduct rises from the sands of centuries; yellow spring flowers burst between the cracks of Crusader walls; and *everywhere lies a potsherd collector's treasure chest. There is so much to excite the senses in Caesarea!*

There was a global spirit in our group: Jews from the United States, Spain, Brazil, Argentina, South Africa, and Germany. There was no common language among us but a common bond nevertheless. There were a few Christians in our group, including one German couple named Israel. The husband had lived among German Jews for many years and had once met a group of German Christians by the same name whose ancestors were Jewish.

The rapport between our driver and guide carried over to the passengers. People were at ease and in good humor. They were interesting tourists and interested in one another. When the scenery was of no special importance, we sang in Hebrew and Yiddish, coaxed by our driver or conducted by two South African girls. When free time was available, we teamed up; no-one was left alone. When it was time to say good-by to new friends, speeches were given and all prayed for peace and prosperity in this nation we had so quickly learned to love.

"Shalom...shalom...*one for today and one for tomorrow.*"

5/2/66

I am on the kibbutz again working in the garden and rooming with an English girl, Gillian Scott. When Gill finished her internship in London, she decided to take a break from medicine and came here for a few months. She paints in her free time and sold 25 paintings at a London exhibition. She's talented and intelligent and works in the garden with me. We are getting on well.

As you've probably read, Israel has been having a rash of trouble with Syrian el-Fatah members. Our nightly guard patrol has increased from 2 to 4 men and, tonight, 40 soldiers are staying on the kibbutz. They have guns and equipment and have set up ambush points. They move about in the area where trouble is expected. As this kibbutz is only 2-1/2 miles from the Jordanian border, the Syrians enter through Jordan. Two nights ago on a kibbutz 10 miles away, dynamite was found planted under one of the houses so now, on our kibbutz, there is a nightly check for dynamite. The room I'm staying in is about 20 yards from the edge of the living area and our toilet is even closer. If I had to go the bathroom in the middle of the night—well, I wouldn't! "Trouble" is expected between 8 - 12 p.m., since the men must recross the border before daybreak.

I know this letter will alarm you, though that is not my intention. I simply want to tell you the circumstances under which kibbutzniks must live. I recall with sour humor

My home on Kibbutz Yizre'el—as plain and simple as could be!

Mom's question: "Don't Israelis feel like they are living on a keg of dynamite?" There was an unfortunate scare several nights ago. One of the soldier girls stationed on the kibbutz was looking at a night guard's gun at midnight. She checked to see if it was loaded and it went off. No-one was hurt, but the gunshot and the Syrian trouble were enough to bring people running. It was a stupid accident that caused a terrible fright.

5/6/66

I found out the 40 soldiers who were with us the other night were here for one of two reasons: either army intelligence had heard of a planned attack on Kibbutz Yizre'el or they came to impress upon the people that they must be alert at all times because the situation is a real one.

There are 98 members on the kibbutz, excluding members' children. Members must be over 18, so the children must apply for membership just as their parents did. There are soldier girls serving their time in the army in kibbutz service, visitors like myself, and various groups that come here from time to time. We now have 50 members of a Nahal division here for a month. Nahal groups are made up of soldiers chosen to work on the development of kibbutzim. Many of them, it is hoped, will come here to live when they have finished their army training in two years. Most of the kibbutzim in Israel were begun by Nahal groups that participated in initial plans before new immigrants came and took them over. Many of the Nahal members do settle on kibbutzim. Of the last group that came three years ago, 21 settled here.

It is difficult to get "in" the kibbutz. Full members have a tightly closed society and do nothing to make newcomers feel at ease. It's strange, too, because they need and want new people to stay on permanently but do nothing to make them feel truly welcome. I didn't expect a large brass band or a royal red carpet, but I did expect some response to my cheery *boker tov* (good morning) or encouragement in my willingness to work anywhere anytime. Thank heavens for the few friends I have here; the rest make me feel like an intruder. None of this is a product of my imagination; Keith had warned me. I don't know if other kibbutzim are similar.

The routine here is simple, but on a temporary basis it's a pleasant change of pace. I'm working in the garden these days and begin at 5 a.m.. About 6, I go to the dining room for tea and bread to hold me over till breakfast at 8. (Hot chocolate pudding for breakfast is super special!) About 10:15, we—the girls in the garden—stop for coffee in one of our rooms or up at the hen house where friends work. Lunch is at noon and we knock off work at 2:30 or thereabouts. Our afternoons and evenings are free; dinner is at 7:15. It's not an exciting life, nor a stimulating one, and a long stretch of it would deaden my mind.

Much of one's joy comes from work, I think, and I do enjoy mine. There is nothing thrilling about hoeing and weeding, but I'm learning, too, about seedlings and transplanting.

I really haven't much to report; my days are rather repetitive. Ramzi Muammar, my Arab friend from Nazareth, paid me a surprise visit, and we drove to Tiberias for the evening to see how lovely the lake is by the light of the full moon. We also saw the excellent movie *To Kill a Mockingbird*. Tonight Gill and two English fellas are going to give a talk on their Easter pilgrimage to Jordan.

Just sold an article about Jews in Iraq to *The Jerusalem Post*, Israel's English language newspaper.

5/9/66

The night of the 7th, I went to bed with terrible stomach pains but woke at 3:45 a.m. yesterday feeling a bit better and decided to go down to the olive groves to wave the white signal flags for the crop plane that was spraying an experimental olive fly killer on our trees. The plane was due at 5, it arrived at 7:15 and, by that time, I was sick all over again. Spent the day in bed sleeping and upchucking, and dear Gill was nurse and doctor all rolled into one. She took my temperature last night and had us all in a panic. It was 104º, or so she thought, until she realized she'd been reading the centigrade thermometer incorrectly! But last night I moved into another room, one that had an adjacent toilet, and she moved in with me in case I needed her during the night. She's really been wonderful. Today she had to go to Tel Aviv, so Keith is bringing me food and good cheer. An Australian girl, who came to visit for a few days, was brought down to keep me company this morning. I like the idea of going back to work tomorrow, at least for a few hours, but I suppose I shall first have to check with the nurse—the real full-time one, not Gill.

The Australian girl, who has been living up north in Kibbutz Dafna, told me of a young Moroccan man there. "I would rather have my mother stay in Morocco where they say, 'Jew, Jew, Jew,'" he said, "than to have her in Israel where they say, 'black, black, black'."

5/14/66

This morning, as happens every Saturday, two truckloads of kibbutzniks went to Ein Harod for swimming in a natural spring. (See Judges 6-7 for the story of Gideon and Ein Harod.) Its stream has been diverted into a large swimming pool, built two years ago by the Gilboa Community Council. It's a wonderful place for a cool, refreshing swim.

This afternoon I played bridge. Evenings are spent in reading or conversation. You can see why I have so little to write about!

5/17/66

This is a sleepless week. We got back at 12:30 a.m. from a Swingle Singers concert at a kibbutz outside Haifa. Tonight is a movie, and that means midnight. Tomorrow night is a wedding. And every morning I'm up at 5. Friday is a *brit*, but that's at noon. The cold beer that follows the baby's bellow is much anticipated by all.

Today was beastly hot from a *sharav*, a dry hot wind that blows in from the desert. And with it, the biting flies and mosquitos make life really unpleasant. Just after work at 2:30, some of the children went swimming at Ein Harod. You are right if you guessed I joined them. It was a joy; didn't even miss my afternoon nap that is almost a necessity here.

5/21/66

The wedding was less than gala. I'm told it's not typical because the bride is not well liked and nobody felt like doing anything. It was a quiet wedding, not too much entertainment. I did the floral arrangement. I do two for the dining hall every three or four days. I am also now giving flower lessons to one of the girls here. I chose for the occasion peach-colored roses, white carnations, white delphinium, and marguerite daisies. The official wedding ceremony was conducted by an orthodox rabbi from Afula. The *chupah*, which consisted of the Israeli flag on poles, was built outside the couple's home. The wedding dinner was in the dining hall and that was followed by the traditional kibbutz ceremony: the older children, carrying flowers, form a horseshoe around the young couple who stand under a similar *chupah*. This time, the poles are replaced by two pitch forks and two rifles. The kibbutz contract is read, a silver trophy is passed on from the last couple married, and the children then present their flowers to the bride. Highlight of the entertainment that followed was a Chasidic wedding dance by the children.

Yesterday at mid day was the partial solar eclipse and the *brit*. People sat on the lawn outside while the *mohel*, also from Afula, did his business. Then there was beer, soda, wine, and snacks. A good time — and a break from work — was had by all.

This weekend a group of 30 high school students are on the kibbutz by invitation. We board and feed them, and they help us cut and bale hay.

Shavuoth never meant too much to me in the states but now I realize how joyous and meaningful the first harvest is. There will be big doings! Gill is preparing a massive art work for the dining hall, and each branch of the kibbutz is supposed to prepare a decorative float relating to Shavuoth and the Story of Ruth.

5/25/66

The Shavuoth celebrations were great fun. I tried staying awake to see Keith model a dress made of irrigation pipes and sprinklers, but what led up to it was all in Hebrew and extremely dull for me. I went to bed early and found out this morning that he was the star of the show and I had missed the spirited Israeli dancing that followed. Late today were the real festivities in the hayfield: presentation-of-the-first-fruits ceremony, dancing by the children, and display of the wagons that were quite clever: eggs piled high atop which sat a hen surrounded by baby chicks; one cattle beet speared with an oversized knife and fork; a calf wearing a pink ribbon and flowered wreath; a sheep and two bags of wool; a simulated tree and ladder; and two men carrying a bag of lemons on an irrigation pipe. This one parodied the official seal of the Israeli government: two men carrying grapes. The wagons were followed by a demonstration of our farm equipment—combine, baler, tractor, plow, etc. Lastly, the contests: a relay of laying irrigation pipes, cutting the wheat with a scythe, pushing the equipment with man power, and driving the equipment in reverse through an obstacle course. A great many guests were in attendance and a few members from the nearby *moshavim*. At day's end, everyone piled on to the vehicles for the short ride back to the living area.

As you've probably guessed, the opinions expressed in my first letter from the kibbutz have changed. I enjoy life on the kibbutz and, while I still wouldn't want to spend my life here, it's not nearly as bad as I had first imagined. By staying here till August, I'm avoiding the tourist season in Europe, and this is a good place to stay awhile. I'm still working in the garden and loving it. This past week I've been trimming peppercorn trees. You can look at all of them and tell how high my reach is. I was far more agile climbing trees as a kid!

5/29/66

The weekend was most pleasant—atypical of kibbutz life. I went into Haifa and visited the Museum of Japanese Art and made arrangements to leave Israel. August 23rd I'm going to Greece via Cyprus and Rhodes. Keith's not convinced I'll leave then either but, as things stand now, I see no reason for a longer postponement. That should get me home before real winter weather starts.

Friday afternoon Miron Galia called to invite me to Haifa for Shabbat. He was leading a group of Pioneer Women. Saturday, he and I and a couple from Skokie, who were on his tour, taxied out to Isfiya, a Druze village on Carmel. There we visited the Druze church and had coffee and candy at the home of the ex-mayor and father of Kamal Mansour, an Arab spokesman in the Israeli government. From there to Pin Hod, the famous artists' colony.

6/1/66

The days are getting quite hot, and I've decided to begin work at 4:30 a.m., so I'm finished by lunch. They've shortened women's working hours by half an hour, which was quite unnecessary but a beneficent gesture, nevertheless.

I took off today and went to Beit Shearim Burial Caves, about 12 miles from Haifa. In the second century A.D., Beit Shearim was the home of the Supreme Court, the Sanhedrin. Many of the learned and famous Jews of Israel were buried in the cemetery of the town, now a lovely grove of cypress and olive trees. Over the centuries the tombs were destroyed, the caves looted, and all were covered by earth and rock. They were unearthed in 1936 and there are still a number of sarcophagi carved with rams' horns, lions, menorahs and/or arks of the covenant. Quite interesting, I thought.

In the afternoon, I went to Beit Shean, similar to Meggido. I made it to the neat and pretty Roman amphitheater but decided not to climb the *tel* to see the remains of other civilizations. It was a blistering hot day, and there wasn't one tree under which I could have found a moment's relief from the sun. Outside the theater was a scattered assortment of broken columns waiting to be pieced together; but their seemingly haphazard method of storage made it all look like a scrap heap of secondhand, out-dated, and useless old columns.

6/4/66

Thursday, on a hot night caused by a *sharav*, a group of us decided quite impulsively to hitch up a wagon to a tractor and go swimming at Ma'ayan Harod. We arrived only to find the pool half filled but with enough water for a not too energetic swim. After, we divided into two groups: Israelis and native English speakers. The latter had a rousing good song fest.

6/8/66

I'm obviously getting acclimated to hard work. My hands are already like those of a laborer and, when a group of us go out to weed cotton, I'm the only one who doesn't complain of the strain. We have 150 acres of cotton and a heck of a lot of weeds, despite the fact that a selective killer was sprayed on just after planting. I always think that the horrid bending will put my back out of commission but, except for the first two days, it really hasn't caused me any discomfort. Knock on wood! But I love the work, and I'm learning much.

It might interest you to know, Mom, that girls on the kibbutz get cake ingredients once a week. We use what is called a Wonderpot for baking that is more difficult and temperamental than an oven. I've had great success with cinnamon nut, apricot upside-down, mocha rum, and raisin-date cakes. We get the basics; the rum or raisins or nuts we must buy in town. I usually keep half for tea time and give the other half to Keith. At one gathering, the hostess served a cake that looked alive, so covered was it with ants. Yet, nobody seemed to take notice. Each piece was served and eaten as if everything was normal. I was stunned but ate it—quickly and with my eyes closed! I guess a little added protein can't hurt!

Life has been a round of parties of late. Sunday night there was a congratulatory party for one of the fellas who flew to Holland to get married. Monday Gill and I had a party for 18 people. Today is a party for one of the New Zealand girls who's leaving. Three are visiting for a month, and the other two decided to stay till after we finish picking pears. We begin that in about 10 days.

6/17/66

I've had the odious job of watering trees—digging trenches, filling them with water, and covering them in again. When there's nothing to write about, something is bound to come up—and it did. While filling in trenches, I misjudged the distance of a pine tree and stuck my left eye in it. Pantocain stopped the pain but not the tearing. The nurse put a bandage over the eye and what a sensation that caused! More upsetting was the need—for the first time in 27 years—to depend solely on my right eye. Even with my glasses, I was worthless. I couldn't judge distances of anything near or far, and that made for some near falls, collisions, and breakages. It was a hell of a situation! This morning I went into Afula to see a doctor who said it was nothing and, while I'm still glassy-eyed and bloodshot, I can again see out of both eyes, and the left one will soon be fine again. You need an experience like this to learn how much we take our eyesight for granted.

6/18/66

I worked in the kitchen today washing and serving and watched a once-in-a-lifetime event tonight. For three weeks, kibbutzniks have been voting on the very important question of whether or not children should live with their parents. It took three weeks because they needed the votes of the members who are now overseas. Tonight they counted the ballots, and it was fascinating to watch the faces of those gathered around the ballot table. 98 voted—64 in favor, 25 opposed, 9 abstentions. Two-thirds was needed and there was excitement at the final results. Now the vote must be approved by the kibbutzim movement and then, most importantly, money must be found to add on additions to the homes. It was an important vote and the decision that children should live with their parents will forevermore change the pattern of life and work on Kibbutz Yizre'el. Having the child live with the mother and father alters nothing but housing and emotions. The mother will still have to work the hours she does now. The next question is at what age the children will live with their parents—from birth?

from two years of age? from five years? There are lots of issues yet to be worked out.

6/19/66

In 27 years—just once—am I allowed a "goof"?

(When my conscience heard it, she nearly hit the roof!

"You stupid thing," she wildly cried.

"Unfilial and remiss.

You don't forget such birthdays; you'll never explain this!")

I was hauled off by a camel...

No, no, that would never do.

Three Arabs came in darkest night...

Untrue! It's so untrue!

I might as well be honest, it was what they always said,

But forgetting family birthdays...

Oh dear, my color's red.

Ahem, dear parents, days slip by, no calendar on my wall;

I didn't forget the dates but the day.

The truth! And that is all.

I do hope I'm forgiven and, if you have a bell,

Ring belated birthday greetings from the land of Israel.

Love as always.

6/25/66

My few days in Tel Aviv were wonderful. I spent time with the family and with Miron. We went for a Rumanian dinner in Jaffa and a visit to the Omar Khayam nightclub, which you and I, Mom, passed by on our walking tour of Old Jaffa-by-the-Sea. The next night we went into the Yemenite quarter of the city and to an

Israeli National Opera performance of Orff's *Carmina Burana* and Ravel's *Bolero*. Seeing a hundred new faces every minute, being able to shop in a supermarket, taste different foods, and dress up like a lady convinced me more than ever I could never be a kibbutznik.

Last night on the kibbutz there was a bar and bat mitzvah for the first time since Yizre'el was established in 1948. It was a happy affair, followed by Israeli dancing.

7/2/66

I'm now on a four-day camping trip up north with Eddie Chambers, an English Catholic who's been living on the kibbutz for a year. He is a friend of Gill's and is now one of my good friends here. We started in Acre. In addition to what you and I saw there, Mom, Eddie and I went to the Museum of Antiquities (located in a once public bathhouse built in 1780), to St. John's Crypt (a Crusader structure from the thirteenth century), and to The Citadel. That was built in the late eighteenth century on Crusader foundations by the Turks and, during the Mandate, was the central prison of Palestine. It was this prison that you saw in the movie *Exodus*. At The Citadel is a museum of the underground movement during the Mandate and the hanging room where the British made martyrs of the Jews. A simple question to the gatekeeper produced a stirring account of the story of Dov Gruner, a Jew in the British Army, who captured a large store of arms at the British prison in Ramla and was later executed for his deed. From Acre we went to the seaside resort of Nahariya for a swim in the Mediterranean, then on to the Achziv camping site for the night. We rented a tent, cooked an early supper, explored the beach area and, when it got dark, made a campfire. We sat around it for a few hours talking, drinking coffee, and toasting bread.

Monday we went up to the Rosh Hanikra Inn on the Lebanese border. There is a great view from there of the Israeli coastline. Then to Mi'ilya, an Arab Christian village and the starting point for a hike into Montfort, a Crusader castle located on a high hill among mountains. Trouble was there were six forks in the road and only two signs. We walked miles out of the way in the first attempt but did manage to see it—and it was a sight worth our tired feet and sunburned noses. In the third attempt to get to it, when we knew we were on the correct trail, we decided it was too late to go. We still had to get to Kibbutz Sasa, which was expecting us for the night. The last bus to Sasa had long since left, and we were told it would be impossible to get to Sasa that day. But, we were lucky; part of the way we hitched a ride with a sympathetic taxi driver and then managed to get a ride right to the gate of Sasa with two Arab Christians who live in the nearby village of Gush Halav. (That's a name to remember, for the two men have invited us to visit the village for a day or two, and Eddie and I may go up there again.)

Kibbutz Sasa was settled entirely by Americans in 1949 and is the highest Jewish agricultural settlement in Israel, in easy view of Mt. Meiron and Safed. I was amused to hear they raise beef cattle and their "cowboys" ride motorcycles. They also have hens, but fruit is the biggest moneymaker. That evening, Eddie and I were with the resident doctor and his wife Geila, the lovely and charming daughter of Molly Bar-David, Israeli cookbook author, and friends of our friend on Yizre'el.

Tuesday morning, Eddie and I went to the second-to-third century synagogue at Kfar Bar'am. It is the best preserved ancient synagogue in Israel, but the stonework at the Capernaum synagogue was much finer. From there we hitched into Safed and took a bus to Hazor, the most extensive *tel* in Israel, site of the biblical settlements of Hazor. From there to Kibbutz Ayelet-Hashahar to visit the Hazor Museum, just half-a-mile from the *tel*. That evening Eddie and I stayed in the Yoram Youth Hostel, located on the shores of the Galilee. Naturally, we went swimming before supper and again before breakfast the following day.

Wednesday was our easiest day. We walked to the Church of the Multiplication of Loaves and Fishes at Tabgha, then hiked up to the Mount of the Beatitudes. The rest of the day was spent exploring Tiberias after an excellent lunch of fresh St. Peter's fish (tilapia) at a seaside cafe; a museum; the hot springs; and the Tombs of Maimonides and Rabbi Yohanan ben Zakkai and his disciples, located in a black basalt walled park. The tombs themselves are a bad joke—white-washed cement, decorated (?) with old scrap iron. Horrible!

> [Happily, Eddie and I are still good friends 50+ years later! The only difference is that now our spouses have joined the friendship. Twice we've been to their home in Leicester, England; they've been to ours in New Jersey and California; and, in 2017, we did a three-day walking tour together in the Yorkshire Dales.]

Eddie and I returned to the kibbutz at 6:15 where there was a message from Miron to meet him in Haifa at 6. He had forgotten my camping trip and had purchased tickets for the Israeli Philharmonic. There was a comedy of errors in getting together, but Miron's determination and a hired taxi did get me to this exceptional orchestral performance conducted by Zubin Mehta with piano soloist Daniel Barenboim. The concert was held in Haifa's Armon Theater with the roof open to the sky. Excellent!

Yesterday I left Haifa and returned to Yizre'el for a half-day of work. Last night I had an impromptu gathering when a few of my friends came over for coffee—they always know when I've baked a cake—and two others on guard duty dropped in for a break.

To ease your mind, I am not putting weight on. Indeed, I haven't looked so well in years: firm muscles, shapely legs, and a nice bronze tan—if I must say so myself!

7/9/66

My greatest moment of accomplishment on the kibbutz came this week when another girl and I finished laying an important and central area of lawn near the dining hall. The exhilaration came a few minutes later when I turned on all the sprinklers. Maybe I wouldn't have been so pleased if we hadn't worked so many days in the blazing sun to complete it.

There was a big party this week to celebrate the marriage of a couple wed 2-1/2 years ago. She, a Christian, and he, a Jew, were married in South Africa a few months before they came to Israel. Because it was a mixed marriage, it wasn't recognized by the State of Israel. She began the long process of converting to Judaism and, on Monday, they received notice that they were legally married according to Israel's laws. Good timing, too; the baby is due in a matter of weeks!

Mom, your letter indicates you're worried about Miron. I'm not sure what it is you're worried about. If it's marriage, he knows I'm not interested. He's a dear friend and being with him in the city atmosphere of nightclubs and concerts gives me the best of both worlds in Israel. Further, it keeps me balanced and stimulates my mind. A steady diet of kibbutz sameness would drive me nuts!

7/16/66

A visit to the Arab village on our property proved to be riveting. There's a church (from what century I don't know) and a stone with some form of writing on it—possibly Aramaic from the time of Christ. Also a Roman bath, several wells, and some areas cut out of stone. Everything is guesswork until further exploration is carried out by the government. It was the capital of kings Ahab and Omri in the ninth century B.C. Its name is linked with one of the first expressions of the concept of human rights recorded in history when the prophet Elijah appeared there and reproached Ahab after a dispute over the vineyard: "Hast thou killed and also taken possession?..." It is the site of Jezebel's summer palace and a Roman fort—the latter quite sensible because it commands a hill overlooking the important road from Cairo to Damascus. From the village of Jezreel (Zir'in, in Arabic) we walked over to the Palmach memorial (also on our property) commemorating the site where eight soldiers fell when taking the town from the Arab inhabitants in 1948. The memorial is a tall column with what looks like a hand pointing toward heaven. There's a stone bench nearby, so it seems to have been a park of some kind years ago, but is now overgrown with weeds. Next to it are several almond trees, but they are no longer tended. Most of the nuts are stolen by young boys from the nearby settlement of Ta'anach. We picked half a kilo's worth, but most were quite bitter. Then we walked down to our lemon orchard to pick a few and returned to make fresh ice-cold lemonade. It was a terrific afternoon!

Two days this week I was in the kitchen on serving duty. It was a pleasant change from working (?!) with the Israeli soldier girls here for a week. They don't work, in truth. They sleep under the trees, go to the toilet or for a drink of water, complain about how hot it is and how hard they must work. I worked with them in both the kitchen and the garden. At first, I tried to be cheery, then amusing, then like a sergeant (that is obviously what they thought when they asked if I was in the army), and then I lost my temper. After that I tried to ignore them. I'm so, so happy they are leaving tomorrow. When I was feeling out of sorts, someone said, "Smile, Wendy. Jews are supposed to have a sense of humor."

Tuesday afternoon I went into Nazareth to visit the Muammar family. Rita, their youngest daughter, is getting married on the 31st and they invited me to come in a few days prior to the wedding, so I won't miss any of the fun.

Also that day I visited the new modern mosque in Nazareth, opened just three months ago. It's not as charming as the older architectural styles but, then, neither are the new, modern synagogues, in my opinion. It took three years to build, and the devotees who built it on Saturdays and after work were paid no money. It was done, as the young guide informed me, for the love of God.

I typed up a newspaper article today about my experiences with the Javedanfars in the ghetto in Isfahan, Iran. (I have, by the way, received a letter from their son, Isaac). It felt good to be doing some real work again. If I could just discipline myself, I might be able to turn all this extra time into money. But people get so lazy here. Friends are always popping in for cake, coffee, and conversation and, in the heat of early afternoon, the only thing one has energy for is sleep. In many ways, it's an easy life on a kibbutz.

Too easy. I shall be here only another month. After that, until the 23rd, I'll be traveling south of Tel Aviv and spending a few last days with the Whitesons. On the 23rd, I sail for Piraeus. I'm eager to hit the road again.

Last night a friend on the kibbutz, who is a teacher elsewhere, was invited to Moledet near here for a party honoring 17 teenagers, children of members, who became members themselves of the *moshav shitufi*. This type of cooperative settlement combines the private family life of the moshav with the communal agricultural life of the kibbutz. Moledet is predominantly inhabited by *yekkim*—a sardonic, somewhat derogatory term for Germans that implies order. It is carefully laid out, and the path leading up to the theater was lined with well-placed bicycles. The other three from Yizre'el took immediate notice of the "order," as did two teachers who arrived from another nearby kibbutz. If you think watching family slides is a bit of a drag, you ought to go to a family gathering of 200 or 300! As each child's picture appeared on the screen, a cacophony of comments pierced the meeting place and quiet was a long time in coming. It happened last night at Moledet; it happened at Yizre'el at the bar and bat mitzvahs.

7/19/66

I was in Haifa again yesterday afternoon to pick up my ticket to Greece, then went up to Ahuza on Carmel to visit Hella Sheres, the Israeli woman who studied pottery with me at the Kyoto institute. Later I went to the Haifa Municipal Theater to see Shakespeare's *Richard III* in Hebrew. A large group from Yizre'el attended. I enjoyed the performance and, since I knew the play, the Hebrew didn't bother me too much. It was well acted and beautifully staged using only props. Shakespeare in Hebrew, with its harsh sounds, is not as flowing nor as poetical as it is in English.

7/26/66

One night last week sixteen of us decided to make our own dinner instead of eating at the dining hall. My contribution was *matzo brei*, which, believe it or not, no-one had ever eaten before! Another night, I went up to the dairy when Eddie was on the night shift and helped him milk cows for a short time, then wandered over to the sheep pen where two other friends were cleaning a freshly-killed sheep for a party we'll have soon. Cows and sheep that are going to die anyway are killed first. The diseased parts are removed and the rest is still good for eating. Thus the makin's of barbecues. Saturday morning I went target shooting with a friend (using a .22), then walked over to the cemetery (no connection in the activities) to see how it was laid out. There are three men buried there: the elderly husband of one of the members who died a natural death, and two young men—one killed by Syrians and one killed in a tractor accident.

One of my friends here was bitten by a poisonous viper. He's coming along well, but the really disturbing thing for everyone is that he was bitten when walking in a central part of the living area. I'm told there is a poisonous snake bite case every year. It's now one down and none to go!

8/1/66

Not too much longer here and an almost steady diet of kitchen duties the past two weeks helped me decide to take a few days' holiday in Safed—high up and cool.

Yesterday I went into Nazareth for Rita Muammar's wedding. (I skipped the pre-marital parties because of transportation difficulties on Shabbat.) I went to her home in time to see Rita put the finishing touches to her dress and veil. Then close friends of the family and relatives came. Sweets and soft drinks were served as guests entered. One woman played the *ud*, a lute-like instrument, and others took turns with the *durbake* hand drum. Several people were requested to dance to the Arab music. I was—and I did! Across the street on the neighbors' balcony, people gathered to watch the festivities and, as young children piled up the stairs for a closer view, a ten-year-old girl, employed to carry the trays of drinks, shooed away the kids. When that didn't help, she cuffed them across the head! Finally, the bridegroom's family came and, as they walked in, the mother sang, or, rather, screamed: "We have come for coffee; we have come for coffee." Coffee served to guests in an Arab home denotes the beginning of a long, close association and, when this ceremony was complete—i.e., the bridegroom's family claiming the bride—Rita was kissed goodbye by the female members of her own family. Rita and her mother and father then got in a car decorated with pink plastic roses and, with horns tooting, the whole cortege of taxis consigned for that moment went to St. Joseph's Church. Rita is Greek Orthodox; Elias, her intended, is Greek Catholic, so they were married in the neutral territory of a Roman Catholic church with an Italian priest conducting the service in Arabic. As Rita arrived, Elias was waiting for her, as were all the other guests who were lined up on both sides of the sidewalk leading to the church. Tourists happily snapped pictures of the Arab wedding couple. After the ceremony, guests lined up to say *mabrouk* (congratulations) in Arabic, and each received a souvenir ashtray and candied almonds.

Rita Muammar, Arab-Israeli friend on her wedding day

Today I went up to Kibbutz Dan, from where one gets a good look at the Syrian mountain project to divert the waters of the Jordan—or, more correctly, the Banias and Hatzbany sources. The third one, the Dan, is in Israeli territory. Work has been discontinued because of attacks by Israeli sniper planes. From there about four months ago, the kibbutz was hit by mortar shells.

I wandered around Safed's famed artist colony, in and out of galleries, and climbed up to the central park near the Metzudah, what's left of a Turkish fortress turned nightclub, to see distant

Lake Tiberias shining in the full moon.

It's a nice, easy holiday...and a lot more enjoyable than making 200 pancakes or doing KP duty for a crowd!

8/7/66

Before leaving Safed, I went up to Metulla, the northernmost settlement in Israel on the Lebanese border and to Tel Hai, the site of the heroic stand in 1920 of eight men led by Josef Trumpeldor, founder of the Russian pioneer movement. Kiryat Shmona (Hill of the Eight) is in the valley below, and it was from the original Arab village there that the attackers advanced and conquered.

Tomorrow six of us will go to Caesarea for a concert of songs, dances, and stories of Oriental communities in Israel. We are taking the kibbutz jeep and will pack a picnic supper to eat on the beach.

8/11/66

My visit to Jerusalem was pleasant. I went to Ramat Rachel, a kibbutz on the Jordanian border from where one gets an excellent view of Jordan and the city of Bethlehem. I also visited Abu Tor, a lookout over the old and new cities of Jerusalem. What a fantastic difference in landscape there is between the two countries. Israel is green with trees; Jordan is gray and barren. But the Jordanians are getting smart; they've begun planting trees in areas near the border. I passed an Arab village split in the middle by a zig-zagged border line. Several months ago, the U.N. met in Jerusalem to see about straightening the line, but Arabs from the Israeli half came en masse to the Knesset to express disapproval of the plan. They have running water and electricity in their homes; their neighbors in the Jordanian half do not. Despite Arab emotions and family ties, they preferred to remain Israeli citizens.

I went back to Yad Vashem and this time witnessed a prayer ceremony held daily at 11 a.m. when the eternal flame is rekindled. It was quite effective, and the cantor's voice resounding on the concrete walls added to it. I also returned to the Church of Dormition on Mt. Zion because I love the mosaics there, then visited the

Cenacle, the traditional room of the Last Supper. The best part of the visit was the Israel Museum, especially the Bezalel Art Gallery so filled with wonderful Jewish ceremonial objects and paintings. I was particularly struck by the display of marriage garments worn by the women of Morocco, Tunis, and Yemen. They were as strange to me as anything in the Orient, but there is a religious bond between those people and myself, and I was greatly moved by this thought.

I would not like to do farming permanently, but I wouldn't mind getting involved with flowers. Tomorrow night we've three wedding parties and the 18th anniversary of the kibbutz—and I'm in charge of all the flowers. In fact, I'm not working anywhere tomorrow except with the flower arrangements, corsages, and boutonnieres.

8/17/66

Shalom...for the last time. I left Yizre'el on the 14th, the day after I was given a farewell reception, announced on the bulletin board with a picture of a teary, bloodshot eye.

Now back in Tel Aviv, I'm getting organized. I will send out a last box from Israel. You have world renown, Mom! Sophie is convinced all over again that nowhere in the world exists a shopper like you.

Well, dear parents, so there will be a family wedding next year! Congratulations are in order to you, I should think, since you will be gaining a daughter. Hope she causes less trouble than this one! Yes, I know about it, and I'm happy because Harv is so happy. Now I must hurry home to meet my future sister-in-law. The ring, as you describe it, sounds beautiful. Leslie will be thrilled to receive it. How does it feel after raising the two of us all these years to know that one is taking that most important step? Let us all pray it will be a marriage ordained in heaven.

8/18/66

Thanks for everything you sent. You were psychic about my needing toothbrushes. As for the deodorant, it worked well today, and I was in the hottest place in Israel and the lowest place on this planet—Sodom and the Dead Sea.

I took a United Tour—with Miron as guide. First stop was the Bedouin market on Thursdays. A hustle-bustle of black cloaked nomads and Jews from all four corners of the world, including Indian Jews in *sari*. Then, down to Sodom with its gigantic mountains of natural salt and salt formations. Lot's wife could have been there if one is inclined to believe biblical legends. According to the Bible and twentieth-century geologists, Sodom was destroyed by earthquakes. Pleasing geological formations resulted, but nothing remains in Sodom today but a few coffee shops, a small hotel for rheumatic winter guests who come for therapeutic reasons, and the Dead Sea Potash Works. The sea, 29% salt, is a pastel turquoise, but it's not natural. It's caused by special green chemicals that are added to aid evaporation. The sea, white salt crystals, white potash, brown dykes, and rusty brown Jordanian mountains are picturesque. The rocks in the water are worn smooth and white, as is the driftwood. I didn't go swimming, but I had fun watching the others. They walk out and kneel and "plip"—their backsides rise to the surface and "poof"—the men's swim trunks puff up. People float on their backs and scull and have their pictures taken while waving with both hands in the air, or reading a newspaper, or gathering chunky salt crystals. Kids can't submerge; adults can't stand. I did go wading. The water has a greasy feel and must be removed well because the salt burns. A sign is posted stating that bathing is permitted with doctors' permission only—10 or 15 minutes maximum. It's hard to understand how a man drowned there in May, for it is almost impossible to sink.

8/24/66

Let me bring you up to date. My trip down to Eilat was brief but pleasant—all 12 hours of it! I had planned to be there longer, but I had to go to the doctor the same day. You remember, I'm sure, the accident to my eye. It's been bothering me periodically, but this past weekend, I was in real pain. I went to an eye specialist and it seems there is a scratch on the cornea near the pupil. Every time it begins to heal, the action of the lid opening reopens the scratch and thus the pain. I'm now on medication—ointment, drops, and pills—for two months to ease the pain, prevent infection, and strengthen the corneal tissue. I expect no more trouble.

[Actually, I had residual issues with that left eye for about 15 years until it was finally repaired properly, carefully, and completely.]

8/25/66

The ship from the port of Haifa sailed three hours late and has been off schedule ever since. I'm told, too, that it is cutting out a stop at Rhodes.

There are three in our four-berth cabin—myself and two women, one Yugoslav and one Polish Jew, Esther. There is no common language among us, but Esther's brother Henry speaks a bit of English. He's a dentist from Warsaw who will soon settle in Israel. Our cabin is small and unbearably hot; I have slept so little these past two nights! The ship itself is small and impossible to get lost on. There are no activities, no organization of any kind, and time is frittered away between deck and dining hall.

I met an English girl, Liz Beeson, when getting on the ship and we've been together a lot. I wanted to see a bit of Cyprus and she decided to join me but, then, so did Esther and Henry. So while the ship went to Famagusta-Larnaca-Limassol, we chose a different route. We disembarked at Famagusta and went to the old city built by the Frankish Lusignans in the thirteenth century. The old city walls are like that of a castle and there is a thriving village today. Then we went to Salamis, a town originally founded in the eleventh century B.C.E. Cyprus now has a total population of 500,000. When Salamis was at its height, there were two million people there. The ruins stretch for nine kilometers but not all are excavated, and part of the city under the sea now lies within view like a mystic coral reef. The best preserved part of the ruins are the gymnasium and baths. The Byzantine marble floors and pagan mosaics are the best I've seen of that style. From Salamis we went to Nicosia for lunch and saw little of the capital city—a bit of the surrounding moat and that's about all. It was then time to get to Limassol to catch our ship, which arrived three hours late. We had time to walk around the town a bit and wait and wait, then finally took a ferry out to the ship, or the "cage," as Liz dubbed it. The Cypriot countryside is nothing to look at, a few villages of gray mud-brick homes but certainly not picturesque. Police barricades frequently stop cars and check the permits of all passengers. Trouble between Greek and Turkish Cypriots is always ripe and these are precautionary measures. The old city of Famagusta is Turkish and is most heavily guarded. Sand bag barriers are scattered about all entrances and exits. We had no trouble in passing with our landing permits.

8/27/66

The ship arrived yesterday at Piraeus at 1 p.m. (four hours behind schedule); it wasn't until 3 p.m. that we finally made it through the visa lines! With the help of Nicolai, a fellow I met on the ship, I managed to find a cheap but clean hotel about a 5-minute walk from Omonia Square. By the time I was finally settled, I was weak from the heat and hunger; Nicolai and I finally had a chance to go for lunch at 5:15! Nicolai's real name is Savvas Nicolaides; he's a 34-year-old Cypriot studying law in London, a pleasant and kindly person. In fact, it's now only 9 a.m. and I am waiting for him to take me to one of those famous Greek beaches.

The Athens area is considerably cooler than Israel and Cyprus, thank heavens! I was quite struck by the view of the Acropolis coming into Athens, but I have done no exploring yet. Nicolai, who said good night at 7, came back at 10 to see if I wanted to go out for dinner and a walk-around, but I was too tired. First time in my history of travel, I think, that I didn't go out to see the sights immediately.

8/28/66

Yesterday was a good day. On the way to catch the bus to the beach at Vouliagmeni, Nicolai and I met Liz, who joined us. We spent about five hours there, then came back for dinner at an outdoor restaurant in the Plaka, the old section of Athens. There were musicians to entertain us and, when the Greeks began to feel their *ouzo*, an anisette liqueur, and *retsina*, an amber wine flavored with pine sap, the glasses started breaking—a Greek drinking custom. I managed to get to bed by 3 a.m., myself a bit heady from the *ouzo*.

This morning I went up to the Acropolis and again met Liz quite by chance. I think I've had a surfeit of antiquities. The Acropolis is impressive, as are all the other ruins in Athens, but I've seen better friezes at Persepolis in Shiraz, Iran, and more wondrous statues elsewhere.

9/1/66

I have come to the horrible realization that when the going gets rough, I am not a sailor. I never get sick—but I sure feel it! The afternoon of the 30th, I took a steamer down to Mykonos. Seven hours of up and down and rock 'n roll! Yesterday's crossing to and from the island of Delos was…well, briefer! Our little ferry tossed about like a cork, and I can understand how the Cyclades figured in Ulysses' *Odyssey*. One funny note: I was sitting in the lounge opposite the captain on the crossing; he was also feeling pretty green!

Anyway, I enjoyed Mykonos. I arrived at night and the whitewashing on streets and houses seemed like fresh-fallen snow and, where it faded in the streets, seemed like trampled snow. I liked the candles flickering in the churches and the lace curtains that danced in shadow play on neighboring walls. Best of all was the little girl reprimanding and swatting at a pelican as high as my waist, who ran along in front of her. I stayed that night in a pleasant *pension*. Delos was marvelous, an archaeologist's dream with extensive ruins.

I arrived back last night but the crossing was calm, or, perhaps there were just too many people for the ship to rock about. Dozens of Greeks boarded at Tinos, the Lourdes of Greece, and all were screaming and diving for chairs. It looked a bit like a refugee ship! Got back only to find my hotel was booked and had to look for another.

9/3/66

I stayed at a *pension* with an illiterate, toothless, and delightful old landlady, who kept patting me on the back and saying "bye-bye" and "goo-night" at least ten times a day. I shared a room with a charming and as-crazy-as-I Greek girl named Poly, a 21-year-old choreographer and dance troupe director. Thanks to her, I saw more and did more than I would have been able or would have wanted to do alone.

The first night we wandered around a part of the island while I kept oohing and aahing over the sunset. The steamer ride to Hydra was enchanting, especially so because the setting sun cast burnt orange and yellow shadows on the scattered islands. It was certainly worth a trip to these Argosaronic Islands; and my one day in Hydra turned to two. After spending the morning at the archaeological museum, I left in the rain—the second in almost six months. The first was just two days earlier. Later, while Poly went to the cinema, I sat on the wharf listening to recorded Greek music, watching a lovely full moon rise over the town and the colorful boats in the circular harbor and watching, as well, the flashes of lightning over the Peloponnese mainland.

One night about 6:30, Poly and I began our "adventure"—certainly one of the craziest things I have ever done and easily subtitled "The Case of the International Icon Thief Suspects." With prior information that it could be done without worry or danger—information wholly false and misleading—we decided to climb the steep mountain foot path to the Monastery of Agia Efpraxia. We got almost to the top in time to watch the sun set over the islands and Hydra take on its lovely night look with the distant lights of Piraeus on the horizon, 3-1/2 hours away by steamer. The climb past 1821 stone wall blockades and watchtowers and twisting around a canyon took us an hour. By the time we reached the monastery, it was dark but for the lights from the summer stars. Persistent knocking on the door brought a nun who berated Poly for coming. She ushered us into the small church where Poly lit a candle at the request of our landlady. The nun, at our request, gave us water and, out of the little goodness in her heart, two small dishes of a fruit jam. All the time she kept muttering to the other nuns that she didn't trust us and that she feared for her icons. (A bit of background information is necessary here: Greece has been having trouble with foreigners who steal valuable icons from the churches and sell them abroad.) Once we finished our small and monastic repast, she ushered us out. I am being euphemistic; "pushed" is the word Poly used. Our whole visit lasted just under four minutes! Exhausted from the climb, we sat down for a few minutes' rest in the outer courtyard. Still not trusting us, the nun sent two boys out to watch us. But perhaps they didn't trust us either because, after a few minutes, they ran back into the monastery and slammed the door to both us and the night. Poly was furious at the treatment given us and vowed never to go to church again, but I burst out laughing at what an impossible situation it had turned out to be.

We had yet to get down the mountain and the moon was being slow about coming up. Staying together and slipping on loose stones and brambles, we made it down in an hour and a half. When the going got particularly rough, Poly, like a pregnant woman, suddenly decided she must have certain Greek delicacies. Periodically we'd call upon God to take pity upon that stupid, inconsiderate woman in black habit. Somewhere along the way, we lost our path down or, at least, the same one we took up. Too late did we realize we were following another one—but how lucky we were! It was much easier than the other. By the time we reached town, my legs were shaking and my thigh muscles were sore. We turned to congratulate each other at our good fortune and our obvious nine lives. The last bit of humor was that we came out, quite by chance, at the restaurant where we intended to have dinner. Poly met a Swedish friend there and told him where we had just been and he, realizing how fantastic the story was, refused to believe her!

I left Hydra early this morning and am now having breakfast on the island of Paros. I'll head back to Athens this afternoon, for tonight I am going to the Wine Festival in Daphne with a Greek fellow I met several days ago—Spiros, by name.

9/4/66

Last night's wine festival was unlike anything I've ever attended. Upon entering, you rent a flask and a glass and then you're on your own. Admission is 66¢, but the wine is free. You can try all 60 samples and drink as much as you like—or, better, as much as you're able! There's a hurdy-gurdy man to entertain with tambourine accompanist and bands that play everything from Greek classics to the modern hully-gully. The wine casks are located in booths, and girls in traditional dress dispense information. What a scene it was! Hundreds of Greeks and tourists all reacting to wine in their own way. Women giggle and sing and get sleepy. Men cry and start fights and sing and stagger, as did a poor American sailor, who could barely walk. Children who come in early enough with their parents can be amused by a shadow play. The most amazing thing is, I think, that this same bacchanalia goes on for all 30 nights in September. People swing from the trees and knock over chairs and do impromptu dances. It is quite a sight, and I was right thinking I would not want to go there alone. "Uncultivated Greek men," which is what the "cultivated" Greeks call all "peasants and low people" are annoying in their unbridled pursuit of women. But, after 10 days in Greece, I'm beginning to think there are a hell of a lot of "uncultivated" men! Greece is the only country in which I have been pinched in the butt repeatedly. Even pinched once on my breast! Walking down any street is unpleasant, and last night I was really grateful for Spiros's presence!

This morning I visited the Athens flea market and the wonderful Museum of Popular and Decorative Arts with its fascinating collection of jewelry and embroidery. I actually drew images of some of the embroidery so I'd remember it. Then to the archaeological museum at the Stoa of Attalos in the Agora, a couple hours of aimless wandering, and now back to the hotel. My legs are still sore from coming down that mountain in Hydra!

9/6/66

The U.S. government has been a bit unkind to my plans these past few days. I had expected to travel about with Herman Fields this week, but he was suddenly sent on assignment to Turkey, and it looks like he won't return before I leave. He is my friend from Ankara, who now lives in Athens—a civilian working with U.S. military forces.

Still plans must go on, so yesterday I went by bus to Corinth on the Peloponnesus. I was quite disappointed. It was a center of art and commerce in ancient times, destroyed by the Romans and rebuilt by Caesar. Went also to Delphi. It's situated on the slopes of Mt. Parnassus among groves of ancient twisted olive trees. I could easily picture the Greeks coming to question the oracle—first Sybil and then the Pythoness. Most fantastic was a climb to the stadium that many people skip. The stadium is well-preserved and conjures up images of fleet-footed races.

9/8/66

I'm getting bored with Athens. I'm not the least bit sorry I'm leaving tomorrow. I had wanted to go to Sounion to see the famous sunset, but the weatherman is against me. We've had almost constant rain these past two days. Perhaps it's the dull, ugly weather that's depressing my spirit.

This morning I wandered around the public market—I don't know why such markets fascinate me so—then went to the excellent Benaki Museum to see the collection of Byzantine icons, embroideries (religious Greek embroideries are the most stunning and complex I've seen), regional costumes, Coptic and Muslim art objects, and Chinese porcelain and ceramics. It is hard to believe that everything in there is a private collection! Then I wandered up via foot and funicular to the highest hill in Athens, the Hill of Lycabettus, atop which is the white-washed Church of St. George. According to legend, the steep rock was detached by Athena from the Pentelikon to reinforce the Acropolis. But, while flying over Athens, she accidentally dropped it where it is now. Even goddesses can be unlucky!

9/10/66

From somewhere in the Adriatic Sea north of the Albanian shore...

This is quite a ship: a two-year-old, tastefully modern Yugoslavian ship, the *Dalmatian*. Not much, in fact, but a luxury liner for what I'm accustomed to! It holds 1000 tons of cargo and 220 passengers, but is now less than half full. There is a swimming pool about the size of six bathtubs, but still a pool; and two bars, one with a dance floor, and a band and singer that entertain nightly. I'm in a comfortable, six-berth air-conditioned cabin — alone! How lucky to get the cheapest berth on the ship, plus a 15% journalist's discount, and end up with a large private room! And that isn't all! This is a cruise ship: Italy-Yugoslavia-Egypt-Lebanon-Greece-Yugoslavia-Italy. My one night on board turned out to be the night of the captain's farewell dinner and dance. The dinner was very good with people oohing and aahing as the waiters displayed each showpiece platter before serving. Included was caviar, lobster, pheasant, and baked Alaska. The pheasant, with feathers intact, was displayed (as my *15th Century Cookery Booke* would put it) as if it "were wont to sit alive" — all that is but for the maraschino cherry stuffed in the beak. The cocktail lounge was all done up with fancy crepe paper twists and balls, and the band was in fine form. It was a pleasant evening.

Tonight at 7:30 we arrive in Dubrovnik. Fortunately, before I left Athens, I called the embassy for a last-minute check on mail, so I did get your letter. I hope you received mine from Greece. Mail to Vienna until 9/25.

Oh, Dubrovnik. I love it! I'm ecstatic! I'm in awe! I'm bursting to share it with you but, no, I must save it for the next letter. Let me just tell you about my arrival. Getting off the ship, I met an American named Ed, about 23 or so. We descended upon the walled city buttonholing all loitering women for available rooms — with his Italian and my smattering of French and German. We were looking for two rooms each with one bed, which no-one could understand. They were more than willing to give us one room with two beds a short distance apart, but we kept saying no and they kept asking why! Ed's retort, extemporaneous and based on the fact that he has a beard, left me laughing. He was a student of religion, he said, and what about his vows of chastity? Finally, a dear lady offered us exactly what we wanted at only little more than we wanted to pay. She's charging us each about $1.30, or 1500 dinars. By the time we schlepped our suitcases up to her home in the walled old city, my arms were ready to crack. We settled in our rooms — mine with a little sitting area and Ed's, narrow and cramped but with a balcony. Then the dear lady brought us glasses of slivovitz, a strong liqueur. Her parting comment (she speaks to Ed in Italian) was that our two separate rooms were also separate from the rest of the house — heh, heh, heh!

A walk around town revealed a hundred ideal photographic angles to snap in the next few days and three ships in the old harbor. Their outlines, neon lit with bright white lights and all, reminded me of gaudy toys on a ship executive's dinner party head table.

Anyway, I love it here, and I can hardly wait till tomorrow.

9/12/66

I'm enraptured about the walled city of Dubrovnik! It's wonderful to be so excited about a place! I'm trying to take in as much as possible in the short time I'm here. (I'm aiming to be in Vienna on the 19th 'cause the Lippizaner horses only perform on Sundays.)

What have I done here? Mostly ramble, but that's such fun in this medieval town reconstructed after the earthquake of 1576 and thus 400 years old. The buildings and streets just breathe with the glories of Dubrovnik's past history. Even the city's flagstone alleys are polished to a sheen by centuries of pedestrian traffic. I keep wondering who once lived here as I sit on the balcony (Ed and I changed rooms), looking up at a pudgy face of an angel with piercing eyes that is carved in relief on the stone wall of this house. I've walked around this city atop the walls, amazed at the wondrous sights that greet every turn. And I've visited museums and churches more wonderful for their natural forms and historical pasts than for their displays within.

I went to Čilipi about 15 miles away, where the men and women wear their traditional clothes every Sunday at church, and I attended Mass with them. I had planned to go out there by excursion bus but then decided to take a regular airport bus. A dear little English woman about 65, Mrs. Walsh, decided to join me. At the airport, we picked up a lift with an Australian of Yugoslav descent. He did an about face of a few miles for us and told us his story on the way. He's a real estate agent, wool farmer, and grazer who has made a good deal of money. He

A woman of Čilipi, Yugoslavia—now Croatia

brought with him several hundred kilos of wool and had more sent from Greece. When the Athens shipment arrived, Customs asked one million dinars for it—roughly $1,000—and he told them to keep it. He's been protesting the charge for a month without results and is on his way to Belgrade to see Tito: "I'm not afraid of no-one!" he proclaimed.

At the nearby island of Socrum, the natural rocky setting and mirror-like Adriatic are perfect for swimming. I don't care what the Greek travel brochures say; the sea is greener and clearer in Yugoslavia! Both plant and animal sea life is lovely. The island is the location of Princess Carlotta's home, to which she retired after her husband, Maximillian, was executed by Mexico's Juarez about 1850. I enjoyed that swim so much I went back today for another.

I visited the beach on the Lapad peninsula and sat at an outdoor cafe listening to musicians play Slavic tunes. I have so enjoyed my stay here and hope to return at a later date for further exploration of the Dalmatian coast. Tomorrow morning I head inland to Mostar for lunch, then on to Sarajevo for two nights. I hope to attend a local synagogue there for Rosh Hashanah services. Then one night up north near Trieste in the town of Postojna for a look at its underground caves and, on the 15th, a night train to Vienna. That is my schedule today. I am curious to see what happens to it.

9/13/66

My dear landlady, Mrs. Mišetić, was up at 6:15 to bid me *adieu*. Then the 6-1/2 hour trip to Mostar, stopping on the way at Trebinje, Ljubinje, and Stolac. What a lovely ride it was through the mountains and past numerous tiny villages, where stone fences, as in Robert Frost's New England, make good neighbors. And the neighbors: gypsies in colorful dress; a woman bent over with the weight of her load of kindling; men with umbrellas to protect themselves from the blazing sun while leading horses and cows or loaded donkeys; farmers pausing to drink—something stronger than water, I suspect—from the wicker-covered bottles that hang from their belts as they scythe hay. Others rest by conical haystacks, each topped with a white plastic cover that remind me of Mom's chicken croquettes with white sauce! The colors: red-tile roofs, occasional mosque towers, gray rocks, verdant greens of trees and shrubs, and the few trees changing to their autumnal colors. There was blue sky and, below it, the pastel green of the twisting, swift currents of the Neretva River. I was in Mostar for only 2-1/2 hours and visited two mosques, the old shopping district, and the wondrous single arch bridge that spans the Neretva, built by the Ottomans in 1566. It is considered an exemplary piece of Islamic architecture in the Balkans. The city is named after the bridge keepers (*mostari*) who, in medieval times, guarded the Stari Most (Old Bridge).

[After Bosnia and Herzegovina declared independence from Yugoslavia in 1992, tensions between Croats and Bosnians increased in Mostar, and the city was divided along ethnic lines. As war escalated, seven of the thirteen original mosques dating from the sixteenth and seventeenth centuries were lost for ideological reasons or by bombardment. The Old Bridge was also destroyed, though it has since been rebuilt.]

From Mostar, I had a 3-1/2 hour trip to Sarajevo along a road that for a good way follows the Neretva and then the wider Jablaičko Jazero. Now I'm settled at the Dom Ferijalaca, a *studentski* center.

9/14/66

I knew it! My plans have changed, and I've already reserved my ticket for Postojna. Seems like the information given me in Dubrovnik was about 13 hours off. The actual route there is so roundabout and involves so many changes, I've decided to go to Zagreb instead. I'm going tomorrow and that trip in itself is eight hours.

First thing this morning I made contact with a Jewish shopkeeper, Leon Atias, through the Turistbiro. I visited him at his store, the oldest warehouse in Europe, built in 1551. He explained to me that the Jewish population before the war was about 11,500 with five synagogues and is now reduced to about 1,100, including children, with one synagogue. The building is in a state of repair that must be finished—I don't know how from the looks of things—in time for the 400th anniversary of the first Jewish settlers' arrival in Bosnia and Herzegovina, which will be held October 14-17 and to which Jews all over the world have been invited. They expect about 400 from abroad. The original settlers came after the Spanish Inquisition, but later the Ashkenazis settled here also. About 50% of the present members are communist and Mr. Atias, a member of the Communist Central Committee and secretary for the anniversary celebrations, explained: "I'm not religious; I'm a communist.

And why not? I'm nationalistic, have been a communist since before the war and would never change my religion." Then the telephone rang; it was communist headquarters calling. After the interruption, he continued: "On Fridays and Saturdays it is very difficult to get a *minyan*. Sometimes they have to go out on the streets in search of men ..." The telephone rang; it was communist headquarters calling again. It was obvious we were getting nowhere and he invited me to return to his store this evening or tomorrow—he wasn't going to synagogue; he's not religious. There was no time to ask the many questions still in my mind.

The rest of the day was spent in finding a room for the night. The youth hostel I stayed in last night was booked solid tonight, if I can read the Serbo-Croatian posters correctly, with arrivals for the Balkan States' Athletic Games which begin tomorrow. I wandered around the old part of Sarajevo that includes the market and visited the Gavrilo Princip Bridge and Museum. Princip, as you may recall, was the assassin of Archduke Ferdinand in 1914. I could not understand what exactly was the nature of the museum since everything was written in Serbo-Croatian, but I had the definite idea that he was being honored. Outside are his footprints where he stood when firing the fatal shot and a plaque commemorating that spot. True at the time that anti-Austrian rule sentiment was widespread, but it seems a bit distorted to so honor the man who launched World War I and the senseless killing of thousands. I also visited the Despitch family home, a good example of eighteenth-century Bosnian architecture, and the same era Serbian Orthodox church that wears beautifully the dark patina of age.

This evening I went to the 45-minute service at Sarajevo's only synagogue—or, rather, in its only room not under mad repair. Actually, that room was a sanctuary, so I'm not quite sure what the rest of the building is used for, unless it houses a larger sanctuary and religious school. Present were 25 men and an elderly rabbi, 10 local women, myself, and three young girls. All wore European clothing. The room was colorfully painted like the tiles of mosques and had painted lacy-looking decorations around the windows.

The painted ceiling reminded me of Persian mosaic boxes. The ark was in an alcove—a bit larger than, but similar to, prayer alcoves in all mosques. During the service, I was thinking about that certain something that has made Jews go on despite all adversities—here in Yugoslavia, in Iran, in Iraq, and many other countries. I was quite awed with the wonder of Judaism's survival, and I don't think I ever felt quite so close to my religion as I did at that moment. It has nothing to do with my five months in Israel but has a great deal to do with Miron. He is deeply religious in spirit, and we had many discussions about Judaism. He made me really excited about my religion and stimulated my interest in knowing more.

This evening I am staying with Mr. and Mrs. Stepić, whom I am forced to communicate with in German. Heaven help us! I gave her those heeled sandals of yours to throw away, but she tried them on before heaving them and returned to tell me they fit and thank you. That reminded me of my chambermaid at the Hotel Rits in Athens. Before I left, she asked me if she could have my brown and black shoes, which you brought me in April, and then preceded to show me how well they fit her. I was amused at the fact that she had obviously tried them on previously and thus knew they were her size. Shades of Cinderella! I always wondered what chambermaids do to amuse themselves while cleaning hotel rooms!

9/15/66

The trip to Zagreb was pleasant; my compartment mates were friendly, though they spoke no English; and the scenery was striking. I stood looking out the window for about five hours of the journey 'cause I didn't dare sit down and miss anything: rolling hills and snug little white houses with red roofs; those comical, conical haystacks; and the farmers with their primitive wooden tools. Saw nothing modern—even the pitchforks were once trees with three branches that met at about the same point. An Englishman I met compared the standard of living here with that of England following World War II but only in the cities, I think. And then Zagreb. My long, agonizing wait to change my ticket from Postojna—unsuccessfully. I took a loss of about $3. Like everything else, the first information was incorrect. It has happened over and over again since my arrival. That long wait and then the information at two tourist offices that there wasn't even a pillow available in Zagreb tonight. The International Trade Fair is being held here now. Walking back to the railroad station slowly collecting my thoughts and thinking that perhaps I could take tonight's train to Vienna when a Yugoslav man, who had been turned away just after I came up, told me he was going to the station to ask the people standing around if they had any rooms. Such is the custom; I've done it myself. We found a man who knew a woman with two rooms and we grabbed them. Got here and found one room with three beds (the same old story) and here I am writing this letter while a strange man whose name I don't know lies in the next bed. I've learned to trust my woman's intuition! Traveling is full of surprises!

9/16/66

Before I comment on Zagreb, I was going to tell you about my last two hours in Sarajevo. I raced down to the market to buy the makings of lunch, then over to the City Museum, which might have been fascinating but for the use of Serbo-Croatian explanations in the Cyrillic alphabet. I am happiest when museum descriptions are in both the local language and English, but they are few and far between on this journey.

I dashed over to see Mr. Atias for morning coffee and questions. Some of the information I received might interest you. Rabbi Romano, is 81 years old and has been rabbi since the war. Before the war (and here Atias's voice changed to a tone of awe and respect), they had a rabbi with a doctorate. Before the war, there were about 70,000 Jews in all of Yugoslavia; after, about 5,000. In Sarajevo, of the 2,000 remaining, 500 went to the U.S.A. and European countries and 600 went to Israel with the First Aliyah. The present synagogue was built about 1912. Money for current reparations came from the Joint Distribution Committee, claims, and the city of Sarajevo. The Jewish Museum, a former synagogue, will have its formal opening during the anniversary celebrations. The $80,000 cost was paid for by the city. The money was given in token of the Jewish community's previous gift of one of their synagogues to the Workers' University and in recognition of past and present contributions of the Jews as citizens of Sarajevo and Yugoslavia. When the present synagogue is completed, it will house a sanctuary and community center. There is no children's Hebrew school because there is no interest in having one. Most Jews in Sarajevo are state employees. Atias, before his retirement, was director of the Turistbiro and now manages the old covered bazaar when it is open during the summer. He invited me to his home but it was just 45 minutes before my train left. Had the invitation been extended the day before, I would have stayed, for he was an interesting man to speak to, informative, witty, and effusive.

Now Zagreb, and all is well. Walked around the city this morning and was particularly impressed with the Gothic cathedral, the Ethnographic Museum, the Museum to the National Revolution, and the Museum of Arts and Crafts devoted to the practical arts: clothing, furniture, utensils, glassware. I was quite amazed at the heavy and ornate furnishings of the eighteenth and nineteenth centuries. I wonder how they relate to the tastes of the Austro-Hungarian Empire. Some of the embroidery designs were similar to what Grandma Koren brought over from the Ukraine. At the same museum, I noticed that in a series of pictures on changing fashions over the centuries, the last one was a photo of John Glenn in a space suit. That's what struck me as odd—it was John Glenn and not Yuri Gagarin.

9/17/66

A general comment about shops in Yugoslavia. Fashions range from chic modern to stodgy peasant, and shoes from leather boots to match mini-skirted dresses to the *sandale*, a leather shoe with a toe that curls up and back and is worn in the villages. There are a number of jewelry shops, but the items suffer more from design than price. The nicest shops are the bookstores and those that sell Yugoslav crafts and cater to the tourists. Restaurants there are aplenty—and far too many "express" shops where you order from a counter and eat or drink standing up.

A summary of my week in Yugoslavia: there was too much to see and do and not enough time. I had no chance to ask citizens how they felt about their country. I only had two reactions: one from a station porter who, when I said in German that Yugoslavia was a good place, replied that America and Germany were better. The other from an English-speaking girl who has been to Vienna three times, Prague about twenty times, and London once. She feels the greatest problem is money and the best thing is the beautiful scenery. She prefers capitalism to socialism but likes Tito—so much, in fact, she wants to cry every time she sees him. Out of love and gratitude, I suppose.

Market day in Yugoslavia—now Croatia

There was not enough time because, unlike holiday travelers, I can't keep up an 18-hour daily pace. They get back to routine after three or four weeks, but this is my routine, my way of life. I can't handle, nor do I want, a frenetic 18-hour daily way of life.

The train ride to Vienna was uneventful. I slept only about two hours and, the rest of the time, I spoke with that Yugoslav girl just referred to. At the crack of dawn, I was up and looking at mountainous Austria and its pretty chalets. I'm staying here with a Servas member, Mrs. Rosenfeld and her daughter. I'm in her son's room while he is in Oslo. She lives far from the center of town—about one hour by two trams and a healthy walk. Her English isn't fluent, but she's very pleasant. I called her when I arrived at 8 a.m. but couldn't come out here till 7 p.m., so I spent the day on the go. Constantly.

Vienna is a wonderful city, as I'm sure you recall. Some of my activities today: wandered round the lovely French gardens at the Belvedere Palace and the walk of the Stadtpark in the center of town; visited the Hofburg Palace apartments where Kaiser Franz Josef and his wife, Elizabeth, lived; to St. Stephen's and St. Peter's Churches; attended a rehearsal of the famed Lippizaner horses at the Spanish Riding School; then on to the amazing Museum of Fine Arts, the only museum in the world I'd like to rob, except there is too much I want to take possession of. What a difference there is in the fineness of work created by Asians and Europeans at the same periods in history. Asian art is so rough and crude by comparison. (I exclude oriental art from this.) All really great museums make me want to cry with joy and, of the hundreds I've visited over the years, I can count on one-and-a-half hands the number that evoke such a response. Looking at the wealth of creativity in this museum, both in items displayed and the building itself, I am dismayed when I think of how civilization has let its truly great artisans go unsupported and has failed to train others in the arts.

It's now almost 11 p.m., and tomorrow is another early-rising day. *Guten nacht.* (Good night.)

9/19/66

I went to Schönbrunn Palace, which I'm sure you must have visited. I was especially fascinated by the way they trimmed the trees. I once had to do some shrubs on the kibbutz that way, and it was almost impossible! I visited the Josef Hayden Museum, the Museum of Ethnology (where I spent most of my time in the Japanese galleries), in the Museum of Austrian Culture—and, oh yes, also the Augustiner Church, past site of Hapsburg weddings; and the Albertina Graphic Collection. I never saw a city with more museums! Vienna is rich in everything and darn expensive! Last night I went to an enjoyable performance of Franz Lehar's *The Merry Widow* at the Volksöper. Met a Japanese woman there with her uncle. We spoke in Japanese, but how much I've forgotten! It's frightful! I shall have to get back to it quickly!

9/20/66

After my first two hectic days in Vienna, these last two have been rather easy. I visited a couple of churches, wandered around a bit, then went to Prater, Vienna's amusement park, and watched three Chasidic Jews smash each other about with bumper cars. I met a very nice Austrian fellow who spoke no English. We rode on the big swings, drove out to a place near my house for coffee, then he drove me home. What a time we had communicating, but I rather enjoyed the effort!

Today I went out to the Vienna Woods to Kahlenberg and Leopoldsberg, where one gets an excellent panoramic view of Vienna and the Danube River.

The Servas house I'm staying in is located across the Danube in Stadlau. Built 14 years ago, it has three bedrooms on the second floor and three rooms on the first. The wood floors are creaky; the bathtub and sink are located in the kitchen but separated by a curtain; hot water comes from a nearby contraption in which water is heated by flames, as in Japan. The kitchen sink has no running water. To wash dishes, water has to be carried from the tub. The living room area has a large rectangular stove encased in porcelain tiles and is used for winter heating.

9/21/66

I went today to the Mozart and Beethoven museums and to the Jewish Museum, where they have stones from the Warsaw Ghetto and Treblinka. At noon I went to watch the parading figures on the Kunstuhr clock in Hoher Markt. Did you see it?

Have decided to go to Salzburg on Saturday after attending Kol Nidre services and will then go to Innsbruck on or about the 27th. I plan to be in Munich on the 1st—don't want to miss that annual beer bacchanalia!

9/24/66

These last few days have been packed. I went to the art museum at the Belvedere Palace; for coffee at the home of Mr. Schmid, Servas Secretary in Austria; to Karlkirche; and did several hours of research on Austrian monarchical history at the American Library. While picking up my mail at the consulate, I met Art Mannion of N.Y.C., who studied international law in Paris for a year and has been traveling in Europe for the past four months. He's a great guy—intelligent, worldly, witty, and pleasant to be with. Because of him, I canceled my train ticket and postponed my departure to Salzburg. Last night we went out to Grinzing to a wine cellar devoted to imbibing new vintage wines. With an Austrian friend of his with whom he worked in NY, we wound up at a party for the International Pharmaceutical Students Conference—mostly reminiscent of wild, swinging, singing college beer parties. It was fun!

Between the time we met and the time we went to Grinzing, I went to the Yom Kippur service at Vienna's only synagogue not destroyed during the war. Remodeled recently, it is modern without being modern—a three-tiered circular building under a dome radiating 16 gold rosettes and 1,056 sun rays. I felt like I was worshipping in a vacuum. There was a small male choir and before the sermon—or, what I think was a sermon—there was a question and answer period between rabbi and individual congregants. The service lasted one hour and 45 minutes. I couldn't understand the German, and the only English speaker I found was an Israeli girl visiting her Viennese aunt. As you can tell, I was far less impressed with this experience than with the one in Sarajevo but amazed by the number of Jews still attending services in Germany.

Today Art and I went to the Hapsburg Treasury and Crown Jewels Exhibition and to a wonderful performance of the Lippizaner Horses at the Spanish Riding School.

9/26/66

My last few days in Vienna were marvelous with full credit going to Art, a brilliant, talented, many-faceted individual with whom conversation never wanes.

Yesterday, I went to the New Hofburg extension of the Fine Arts Museum with its fantastic collection of old musical instruments and then to the Silberkammer to take a look at the Hofburg's eye-popping collection of tableware and gilded silver serving pieces. Oooo-aaaah! Art and I met again after that and blew our budgets on a coffee and cake at Demel, Vienna's famed *konditorei* since 1846. That evening we returned to Grinzing, this time to a more authentic and less touristy *heurigen*.

This morning we went to the beautiful Grand State Room at the National Library, where they also held an exhibition of paintings and studies by the artist Ernst Fuchs. After a farewell beer, I boarded the train to Salzburg.

I'm staying with the wife of a Servas member. He is Eduard Bäumer, professor at the Academy of Arts in Vienna and a painter. His wife, a charmer, is also a painter and speaks no English. We're relying on my gutsy German! The Bäumers have three children, all living in Munich. Two are married, and there are three grandchildren. Since rooms are nonexistent during Oktoberfest, she brought up the possibility of my staying in Munich with her older daughter and family. The Bäumers live in a lovely four-year-old home in the suburbs of Salzburg, and Mrs. Bäumer gave me a full tour (including the linen closets!) with explanations of the many pieces of art that fill the home and that she or her husband created. Her studio is in the house; his is in an adjacent building with the top floor devoted to a 12' desk, bookshelves, a bed, and a sunken bath and shower—the latter two for her husband to unwind while at work. The first floor is where he creates. Mrs. Bäumer shared many family photos and stories of the war. She was born of Jewish parents (her mother died in a concentration camp at the age of 62), but she is now Lutheran. Her children are the same and I assume so is her husband.

9/27/66

My head is slightly spinning with all that I've seen today, but a quick run down will give you an idea of what Salzburg offers. First, it's in a charming setting among mountains with the Salzach River running through city center and crossed by eight bridges. Rising in the center of the city and visible from everywhere is a 394' dolomite rock upon which is the large and lovely Castle of Hohensalzburg, begun in 1077. Second is the fact that Salzburg is, without question, the city of Mozart—his statue, his birthplace and museum, his family home, the Mozarteum, and all the Mozart concerts throughout the year. One can hardly pass a shop that doesn't sell Mozartkugeln, a chocolate-covered marzipan and nougat candy.

I went to the castle fortress, finished in 1681 and, while up there, also to the State Apartments, Torture Chamber, and Museum. The Residence, circa 1600, had a collection of baroque paintings and a fine graphic collection of Anton Steinhardt, a friend of the Bäumers before his death. Nonnberg Cloisters is famous now—not because it was founded in 770 and is the oldest nunnery in the world existing without pause—but because Maria von Trapp was a novice there and all the world has seen *The Sound of Music*. I visited the beautiful Salzburg Cathedral; "The Dome," consecrated in 1621; and the cemetery and catacombs of St. Peter, where the oldest church in Europe is located. It was founded about 250 A.D. by Roman soldiers who had come here during the persecutions. I went to Mozart's Museum in his birthplace and past the frescoed wall of horses in a nearby square. Then to the rococo and baroque Church of St. Francis and the seventeenth-century Saint-Gaetan Church.

But tonight was the real joy. I attended a Mozartspieler performance of works by Haydn and Mozart in the Mirabell Palace, circa 1606. The Marmorsaal, where the concerts are held, is baroque gold and white, designed by architect Lukas von Hildebrandt in 1726. With nought but the flickering candles in the two eight-branched candelabras and a light for the five musicians to read by, it was reminiscent of by-gone days and, indeed, Mozart did perform in this room. As Austrian radio put it in 1965: "Again this year there was the same atmosphere of relaxation and fruits of a great idea superbly executed, which is why they have no counterpart elsewhere in the world."

Tomorrow I'm going to the salt mines in Hallein and to a performance of Mozart's *Don Giovanni* by the famed Aicher Marionettes.

9/29/66

These last two days have been such fun! At the salt mines in Hallein, a ropeway takes riders up to Mt. Dürrnberg to begin the descent—traveling 200 meters below the earth and crossing the Austrian-German border without a passport. Where am I? In the bowels of the mountain dressed in baggy white pants and a baggy white jacket with hood. Why white? So each person can see the person in front of him. There are only two lanterns carried by miners. Once inside, you walk along mine shafts and slide down seven "roller coasters" totaling 380 feet. The summer and winter temperature is 50ºF, but your bottom gets darn hot each time you've finished a slide! You ride on a ferry across a salt lake and on the "Salt Mine Express" that isn't much more than a board on wheels. The mine has been worked for over 7,000 years. There are still 20 salt lakes in production; 90 miners and 70 men in the factory. The whole trip beneath the earth covers 4 kilometers. It's great fun, a novel experience, and extremely engaging.

From there I went to the Hellbrunn Palace, which has the most imaginative and far-fetched fountains. Water pressure imitates bird whistles and moves carved figures and unsuspecting tourists. Fountains are in the unlikeliest of places and when least expected—from sidewalks, stone figures, and deer horns from behind, over, and under you.

Mrs. Bäumer wanted me to see Wolfgangsee—and what a glorious time we had! We went by bus to St. Gilgin and by boat to St. Wolfgang. After a good trout lunch, we went to the Church of St. Wolfgang with its sculpted and painted Gothic altar from 1481. We headed up into the hills past handsome wooden fences and scattered farmers' homes. The rolling hills were pretty, and I recalled *The Sound of Music,* for these fields were also covered with wildflowers. She showed me a trick that Austrian children do with the "clutch" flower, and I demonstrated the buttercup game. We met a farmer and his wife knocking plums from their two trees. After allowing us to pick up as much as we could carry, we paid them a few shillings. Austrians are cordial and a standard greeting is *Grüss Gott* (God's Greetings). People are open and friendly. (That's such a contradiction when I can also picture their history during WWII.) We found a rushing stream, a little waterfall, and a crude bridge put together, I suspect, by the farmer who lived nearby. It was, as Mrs. Bäumer put it, a perfect autumn adventure.

Mrs. Bäumer has been a joy to live with. It is always coffee or tea time when I return home regardless of the hour, and she has been so patient with my German. I was five months in Israel and learned about 50 words of Hebrew. I have been only 3-1/2 days with her and already I'm translating words for foreigners on buses (who thank me in German). My German is non-grammatical and just one-or two-word sentences, but it seems I'm not having much trouble being understood. I'm sure that when Grandpa lived with us for three years in the 1950s and spoke mostly Yiddish to me, it helped ease my way into the German language. Even my Japanese came slower, but that may mean I'll forget the German that much quicker.

Tomorrow I am definitely leaving for Innsbruck—for all of 24 hours. I had planned four days there but all this extra time in Vienna and here cut out all four days and has now put me a day behind my hoped for arrival in Munich. Oh well, I don't regret these extended stays; they've been the best of my two weeks in Austria.

9/30/66

Since it was my last morning with Mrs. Bäumer, she wanted to have a special leisurely breakfast. She gifted me with a little wooden scoop for sugar or flour that I was reluctant to accept. Servas hosts are not required to be lovable and motherly. I gave her two pairs of stockings. I give all my Servas hosts a gift—usually from a stock of small items from Japan that I carry with me. That woman will always hold a special place in my heart—like Mrs. Javedanfar in Isfahan, Iran. Almost forgot that when I left Mrs. Bäumer, she presented me with one freshly picked red rose from her garden—the final elegant touch from an elegant lady.

It certainly was a lovely ride from Salzburg to Innsbruck, particularly the areas of Zell am See and Kitzbühel. I sat with two Yugoslav girls and spoke with them in both German and French. Unfortunately, by the time the train arrived here, it was raining and the low clouds put off my trip up to Mount Patscherkofel (7,415′) until tomorrow morning and possibly forever! I cannot sit here and wait for the weatherman to cooperate! Instead, I went to the Imperial Palace built by Empress Maria-Theresa. Just more of the same. But the Court Church—now that's something! It's hard to find a really unique church in all the thousands. This one was built 1553-1563 under Emperor Maximilian I and contains his memorial tomb and sarcophagus with its sides covered by 24 scenes in marble high-relief depicting the Emperor's deeds. On either side stand 28 bronze figures, each about 6-1/2′ tall representing his relatives and ancestors. On the balcony overhead, 23 two-foot high statues represent the Hapsburgs' saints and 20 busts of Roman emperors signify the important patrician rulers of the empire, as well as the imperial dignity of the Hapsburgs. All are in bronze.

From there I went to the excellent Museum of Tyrolean Art with its wonderful collection of national costumes, peasant rooms, furniture, and crèche scenes. It was a good lesson in comparative tastes. In Japan the beauty of wood is in its natural state—simple elegance. In the Tyrol it is what can be carved out of the wood, and the ornately intricate designs are awesome. I was particularly fascinated by the wooden rolling pins and stamping boards for breads and cookies. I had to purchase one!

When all that was accomplished, as well as a walk in the old section of Innsbruck, I arranged for a room in the home of a Mrs. Franke. She's a woman about 75 and stands all of 4-1/2' tall. She's a jolly old thing and very cordial—typically Austrian!

I haven't seen all there is to see in Innsbruck, but I know I've hit the most important, and I can expect no more in the short time I've allowed myself.

10/2/66

Munich—home of the Oktoberfest. I was told by the information office here, as I expected, there were no rooms available. I had no luck on my own and went back to ask where the area was with all the inns. I was told it was a bad area, and I mustn't go there. I told them it didn't matter; I had to have a place to sleep. Voila! There was a room! And where? Of all places, in the home of an Iranian bachelor in his late 30's. Mr. Afshar has been here for 10 years; he's an importer of Persian rugs. Actually, I don't even have a private room but a couch in his living room. This is the first time he's had a guest (not allowed by his landlord) and, while it isn't exactly desirable, it's all that's available! (Ah ha!—word is that he has a German wife and daughter now in Iran. That's the second story.) Yes sir, the Munich Information Office certainly takes care of its guests.

Last night Mr. Afshar went with me to Oktoberfest, and this afternoon I went back alone to take pictures and stayed till 8 p.m. Let me just quote the notes I made at the time: "A wild, fun-swingin', free-for-all with slaps on the back and flicks of the hair, as I wore my long hair down. Smiles and singing and standing on tables. *Prosit*! *Prosit*! Amusement park is a blare of lights and happy people with big pretzels and chocolate hearts hanging around their necks. Whumps on the head with sponge rubber mallets. Beer halls that hold hundreds of bands. An oom-pah-pah fest! Three-foot feathered hats and cherubic angels in the Hofbrauhaus overlooking not so cherubic subjects. Rotating angels and roses and breads. This is *gemütlichkeit* by all that is Germany! For American ex-college students, this beats 15 fraternity weekends! Old men kiss their wives again but, by the time they get home, these rejuvenated gents probably roll over and fall fast asleep. Beer wagons are pulled by six giant horses. Oktoberfest makes the Daphne Wine Festival look like a D.A.R. tea party!" Unquote.

According to Mrs. Bäumer, I wouldn't like the Oktoberfest because it's "primitive" and I have "culture." Wrong on one count, anyway. Yes, it's primitive—but so much fun! By the time I left the table tonight, I was friendly with all the Germans. One was a soldier in WWII and fought in Crete. Oktoberfest is an experience—and one worth having. So glad I came for it.

While at the amusement-park-half of the fest, I went to a genuine flea circus. Having never seen a flea, I can only suppose that the tiny thing I saw by magnifying glass was really a flea. One walked around a carousel when blown upon; another wiggled paper about. "Theodore" threw off his paper at his master's bidding—football for fleas—and for the grand finale, three of them pulled toy cars while two others wiggled colored paper around like Lilliputian belly dancers. The show was novel and amusing.

Today I visited the Alte Pinakothek with its exquisite collections of Rubens, Tintoretto, Pacher, and others; the wonderful rococo Residing Theater; the complete City Museum; and the tower of St. Peter's Church for a panoramic view of the city.

Munich is a good looking city with many smart and expensive shops. There is quite a bit to see here, so I shall probably stay till Thursday before pushing north to Heidelberg.

10/3/66

This morning I went to Dachau. It was not pleasant; I cried. Memorials from all three religions; a museum; an execution site with a blood ditch; gas chambers never used; and crematoriums used too many times. In May 1938 there was a public burning of books by "undesirable authors." In 1820, more than a hundred years earlier, the German poet Heinrich Heine wrote: "There was but a prelude, where books are burnt, humans will be burnt in the end." Dr. Rascher kept excellent charts of his medical experiments: water and body temperatures at time of submersion and at death. And the prisoner's diet:

- Morning: 350 grams daily ration of bread, 1/2 liter of a coffee substitute

- Noon: 6 days a week: 1 liter rhubarb or cabbage soup
  1 day a week: 1 liter noodle soup

- Evening: 4 days a week: 20-30 grams sausage or cheese and 3/4 liter of tea 3 days a week: 1 liter of soup

As I said, Dachau was not pleasant, but I felt it was a required visit.

[Many years later, Marty and I went to Dachau with Helga and Andy, our German sister-in-law and nephew. This time the "museum" had been decontaminated. It was more sterilized than in 1966, having been scrubbed and scoured for the benefit of visitors. In 1966 it was more real and raw and powerful. Helga told us her own experiences as a child in WWII in an anti-Hitler family; Andy was reviled, disgusted, saddened, and angry.]

In a 180° change of emotion, this afternoon I went to the botanical gardens with flowers and trees from all over the world. The only thing missing, I think, was the Venus Fly Trap...and that might have been in the back rooms catching flies!

This evening I had dinner with Erika Fiedler whom I met at the Pharmaceutical Convention festivities in Grinzing near Vienna.

10/4/66

Dad, that letter was a surprise—and a pleasant one, too! Thanks. I did not know Sarah Knight is in Munich—or, perhaps, I have forgotten—but I already tracked down her phone number and will try to contact her tomorrow.

I am staying in Munich until Sunday, the 9th, and have moved out of Mr. Afshar's apartment. I'm now in the rent-free cold-water flat of Hansi Feldmaier, a friend of Erika Fiedler, who is at her mother's apartment for a week.

Today I went to the National Museum, the new Alte Pinakothek with its fourteenth- and twentieth-century paintings, and to an Herbst Sammlung autumn collection of op and pop art. That was my first face-to-face experience with claptrap and what a reaction I had! Later I visited Bettina Bäumer, who is as charming as her mother.

10/5/66

Did little today but get a ticket to Saturday's performance of *Lohengrin,* buy some dress material, and wander through the Englisher Garten with Erika. It's a lovely and extensive patch of green in this city. And, oh yes, I watched the dancing and jousting figures on the tower clock at the Rathaus—a requirement for tourists.

But this evening was something special! I went out to Sarah Knight's home (hoping she'd be there for the surprise) and, after 12 years and in another country, she took one look at me and called me by name! She was hesitant, but she was almost certain it was me. Remarkable! Her sister Ruth is visiting, and we spent a chatty evening together. She looks wonderful and is happy, but may be leaving Munich within the year.

Tomorrow morning I am going to the Munich synagogue for Simchas Torah. Tomorrow is also October 6th and marks my second anniversary. It will be exactly two years since I left the states. Incredible! Incredibly wonderful!

10/7/66

Yesterday's Simchas Torah service was long but interesting. One woman there invited me to attend the afternoon party but, when I returned for it, the place was locked up tight. The only explanation for this, I think, is that we were speaking in German and I probably misunderstood.

I had a pleasant lunch with Sarah, then met her again for dinner, which was very American. The other two guests were the principals of the American elementary and high schools. It wasn't a terribly stimulating evening, but I enjoyed being with Sarah. I slept in the living room with her collection of antique German cuckoo and "bong-bong" clocks. The cacophony each and every hour was not exactly conducive to a restful sleep!

Today I visited the Residenz with its particularly fine porcelains and suites of period rooms from the sixteenth to nineteenth centuries and the Treasury with its lovely reliquaries, jewels, and a breathtaking collection of cups and boxes in lapis lazuli, jasper, amber, etc.

10/9/66

I went to the Nymphenburg Palace with its beautiful grounds and small summer villas, then to the Deutsches Museum, the largest science and technology museum in the world. I believe it! My four hours there hardly scratched the surface. Later I went to an enjoyable performance of *Lohengrin*.

Today: Munich's zoo, the largest in Germany, and, rather than spend my last night in Munich at home alone, stopped into the Hofbräuhaus again. I met a number of people and ended up at a private party in a *pension* with two American males, two Canadian females, and an Austrian fellow. I love how easily the comaraderie among strangers develops.

One of the Americans, a 25-year-old soldier, asked me where I'm living now and the answer was that my present address is the world. 27 and unmarried! It amazed him, and then he had an explanatory flash. "Oh, I know," he said, "You've been married already." "No. I'm not traveling on alimony payments." Those who've never tried this life find it hard to believe.

10/10/66

Heidelberg: home of *The Student Prince*. Like Salzburg, Heidelberg, too, has a castle, but this one is not as well preserved.

It was partly destroyed in the Battle of Orleans in 1693. Inside is a fascinating historical collection in the Apothecaries' Museum and an eighteenth-century beer cask that holds 220,000 liters! Imagine! It's about 30' in diameter. That reminds me that all I've done since arriving in Germany is drink beer!

I visited the nineteenth-century Holy Ghost Protestant Church and the Old Bridge from 1786. In my wanderings, I found some pretty homes in the students' quarter and across the Neckar River. As in Salzburg, a river cuts across the city.

Heidelberg is nice but, after Salzburg, I'm afraid I can say nothing more. It's not nearly as picturesque as I'd expected. It doesn't have the atmosphere of Salzburg or the *gemütlichkeit* of Bavaria. I expect to leave here on the 12th.

I'm staying in a *pension*, and I was lucky to get it. Again my timing was off—there is now a nurses' and social workers' congress meeting here.

I have decided again to take the foreign service examination for USIA. As it stands now I will take it on December 3rd in Oslo. Actually, I had planned to be home in early December but I must wait in Oslo till the 3rd, since it is given the same date all over the world and, also, because the only consular post in Norway is in the capital.

Unemployment. Unless something super special comes up in Rochester, I've decided to return to N.Y.C. I just can't think of a better place for a single girl and, besides, I love The City. Thank heaven I have friends to stay with. I am taking the foreign service exam not because I'm convinced I want to work with USIA, but because it is foolish for me to close doors already. I'm still not sure what type of work I want to do, so I'm open to almost anything other than secretarial. I am not opposed to working in Rochester, but the job must be a good one. Dad, in line with this, keep your eyes and ears open to anything in broadcasting, public relations, or working with people. ("Working with people"—how much more general could I get and still say something?)

10/11/66

Today I went to Tiefburg, a little moated castle—or, perhaps, it's better to say a moated little castle; to the eighth-century Church of St. Vitus; to the eighteenth-century Jesuit church; to the Palatinate Museum; and to the top of Mt. Köenigstuhl. I met a Dutchman I'm seeing again this evening.

A point of humor: many German cars carry a red and white sticker on their trunks proclaiming *"Ich hab' den* (picture of a tiger) *im Tank!"* Translation: "I have an ESSO tiger in my tank!"

A point of interest: this is the area of marzipan and it comes in a thousand shapes and sizes and colors: fruits, vegetables, animals, sausages, sea shells, flowers, playing cards, and even *München kindl* (the little symbols of Munich children in brown and yellow monks' robes). Candy stores in Austria and Germany are fantasy shops of wondrous delight. For that matter, so are the *konditorei* that sell little cakes and sugared treats.

10/13/66

Frankfurt is certainly a disappointment. I had planned on two or three nights here, but I'm leaving this afternoon. This morning I emptied my suitcase into an automatic washing machine in an attempt to clean and whiten underwear. I've been too long without hot water and my clothes show it.

Frankfurt is a modern city and building still. There is less here than in the other cities I've been in to remind one of the charm of pre-war architecture. Because this is so, there is little to see here and I found, to my surprise, that I saw almost all the interesting sights in just one afternoon. Goethe Haus, the birthplace of the German poet, was destroyed during the war but has been rebuilt. It is not of any great interest. The Eschenheimer Tower, however, is a well-preserved remnant of the original city fortifications erected in 1426. The Römer, City Hall on the Roman Hill, was rebuilt after the war in the original design and has one room, the Kaisersaal, with portraits of German emperors from Karl the Great in the eighth century up until the nineteenth century. Nearby St. Nicholas Church dates from the thirteenth century. The most compelling place in Frankfurt, to my mind, is the great Cathedral of St. Bartholomew built in the fourteenth century. There are a number of elegant carved wooden altars from the sixteenth century and shields from the first families of the church. One particularly moving carved altar depicts the Dormition with mourning figures standing by Mary's bed, one man kneeling by her side holding one of her hands, while one tiny angel closes Mary's eyes and another hovers behind. A tour of the church that I joined as an afterthought takes you into the back rooms: the bishops' coronation room and the room that holds several mantles dating back to the fourteenth century. The door to this room was built in 1842 and three keys are needed to unlock it. The lock system is from the time when even an elementary creation such as that was a work of art. Behind these cases is another door and display case filled with religious objects, including a miniature crown presented by Empress Maria-Theresa and a cross presented to the church in 1833 by the people of Munich on the 700th anniversary. During the war everything was hidden in bunkers 60 kilometers from Frankfurt.

Bear with me, folks, on all these details. I write for me as well as for you. This has been such a precious time in my life I want to remember it all. Although it may seem like I have included every detail, minor and major, I really have left out a great deal.

Much to my regret, the ships up the Rhine are no longer running, so it seems that I shall miss the famous views of the Rhineland castles. October and November weather in Europe is not notably grand, anyway, and the unpleasantness of rain and fog has begun.

Today I head for Rüdesheim, a small village on the Rhine…and another youth hostel.

10/13 ... but later

Whatever castles were visible between Mainz and here rose out of the mist like Brigadoon. Only here, they never became 100% visible! The castles I saw were impressive and the river itself seems to be an endless traffic jam of colorful barges. I took the ferry across the river to the town of Bingen and visited its castle. My guess from the towns of Bingen and Rüdesheim is that the Allies bombed the river area itself to prevent traffic from moving supplies but weren't much interested in the adjoining towns. A lot of the architectural charm I mentioned before is present here. The towns seemed to have survived both wars and it is to their present (and, of course, past) advantage. I have not explored Rüdesheim much but will do so tomorrow. I treated myself to a gala meal for all of $1.35. It was steak tartar. I'm getting so bored with the wursts! Then I walked up to the youth hostel, situated overlooking endless grapevine fields and with a commanding view of the Rhine. Night lights, at least, are visible through fog! There is no hot water at the hostel, which proves all over again my theory (actually, it's not theory; it's fact) that travelers cannot procrastinate and hope for a shower in the next place or a cleaner toilet in the next town. Often what's there is all there is. Good thing I paid for a hot shower this morning!

10/14/66

This will be just a quick note before saying goodnight. Now in Cologne at a decent hotel, I visited the famous two-spired Gothic cathedral, which matches its notable reputation; the second-century Dionysos Mosaic; and the fine Wallraf-Richartz Museum with its collection of paintings from the seventeenth to twentieth centuries. Now there is also a temporary collection of English Stewarts, Gainsboroughs, Hogarths, and others.

10/15/66

Before leaving Cologne, I went to the religious museum at St. Cecilie and the City Museum, which has among its exhibits a collection of Jewish artifacts and paintings of Jewish subjects. One was the synagogue in Prague in the 1860s. 75% of Cologne was destroyed during the war, so there isn't much that's old there. And, like Frankfurt and Munich, the city is being ripped apart again—this time in the building of a new and super subway system.

I enjoyed the ride from Cologne to Brussels. There are some pretty spots of countryside in Belgium that I wasn't aware of seven years ago when I was last here. I passed one particularly picturesque chateau by a stream with a gate and drawbridge; cows grazed on the rolling green lawns in front.

When I arrived in Brussels, I was greeted as I got off the train by Claudine, her mother, and her older daughter, Isabelle. Claudine looks wonderful but is terribly thin. "All this activity with the children," she says. Her mother, because of a long-time wish to learn English before she died, started English lessons in September. Claudine's husband, Jean-Pierre, is a tall, good-looking man of 36 who works in the family gear manufacturing business.

On the way to Claudine's, we stopped at her mother's apartment for a drink, then went home where Jean-Pierre and Corinne, their younger daughter, were waiting. Once the children were ready for bed, we took them to Jean-Pierre's parents for the evening, then went for dinner and a gathering at the tennis club where Claudine and Jean-Pierre met.

Claudine DeSmet and husband John-Pierre DeDecker. Claudine was a high school exchange student from Belgium in Rochester, NY in 1956-1957. We've been good friends ever since with multiple visits in Belgium and the United States.

Claudine has a two-bedroom apartment in a three-story building. The third floor has only a bedroom, toilet, and wash area—unoccupied at present—so Claudine asked her landlord if I could stay there and, while I was willing to pay for the use of it, he wants no money. It is, of course, the most convenient arrangement, and I am able to spend the maximum amount of time with Claudine's family. Even now I am trying to write this letter while playing with Isabelle. Most difficult is not the play but the verbal communication!

Claudine and I have already been through our *Monroe Log* yearbook. This is such a wonderful reunion; we are thrilled with the chance to be together again. We've done nothing but talk, talk, talk. When Claudine went to work (she helps out at Jean-Pierre's office two mornings a week), I went downtown and visited the Royal Museum of Art and History and the City Museum, which houses the collection of clothes that have been gifts to the famous and popular Manneken Pis, the 2'-tall bronze statue of a naked boy who urinates into a fountain's basin. Then I walked over to see that uninhibited young man who's been peeing in the fountain for 350 years! These past two mornings I stayed home despite Claudine's absence, because I so appreciate this touch of "home" in an otherwise kinetic schedule. We have had a wonderful time together and have renewed and deepened our friendship.

10/22/66

The night train to Berlin was anything but restful what with noisy travelers and border checks passing through the Russian zone. I was so tired by morning that my compartment mates had to wake me so I wouldn't miss the Berlin station and head for Moscow.

I visited the twentieth-century art museum, the zoo (especially fine), and the Jewish Center. Built in 1959, the Center replaced the largest synagogue of Berlin destroyed by arson on Crystal Night, November 9, 1938. There are, in addition, four synagogues in West Berlin now and one in East Berlin. In West Berlin there are 6,000 Jews; in East Berlin, 700. In 1930 there were 100,000 in the city. When I asked Jews in Munich why they remained in Germany, they said because it was their home. But it is difficult for me to understand their repression, their recalcitrance, or their resilience.

Damn it all, but the Russian manufacturers of barbed wire must be writing their books in bold black! The morning began with a long walk around a portion of the Berlin Wall. Memorials mark sidewalk deaths for would-be escapees; observation towers where one can see East Berlin; an overgrown cemetery with a solitary large yellow watchdog, barbed wire, and walls of brick topped with glass shards; and an East Berlin street where a woman about 50 yards away watched me as I watched her. How I wished to know her thoughts and to call to her, but a Russian guard was also observing me. Warning signs face both East and West Berlin. Soldiers—French and West German, since this part of the wall is in the French sector—patrol the area guarded by an armed Russian soldier. West Berliners can ride under the eastern sector, but they cannot disembark unless they hold a police permit and, even then, only one station on the U-Bahn line is now in use. As the train whizzes by closed stations, you can see armed guards standing by.

This marks the spot where Ernst Mundt was killed trying to escape over the Wall from East Berlin. There were many similar memorials by the Berlin Wall.

East Germany beyond the barbed wire. The sign reads: Securing peace in Europe requires respect for existing borders.

On Gartenstrasse next to the wall, car owners line up their cars for washing at a sidewalk pump. While just around the corner is Bernauerstrasse, an unpleasant street of once-houses. All that remains on one side are building fronts with windows cemented shut like a horror movie set, now a part of the wall and a vivid image of what the Russians have done to keep their citizens confined. On one part of the wall someone whitewashed the letters K-Z, the initials for *Konzentrationslager*, and that, as you can guess, means "concentration camp."

Once I took this walk, I felt prepared enough to go into East Berlin, and chose this day to take the S-Bahn to the Friedrichstrasse checkpoint. The S-Bahn is the Soviet-operated tram that runs through all sectors. While the U-Bahn stations are modern and clean, the S-Bahn stations are old, dirty and overgrown. The fare to East Berlin is just 12¢ to another world.

Foreign visitors to East Berlin must cash a minimum of $1.25 (5 Deutsche marks), non-refundable. I had some money left over, in fact, and the Russian guard told me to go eat or drink something. When I refused, he directed me to a Red Cross coin box. While waiting for my passport to be checked, an Austrian man asked if I was an American on holiday. When I replied yes, he asked, "Couldn't you think of a better place to spend your holiday than in East Germany?" There are no policemen, only Russian soldiers—a surly lot. There are no traffic jams, no neon signs, no gay sidewalk strollers—unless they are foreigners and, even then, it is hard for anyone to feel gay in East Berlin. I was invited to go nightclubbing tonight and, while it would have been intriguing, my escorts were Syrian and Egyptian and that left me with no comfortable thoughts whatsoever. There is more I wish to see in East Berlin, so I am returning tomorrow, this time through the more well-known Checkpoint Charlie.

The area bordering Avenue Unter den Linden was the cultural center of Berlin in pre-war days. It is a wide street with a park in the center and fashionable shops on either side. I walked down to the Brandenburg Gate, or as close as I was allowed to go, then walked back the other way to the Historical Museum, devoted to German history and filled with pictures, books, graphs, tools, etc.—all explaining how wonderful the workers' revolts have been throughout the world, how Russia "saved" Berlin from Nazi domination, and how Russia aided the workers in the Spanish Civil War. It also has displays about the terrible factors of imperialism and the rise of Marx, Engels, and other communist heroes. How I wished I had an interpreter with me there! I watched the changing of the guards at the Soviet Memorial, which houses a large stone symbolizing I know not what. I visited the excellent and vast Pergamon Museum, St. Mary's Church (formerly one of the oldest Protestant churches in Berlin but now a bombed-out shell), and the display at the *Berliner Newspaper* office about the horrors of the Vietnam War.

10/23/66

I don't think I have ever been so moved by political injustice as I have been in Berlin. I can think of no greater indignity, insanity, or invalid action than the Berlin Wall and what has resulted from the horrid day on August 13, 1961, when people woke to find they were barbed-wired in and held back at gunpoint from crossing the street to freedom. Construction of the wall cut off East Berlin from West Berlin and West Berlin from the surrounding East Germany. East Germans claimed the wall was erected to protect its population from fascist elements conspiring to prevent building a socialist state in East Germany. In practice, the wall served to prevent the massive emigration and defection from East Germany and the Communist Eastern Bloc during the post-World War II period. Before the wall was built, 3.5 million East Germans crossed the border from East to West Berlin, from where they could travel to West Germany and other Western European countries.

Checkpoint Charlie is in the American sector and the examination here by Russian Army soldiers—actually, both Russian and German—is more intense than that at the Friedrichstrasse station. For cars it is almost agonizing when even the seats must be removed. The Volpos (Volkspolizei, the dreaded East German Police with sub-machine guns) have the measurements for every part of every car. No longer can escapees hide under the seats or in the hood. 129 people have died in escape attempts. The Volpos want no more deaths and no more escapes. The sign in the German Democratic Republic border office says: The Socialist Unity Party is the Party of Peace, of National Dignity, and of National Unity. It staggers the imagination!

I walked down to Potsdamer Platz, once Berlin's central square, and was startled to realize that at 12 noon I was the only person on the once-busy Leipzigerstrasse. But that was true everywhere—even on East Berlin's main Alexander Platz and Strausberger Platz, there were only scattered strollers. One store with sales demonstrations and fashion shows only had a group of about 30 people. Three Germans were fishing in the river; mothers walked their children; and young lovers held hands. There were only a few signs of what I'd label "normalcy." I did see a few neon signs today, but they brought no life to this already dead city.

Despite the fact that East Berliners are held back by enough barbed wire to span the earth, life still goes on. There are nine main theaters, including one named Maxim Gorky Theater, that feature drama, comedy, and such diverse musicals as *My Fair Lady* and *Don Giovanni*. The Berliner Ensemble continues the Theater of Bertolt Brecht and is now headed by Brecht's wife. There's a puppet theater, dances and concerts, and lectures are held at the Central House for German-Russian Friendship.

A variety of magazines are available, but they are printed in Russia or in the Russian sector of Germany. Most are in Russian or German, but I did notice a Chinese-language newspaper.

When window shopping, none of the brand names were familiar to me, but I assume that most are Russian. I don't know what the actual value of the East German mark is (the weight is that of tin toy money), but visiting foreign nationals must exchange their marks at the rate of 1:1. This is undoubtedly to the DDR's advantage.

Back in West Berlin and opposite Checkpoint Charlie, I went to an exhibition titled "Freedom Must Not End Here!" It was set up by students and political refugees and has many pictures of escapes or other incidents at the wall, displays of items used in escapes, a movie about the wall, children's drawings, and two TV cameras on the roof that show what present life is like on Friedrichstrasse in East Berlin. It is a very moving exhibit.

I ended the day on a much happier note—dinner in the first Japanese restaurant I've found since Hong Kong, then a sold-out performance at the Jewish Center by Belina, an Israeli, who sings in Hebrew, Russian, Yiddish, and English, and Bahrend, a German guitarist.

[Checkpoints were opened in 1989. In 1992, demolition of the Berlin Wall was completed.]

10/25/66

I've really made tracks these last two days: to the museums at Charlottenburg Palace; the Berlin Pavilion of black and white photos of West Berlin; the State Porcelain Industry Showrooms; the Berlin City Museum; the excellent Dahlem Museum; "The History of the World" exhibition in Amerika Haus (in the same room where East Berliners once came to read "Free World" literature); and to Hansa, a modern living area constructed for the 1957 Berlin International Building Fair.

I've met few people in Germany. Most of my evenings are spent alone or at home, and I think there is a simple reason. I am easily mistaken for a German, and German girls (or natives) are not as readily approached. I know that I don't talk to many people because I'm not sure whether they are German. Because I have a ubiquitous European face, I had much more fun with contacts in Asia where I was decidedly foreign. Also, in Europe, there are always hordes of tourists, and we are not such novelties as in Asian hinterlands.

10/27/66

Before leaving Berlin yesterday afternoon, I went to the Reichstag, now being rebuilt, and Congress Hall, a graceful nine-year-old building designed by American architect Hugh Stubbins. I walked over to the western side of the Brandenburg Gate and watched Russian officers on the eastern side discussing the wall, or so it seemed. Near the Gate and in the west is the Russian Memorial guarded by the Russians, who are guarded by the British, and surrounded by a barbed-wire fence.

There was nothing special about the ride to Hamburg but for the scenic calm of Potsdam and a Russian tank on a flatcar surrounded by guards. My traveling companion was fascinating—an Islamic historian, author of several books, and an associate professor at the University of Hamburg. He was just returning from a three-week research trip to the Soviet Union and could not emphasize enough how different the Russians are in East Germany and in the U.S.S.R. We spoke almost the entire six hours of the trip, and I learned a great deal from him.

I had planned to stay with a Servas member here but again, as in Berlin, I struck out! The only Servas contact in Hamburg is now in France for ten months!

I didn't do much today but visit the Hamburg Art Gallery, the Museum of Art and Craft, and decide I was anxious to get to Denmark. I will leave here tomorrow.

My first stop, however, was the American Consulate. You mentioned my world correspondence. I received letters from the U.S., Israel, Japan, India, Denmark, and Greece! I love my global friendships! They are a privilege and a source of great joy!

Other mail today was a letter from my former WRVR boss telling me that my Japanese series was about to begin and could he count on two specials on Israel after I return. How like him and the whole system of educational radio to count on something without mention of payment! I also received a very sweet note from Yoyo Nakamura, the *sumi-e* (ink painting) artist and Living National

Treasure, whom I twice visited. The letter was written in graceful brush strokes (as opposed to the modern pen), and I had to take it to the Japanese Consulate here for translation.

10/28/66

It is as I knew it would be. I am already enraptured with Denmark! The ride from Hamburg to Ribe was enchanting, as was St. Michaelsdown and its pretty windmills and pasture-lands for sheep, sows, and cows. The cows are Holstein, for this is the North German peninsula of Schleswig-Holstein, an area of pastoral serenity and irrigated meadows whose color, even in mid-morning, retained the golden glow of the rising sun. In some little nameless town, the irrigated ditches became a widening river, and a fleet of colorful fishing boats rocked at rest in the tiny protected harbor. In Niebüll I saw evergreen branches being loaded on a freight train; they were no doubt headed for Hamburg florist shops to be sold as greenery with autumn flowers or considerably enhanced with Christmas ornaments. A little two-car train brought me across the border to Tønder and, since there were only five minutes to get through Customs and on the next little two-car train to Ribe, they had to call and have the train held for me. In Denmark, the only additions to an already picturesque countryside with groups of identical red-brick houses with red-tiled roofs were the cows wearing gray saddle blankets tied under their breasts in front of their forelegs.

Ribe, Denmark's oldest town, is charming, really charming. It's what I expected to find in the Rhineland and didn't. It's a twelfth-to-thirteenth-century town with numerous old, historical, half-timbered houses and flagstone alleys. It is famous for the storks that nest here on the chimney tops, but they are smarter than I; they have already gone south to warmer climes. There are three small historical museums and a local art museum and not much left of an old castle. But there stands a statue of Queen Dagmar in the prow of her boat, her hand shading the sun from her eyes as she looks at Jutland's shores. On the shore of Ribe's little river, laughingly called her port, stands an old wooden column indicating flood levels in 1634 (above the doorways), 1825, 1904, 1909, and 1911. Where the river flows into the town is a very old, out-of-order water wheel. I am staying at Ribe's youth hostel, complete with indoor tennis and hockey court.

10/29/66

When I awoke this morning, a heavy coat of frost blanketed the land, and garden dahlias and roses hung as if they'd been preserved for all time in a deep freeze. When I boarded the bus, I saw several little girls saying goodbye to an elderly man. The girls shook hands and executed quick and practiced curtsies. Breakfast was a big slice of Danish blue cheese and a small loaf of hot, fresh bread.

The ride to Odense was short and uncomplicated, and I am now on the second largest island, "The Garden of Denmark." First visit today was to the home of Hans Christian Anderson, then to his boyhood home, and then to Funen Village, a charming museum community of 22 structures, some dating back to the sixteenth century: water mill, smithy, shoemaker, vicarage, weaver's house, windmill, maypole, district jail, and others. Odense is hardly the quaint city I've read about, but it's worth a visit, nevertheless. It's grown too big and industrial to be considered quaint.

Guess what Danish cars have in their ESSO-filled tanks? "*Kom em tiger i tanken.*" Here, too!

10/30/66

I took the bus down to Fåborg this morning, a town that dates back to 1225. It was destroyed by fire in 1715 so the old homes only go back 250 years. Only 250 years! The town is supposed to be similar to Ribe, but isn't nearly as charming. The drive down to Fåborg reveals rolling hills and grazing cows. There are lots of old thatched houses on the way, similar to what is in the Funen Village, which means that Funen Village isn't a museum at all. It's simply a place for tourists who don't get into the real Danish countryside.

I'm now in Copenhagen with Joanne and Mel Zax. **[another niece** and nephew of friends of my parents.] They live in a villa on the edge of a lake and, while there are few American luxuries like a large refrigerator and closet space, it has a remarkable second-floor terrace and an indoor fireplace. The rest of the house is a museum piece.

11/4/66

I've managed to enjoy Copenhagen despite bad weather, short museum hours, and the winter closure of the world-famous Tivoli Gardens.

On the 1st, I went to a luncheon with Joanne. On the 2nd, I explored the university area. That evening Joanne and I went to a performance of *La Traviata*. On the 3rd, I visited Christianborg Palace, the state rooms and the ruins beneath of the twelfth-century Absalom's Castle and the first two Christianborg Castles destroyed by fire. Then on to Thorvaldsen's Museum filled with his sculptures, with time to wander around the oldest part of Copenhagen. One house entrance is covered with frescoes depicting some of the owners since 1379. Last night I spent a pleasant evening with John and Bergljot Heaslip. Bergljot is a friend of Claudine's. She is Danish; John is American.

Today I was at the City Museum, then took a fascinating walk through Nyhavn, the sailors' quarters filled with bars open from 5 a.m. till 1 a.m. the following morning and where, at 10 a.m. already, drunks are weaving down the streets. Two tattoo parlors display in their windows all the gross arty pictures that can be permanently needled into one's skin. Ships lie in the river and the harbor, and horse-drawn carriages from the Carlsberg Brewery wait to be unloaded. It is picturesque, all located just a stone's throw from Amalienborg Palace, where the king and queen reside and where the Royal Life Guards pace back and forth.

John and Bergljot have convinced me to stay in Copenhagen for about a month. If I do not find a temporary job, it will not be because Bergljot hasn't tried. Already she's set up interviews for me and is still thinking of other possibilities. Tomorrow morning I go to Japan Air Lines and SAS, which is as much as I can do on the weekend, and will then see about finding a place to live.

11/7/66

I moved into a hotel in downtown Copenhagen, a remarkably decent hotel and am paying just $18 for one week, baths, phone, and tax included. I have nothing to report on a job and, if I don't find one within the week, I'm leaving.

I went to the Copenhagen cathedral for Vespers but, more specifically, to hear the Copenhagen Boys' Choir. There are about 100 boys aged 7-17. Boys will be boys regardless of their talents and, once they filed out of the church and donned their coats, they clattered down the stairs as if they were running to a newly-organized sandlot football game!

I visited the Round Tower, the top of which is reached by a broad, spiral, flagstone ramp. It was built in the seventeenth century by Christian IV for the adjoining Church of the Trinity and as an observatory. I watched the Changing of the Guards at Amalienborg Palace, then went to the Museum of Applied Arts and the Freedom Museum about Denmark's Fight for Freedom in 1940-45. Tonight I'm finally going to see *Doctor Zhivago*. There are so many good movies here now; I couldn't begin to catch up on all I've missed these past two years!

11/11/66

I went to see Jens Olsen's World Clock in the City Hall. Olsen was a locksmith with an interest in clocks and astronomy. It took him 23 years to design this and it is so accurate it will lose only half a second every 300 years! It gives information on world and local time, dates, stars, planets, moon, sun, and leap years.

Yesterday I went out to Roskilde, Denmark's capital until 1444 and the seat of a bishopric. There's a fine Romanesque cathedral there begun by Bishop Absalom in 1170. It's on the original site of a wooden church constructed around 960 by King Harald

Bluetooth. (How's that for a handle?!) Bluetooth is now buried in the red brick cathedral along with 35 other Danish kings and queens who lie at rest in sarcophagi of marble and alabaster. More wondrous than the sarcophagi, I thought, were the choir stalls in carved wood. Old European churches have the most striking choir stalls. Most people pass over them, but they're the first things I look for. An amusing digression: Roskilde has a Home for Unmarried Ladies of Rank, an institution founded in 1699. That's a fancier name than "old maids' home"!

I went to the wonderful old Theater Museum in Christiansborg Slot (Castle). The theater dates back to the 1700s. Fascinating as it was, it would have been more so were I a devotee of Danish theater.

As I anticipated, today was a really fun day. I always feel like a part of the community when I'm riding a bike, and I rented one for the day. Bicycling is very common here, but try manipulating in rush hour downtown traffic. It's a brake and a prayer all the way!

I toured the Carlsberg Breweries—incredibly artistic for a factory. J.C. Jacobsen and his son, Carl, the first owners of the two breweries, which are now amalgamated, were benefactors and philanthropists of the noblest character. I never realized how much they have done for Denmark, as well as scientists all over the world. J.C. endowed science; Carl endowed art; and now all their labs and museums are a part of the Carlsberg Foundation administered by five professors from the Danish Academy of Arts and Sciences. Incidentally, each of the 3,500 workers at Carlsberg gets six free bottles of beer daily, all of which must be consumed on the premises. Free beer in endless quantities is given to all visitors also. I met two Italians this morning who had come for their third tour and third round of free beer—the obvious ulterior motive! I went to see the Fredericksberg Town Hall and the Statens Museum with a collection of Picasso graphics. Then I cycled along the Langelinie ("long line"), a half-mile-long promenade that runs along the harbor and through Citadel Park. At the head of Langelinie, Hans Christian Andersen's famous Little Mermaid bronze sculpture from 1913 sits on a rock.

I went to the wonderful Ny Carlsberg Glyptotek with an excellent collection of French impressionists, French sculptures, and Egyptian, Greek and Roman art—all the personal collection of Carl Jacobsen mentioned above.

Tonight I'm attending one of the two concerts in the Copenhagen Jazz Festival to hear the Dave Brubeck and Stan Getz quartets.

Know who Anders And and Peter Plys are? Danish children do! They are Donald Duck and Winnie-the-Pooh!

I noticed an unusual item for sale in Copenhagen's supermarkets. Meats in plastic wrapping come with prunes, orange or lemon slices, and bay leaves for seasoning while cooking. It saves buying a whole orange when only two or three slices are needed. How convenient!

11/12/66

I went out to Elsinore today to Hamlet's legendary castle and toured the state rooms, the dungeons, and the museum. I'm good at mentally reliving the days when Elsinore's guns were pointed on the Sound and for 400 years forced through-going ships to pay Sound Dues. Elsinore—in fact, Kronberg Castle—is located 25 miles north of Copenhagen and 2-1/2-miles from Sweden in a town called Helsingør. There I also visited the Marienlyst Palace, which was once connected to Kronberg by a 1-1/2-mile underground tunnel. Then on to the churches of St. Olai and St. Mary. Dieterich Buxtehude, a Danish-German organist and composer of the baroque period, played in St. Mary's for eight years. His compositions are a central part of standard organ repertoire, and his organ there has been restored. Also in St. Mary's according to the travel brochure, though I couldn't find it, is an "interesting portrait of Admiral Hans Pothorst who discovered America in 1472." Really?! 1472? Everybody's getting into the act!

I found a poster in the Elsinore Town Museum from 1800 that I'm sure you'll enjoy.

OFFICE RULES:

1. Gentlemen upon entering will Leave the Door Wide Open, or apologize.
2. Those having No Business should remain as Long as Possible, take a chair and Lean against the wall; it will preserve the wall and may prevent its fall upon us.
3. Gentlemen are requested to Smoke especially during Office Hours; Tobaccos and Cigars will be supplied.
4. Talk Loud or Whistle, especially when we are engaged, if this has not the desired effect Sing.
5. If we are in Business Conversation with anyone you are not to wait until we are done but to Join in, as we are particularly fond of speaking to half a dozen or more at a time.
6. Profane Language is expected at all times, especially if ladies are present.
7. Put your Feet on the Tables, or Lean against the Desk. It will be of great assistance to those who are writing.
8. Persons having no Business with this Office will call often or excuse themselves.
9. Should you need the Loan of any Money do not fail to ask for it, as we do not require it for Business Purposes, but merely for the sake of lending.
10. Spit on the floor, as the spittoons are only for ornament.
11. Our hours for listening to Solicitors for Benevolent Purposes are from 11 a.m. to 3 p.m., Book Agents from 1 to 3 p.m., Beggars, Peddlars, and Insurance Agents all day. We attend to our business at night.
12. The Lord helpeth those that help themselves, but the Lord help any man caught helping himself here.

11/12/66

This morning I went to services at Copenhagen's large, 133-year-old synagogue. Like the Vienna synagogue, it has been recently repainted but, unlike the synagogue in Vienna, this one is tastefully done.

This afternoon I went out to Klampenborg Park and visited the Ordupgaard Museum of French impressionist masterpieces and Danish art. The museum was established by a Mr. and Mrs. Wilhelm Hansen in 1918 and, in 1952, it became state property in accordance with the provisions of their will.

Near there is the Galopbanen race track, and I decided to go to the races. It was a foggy, cold afternoon, and the combination of red-gold fallen leaves, snorting, steamy horses, and crisp winter air made it all fresh and exhilarating and, yes, enchanting. The horses race on grassy turf.

11/14/66

Yesterday's trip to Stockholm was a long 10 hours and uneventful. I spent the entire time embroidering. Arrived at 9:45 p.m. and — par for the course — found the Servas contact unreachable. But I spoke to him today — by the sound of his voice, a man in his 50s — and discovered that just this evening he returned from his honeymoon. He was married on Saturday! Have had no success with other Servas members and spent these two nights at the KFUM (YMCA) Hostel. Tomorrow I'm moving into the Af Chapman Youth Hostel, a nineteenth-century sailing ship.

This hostel is $2 a night and, while it may not seem so, there is nothing other than the ACYH that's cheaper in this expensive city. Last night I had my own room and tonight I'm sharing it with an elderly Swedish woman, who is the only other woman I've seen here. I remember my first night in Europe in Paris seven years ago at the Maison des Étudiantes — how shocked I was to find that men and women shared the same toilets and showers. I'm seasoned now. Didn't even blink this morning when I found a man standing in his shorts and shaving. I'm still not comfortable in the easy-to-see-over-the-top toilet stalls. As for showers or bathtubs, there aren't any!

Sweden's capital is old and charming. It rambles over 12 islands connected by 42 bridges, and the sun doesn't shine in November. At least, it hasn't yet and, by 4:30, it's already night — only bothersome in terms of photography.

First stop—or ride up—this morning was in Katarinahissen, an outdoor elevator that takes you from one level of the city to another. Quite unique it is!

Stockholm is 700 years old and my next stop was the Old Town, the "City Between the Bridges," consisting of the center island and the two tiny ones of Riddarholmen and Helgeåndsholm. The center of the Old Town is Stortorget (Great Square). Here on November 8, 1520, Danish King Christian II, following his coronation in Stockholm of United Scandinavia, had 94 Swedish noblemen arrested, men who had just sworn their allegiance to him. They were put on trial (with the verdict and sentence long since prearranged) and beheaded. Then, with grotesque dramatic flare, the heads were piled up in pyramid fashion in the center of Stortorget. That—the Stockholm Massacre—marked the beginning of the Swedish battle for independence.

Though Sweden, Norway, Finland, and Denmark are now independent of each other, traveling between them involves no formalities. It's as easy as going from New York to Pennsylvania. Bank books good in one country are just as good in another.

The Royal Palace in the Old Town was finished in 1700. It's elegant and large—with almost 700 rooms. The apartments of King Oscar II and Queen Sophia are open to the public, as are the rooms for guests of the king. They are still used today when the gentry come calling!

Next to the palace is Storkyrkan, the Great Church or Stockholm Cathedral, founded in the thirteenth century, though the present exterior only dates back to 1743. Until this century, Storkyrkan was the coronation place of almost all the kings of Sweden and countless royal marriages, as well. Its royal pews are especially striking. From there to the House of Nobility, where the 2,345 crests of Swedish nobility are kept.

P.S. Again in Sweden: *"In med en tiger i tanken."*

11/15/66

Having had my fill of museums in Stockholm, this morning I went to City Hall, a most unique building designed by Ragnar Östberg, who, after a trip to various European cities, convinced a group of Stockholm millionaires to finance the building. Then he went to the city government. It was completed in 1923 at a cost of $3,600,000. Five hundred artists, sculptors, and craftsmen from all over Sweden contributed their talents to its creation and are now anonymously immortalized in stone over the doorways. Each of the red bricks was chiseled by hand, and the mosaic designs depicting Swedish history were done by a then unknown 27-year-old artist. The room now serves for Nobel Prize dinners and other state functions. The large marble hall downstairs is used for balls. The nicest thing is that any group can rent the halls for a nominal fee. Town Hall belongs to the people. They can use the room but not the kitchen facilities, which can feed 2,000. It is a fantastic building.

I did more exploring of the Old Town, then went to Riddarholm Church, originally founded in the thirteenth century as a Franciscan abbey, now the burial place of Swedish monarchs. I also went to the Post (Office) Museum, which was surprisingly interesting. Another surprise—displays were subtitled in English.

The subway system in Stockholm is the loveliest I've seen. Long, sleek escalators carry passengers to and from the underground platforms, and the walls are covered with modern, tasteful art. Tile patterns and caricatures of Swedish actors are carved in stone, for instance. I appreciate that the Tunnelbana (subway) is always spanking clean.

11/16/66

At the hostel yesterday, I met a very nice American, Nina Tanner, who is looking for someone to go with her to Russia. I told her I didn't want to hear about it! But she kept talking and, what's more, she was making sense. To make a long story short, we're going. This day was spent in making arrangements. We even went to the Russian Ambassador to find out the maximum amount of time we need to get a visa. What a shock to find he spoke no English! Fortunately, he spoke German and that saved us. In the middle of all this running around, I said to Nina, "How will I ever explain this nonsense to my parents?" Then I laughed, for I suddenly recalled your comment, Mom, that you could understand my going to Russia 'cause it's so close ... but not Lapland! I distinctly recall that in your last letter! Anyway, the scoop is that Friday afternoon Nina and I are taking a ship to Helsinki. We'll stay in Finland—Helsinki and Turku—until the 24th and then catch a train to Leningrad. We'll be in Leningrad until the 30th, then by train, freighter and bus return directly to Stockholm. We arrive on the 1st and that same day I head for Oslo. The point is to get there in time for the exam on the 3rd.

In Russia, of course, we have to travel with Intourist and that costs! As for Moscow, I have neither the time nor money to include it. Besides, Leningrad is historically the most important city.

Once all these arrangements were completed, Nina and I went to the markets in Hotorget and then to Djurgården. There we visited the Warship Vasa, built in 1628 for the wars, but it sank on her maiden voyage. In 1956 she was found half submerged in mud in Stockholm's harbor and, in 1961, a salvage fleet raised her to the surface. The archaeologists then excavated the ship and she is now housed in the harbor. During this process of preservation, she is sprayed every hour, 24 hours a day, with a special fluid that protects against shrinkage and attack from fungi.

Then to the embassy for mail, dinner and back to the hostel where I spent an hour speaking Japanese to some guys from Osaka. Landsmen!

The Af Chapman Youth Hostel is an old sailing ship moored within the area of a Swedish naval station. She was a rigged sailing ship, the *Dunboyne*, built in 1888 in England. She's now a popular and delightful youth hostel—perhaps the nicest hostel with the nicest view in the nicest of cities!

11/17/66

In Märsta my first thoughts were of a Swedish Levittown—numerous faceless, shapeless, three-story apartment buildings. Fifty percent of the Stockholm population own both summer and winter homes. Märsta is close to the archipelago with its 24,000 islands and, for that reason, the building continues, I suppose. A hometown Miss Rhinegold-type contest was taking place. Five local teenagers were competing to be selected as Lucia for the St. Lucia Day festival of lights on December 13th. The winner gets $10 and will wear a white dress with a red sash around her waist and a crown of candles on her head.

Then on to Sigtuna, site of some of the first Christian churches in Sweden and capital of Sweden in the Middle Ages. The remains of two stone churches and a rune stone are still there, and the main street still follows the course of a thousand years ago.

11/19/66

The boat ride to Helsinki was uneventful. Nina and I had our own closet-size stateroom that had neither closet nor porthole. It was a 20-hour ride and we awoke at 6:30 this morning to watch the sun rise. By 7:30 it was still black as night; the sun never did come out! But we had a moon tonight for the first time in about a week, and for that we were thankful. Yesterday, incidentally, we were treated to a picturesque sight of gulls following our ship, the *Aaltostar*, their reflections shining on the wet deck.

First stop this morning was at our travel agent's agent where we were told that our confirmation from Intourist had not come in yet and that, contrary to what the Russian Consul in Stockholm had told us, the consulate here was not open on Saturdays. And that's why we came running to Helsinki!

We wandered around the stores, visited the National Art Museum, set ourselves up in a private home, went to a piano competition at the Sibelius Academy, and then to a mediocre performance of Karl Millöcker's operetta, *The Beggar Student*. We had gone because the tourist office told us it was *The Student Prince.*

Helsinki is not particularly attractive, but it is old in many respects and has a minimum amount of charm. Damning with faint praise!

11/20/66

It was a good day today, not in terms of weather, but in what we did, starting at the Exhibition Hall, where the second day of a two-day dog show was taking place. So many dogs and so many strange and varied breeds. From there we took a tour of the Parliament with its five nude statues in the chamber hall called Pioneer, Intellectual, Future, Faith, and Harvest. Not sure how the nudity relates! Then to the National Museum, the Amos Anderson Art Gallery for the special exhibition of lithographs by Edvard Munch, to dinner, and home.

Nina and I have been having a terrible time with Finnish, which is closest to Hungarian. Finnish and Swedish are both official languages here and not many speak English. We were talking about the number of Ravintola in Helsinki, assuming it was a restaurant chain, and the different types of restaurants in the chain—expensive, cheap, Hungarian, Finnish. It suddenly occurred to us at the same time that *Ravintola* is simply the Finnish word for "restaurant."

Nina and I are alike in so many ways that it's an endless source of laughter. She hails from L.A. and is a 1964 graduate of U.C.-Berkeley, having majored in African Studies that included Xhosa, the South African click language that Miriam Makeba sings. Nina worked in Boston for the Unitarian Universalist Association. Coming over on the ship, she mentioned a girl she worked with named Carol who graduated from Syracuse University in '61. Suddenly it all fell into place—she was speaking of my S.U. friend Carol Hurlburt, née Johnson. The world is incredibly small!

In Stockholm, night fell by 4 p.m.; in Helsinki, daylight lasts till about 5 p.m. (on a good day). The gray skies of Finland match the gray buildings that match the gray streets. And Finland's Finest (i.e., army) complete the drab picture with dull gray uniforms. I've found nothing in Finland to love—but, then, I haven't tried a sauna yet!

11/21/66

Nina and I have received such differing information that we don't really know what's going on. We left Stockholm hurriedly because we were told by the travel agent that it takes a week to get our visas, that we couldn't get our visas without confirmation from the Intourist agent, and that the U.S.S.R. Embassy was open on Saturday mornings (so said the Russian Consul). Further, that confirmation would take about one week (travel agent) and could be sent to us in Helsinki. We raced to Helsinki to take the confirmation to the embassy on Saturday morning, so that we could get our visas and still be in Leningrad on the 24th. So what happens? The embassy is not open on Saturday; it's five days later and still no confirmation; we find we don't need confirmation to get a visa as long as we have an Intourist voucher (from Stockholm travel agent and confirmation from Leningrad); that the visa can be had in only two days; and that we can even go to Leningrad without confirmation by simply presenting ourselves to Intourist upon arrival. We could have stayed longer in Stockholm and saved ourselves worry. The whole business has, from the start, been a bit wacky!

Now we have had a sauna experience—at a neighborhood sauna in Turku. The sitting boards are on three cooking levels—rare, medium, and well done—the last being on top. Water is thrown on the coals or hot bricks to increase the heat, while each person carries a pail of lukewarm water to cool off the boards before sitting on them or to cool one's face as sweat pours from every pore. If desired, one can be flagellated with a bunch of birch branches, which further opens the pores to the intense heat. The birch leaves are fragrant and lie around the wet floor or stick to one's body as a result of the whipping. A session in a sauna is both relaxing and refreshing, and it was fun to share the experience with another neophyte. (Rereading this, it sure doesn't sound like fun!)

Turku is located in southwest Finland on the Aura River, a three-hour train ride from the capital. After 1155, Turku became the religious center of Finland and remained so until 1809 when Sweden surrendered Finland to Russia and Helsinki was made the capital. Historically, Turku is the oldest city and is once again an important seaport. We haven't had much of a chance to explore this city of 140,000 people, but the architecture we've seen so far is unique: red wooden houses with white trim or one-color wooden homes with fancy carved trim or stained-glass windows.

11/22/66

We visited Turku's medieval castle, Finland's only castle. Originally built in the thirteenth century, what's there now was reconstructed only five years ago. It's been designed for present-day use but, as castles go, this one's a bust!

The attractive community of Suostarinmäki (Cloister Hill) is a museum town of eighteenth- and nineteenth-century homes and shops: shoemaker, pipe factory, cooper, tailor, bakery (where by some magic the smell of fresh bread lingered), print shop, wigmaker, etc. That was followed by a visit to the Sibelius Museum, Turku's instrumental collection to which Sibelius loaned his name.

After dinner we went to another sauna—more deluxe and more expensive. As the heat rose, I gasped for air, but every inhale caused a burning sensation in my nostrils, and I jumped down to the lowest level until I could breathe again and regain my composure. Then back up top for a roasting. Had a soapy rub-down by a female attendant and then, while Nina underwent the same procedure, I went back into the sauna. A lukewarm shower to finish it off, and we were both enervated.

It snowed last night and the whiteness brought some life to an otherwise gray landscape. There was even enough to make snowballs! In many ways, Turku deserves a longer stay than Helsinki. The capital is like so many other cities but not as attractive nor as interesting, while Turku is quite different. We planned it wrong, but we must leave tomorrow to pick up our Russian visas. We want no slip-ups or delays.

From the Department of Worthless Information: The word *Oy* is Finnish for Limited or Incorporated. So signs read "Kodak Oy" or "Oy Valkarkis." We've been looking everywhere without success, for a sign reading "Oy Veh"! We did locate in the phone directory a company called Vei Oy! It was a silly activity that amused us.

Nina is a great person to travel with. We're so much alike that neither one of us can act as a stabilizing influence, and she's a great audience for my humor. There hasn't been a serious moment between us; it always ends in laughter!

11/23/66

Up at 6:15 and on the 7:20 train to Helsinki, where we first went to the Russian Embassy to pick up our visas. Not a hitch! We did a bit of wandering and shopping — window and otherwise.

For dinner we went to Kestikartano, a national-type restaurant with wood taken from the forests of Karelia before it became a Russian possession. While at the restaurant, we saw a rehearsal of "The Bear Feast," a story taken from the *Kalevala*, a book of Finnish mythology extending from the creation of earth to the conquest of paganism. The forest folk were to be placated for the loss of their beloved bear, so the hunter and villagers pretended that the bear had killed himself through an accident and came into the village as an honored guest. In eating the bear's flesh in a stew, the Finns believed they were acquiring the attributes of the bear: sharp ears, keen eyes, high forehead, long tongue, and wide mouth. There was even a bride, a young village girl for the bear, called Otso or Otonen. The hunter was named Väinämoïnen, the ancient bard-hero of *Kalevala*. The little play will be given tomorrow night by the Kalevala Organization, which raises money for the preservation of this mythology. Incidentally, we ate a Karelian stew of mutton, beef, veal, and smoked reindeer meat; it had a strong and unpleasant taste.

11/26/66

Leningrad, U.S.S.R. I'm glad I came. The history. Perspective. Personal contacts.

The train trip to Leningrad was not very exciting, but interesting nevertheless. Russian trains have hard cars and soft cars—2nd and 1st class, respectively—but, since the revolution, this has been a classless society and that includes train coaches! When the medical certificates were checked at the border, Nina realized she had left hers in Germany 'cause she didn't think she'd need it. Consequently, she had to get a smallpox shot on the train by a nurse with the biggest, fattest hypodermic needle I've ever seen! I was so grateful that I could avoid that! In Vyborg, we had a 40-minute station stop for dinner. Guards were all over the platform and building. That was our holiday meal on the way to Leningrad—beef stroganoff with our own concocted turkey stuffing of stroganoff gravy, dunked bread, and almonds! What a Thanksgiving!

We were met at the station by an Intourist guide and taken to the Hotel Astoria, where no-one was expecting us and no-one spoke English. Our guide left us there. Nina, who speaks ruptured Russian she learned from her grandmother, asked the maid where the heat was—well, that's what she thought, anyway. A most unusual look in response prompted Nina to recheck. She had asked where the maid's heart was.

The Hotel Astoria is where Hitler had planned his victory dinner in June 1941. He had already had the invitations engraved, but the Germans never entered Leningrad till 1944—and then as POWs. In the interim, the city suffered a 900-day siege and 700,000 people died of starvation.

While I think of it, I discovered another style of English to add to my list of Menu English and Passport English: Fruit Import English. The Russian woman told us we had to eat our fruit because it couldn't be taken into Russia. And that was the only English she knew!

Leningrad was founded in 1703 as St. Petersburg by Peter the Great. It's an expansive city and drab. Lack of competition leads to dreary shops and store windows and, in fact, the largest department store here was once a building housing numerous small shops in the days of Catherine the Great in the eighteenth century. All the connecting walls have been knocked down and the two floors circle the block overlooking the courtyard. Many of the buildings were once homes of the aristocracy, now reconstructed inside for other purposes but not retouched or beautified outside. Though Leningrad is reputedly the most beautiful city in the U.S.S.R., we have not found it to be so special. Big fluffy snowflakes help to beautify the scene, but only in the country or on cathedral domes does it not turn to slush.

Since we are first class tourists—that is tourist class in the western world—we get a guide and a car for three hours every two days. Yesterday, before joining our guide, we went into the small park in the square opposite our hotel, took some photos of Russian children, then walked across the street to the early-nineteenth-century St. Isaac's Cathedral, one of the most glorious cathedrals I've ever seen—second only to St. Peter's in Rome. I was awed by its magnificence and, particularly, by the solid columns of polished malachite.

With our guide, we took a brief drive around the center of the city and stopped first at the Palace of Weddings. Here in the presence of a city deputy and a woman from the Palace, young couples are married. In the downstairs registry room, they apply for marriage, then are given 15-30 days to think it over. Upstairs in the souvenir shop they can buy their wedding rings and other accessories and, on the day of their marriage, they return to the gold and white baroque Palace of Weddings. They must take their turns and, when we were there, four brides in white occupied four couches in the brides' room, each girl surrounded by a few friends and family. In the next room sat the four grooms. On cue the canned music begins and the couple, followed by their simply dressed small entourage, march up the carpeted staircase to the waiting room. Music fades on cue. The couple is invited into the room. Music up and under. Guests sit outside and couple stands in center. Music out. Bride asked if she'll take this groom. She says, *"da."* Groom states what name she'll take. They sign certificate. Witnesses also sign. Woman gives speech to young couple about difficulties ahead. City deputy presents certificate. Ceremony over. Applause. Music up for 30 seconds and out. (Shades of all my radio shows!)

From there to the tiny house Peter I built in 1703 on the shores of the Neva River, which runs through the city. The door isn't much taller than I am! Amazing, since we were told that Peter was really Great at 7' tall! I stood next to a desk designed especially for his height and, where it opened out, there was my chin!

The Museum of the Great October Socialist Revolution is filled with statues of Lenin (as is the entire city) with paintings, papers, and photos. There is also a small photo exhibition of America's war in Vietnam. "Why?" our guide finally demanded to know, "Why? Just tell me why are you fighting in Vietnam? Tell me!"

Last night for just $3.18 apiece, Nina and I went to see the Kirov Ballet with two French guest dancers performing a near-perfect "Swan Lake." We were one seat away from the best seat in the house in the central box. The Kirov Theater, formerly the Marinski Theater, is designed in white and gold. I was amused to see the loge audience promenading between acts—a quick stroll on a carpet that runs around a hall, and they just go round and round and round.

After the ballet we boarded a very crowded bus and, since we didn't know how to pay, I assumed the woman behind who tapped me on the shoulder was collecting. So I gave her 10 kopek. "*Nyet*!" So I gave her 30 kopek. "*Nyet*!" Then I grappled for my wallet and pulled out a ruble ($1.11). "*Nyet*!" And then I realized she wasn't collecting my money; she was trying to give me her money to pass on to someone to put it in the machine for her ticket. The fare turned out to be just 10 kopeks for the two of us. And we never paid. As we were pushed on, so were we pushed off!

If the controller comes on the bus or tram and you don't have your ticket, it's a 50-kopek fine. The Metro is another matter. If you don't pay the 5-kopek fare, the metal gates slam shut on your knees. Nina tried it.

Before the ballet, based on incorrect information, we went to Leningrad's only synagogue. (Nina is of Jewish ancestry but is Unitarian.) We found the building, but the only open door led into the trash room, which ultimately led to the caretaker's apartment. "No service tonight; come tomorrow."

So we did. The synagogue is the most unique I've seen and among the oldest. It dates back to the mid-1800s and reminds me in many architectural ways of a mosque. We spoke with a group of women—Nina in Russian and I in German and Yiddish—who were very emotional. They cried and kissed us. About 150 men and women were there today, although the synagogue holds 1,300. Now Leningrad has 300,000 Jews and most of them—in fact, all of them present this morning—were born before the revolution. They said life in Russia was not bad and that they received matzo during Passover. I told them I had lived in Israel, and one woman surprised me with the question, "Life isn't good there, is it?" I asked why she thought that, and she said she had read that Israel wasn't a good country.

Back at the hotel for a long lunch, we met a young Japanese man who joined us on our afternoon excursion. With guide and car, we drove out to the town of Pushkin, 25 kilometers from Leningrad, to visit the Palace of Catherine the Great. Then to the nearby town of Pavlovsk and a visit to the palace Catherine built for her son, Paul I. The 25-kilometer ride back to town took an hour and a half with four railroad crossings. And it didn't save time either when the driver took the wrong turn and got lost!

Early evening, Nina and I went to the blue and gold Russian Orthodox cathedral. On the first floor were many small chapels decorated with icons. At each, women prostrated, made the sign of the cross, and polished the covering glass with hand-embroidered cloths hanging on either side. There were also five coffins adorned with wilting flowers, perhaps the coffins of past bishops. Upstairs was the cathedral itself. There must have been at least 1,000 people in attendance, so Nina and I wondered if it might be a special holy day. Some stood; some kneeled; one man, in grotesque contortions of prayer, begged for his eyesight. Most were women over 50. We saw one child about six, a few young adults, and a few in their 30s and 40s. The head priest was an elderly man with a long white beard; the others, middle-aged; and all clergy wore robes of gold and maroon. The choir was made up of about 25 singers of varying ages. There was such genuine, or maybe just desperate devotion—crossing and bible kissing, collecting money in metal boxes with a single candle, tears, and congregational singing. These poor, old souls who don't know that for them their God is dead. On my way out, one woman reprimanded me for wearing a bright green coat. Perhaps it is customary to wear dark or drab coats to church. Perhaps they are in mourning—for God and for religion. It is customary to wear dark or drab clothing when mourning, isn't it?

Following this, Nina and I wandered into another department store. More people, more Christmas decorations of tree lights and bulbs, and statues of Grandfather Frost and the Snow Maiden. They have surely taken the Christ out of Christmas.

I discovered that the pamphlets we stole from the train coming into Russia and hid in our suitcases were free for the taking; that with Intourist the customer is never right; that Russians don't smile easily, especially those who work in hotels and stores (the ones on the street are friendlier—indeed, we have dates with two of them tomorrow night); that Intourist does not dog one's every step; that guides bait the foreign tourist (our guide today said, "Tell me, what's the difference between your two political parties. Tell me! What's the difference?"); that Russians think each of the 15 republics in the U.S.S.R. are represented in the United Nations; that Russia is a varied and eye-opening place for foreign tourists; and that bibles in large numbers are unwelcome.

We have been having a great time with food—breads, pastries, blintzes, borscht (not with red beets and sour cream but meat and cabbage), caviar, fish, sturgeon, beef stroganoff, kasha, and other wondrous delicacies.

11/30/66

The past few days have been so full that I haven't had a minute to write, but I've accumulated five pages of notes, so bear with me. If the writing is now a bit fuzzy, it's because I'm on a train to Turku after just two hours in Helsinki. But I have many things to cover before speaking of the present.

On the 27th, Nina and I went to the Peter-Paul Fortress erected by Peter I against the Swedes. The cathedral there was built 1712-33. All the Russian emperors from Peter I to Alexander III are buried there, except for Peter II who lies in Moscow. The gold baroque cathedral holds 27 marble sarcophagi that include the wives and children of the emperors or czars. Then back to St. Isaac's Cathedral for a second, longer look. Its 300-foot gilded cupola is decorated with 112 monolithic columns.

The evening before I was stopped on the street—I'm an obvious foreigner in a bright green coat in a land of drabness—by a Russian who wanted me to take a letter to Finland for him. I refused, and Nina and I walked on. But the young man caught up with us and asked if he could show me a bit of Leningrad that evening. I said no again and that I was going shopping with my friend. So he asked about Sunday night and mentioned a friend of his and asked if they could pick us up after the ballet. Nina and I exchanged quick glances, and I said yes.

That evening we saw a fine performance of *Giselle* and *Chopiniana*. The two young men Eric (Archil) and Michael (Mischke) met us in front of the theater about 10:30. We went to a Russian restaurant off the main street Nevsky Prospekt, named for Alexander Nevsky, a war hero of three battles in 1240 and 1242 and there talked, drank vodka, and ate sprats.

Eric, the one I met the night before, and Michael, whose father is a scientist and was at that moment at the Kremlin, are students at the Ship Building Institute. Eric said he was glad of the revolution because now he can be an engineer. He told me he was a communist because that's the only way to get anywhere in the U.S.S.R.

He had been a member of the Young Pioneers, but I do not know if he now belongs to Komsomol, the All-Union Leninist Young Communist League. The name comes from the first syllables of three Russian words meaning Communist Union of Youth. He wants to be prime minister some day, and his conversational offerings made him somewhat of a propagandist. Almost every sentence included the word "worker" and it was difficult to explain what an American worker was in answer to his probe. Eric thinks the Soviet government plans for the future but "plans slowly" and doesn't understand why they discourage contact with foreigners. He believes that to be a modern man he must know other nations and is, therefore, hoping to do graduate work in France or the U.S. in sociology. Sociological studies are only two years old in the U.S.S.R., thus his desire to study abroad. He went into engineering simply because he didn't want to go into the army or marines for four or five years. Now he doesn't want to be an engineer because his ready access to "secrets" will, perhaps, cause the government to prevent his visiting other countries.

At this restaurant most of the clientele were young adults. A band played and there was dancing. The Russians are wild twisters! While drinking vodka, we learned two slang phrases: *"Poddadim"* (D'ya wanna' drink?") and *"Zdaróvye"* (To your health.") The total bill came to 3 rubles, 82 kopeks—a bit high for students who are given a monthly government stipend of 50 rubles, or $55.50.

Peter the Great was immortalized in Pushkin's poem "The Bronze Horseman"—and Monday we walked over to the statue of The Bronze Horseman in Decembrist Square, named for a revolt in 1125. The rebellion was led by army officers who wanted representation for the privileged class rather than have total government control in the hands of the czar. The revolt was put down after a few hours; 1,000 men were arrested; 12 were hung.

Back to the hotel to pick up our car and guide, then on to Smolny Institute, built by Catherine the Great as a school for daughters of the nobility. It was a finishing school to isolate the "noble" child and create "a new species of humanity." Before the building was constructed, the area was a ship-building yard with much tar about. "Tar," in Russian, is *smolnia* and thus the name Smolny. But comes the revolution, the daughters leave, and the place is occupied by the Revolutionary Government. Lenin and his wife lived in two small rooms there in 1917-18, and these are now open to the public. At present, the party administration—i.e., the city soviets, regional administration, and regional soviets—is housed there. 650 deputies in the city commission are each elected for two years. They come from all professions but "no professional politicians"—quotes from Sonya, our guide. Cities get their budget from the central government and profits from little enterprises. There's a graduated income tax starting at 0.5% up to 13%. Those earning under 60 rubles a month (museum guards was the example given) pay no taxes.

In visiting the museum part of Smolny with photos and drawings of events leading up to the revolution, we teamed up with a Japanese delegation. Their Russian interpreter said something to me in Russian. I surprised them all by saying in Japanese that I spoke no Russian but did speak Japanese. From then on, he spoke in Japanese to the delegation, and I translated from Japanese to English for Nina. Love when this happens!

We then went to the Kazan Cathedral, the colonnade of which was built in honor of Russia's victory over Napoleon. It is a repulsive museum of anti-religion and atheism divided into four parts: astronomy, history of Russian Orthodoxy, tribal religions, and contemporary religion in the U.S.S.R. For the point it is trying to make and succeeds in so doing, it is ingeniously planned: paintings of historical religious injustices and uprisings; iron crosses and religious shackles worn by sinners; vicious satiric lithographs; posters of workers knocking out religions and urging post-revolutionary citizens to give up these things; photos of people turning away from religion—replacing icons with radios, reading atheistic newspapers, etc.; clothing and photos of a counter-revolutionary religious sect; a kiosk with a wax monk selling Catholic votive trinkets and postcards of St. Peter's; a diorama of monks playing in a jazz band in the choir loft under which teenagers jive behind the rows of pews; photos of James Meredith after a beating; demonstrators threatened; and bread lines of '62. The last three in the U.S. Also, a declaration (from the constitution?) providing for "freedom of conscience." It's all there. No religion is spared.

Interspersed among the exhibit were these maxims:

Gorky: *The church educates men not to think, but puts them in a religious stupor.*

Engels: *It behooves factory owners to train workers to obedience because obedient people are not thinkers—not dangerous to profits.*

Lenin: *It is necessary to circulate atheistic propaganda because the peoples of the world have been told for centuries what religion is; now they need a chance to be told what atheism is."*

One thing can be said for the Soviets: despite their outward hatred for things religious, they seem to have done a remarkable job of preserving, without condoning, memorials of the past. St. Isaacs, for instance. They have apparently felt no need to erase these reminders of a long-gone past. Our guide said the Russians have never been very religious and that, even from the beginning, there was an atheistic movement.

That afternoon Nina and I went to the world famous Hermitage Museum. It was founded in 1764 when a collection of 225 paintings were purchased by Catherine the Great. Hermitage means "a hermit's dwelling" or "a solitary place," and, indeed, the first Hermitage was a palace museum accessible only to those closest to court. The Hermitage, now greatly expanded especially since the revolution nationalized all private collections, is located in the Winter Palace. That structure was built in the eighteenth century at the wishes of Catherine and designed by the same architect who planned her summer palace in Pushkin. The green baroque palace, now a museum, has 300 rooms; 2,300,000 exhibits; and 8,000 paintings. It has the finest collection of French paintings outside France—complete rooms of Rubens, Rembrandt, and Picasso— and art from the ancient world to the present. It is magnificent— the exhibits as much as the palace rooms themselves.

The Winter Palace is situated on the main Neva River. Behind it in Palace Square is the Alexandrovskaya Column, the world's tallest monolithic stone monument—154' high, weighing 600 tons. It commemorates the Russian victory over Napoleon in 1812, as does the adjacent Triumphal Arch.

With extra Intourist meal coupons that had to be spent or destroyed, Nina and I started living (eating) big. We've been doing pretty well, anyway, but that night we ordered past favorites, including a "special dish of mushrooms and wine from Crimean vaults."

Following this we met Eric and Michael again at the Dom Knigi, Leningrad's largest book haunt, and went to a distant movie theater to see one part—Natasha's love story—of the three-part Soviet version of *War and Peace*. If that is one of Russia's best cinematic efforts, they have a long way to go—blocked-out screens, fuzzy borders on some of the frames, and varying illogical changes in sound volume.

Incidentally, Michael and Eric asked us if we would change money for them because at the dollar shops all things are considerably cheaper—a book for 7R50, or $2.33; a watch for 165 rubles, or $17. We wouldn't do it. The government penalty is high.

American cigarettes are valued gifts, and I'd given a pack to Eric. While we were talking in front of the hotel, a policeman and another man came out of the hotel and stood talking on the stoop next to us. Eric suddenly put his finger to his lips in the age-old sign of "quiet." His back was to the policeman, and he motioned me across the street. He explained that he ought not speak to foreigners, that he and Michael had already been reprimanded, that the government was afraid "secrets" might be told. Then he suddenly looked me straight in the eye and with absolute seriousness asked, "Are you a spy?" "No, of course not!" With earnest, he responded, "I believe you."

Nina bumped into Dick Longworth in the hall and the evening turned into a late one as we adjourned to the downstairs bar till 2:30 a.m.. We had met Dick the evening before when the three of us shared a taxi to the ballet. He is from Chicago originally but is now on a three-year assignment in Moscow with UPI (United Press International). His wife had gone to Helsinki for a week to stock up on basic necessities and Christmas gifts unavailable in Russia, and he had come to Leningrad for three days, his first visit in the year-and-a-half he's been in this country. Student Eric thinks Moscow is great for journalists since so much is always happening there, but generally classifies Moscow as a "dump." Would that I could have seen it and judged for myself!

At the dollar shops, misnamed because they'll accept about 12 different kinds of stable currency, change can come in any form. I was given a French *franc* after a payment in dollars and, when I paid for something with the *franc*, I received a piece of chocolate in change since the cashier had no *centimes*. They want stable currency desperately and bend backwards to get it.

The next day we began our last full day at the Peasants' Free Market. Each peasant reserves from the state about one acre of land to raise anything he chooses. Collective farms and free enterprise. The products from these farms are usually the best offered, but we were revolted by the thousands of rotten fruits—apples, tangerines, pomegranates. Dick was also surprised, for he said that is rarely the case. The prices are higher, but the quality is better. Soup greens were put in bunches, just enough for one pot, and sold for 10 kopeks a bunch.

Back in the heart of town, Nina and I separated, and I went meandering to the supposedly poor replica of Moscow's St. Basil's Cathedral. It was so unique!

On the way to the Hermitage Museum again, I was surprised when a sidewalk construction worker smacked out a loud kiss and blew it in my direction. Didn't quite expect that from the Soviets!

That evening Nina, Dick, and I had our final "blow out"—vodka, caviar, crab salad, tongue, 40-minute chocolate soufflé, and two bottles of champagne. The three of us had coupons worth a total of 22R60. Without keeping track, our bill somehow, incredibly, totaled 22R61! A grand total of $8! Money's no object but, with us, it was coupons. It was a fantastic meal, and the first time I've ever had enough champagne to feel giddy. During the meal, Dave Levy of the Canadian Broadcasting Company joined us briefly. He, too, is stationed in Moscow and was filming a TV show in our hotel dining room.

When Dick, Nina, and I were almost the last ones awake in the hotel, we were entertained at 3 a.m. by the bar guitarist, who had moved to the quiet and better acoustics of the small hotel cloak room.

I had a bit of a scare yesterday evening when I returned from the Hermitage before Nina and I went to pick up our passports at Intourist. After a careful (?) check, I was informed they didn't have them and that surely Nina must have picked them up. I was sure she hadn't. Nervous tension for 15 minutes until they called the room and apologized. They had them.

That brings me to today but not nearly to the end of this novelette. We were out of the hotel at 7 a.m. and by 8 we were on our way to Helsinki. After having already taken several scenic photos from the train, we were told to stop, but I surreptitiously snapped another of the barbed wire and a watch tower at the Finnish border.

The most frustrating thing about the train ride was that the sun came out in all its golden glory—the first time we've seen the sun in three weeks! By the time we got to Helsinki at 4 p.m., it was already night. A two-hour stopover there; the train to Turku; a 2-1/2-hour wait there, where we were amused by a family of Finnish gypsies (that's sardonic); and now the ship to Norrtälje.

Russia was a sobering experience. Nina and I didn't fully relax until we were on our way out. There's not much joy in the U.S.S.R. and it seemed to effect us.

I have numerous odd notes and thoughts that I'd like to get down, so if you'll just bear with me, I'll start subject hopping.

There are 17 places of worship in Leningrad: 1 Baptist, 1 Lutheran, 1 Mosque, 13 Russian Orthodox churches, and 1 synagogue.

The largest department store in St. Petersburg (from the time of Catherine) is the Gostiny Dvor.

Men's fur hats are called *shapka*; women's, *shlapa*. The fur is called *meh*.

UPI journalists or other press-types use the phrase: "Do you know a pigeon?" when looking for people leaving the U.S.S.R. who can carry stories out.

Salaries. Beginning wage for engineers is about 100R ($111.11) with a raise to 150R in three years. Teachers earn about 80R; dental technicians, 90R; Intourist guides, at least 150R. But a good coat is 100R; decent boots, 60R; tablecloths, 10R; automobiles, 5,000R. Clothes are outrageously priced; dress patterns, outrageously designed. Quote from a women's magazine: "Even in a crowd of visitors, you can always recognize the Leningrad woman by the style of her clothes and the casual way she wears them." We laughed to think of the outmoded, drab, dumpy fashions and the tucked-under-the-chin babushkas.

Department stores have long queues at various counters, which might lead one to assume that they are lining up for "specials." But no, just hats, newspapers, new Metro maps, and food. All shops have special cashiers; no money is handled by the salesgirls. There are long lines on Sundays for the museums. We had wanted to visit the Hermitage on Sunday but were quickly discouraged by the round-the-block queue.

The nicest store we were in was a specialty food store on Nevsky Prospekt, which had high prices but a pleasant and cheery interior with large, airy showcases and neon lights in the shape of lilies hanging from metal stems.

According to Dick (from UPI), the Russians know the merchandise is lousy, and they buy a minimum of goods. He claims there is a great deal of unspent money around and, if the market opened, the worst inflation in the history of the world would hit the U.S.S.R.

Beryozka is the name of the foreign currency shops at Intourist hotels.

The U.S. has consular representation only in Moscow. When the ambassador travels to other parts of the Soviet Union, it is merely a gesture of goodwill and as a guest of the government.

Soviet authorities consider the three million Jews an ethnic, not a religious, group. Policies of persecution followed (especially 1940-53) with the aim of eradicating Jews who might have loyalties outside the Soviet Union. Direct persecution of the Stalin era has eased, though official discrimination persists. Dick feels that pressure by American Jews helps ease the situation because the Soviet Union is concerned with public opinion.

Leningrad overlooks the Gulf of Finland. The capital was built there when Peter the Great realized the need for a European seaport for development. At the time, the city was called St. Petersburg. It was renamed Petrograd in 1914 at the beginning of World War I, then Leningrad after the death of Vladimir Lenin in 1924.

[And in 1991, when the Soviet Union collapsed, its name was changed back to St. Petersburg.]

Before World War II, three million people lived in Leningrad. One million evacuated; one million were killed, about 700,000 by starvation. The sole source of supply during Germany's 900-day siege was a precarious ice highway across frozen Lake Ladoga, because a section of the eastern shore remained in Soviet hands.

The city of Leningrad is made up of 101 islands, 350 bridges, and 200 miles of waterway.

The Leningrad Metro, a marvel in marble, is not as colorful as the one in Stockholm, but its efficiency may be second only to the famous Moscow Metro. The automatic coin collectors and escalators are sleek and fast; the underground stations of marble, glass, plaster, steel, and lighting are designed to create varied effects of socialist symbolism.

Pushkin, where Catherine the Great's Summer Place is situated, was formerly Tsarskoyeselo (Village of the Tsars). Prior to the 1917 revolution and his forced abdication, it was the permanent residence of Czar Nicholas II and his family.

Boris Pasternak's *Dr. Zhivago* has never been published in the U.S.S.R., but our first guide had read it, which means books do get around even here.

We were approached on the street by boys requesting chewing gum and pens. They were willing to pay for the latter. It was all their gain—foreign pens have a high resale value.

A Young Pioneer stuck a pin on Nina's sweater while she was reading a map at the Hermitage. His comment in English: "We like you in Leningrad."

Enrollment in the Young Pioneers is 19 million youths, 9-14 years of age. They have lectures on Soviet leaders, the army, and elementary instruction in communist doctrine. The groups sometimes help in collecting scrap metal or in the work on collective farms. They are led by the 21.1 million members of Komsomol, 14-28 years of age. Their aims include the mastery of revolutionary theory and the study of the teachings of their leaders. They must be ready for defense and must be eloquent propagandists.

Exploitation of the masses is forbidden. One man may have his own shop, but he may do no hiring.

Russian litterbugs who are caught must pay a 50 kopek fine. If they argue with the policeman, they must pay 1 ruble. And if they continue to argue, their punishment is 15 days in jail—for a piece of paper!

Eric asked me the meaning of three American words he'd picked up from Paddy Chayefsky: slob, snob, and barf. The "workers" will never be the same!

Intourist hotel menus are written in Russian, German, English, French, and Chinese; but few of the personnel speak anything but Russian.

The Anichkov Bridge along the Nevsky Prospekt crosses the Fontanka River and has at each of its four corners fine bronze sculptures of a man training a horse.

Expectant mothers receive a month's paid leave before childbirth and two months after. When the newborn child is registered, it receives a medal. Awards are given to mothers with more than ten children.

The state spends 90 rubles a year for the education of every pupil in an ordinary school and more than 600 rubles a year in a boarding school. Who is entitled to go where and why I don't know.

There are 33 children's railways in the U.S.S.R. Places include Yuzhno-Sakhalinsk, Rostov, Sumgait and Dnepropetrovsk. Both passengers and drivers are children who are interested in becoming railwaymen. In Gorky, the children run a boat service and have transported 200,000 young passengers.

According to Intourist, the visitor can do anything she wants, but we couldn't get permission to visit a radio or TV station, a prefabricated housing production plant, or the Young Pioneer Palace. We were told the latter was under repair: "See all the scaffolding?" we were asked by our Intourist guide. But it sure didn't look that way when we drove by; there was no scaffolding anywhere!

Intourist also gets the visitors' money. Not only are coupons non-refundable and an exorbitant tax added (the price of an extra night), but a train reservation (an absolute necessity) requires an absolute extra fee of 2 rubles!

12/1/66

Having left Russia, I shall drop the subject. I apologize for this unintentional tome I've written, but you were warned! It was important to get everything down while still fresh.

Nina and I had another small room on the good ship *Scandia*. It was below the car deck and next to the engines, which had a tendency for extreme fits of noise! There was a sauna on the ship but, while Nina took advantage of it, I felt I had to keep writing. We arrived in Norrtalje at 8:10 a.m., took a bus to Stockholm, and arrived there about 9:45. With great reluctance and regret, Nina and I said goodbye, then I went out to the apartment of a friend of a Servas host to pick up my suitcase.

[Nina and I reconnected again in 2018 when we were both living in the Bay Area of California. Our ease with each other rekindled good memories of a very interesting adventure more than 50 years ago.]

I mailed three packages of book materials, most of which were communist propaganda I'd brought out of Russia.

I left Stockholm on schedule at 4 p.m. and am now on the train to Oslo, thus the wavering hand again.

12/3/66

So now Oslo, a capital city with the appearance of a small town. Small main streets hung with Christmas lights, small stores, but some excellent specialty shops. The anachronously large Royal Palace is situated on a sloping hill in a park at the end of the central main street Karl Johans gate, named in honor of King Charles III John, who was also King of Sweden as Charles XIV John. (Norway was under Sweden's control at one time.) At the palace I watched the Changing of the Guards—each guard with a black feather in his cap, Yankee Doodle Dandy style. It was particularly amusing on this rainy, slushy day because one of the guards stood anchored in a large puddle. Every time his left foot came down on command, muddy water sprayed up. But this particular dandy never cracked a smile.

I also visited City Hall with its outer ounce of modernity and its inner monstrous murals. On the walls of the outer courtyard are carved and painted squares of wooden figures depicting legends from Norwegian mythology. The inner main hall has large and homely frescoes, two of which are titled "Work, Administration, and Leisure" and "War and Occupation." City Hall took 20 years to complete; it was finished in 1950 in time for Oslo's 900th birthday. It is "an attempt to summarize in brick, stone, and paint the men and ideas of modern Norway." Every contemporary Norwegian artist of note had a hand in the decoration, which proves, in this instance, that too many cooks can spoil the broth.

I was more impressed by the native art I saw in the National Gallery of Art. The painters were all intensely nationalistic in their great respect and love for the natural beauty of Norway. I have seen no finer local landscape collection anywhere.

Oslo, once called Christiana, was named for Christian IV when Norway was under Danish domination. Yes, Danish, too. It is confusing!

After a bit of window shopping, I went to one of the public baths for a good sauna and soap rubdown, then came home and went to bed early. I had to be well rested for today's exam.

Nothing ventured; nothing gained. I ventured to take the exam, and I gained nothing. In difficulty, it surpasses its reputation, but it's a good exam that tests applicants' broad knowledge of everything. I was weak on American history, economics, and philosophy. Having taken the exam, however, I have greater respect for our foreign service officers.

When my proctor saw that I had been a Radio-TV major at Syracuse University, he informed me that Dr. William Bluem, one of my former professors, was in town. I went to five hotels in search of him, found him, and spent several hours conversing with him. It was a good reunion, an unexpected one—and, possibly, a worthwhile one, as well. Since I last saw him, he's authored two books, is referred to as "the poor man's Marshall McLuhan," is editor of *TV Quarterly*, TV critic for *The Nation*, and is in Europe now as a guest of the State Department. He has contacts with a capital C and wants me to get in touch with him after the first of the year. He might be a good referral.

The Servas home I'm staying in reminds me of that children's story about the little old house that refused to move, so it just stayed between two towering skyscrapers. This nineteenth-century home wasn't even found by the Germans, for it's invisible from the street and the entrance isn't where the address is. Further, it's surrounded by taller apartment buildings. It's old and charming. The man who lives here is now in Denmark, but there's a Norwegian student renting a room here and he was expecting me. I have my own room, a cot, a sleeping bag, and kitchen privileges.

This morning I went to the unusual Gustav Vigeland Sculpture Garden in Frogner Park. Oslo decided to do what no other city had ever done before. They offered Vigeland a contract which permitted him carte blanche to develop his art. The city gave him a studio, hired assistants and workmen in large numbers, and put them at the sculptor's disposal. Then they gave him a large park in which to display his work. The artist labored for 40 years. The city ran out of funds a number of times, but there were drives to raise money in order to keep his project going. In the end, no less than 150 sculptural groups were assembled in Frogner Park. The groups are divided into four sections: the main entrance, the bridge, the fountain, and the circular stairs. The most famous work is the monolith, a mass of writhing figures striving to reach the top. The stone is over 50' high and was cut from a single block of granite that weighed 170 tons before the carving began. It took three stone masons 15 years to complete and was finished in 1943, the year of Vigeland's death. Vigeland was attempting to depict in stone and bronze the full cycle of human life: birth, growing up, decline into old age, and death. There are hundreds of nude figures—some alluring, others grotesque—in a picture of mankind's pathos, agony, and moments of joy.

I also went to the Holmenkollen Tower just outside Oslo. The ski jump, built in 1952 for the Winter Olympics, is on a hill that has been used for ski jumping since 1892. It is currently used only once a year—the first Sunday in March for an international competition. According to books, there's a wonderful panoramic view of Oslo, the mountains, and fjords, but I saw nothing but thick fog. There were children playing at the bottom of the jump, but I only heard laughing voices. The tram ride up to the top was pretty because of the many large and well-situated homes. Up top there was lots of snow, and every tree and bush was covered with a mantle of crystallized frost flowers.

I have now tried everything! Stainless steel urinals for women?! The most aggravating thing is that they weren't designed for women under 5'3"!

Tomorrow I'm taking a 9-1/2-hour train ride to Trondheim, where I'm staying at a Servas home. Trondheim is the farthest north I'm going on this trip. It's on the same latitude as Southhampton Island north of Hudson Bay, Iceland, and the U.S.S.R.'s Stanovoi Mountains.

It was a fascinating day. A contributing factor was a bit of blue sky and sun, which I've come to realize is unusual at this time of year. I went out to Bygdøy, a peninsular suburb on the Oslofjord. The Viking Ship Museum there has three long ships from the

Viking period and many articles found in the burial mounds with the ships. Two of the ships are well preserved: the *Gokstad*, a ninth-century seagoing war vessel 77′ long and 16′ wide, and the highly decorative *Oseberg*. The latter was buried with a Viking queen and was intended to carry her to Valhalla. Buried alive with this queen were a servant girl, 16 horses, 4 dogs, and an ox. Also, everyday materials to carry on life in death: a carved oak bed, yarn and a loom, tapestries, royal garments, and cooking utensils.

The Kon-Tiki Museum was of most interest to me. It houses the balsa raft which carried Thor Heyerdahl, five other men, and a parrot from Peru to Polynesia in 1950. Norse seamanship at its most exciting and daring!

The Norwegian Folk Museum, also in Bygdøy, has an open-air collection of 150 old wooden buildings from all parts of Norway. The oldest, and my favorite, is the stave church from 1200. Its architecture is very distinct with dragon eaves and wood carvings and is found only in Norway. The design may have originated, according to one book, from old Norse pagan temples.

Back in the city, I visited the Edvard Munch Art Museum. I have never, until today, been excited about Munch's paintings, though I have long liked his lithographs. But seeing so much of his work at one time I realized how much depth he has and how uniquely he uses color.

This evening I went to see a film titled *Common Racism*, startling in its pictorial content. In it was a fantastic news film of Mussolini giving a speech and manifesting with facial expressions what a pompous ass he was! The film deals mostly with the Russo-German conflict and ends with a big question mark for the future. It was produced by a western nation, though I'm not sure which one. I do know that it comes in an English version. It's an important film in its implication, and I was quick to note that it's playing to packed houses in Oslo.

12/5/66

If I have been interpreting your letters correctly, I think this is the moment you've been waiting so long for. I'm coming home. I repeat: I'm coming home! Here is the schedule from start to finish: Wednesday, the 14th, I leave Oslo by Loftleidir **[Icelandic Airlines]** at 9:15 p.m...arrive in Reykjavik, Iceland at 12:15 a.m...change planes...set out again at 1:45 a.m....arrive in N.Y.C. at 5:30 a.m. on Thursday, the 15th...then over to LaGuardia for the 8:45 a.m. American Airlines flight #453...arriving in Rochester at 9:45 a.m.

12/6/66

I'm beginning to understand why all the talk about Norway's fjords. The fjords we passed on the way north were so beautiful, their fir-green coastlines darting in and out of the icy blue waters like reluctant swimmers who can't decide to take the plunge. Still farther north, when the train was almost void of passengers, the light patches of snow and iced dirt turned to full-blown snows of winter—snows that covered everything with a fluffy coat. The whirling snowflakes seemed as if they would never stop. The train scattered fresh fallen snow on the tracks, while the snow-catcher sent puffs of white flying to the sides. By 3:30 the sky was a deep blue and the snow had a bluish mantle that here and there held dots of suspended golden light. There were few towns and fewer houses. The train stopped at almost every station, if only for one minute, but most of the time I saw nothing more than a box-size station. I was on a mail train, so the rural stops seem sensible. I was anticipating heavy snows in Trondheim and I thought at last, at last! The farther north, the more snow! Right? Wrong! Not a patch of white anywhere and the only thing I can blame is the Gulf Stream. The wind is now blowing with ferocity outside my window, but still I see no lacy white flakes.

The approach to Trondheim was spectacular. Though I couldn't see exactly where we were, I assume from the view that we must have been on a mountain. The lights of the city spread below us like an animated pinball machine, creating a vivid sensation of flying in for a landing.

I'm now staying in a suburb of Trondheim with Mr. and Mrs. Jon Skjølsvold. Mrs. S speaks no English whatsoever, while Mr. S speaks a little. "I like snow," said I. And he, "You likes Norway?" If you slur the "likes" and "Norway" together, you'll get the right idea! Mr. S told me he was from the town of Røros, so I looked it up in the French guide book I had picked up at the station. I read that Røros has been written about in books about Norway's famed author Johan Falkberget. It turns out that he's Mr. S's brother-in-law, and then I was shown photos of him with King Olav. Watching a TV concert this evening, Mrs. S tapped me with excitement every time they showed a close-up of the king.

Their home is small, the upper floor of a two-family house. It's cluttered with knick-knacks and family photos and a surplus of 1940-ish furniture. I have my own room, however, and both Mr. and Mrs. S are pleasant people.

Incidentally, we watched the NBC special "The Pope and the Vatican," and that prompted them to ask if I were Christian. They know the "sign of David" and pumped me with questions, as best they could, about what the Jews believe.

Tomorrow, I begin exploring this old town founded in 977, then the capital of the country for the Viking king, Olav Trygavson. It was from Trondheimfjord that great Viking fleets sailed out on raids and expeditions.

I suppose I had better mail this tomorrow to assure it arrives before I do. I can hardly believe this is the last of the letters to be sent. I shall continue to write, however, until the bitter end.

12/7/66

It seems a bit odd writing to no-one in particular. But force of habit and a desire to get everything down on paper compel me to keep at it.

The sun rose this morning at 9:45 a.m. and set at 2 p.m.! It was a short day but a sweet one. The fluffy morning clouds were edged in pink—missing were robust Rubens' angels gamboling about with harps and lutes! The sun, when up, hung in the sky just over the mountains and gave a golden glow to Trondheim's colorful wooden houses and the snow-flecked hillsides that rose out of the Trondheimfjord.

12/9/66

The days are going quickly but, oh, so pleasantly! On the 7th I did most of my sightseeing, starting with the magnificent Nidaros Cathedral, Scandinavia's largest medieval building. Begun about 1150, the cathedral combines Norman and late English Gothic-style elements. According to one book, the monarchs of Norway are crowned at the cathedral and buried there, as well. Then on to Nordenfjeldski Museum of Applied Art and the Trondhjems Art Society. Part of the four hours of daylight were spent wandering in the narrow side streets enjoying the little houses and the hundred-year-old warehouses that rise on stilts along the Nidelven River. Trondheimers are very friendly.

I had wanted to attend synagogue on Chanukah, so the tourist office made the contact. I spoke with David Hirschberg who explained there was no service but invited me to his home that evening.

David and Levana Hirschberg have three children. They are Israelis but in Trondheim for a few years, since David is the spiritual leader of the 100-member Jewish community here. (There are 1,000 Jews in Norway now; 1,600 before the war.) That evening there was an additional guest, Trondheim's wealthy and eligible 41-year-old Jewish bachelor, Abba Bekker. David is a conniver of the highest order! He has arranged my meetings with Bekker, and he has asked friends to invite Bekker to their home on Saturday evening, for I'll be there, also.

Yesterday I went up to Skistua somewhere out of and up over the town. The view was terrific and the few hours of complete relaxation were pleasant. The drive back was even more startling for blinding rays of vivid orange-yellow sun pierced through charcoal gray clouds and shone like a spotlight on a part of town.

The clouds moved quickly through the sky, pushed by a rotund old man with puffed cheeks of wind. By the time I returned to Nardo, it was night. But what a strange night sky—the blackest black with startling white light forms over on the horizon. David explained that this far north we were at an angle of the world. While night here, several hundred kilometers south it was still day. Both night and day, then, in the most unusual and strangely wonderful skies I've seen.

Bekker took me to dinner last night at the elegant Britannia Hotel. The eyebrows of Trondheim's citizenry were raised to see Bekker with an unfamiliar young woman.

Today I spent the afternoon with Meira (Mary) Buchman, an Israeli-turned-Norwegian citizen. She married a Trondheim Jew 15 years ago and has been here since. She's a charming, interested, interesting, and intelligent woman.

Bekker asked me out for tomorrow evening, but I'm going out with Levana and David, who had already planned for just such a situation and arranged with the host to ask Bekker, as well. Furthermore, Bekker seems to have decided to attend Sunday's Chanukah party. What, I wonder, has influenced his change of plans?! David and Levana let no opportunity go by; they are always telling me how wonderful and wealthy Bekker is, how devoted he's been to his aunt and uncle with whom he's living, and how bighearted he is. Even Mary Buchman is acting as his press agent!

I tried a Trondelag specialty: *lefse*, a traditional soft and doughy Norwegian potato flatbread covered with margarine and sugar, rolled or covered with margarine and cinnamon, topped with another slice of bread, and served like a pie wedge. I've enjoyed trying different native foods as I've traveled around the world.

Mr. S played "Stars and Stripes" on his viola for my benefit on the last night I stayed with them and continued struggling through English. I tried explaining the story of Chanukah to them, but he couldn't understand the word "oil"—and what could be more basic to the story? He asked Mom's name and I told him it was Anne. "O - n - d?" he asked.

Quote from the Dec. 5th New York Herald-Tribune Christmas supplement: "In France the principal Xmas meal is called the *reveillon* and takes place in the small hours of Christmas Day following a midnight ass on Xmas eve." That's not my typo!

Norway is 1,100 miles long, but her fjord-studded coastline measures more than 12,000 miles. There are 150,000 islands and reefs; 100,000 lakes; hundreds of rivers, waterfalls, and forests; and 3.5 million people, two-thirds of them along the coast, who make their living from the sea.

I have found Norway and the Norwegians enchanting.

12/12/66

Oslo, Norway. But my thoughts are still in Trondheim with new friends. The greatest tragedy in traveling is having to leave those one becomes close to.

The 10th was a visiting day, and I was quite exhausted by the end of the evening. I went to the Skjølsvolds and then to the home of Mary and Bernt Buchman. We watched the Nobel Award Ceremony in Stockholm on TV, with grateful thanks to Eurovision. It was an emotional experience, as well, since the literature award was shared by Josef Agnon and Nellie Sachs, who write of Jewish life and thoughts. Mary showed me the work of her sister Esther Lurie, who spent time in various concentration camps and painted scenes from them. I also saw Mary's art: jewelry from beans, corn, seaweed, and other odd objects. Then, with the Hirschbergs and Bekker, I went to the home of friends.

Last night was the Jewish community's Chanukah Party at the Hotel Astoria. Mary came only because of me, so I spent most of the time with her. Bekker showed up the last hour for no apparent reason. We spoke, we danced, but we went home separately much to the chagrin of David and Levana, who had hoped for a *shiddach*. Neither of us was as interested as they.

By the way, I never did give that bright green winter coat away and, though it's badly worn, falling apart, and faded, it's still keeping me warm. Levana, however, called it a *schmatte* (a rag), and wouldn't let me wear it the entire time I was with her, but gave me another.

This morning I took the train back to Oslo. On the way to Trondheim, I saw the fjords; on the return trip, I was treated to the beauty of Norwegian mountains covered with deep fresh snows and forests of pines and birches. The robin-egg blue sky was spotted with peach-colored clouds of fluff under which sat those wonderful wooden Norwegian houses in barn red, yellow, blue, green, and burnt orange. Even the train stations had charm — brown wood with pastel painted shutters covered with snow-like icing on a cake. Waterfalls on the sides of the train tracks had frozen in their fall, reminding me of a magician that, with a few abracadabra words, had made the world stop its movement. I have written so much about the natural beauty of Norway, because I am most awed by the natural wonders in this mountainous, fjord-studded country. I must return.

> [And so I did—more than 50 years later in October 2015. On a tour of Scandinavia, Marty and I extended our stay in Norway into the fjord region to explore, hike, and kayak. We were there in the midst of a California drought back home and were particularly awed by the abundance of rushing waterfalls and rivers. Mother Nature outdid herself in western Norway! After God created Norway, we were told, He thought it was so beautiful He had to water it every day!]

12/13/66

After going to the cathedral and flower market, I visited with Nancy Berger Hauger and Sue Balter Bøvre, formerly of Rochester. It was a brief hometown reunion but pleasant. Later I saw the very small St. Lucia Day parade with two mounted policemen, about thirty children carrying torches, a band truck, and a truck carrying the newly crowned St. Lucia and her five-girl cortege, all wearing white gowns with red sashes, white coats, and white mittens. They smiled and waved at a non-existent crowd.

12/14/66

Dateline: Oslo, Norway

What does a woman do on her last day overseas? She sleeps late, goes to the Roman baths for a sauna and oil massage, and has her hair done. Today is an occasion—and so is tomorrow!

I have lain awake these past two nights with memories revolving in confusion. Was this past year real? Am I beginning a new phase of life tomorrow, or am I simply awakening from a fabulous dream? If it has been a dream, then I am sorry to break the spell. But if it has, in fact, been life—oh!!!, then how lucky I've been to have my life so colored, so changed with the makings of this dream!

12/15/66

POSTSCRIPT: The Trip Home

I suppose it was inevitable that even the last journey home would not go smoothly. The number in Oslo of Taxi Central was answered by a recorded voice speaking Norwegian so, in desperation, I dialed the first number I found in the phone directory. That was Post Office Control. After 40 minutes I not only had not hailed a taxi, but I had already missed the airport bus. When the Loftleidir flight finally departed with me on it, a light snow was blowing in the wind.

Reykjavik, Iceland's Keflavik Airport greeted us with stiff winds and much rain. Departure for the next flight was delayed. We eventually took off, but somewhere, about 40 minutes over the Atlantic, it was announced that, because of mechanical failure, the plane would have to return to Reykjavik. By the time of arrival, the ground was already covered with an inch of snow. We waited in the airport for the buses to take us to a hotel, sent out telegrams, and endured the hour's drive into the city. Again—and a day later— departure to the U.S. was delayed. A bit worse for wear and to make a long story short, we finally arrived in New York City.

U.S. Customs was a snap. When the young man heard I spoke Japanese, he asked me how one says "food" in Japanese—as in

"Have you brought any *tabemono*?" He merely tapped one suitcase and let the other pass.

Again Loftleidir put me up in a hotel. The next morning's flight brought me home on the 15th of December 1966, exactly 24 hours and 15 minutes later than originally scheduled. Aunts and uncles had planned the family equivalent of a brass band welcome with signs and cheers but, when I actually arrived a day later, there was no big finish— just a quiet welcome-home from my parents and a close friend.

* * *

It is a strange thing to come home. While yet on the journey, you cannot at all realize how strange it will be.
> ~Selma Lagerlöf, Swedish author and Nobel Prize winner

Man cannot discover new oceans unless he has the courage to lose sight of the shore.
> ~Andre Gide, French author and Nobel Prize winner

I had changed much more than my sky; my chores, habits, meals, and even my speech were different now. ...I would sometimes pull back and marvel quietly at who I had become...I had moved so far, and in such an unexpected direction from my previous life that I felt an almost disbelieving happiness.
> ~Thomas Swick, author

I believe it is in our nature to explore, to reach out into the unknown. The only true failure would be not to explore at all.
> ~Ernest Shackleton, explorer

Everything you do that leaves a handprint or heart print is your legacy. And there's a chance to make a difference daily, building a legacy as a giver to and supporter of others.
> ~Oprah Winfrey, producer, media personality, author, actress

A mind that is stretched by a new experience can never go back to its old dimensions.
> ~Oliver Wendell Holmes, jurist, historian, philosopher

We live in a wonderful world that is full of beauty, charm and adventure. There is no end to the adventures that we can have if only we seek them with our eyes open.
> ~Jawaharlal Nehru, Prime Minister of India

We travel not to escape life, but for life not to escape us.
> ~Anonymous

The purpose of life is to live it, to taste it, to experience to the utmost, to reach out eagerly and without fear for newer and richer experience.
> ~Eleanor Roosevelt, political figure, diplomat, activist

And I think to myself, what a wonderful world.
> ~Louis Armstrong, musician

1966 TRAVEL ITINERARY

Taiwan	01/10 - 01/11
Hong Kong	01/12 - 01/26
Cambodia	01/26 - 01/30
Thailand	01/30 - 02/05
Malaysia	02/05 - 02/14
Thailand again	02/14
India	02/14 - 03/06
Iran	03/06 - 03/17
Iraq	03/17 - 03/22
Syria	03/22
Turkey	03/22 - 04/04
Israel	04/04 - 08/23
Cyprus	08/24 - 08/25
Greece	08/26 - 09/09
Yugoslavia	09/10 - 09/16
Austria	09/17 - 10/01
Germany	10/02 - 10/15
Belgium	10/15 - 10/20
Germany again	10/20 - 10/27
Denmark	10/28 - 11/13
Sweden	11/13 - 11/18
Finland	11/19 - 11/25
U.S.S.R.	11/26 - 11/30
Finland again	11/30
Sweden again	12/01
Norway	12/01 - 12/14
To USA	12/14 - 12/16

THE DARUMA DOLL

My trusted 1-3/4" daruma doll and lucky charm that safeguarded me when I traveled around the world. Before I left Japan, as tradition dictates, I made a wish for a safe trip home and painted in one eye. I painted in his other eye when I arrived safely in the U.S.—my wish granted.

This is one of Japan's oldest and most common toys—available in many sizes, shapes, and materials, though mostly made of clay or papiermâché. It has a weighted and rounded bottom so that it will always come back to its upright position. Because it comes up and never stays down, it represents the Japanese appreciation for resiliency of spirit. It is also used as a good luck talisman. It's named Daruma after the famous Chinese Buddhist priest Dharma of the sixth century. He is reputed to be the founder of the Zen sect of Buddhism. Legend says he sat in meditation for many years on a piece of rock, which caused him to lose the use of his legs. He came to be represented in this stubby, legless statue in a sitting posture. The doll is usually painted red all over, except the round face with two big round white eyes. When you buy the doll, the eyes are intentionally blank. It is up to the owner to paint in the eyes, but not at the same time. Here's how it works: have a goal or make a wish and paint in one eye. When the wish comes true, paint in the other eye as a token of your appreciation.

EPILOGUE

Travel is all about making connections: across pathways, places, borders, languages, points of view, cultures.

Travel stimulated my independent nature and my drive for adventure. I had amazing experiences and terrifying ones. I cried with laughter and cried because there was nothing to laugh about. I found myself on the wrong train heading to a bad part of town, been stuck at night without a place to sleep, and felt moments of deep loneliness. But I also had been welcomed by strangers with open arms, friendship, and trust. I was revitalized by the kindness and compassion of strangers. I felt the forces of history. My world and my place in it broadened and deepened with each new perspective, and my admiration and appreciation grew for the wonders I witnessed. Most important, I thrived on the friendships made—some lasting many years.

I rode the back of a motorcycle in India while monkeys screamed from the trees above. I triumphed over a rape attack in Turkey. I stood up to threatening border guards in Iraq. I ignored warnings about single women in certain places that turned out to be joyful experiences. I turned down marriage proposals. I patiently put up with men and women touching my red hair to feel the texture. I listened to Russians reprimand me for wearing a bright green coat in their dull gray winter. I was privileged to attend lifecycle events in different countries and cultures. And there was more. So much more. Each experience was a treasured *ichigo ichie* (once-in-a-lifetime moment).

Lewis Carroll expressed it well when he wrote: "If you don't know where you are going, any road will get you there." And so it did. Life was filled with new beginnings and endless surprises, an open road with twists and turns that lead to unexpected adventures—some of significance, some not so much. My time on this trip was a blank dance card waiting to be filled.

There were occasions when I stood alone in a dusty bus station or remote location wondering what my next move should be and asking myself what a nice girl like me was doing in a place like that. It was a hypothetical question, of course; I always knew the answer. I was overjoyed with the freedom to do what I wanted—when, where, how, and with whom. I could be impulsive or cautious, carefree or controlled. Traveling solo tested my limits of what I thought I knew about myself and connected me with the person I truly am.

How ironic, yet so appropriate, that one meaning of my name Wendy is Wanderer! I reveled in the thrill of wanderlust—no traditions, no demands, no expectations, no definitions, no limits—just me and the world and my connection to it. No past, no future, only right there and then.

When women travel abroad, we don't know what's expected of us or the local rules for dealing with overly friendly or sexually aggressive men. Safety concerns specific to females are all about protecting oneself. Our instincts need to be target sharp regarding the dangers that could exist in any interaction. Dating American men overseas was so much easier because I understood the rules of the game. With men from Asian and Middle Eastern cultures, it wasn't as relaxed. Women must adjust their behavior, habits, appearance, and choices creating rules of the road that are as varied as the women making them. We test our intuition, confidence, strengths, courage, taste for adventure, and sense of self. If I was in a place where women never went out alone at night, I didn't either. On the other hand, the more open, curious, and willing I was, the bigger the travel payoff. I learned to trust my judgement and, fortunately, it rarely failed me. It needs to be restated, however, that these solo travels were in the 1960s. It was a very different world back then—more open and giving, less fearful and angry.

My parents never knew where I was, whom I was with, or how to get in touch with me. There were no cell phones or email in the 1960s. In fact, I phoned my parents only twice in the 27 months I was overseas. I sent letters that you've read here but, as I moved from one country to the next, I had often already moved on by the time my parents received them. I'd pick a place several weeks ahead that I knew I would visit, and they wrote to me care of the

General Post Office, American Express, or American embassies. Letters frequently crossed, but I don't think one ever went astray.

Travel is transformative. It's about relating to dissimilar people with opposing values; about embracing differing points of view and ways of doing things; about savoring a new range of arts and culture and cuisine; about relying on strangers to help find my way, both directional and spiritual; about approaching unfamiliar cultures and people with curiosity, respect, and an open heart and getting that back many times over; about loving the global mosaic and being a citizen of the world. That is the essence of who I am.

ONE FINAL NOTE

Before I left Kibbutz Yizre'el in August, guests were given the opportunity to send Jewish New Year greetings to anyone anywhere in the world. I sent a postcard to Marty telling him that I'd be home when I ran out of money, and I'd probably run out of money in December. Three days after I arrived, he called my mother to find out when I was coming home.

Despite all the viable career options I wrote about and the possible life plans I had thought through, six months after my return to the United States, Marty and I were married. We moved to New Jersey, and I resumed my career as a freelance educational broadcaster in New York City.

And thus began another adventure…and another…and another…and another…and another…

When the world has been your oyster and the scattered seas your friends,
It is time to come home proudly, but never make amends
For having spent long months in traveling, learning, loving all you meet
In harbors, cafes, parks, and shrines, a thousand winding streets.
Two long years and forty-one days in varied lands and climes —
There could be nothing grander, nor a life that's more sublime.
Why need I apologize to those who dream but stay
When I have friends in every land — a simple smile away?

www.ingramcontent.com/pod-product-compliance
Lightning Source LLC
Chambersburg PA
CBHW071952290426
44109CB00018B/1993